EVEN IF
YOU "LOSE" THE FIGHT,
YOU WIN!

—as long as you fight *fair*! You may know couples who
wrangle continually, in unproductive, embarrassing ways
—in fact, you may be in that kind of relationship yourself—but the answer isn't to stop fighting. The answer is
to fight often, to fight hard . . . and to fight fair!

Now Dr. George R. Bach and Peter Wyden have de-fused
the bombs which poison battles between intimates, in a
book that tells why couples who fight together *stay* together—if they use the right fight techniques.

THE INTIMATE ENEMY explores the rules of the "Fair
Fight" through clear, easy-to-understand analyses of over
a hundred case histories and actual fights, plus the authors' own skilled observations on couples who either
can't fight, or who "go for the jugular" when they *do*
fight. Here are the rules for fair, healthy fights which
will promote understanding and intimacy in every relationship!

"Brilliant . . . Superb observations,
insights, and
new perspectives."
Psychology Today

Other Avon Books by
Dr. George Bach

CREATIVE AGGRESSION
PAIRING

THE INTIMATE ENEMY

How to fight fair in love and marriage

Dr. George R. Bach
and Peter Wyden

 AVON
PUBLISHERS OF BARD, CAMELOT AND DISCUS BOOKS

Excerpts from this book have appeared in the *Ladies'
Home Journal* under the title, *Marital Fighting.*

AVON BOOKS
A division of
The Hearst Corporation
959 Eighth Avenue
New York, New York 10019

Copyright © 1968 by George R. Bach and Peter Wyden
Published by arrangement with William Morrow &
Company, Inc.
Library of Congress Catalog Card Number: 69-14232
ISBN: 0-380-00392-9

All rights reserved, which includes the right
to reproduce this book or portions thereof in
any form whatsoever. For information address
William Morrow & Company, Inc., 105 Madison Avenue,
New York, New York 10016

First Avon Printing, May, 1970
Twenty-third Printing

AVON TRADEMARK REG. U.S. PAT. OFF. AND IN
OTHER COUNTRIES, MARCA REGISTRADA,
HECHO EN U.S.A.

Printed in the U.S.A.

To Peggy and Barbara

About the Collaboration that Produced this Book

Dr. George R. Bach, the senior author of *The Intimate Enemy*, received his Ph.D. degree in psychology from the University of Iowa. He has taught there and at four other universities. His authoritative textbook, *Intensive Group Psychotherapy*, is widely used. Dr. Bach is the founder and director of the Institute of Group Psychotherapy in Beverly Hills, California. There, working with his private clients and a small group of scientists, he developed the theory of "constructive aggression" on which the present book is based. Dr. Bach is an editor of three scientific journals; past president of the west coast chapter, American Academy of Psychotherapists; and past president of the Group Therapy Association of Southern California.

Peter Wyden, Dr. Bach's collaborator, is executive editor of the *Ladies' Home Journal* and has written extensively on contemporary problems. His previous books are *Suburbia's Coddled Kids*, *The Hired Killers* (Introduction by Karl Menninger, M.D.), *The Overweight Society*, *How the Doctors Diet*, and *Growing Up Straight: What Every Thoughtful Parent Should Know About Homosexuality*. To prepare himself for the present volume, Mr. Wyden participated intensively in Dr. Bach's work. However, in fairness to the doctor and his staff, Mr. Wyden would like to make clear that the first-person plural, as used throughout this book, refers principally to them.

The substance and most details of the case histories presented in these pages are authentic. But the material has been greatly condensed to save the reader's time; and names and incidents, as well as other details, have been disguised with utmost care so that the privacy of clients remains more than adequately protected.

Contents

List of Charts

ACKNOWLEDGMENTS

The senior author gratefully acknowledges the expert help and professional encouragement he has received from staff members of the Institute of Group Psychotherapy and also from independent consultants and advisors. Most personally stimulating in the incubation and development of conceptual tools and theory were: Henry Altenberg, M.D.; Eric Berne, M.D.; Robert Boguslaw, Ph.D.; Albert Ellis, Ph.D.; Frank Harary, Ph.D.; Abraham Kaplan, Ph.D.; John Warkentin, M.D.; Carl Whitaker, M.D.; and Lewis Yablonsky, Ph.D. Others who aided in the development of the practice of therapeutic aggression and research included: Roger and Lauren Bach; Yetta Bernhard, M.S.; Ildri Bie, M.A.; Meyer Elkin, M.S.W.; Walter Gaudnek, Ph.D.; Leonard Gluckson, M.D.; Marshall Hodge, Ph.D.; Richard Hogan, Ph.D.; Robert Kovan, M.D.; Alvirdo Pearson, M.D.; Everett Shostrom, Ph.D.; Marshall and Claire Shumsky, M.A.; Frederick Stoller, Ph.D.; and Robert van Vorst. Last but not least, I am deeply indebted to Shana Alexander who summarized my work for *Life* magazine and gave constant encouragement for its detailed publication in book form.

1. Why Intimates Must Fight

Verbal conflict between intimates is not only acceptable, especially between husbands and wives; it is constructive and highly desirable. Many people, including quite a few psychologists and psychiatrists, believe that this new scientific concept is an outrageous and even dangerous idea. We know otherwise, and we can prove it. At our Institute of Group Psychotherapy in Beverly Hills, California, we have discovered that couples who fight together are couples who stay together—provided they know how to fight properly.

The art of fighting right is exactly what we teach couples who come to us for marriage counseling. Our training methods are not simple and cannot be successfully applied by everyone. They require patience, good will, and the flexibility to adopt some challenging and unconventional ways for dealing with humanity's most personal drives. Most of all, they demand hearts and minds that are open—open to reason and to change. The great majority of our clients master the art of marital combat quickly. For them, the payoffs are warmly rewarding, and we believe that any couple with honest and deep motivation can achieve the same results.

When our trainees fight according to our flexible system of rules, they find that the natural tensions and frustrations of two people living together can be greatly reduced. Since they live with fewer lies and inhibitions and have discarded outmoded notions of etiquette, these couples are free to grow emotionally, to become more productive and more creative, as individuals in their own right and also as pairs. Their sex lives tend to improve. They are likely to do a better job raising their children. They feel less guilty about hostile emotions that they harbor against each other. Their communications improve and, as a result, they face fewer unpleasant surprises from their partners. Our graduates know how to make the here-and-now more livable for themselves, and so they worry much less about the past that cannot be changed. They are less likely to become victims of boredom or divorce. They feel less vulnerable and more loving toward each other because they are protected by an umbrella of reasonable

17

standards for what is fair and foul in their relationship. Perhaps best of all, they are liberated to be themselves.

Some aspects of our fight training shock trainees when they first begin to work with us. We advocate that they fight in front of their friends and children. For many couples we recommend fighting before, during, or after sexual intercourse. Some people who learn about our work by way of hearsay get the impression that we encourage trainees to become expert at the sort of sick and chronic insult exchanges that proved so readily recognizable to audiences of Edward Albee's play and movie, *Who's Afraid of Virginia Woolf?*. But this we never, never do. People fight in the *Virginia Woolf* style before we train them, not afterward.

The wild, low-blow flailing of *Virginia Woolf* is not an extreme example of fighting between intimate enemies; in fact, it is rather common in ordinary life. Let's listen in on a fight that we have heard, with variations, literally hundreds of times during nearly 25 years of practicing psychotherapy. We call this a "kitchen sink fight" because the kitchen plumbing is about all that isn't thrown as a weapon in such a battle.

Mr. and Mrs. Bill Miller have a dinner date with one of Bill's out-of-town business associates and the associate's wife. Mrs. Miller is coming in from the suburbs and has agreed to meet Bill in front of his office building. The Millers have been married for 12 years and have three children. They are somewhat bored with each other by now, but they rarely fight. Tonight happens to be different. Bill Miller is anxious to make a good impression on the visiting firemen from out of town. His wife arrives 20 minutes late. Bill is furious. He hails a taxi and the fun begins:

HE: Why were you late?

SHE: I tried my best.

HE: Yeah? You and who else? Your mother is never on time either.

SHE: That's got nothing to do with it.

HE: The hell it doesn't. You're just as sloppy as she is.

SHE (*getting louder*): You don't say! Who's picking whose dirty underwear off the floor every morning?

HE (*sarcastic but controlled*): I happen to go to work. What have *you* got to do all day?

SHE (*shouting*): I'm trying to get along on the money you don't make, that's what.

HE (*turning away from her*): Why should I knock myself out for an ungrateful bitch like you?

The Millers got very little out of this encounter except a thoroughly spoiled evening. Trained marital fighters, on the other hand, would be able to extract from this brief volley a great deal of useful information. They would note that while the trigger for this fight was legitimate (the lady *was* very late), it was also trivial and not indicative of what was really troubling this couple. The aggression reservoir of the hapless Millers was simply so full that even a slight jar caused it to spill over. Both partners had been keeping their grievances bottled up, and this is invariably a poor idea. We call this "gunny-sacking" because when marital complaints are toted along quietly in a gunny sack for any length of time they make a dreadful mess when the sack finally bursts.

Our graduates would also be able to point out that Bill Miller quite unfairly reached into the couple's "psychiatric museum" by dragging the totally irrelevant past (his mother-in-law's tardiness and sloppiness) into the argument; and Mrs. Miller added to the destruction when she escalated the conflict by going out of her way to attack Bill's masculinity. She did this when she castigated him as a poor provider (we call this "shaking the money tree").

Obviously, both of these fighters would benefit from the principal recommendation we make to our trainees: to do their best to keep all arguments not only fair but up-to-date so that the books on a marriage can be balanced daily, much as banks keep their debits and credits current by clearing all checks with other banks before closing down for business every evening. Couples who fight regularly and constructively need not carry gunny sacks full of grievances, and their psychiatric museums can be closed down.

By studying tens of thousands of intimate encounters like this one between the Millers, we designed a system for programming individual aggression through what we call constructive fighting. Our system is not a sport like boxing. It is more like a cooperative skill such as dancing. It is a tool, a way of life that, paradoxically, leads to greater harmony between intimates. It is a somewhat revolutionary notion, but we believe that it can serve not only to enrich the lives of husbands, wives, and lovers; it could become the first step toward controlling the violent feelings that lead to assassinations and to aggressions between entire peoples. A Utopian dream? Perhaps. But we submit that humanity cannot cope with hostilities between nations until it learns to hammer out livable settlements for hostilities between loved ones.

About eight years ago our Institute pioneered in the management of intimate aggression. We have worked successfully with more than 250 couples, and many therapists throughout the United States and abroad now use our system. But, since our methods are still widely misunderstood, we would like to emphasize that our kind of "programming" is neither as precise nor as rigid as the type achieved by computers. Anyone who tries to "program" people in a machinelike way is either kidding himself or trying to play God.

Our system amounts to a set of experimental exercises. We suggest format, but not content; the frame, but not the picture. The picture is filled in by each couple as they fight. This is known as the heuristic approach to education, a system that trains students to find out things for themselves. We train attitudes and suggest directions for further inquiry through trial and error. We formalize and civilize impulsive or repressed anger; but we preserve the spontaneity of aggressive encounters. This is vital because no fight is predictable and no two are alike.

We will describe the at-home fight exercises that we offer our clients; when, where, and how to start a fight; when and how to finish it when it has gone far enough; how couples can regulate their "closeness" to each other while they are between fights; how to score 21 kinds of results of an intimate battle. Our program does not, however, offer hard-and-fast recipes in cookbook style. It can be tried, always with due consideration for the vulnerability of the partner, by anyone without a therapist. But when a therapist is present, as is always the case at our Institute, he is no distant father figure. He participates as trainer, coach, referee, cheerleader, model, and friend.

Some readers may wonder whether all this adds up to complicated machinery constructed by psychologists who cannot bear to keep things simple. Our clinical experience suggests otherwise. Many intelligent, well-to-do trainees tell us of fights that are so abysmally crude and hurtful that it is impossible to doubt the need for fight training. But these kitchen-sink fighters are not the ones who are worst off. We have far more clients who live in a style that can be infinitely more threatening to intimate relationships. Again paradoxically, these unfortunates are the partners who fight rarely or not at all.

Although the Bill Millers, for example, sustained painful emotional injuries in their taxicab fight, they became aggressors ("hawks") under pressure. This is a point in their favor, not against them, for even this destructive encounter produced one positive result. In its way, the taxicab fight gave the Millers a rough—very rough—idea of where they stood with each other, which is the essential first step toward the improvement of any relationship. This knowledge placed them way ahead of many couples. Approximately 80% of our trainees start out as natural nonfighters or active fight-evaders ("doves"), and these people usually know much less about each other than the Millers did. After their fight the Millers knew at least how far apart they were and how far each would go to hurt the other.

In intimate relationships ignorance is rarely bliss. At best it leads to the monumental boredom of couples who are living out parallel lives in a state of loneliness *à deux*. The quiet that prevails in their homes isn't really peace. Actually, these people are full of anger much of the time, like everyone else on earth. After all, what is anger? It's the basic emotional and physiological reaction against interference with the pursuit of a desired goal; and an expression of strong concern when things go wrong. When partners don't fight, therefore, they are not involved in an intimate relationship; honest intimates can't ignore their hostile feelings because such feelings are inevitable.

One typical evening in the home of nonfighting pseudo-intimates began like this:

HE (*yawning*): How was your day, dear?
SHE (*pleasantly*): OK, how was yours?
HE: Oh, you know, the usual.
SHE: Want your martini on the rocks?
HE: Whatever you want to fix, dear.
SHE: Anything special you want to do later?
HE: Oh, I don't know . . .

In this fight-phobic home nothing more meaningful may be exchanged for the rest of the evening. Or practically any evening. For reasons to be discussed shortly, these partners won't level with each other. Their penalty is emotional divorce.

There is another group of fight-evaders who do exchange some important signals with their mates, but usually with unfortunate results. We call them the pseudo-accommodators. Here is one such husband who is about to dive into appalling hot water:

WIFE (*settling down comfortably for a sensible discussion*): Mother wants to come visit from New York.
HUSBAND (*shrinking away and accommodating*): Why not?

The dove-husband in this case was saying to himself, "Oh, my God!" He did not say it out loud because he "can't stand hassling." So his mother-in-law arrives and the fights triggered by her presence are far more terrible than the original fight with his wife which the husband managed to avoid. This husband was also practicing another technique that is popular among intimates. He expected his wife to *divine* how he really felt about the mother-in-law's visit. He was saying to himself, "If Emmy loves me she will know that I don't want her mother to come until later in the year when I'll have less pressure on my job." Too bad that most people are not talented in the extrasensory art of divining. But they're not, and many intimates therefore never really know "where they're at."

Throughout this book we will demonstrate how they can find out. Here we would only like to demonstrate the dangers of not trying.

Surprisingly few couples seem to realize how their failure to level with each other can lead to a totally unexpected, dramatic marriage crisis and perhaps even to divorce. This is what happened to another pair of doves, Mr. and Mrs. Kermit James. While making love, many husbands and wives pretend more passion than they really feel. In some marriages, both partners engage in this charade. In the case of the James family, the wife was the one who did the pretending. True intimates would confess their sex problems to each other. Pseudo-intimates, on the other hand, just go on pretending. The trouble is that unless two partners are really beyond the point of caring what happens to their union, the pretending eventually wears dangerously thin.

The Jameses had been married for eight years. One night after they had sexual intercourse Mr. James patted himself innocently on the back for his skill at love-making. Mrs. James happened to be furious at him because at dinnertime he had refused to discuss an urgent financial problem and later he had left his clothes strewn messily all over the floor. Normally she ignored such provocations just to keep things peaceful. This time, her anger at her husband got out of control. She was ready to "let him have it." She had been gunny-sacking so many additional grievances for such a very long time, however, that she reached unthinkingly for the trigger of an atomic bomb. The danger of a nuclear explosion hovers over every nonfighting marriage. Mrs. James unleashed the lethal mushroom cloud when she casually said:

"You know, I never come. I fake it."

Marriages have split up with less provocation. The Jameses

gradually repaired their relationship by entering fight training at our Institute. One of the first bits of advice we gave them, incidentally, is that wise marital combatants always try to measure their weapons against the seriousness of a particular fight issue. Nuclear bombs shouldn't be triggered against pea-shooter causes; or, as we sometimes warn trainees: "Don't drop the bomb on Luxembourg!"

Fight-evading can also lead to disaster without any blow-up whatever. A somewhat extreme example are Mr. and Mrs. Harold Jacobson, a prosperous suburban couple who had been married for more than 20 years. They had raised two children and were socially popular. Everybody thought they had a fine marriage. Mr. Jacobson was a sales manager with an income of well over $20,000. His wife dressed well, played excellent bridge, and did more than her share for local causes. Both were considered well-informed conversationalists in their set, but at home Mr. Jacobson rarely said much. Peacefully, he went along with whatever his wife wanted to do.

Shortly after their younger child went off to college, Mr. Jacobson packed his clothes while his wife was out shopping and left home without leaving a note. It took Mrs. Jacobson some time to discover through her husband's lawyer that he meant to leave for good. As usual, he just hadn't felt like arguing about it. His wife was incredulous and then horrified. Their many friends were flabbergasted. None would have believed that this marriage could break up. Over a period of weeks, several of them brought sufficient pressure to bear on the Jacobsons to enter our fight-training program.

Mr. Jacobson was persuaded to start first. He joined one of our self-development groups, along with eight other individuals who were involved in marital crises but were not yet ready to work on their problems in the presence of their mates. The senior author of this book was the therapist. Together the group convinced Mr. Jacobson that the "silent treatment" which he had given his wife was not cooperation or strength but noncooperation or something worse: hostility camouflaged by phony and misleading compliance. He admitted that he had never leveled with his wife, and never clearly communicated his feelings about the way she dominated most of the family decisions; it riled him no end when she decided what they should do to "have fun," to "be creative," and all the rest. Almost invariably he went along, even though he resented it terribly in what we call the "inner dialogue" (conversations and fights which all of us keep going within ourselves). On the few occasions when Mr.

Jacobson did protest mildly—always without making the true depth of his feelings clear—he found that his wife became even more assertive when she was resisted. So he became even more quiet.

At first Mr. Jacobson resisted fight training. He said that it would be "undignified" to let himself go and engage his wife in "useless" arguments. It was against his "values." It turned out that his German-born mother had taught him the virtue of the old adage, *"Reden ist Silber, aber Schweigen ist Gold"* (Talk is silver, but silence is golden). Mr. Jacobson still lived by this peasant saying, which was useful in feudal times when speaking up was indeed dangerous for serfs. He therefore believed that self-control was more virtuous than his wife's "noisy dominance."

In the course of six weekly sessions, the group thawed out this typical case of "etiquette-upmanship." We were able to convince Mr. Jacobson that speaking up in a good cause is more effective and valuable than "golden silence" that leads only to hopelessness. In his therapy group he then practiced "speaking up" and "fighting back" on a particularly domineering lady who became, in effect, a substitute for his wife. He reasoned with her. He argued. He refused to be squelched. He was elated when finally he succeeded in getting through to her, and boasted that she was "much worse than my wife."

Then Mr. Jacobson entered a second type of group. Here, four to six married and unmarried intimates work at their problems not as individuals but as couples. Having learned the value of asserting himself aggressively in the self-development group, Mr. Jacobson found that he could now face Mrs. Jacobson on a new basis. During the group sessions he noticed that the wife whom he had always considered overwhelmingly argumentative and domineering could be managed, even tamed. To his surprise, he discovered that she actually *preferred* him to speak up assertively and to share the responsibility for family decision-making. It also made him generally more attractive and stimulating to her, with pleasing sexual fringe benefits for both.

Eventually, Mr. Jacobson, like most intelligent people, came to enjoy the give-and-take of true intimacy. He dismissed his divorce lawyer and, most likely, will carry on his marriage for another 20 years, but on a fresh, realistic basis. We felt that the Jacobsons had gained a brand-new marriage without a divorce.

Like most people today, Mr. Jacobson considered "aggression" a dirty word, just as "sex" used to be. Most people feel secretive about their anger and their fights. When we first initiated fight training, we asked couples to put some of their fights on tape at home and bring us the tapes for interpretation and discussion. This system did not work too well. Some partners were too clever; they turned on the tape recorder only when it was to their supposed "advantage" and turned it off when they felt like acting as censors. Other couples resisted the tape-making at home simply because they were too embarrassed to put their anger on record and then listen to it.

The fact is that anger is considered taboo in modern society. It isn't "gentlemanly." It isn't "feminine." It isn't "nice." It isn't "mature." This is supposed to be the age of sweet reason and "togetherness." The very word "fighting" makes most people uncomfortable. They prefer to talk about "differences" or "silly arguments." And they will go to considerable lengths to maintain the quiet that isn't peace.

Partners say, "Darling, I love you too much to fight with you; you're not my enemy!" But they usually say this in their inner dialogue, not out loud to their partner. Then, when they get angrier, their next step may be a demand, also directed toward the partner but still usually unspoken: "Act nice, no matter how angry you feel!" When an intimate feels even more threatened, he may finally speak up with a plea: "Don't get angry with me!" Or he may demand to turn the partner off: "I can't take you seriously when you're angry!" In an extremity, he may link his demand to a threat: "Don't raise your voice—or else!" All this is part of the strategy of "peace at any price."

The wish to be above personal animosity is fed by many mistaken beliefs. Control of anger, rather than its expression, is considered "mature." Hostility feelings toward an intimate are not only considered the antithesis of love ("If you really love me you should tolerate me as I am"); often such "hate" emotions are considered "sick," requiring psychiatric care. If an angry partner is not seriously enough afflicted to be led away to the head doctor, he is considered at least temporarily irrational. After all, everybody "knows" that what is said in anger cannot be taken seriously; a "mature" partner discounts it as the gibberish of an emotionally upset person, much like the ranting of a drunk.

Nonfighting marital stalemates are rooted in the romantic belief that intimates should take one another as they are. Folklore and etiquette insist that one should not try to change the beloved but accept him or her, warts and all, and "live happily ever after." Once one somehow acquires the magic ability to accept the other's frailties, automatic bliss is supposed to ensue. This charming idyll is promoted not only in fiction and on the screen but even by some marriage counselors and other professionals.

The dream of romantic bliss is an anachronistic hangover from the Victorian etiquette that tried to create gentlemen and gentleladies by social pressure. But the notion that a stress- and quarrel-free emotional climate in the home will bring about authentic harmony is a preposterous myth, born in ignorance of the psychological realities of human relationships. Fighting is inevitable between mature intimates. Quarreling and making up are hallmarks of true intimacy. However earnestly a mature person tries to live in harmony with a partner, he will have to fight for his very notions of harmony itself and come to terms with competing notions—and there are always competing interests.

Everybody has his own ideas about what makes for harmonious living. Being human, one likes one's own ideas to prevail except perhaps in cases of aggression-phobic fight-evaders or excessively submissive partners who act like doormats. The mature partner may yield some of his notions, but usually not without a fight. The classic battle about where to take the family on vacation is a perfect example of such an authentic encounter.

"The mountains are most relaxing," shouts the husband.

"The beach is more fun," shouts the wife.

Such conflicting notions make it perfectly natural for everybody to be angry at his mate some of the time.

Yet many couples still consider intimate conflict revolting. "We never fight," they tell us indignantly. They are, in truth, afraid of fighting. Sometimes they fear just the stress of "hassling"; few couples know about the modern research that shows stress is valuable for keeping the nervous system toned up in the psychological sense. More likely, intimates fear that anger is a Pandora's box. They fear they "can't afford to fight" because they have so many years invested in each other. They worry that if one partner raises his voice, the other must raise his. There might be tears. The fight might escalate out of control. It could lead to rejection, even separation!.

As a matter of fact, our trainees find that they tend to feel closest after a properly fought fight. Only our newest recruits wonder whether we're being facetious when we tell them, "A fight a day keeps the doctor away."

Fascinating new experiments document this paradoxical-sounding thesis. In one famous series, Dr. Harry Harlow of the University of Wisconsin reared several generations of monkeys and showed that an exchange of hostilities is *necessary* between mates before there can be an exchange of love. Harlow's calm, mechanical, totally accepting and nonfighting monkey mothers raised off-spring who grew up "normal" except that they couldn't and wouldn't make love.

Another distinguished researcher, Konrad Lorenz, made similar observations about "bonding" (loving) behavior: "Among birds, the most aggressive representatives of any group are also the staunchest friends, and the same applies to mammals. To the best of our knowledge, bond behavior does not exist except in aggressive organisms. This certainly will not be news to the students of human nature ... The wisdom of old proverbs as well as that of Sigmund Freud has known for a very long time how closely human aggression and human love are bound together." Indeed, one of the leading theorists on emotional maturity, Erik Erikson of Harvard University, blames the failure to achieve human intimacy on "the inability to engage in controversy and useful combat."

Oddly enough, anger can be useful just *because* it pours out with a minimum of forethought. Unless a partner hides it behind a falsely neutral or false-friendly (and ulcer-producing) façade, his anger—like spontaneous laughter or spontaneous sexual arousal—cannot be dishonest. Making a person angry is the surest way to find out what he cares about and how deeply he cares. Since intimates keep measuring and remeasuring how much they care for one another ("Are you getting bored with me?"), they can make each other angry in normal but usually unconscious tests of the depth of their involvement.

The process starts right in the early phase of courtship when one partner tries to get the other "sore," not necessarily to "pick a fight," but just to "tease," to test the other out. How far can he go? What does she care enough about to get her "good and angry"? These fight games can be informative if they are played fairly and in a spirit that seeks not to inflict hurt but to resolve realistic conflicts. Lovers also find out by this process that affection grows deeper when it is mixed with aggression. Both feelings then become part of a natural, genuine relationship that allows for expression of the bitter as well as the sweet side of emotional involvement.

We believe, then, that there can be no mature intimate relationship without aggressive leveling; that is, "having it out," speaking up, asking the partner "what's eating" him and negotiating for realistic settlements of differences. This does cause stress, but our successful trainees learn to accept one of the realities of the human condition: the pain of conflict is the price of true and enduring love. People simply cannot release all their love feelings unless they have learned to manage their hate.

"Hate" sounds like too strong a word, but it isn't. When a partner performs according to one's expectations, one is "turned on" and feels love. When these expectations are frustrated, one is "turned off" and feels hate. This is what people recognize as the ups and downs of marriage. We call it "the state of marital swing." Unfortunately, it is usually a state viewed with vast resignation; hence the saying, "You can't live with 'em and you can't live without 'em." This hopelessness is unwarranted. At our Institute we discovered: (1) It is not a partner's sweet and loving side that shapes his bond with an intimate; it is the talent for airing aggression that counts most. And (2) aggression management not only can be learned; it can be used to *change* a partnership constructively.

Contrary to folklore, the existence of hostility and conflict is not necessarily a sign that love is waning. As often as not, an upsurge of hate may signal a deepening of true intimacy; it is when neither love nor hate can move a partner that a relationship is deteriorating. Typically, one partner then gives up the other as a "lost cause" or shrugs him off ("I couldn't care less"). Indifference to a partner's anger and hate is a surer sign of a deteriorating relationship than is indifference to love.

The problem of regulating personal aggression is rarely discussed. It hovers too uncomfortably close to home for most people. Almost everybody has a greater or lesser "hang-up" about admitting hostile feelings, even to himself. It is part of humanity's embarrassment about its inborn aggressive side. Frequently, therefore, people displace their hostilities onto others. We call this "blamesmanship" or "scapegoating," and intimates usually find the process baffling and infuriating.

Suppose it's Wednesday night. Mrs. Jones has had a trying day. She doesn't feel like making love and has decided to withhold sex from her husband. Instead of negotiating with him, she contaminates the situation with an extraneous issue and engages in blamesmanship between the sheets.

SHE: Not tonight, dear. Besides, I can't ever feel anything anyway. Your stomach is in the way.
HE: That's just your excuse. It all depends on the position.
SHE (*heatedly*): You know perfectly well that I can't make it with those acrobatics. Everything would be very simple if you'd just stop stuffing yourself.

HE (*furious*): I'm comfortable the way I am and you're not going to take my gourmet tastes away from me.

SHE (*icily*): Well, something's got to give.

HE (*angry but resigned*): Oh hell, there we go again . . .

Children are a favorite target when intimates displace their own fights onto other people. Most parental fights about children, for example, are not about children at all. The disagreement is between the parents; the child is only the battleground. Tom and Myra Robinson learned this when they conducted the following fight before one of our training groups:

SHE: You simply must start to enforce discipline around here and make the kids toe the line.

HE: Why me?

SHE: Because I want you to be the power in this house!

HE: I like to be and I am.

SHE: No, you're not—I am! I have to be!

HE: No, you don't have to be, and you're not!

SHE (*getting angrier*): Don't be stupid! Who disciplines the kids? Me! Who takes all the responsibility for discipline—me!

HE (*pacing and pulling hard on cigarette*): I am glad you do, but that just makes a cop out of you . . . it doesn't really impress the kids at all.

SHE (*very red in the face*): You're driving me out of my mind! That's my point! You let me do all the dirty work. That makes me a "mean mother" in the eyes of the kids. You get all the goodies: you're their loving "super daddy." I don't like it!

HE (*flopping resignedly into an armchair*): Why shouldn't you like it when the kids and I have a terrific relationship? I don't understand you. That's one of the main attractions for coming home. I love those kids and you'll never make a "heavy" out of me!

SHE: OK! But I can't do it all! You have to back me up and you never do! Listen to what they just did today . . .

HE (*disgusted with her but not with his children*): Cut it out!

SHE (*totally exasperated*): Why? Don't you want to hear? Don't you want to be part of this family? Don't you want to take any responsibility?

HE (*getting up again to counterattack*): I take enough

responsibility earning our living. And I don't like
you when you tattle on the kids! In fact, I can't
stand it . . .

The Robinsons thought they were battling about their ideas
of "parental authority," "doing a good job of raising the
kids," and the role of the "man of the house." But these are
only superficial cultural stereotypes. Once the therapy group
began to probe what was really bothering Tom and Myra, we
discovered some much deeper intimate issues which the couple did not dare confront.

It developed that Myra was jealous of Tom's love for the
kids because he was not making enough passionate love to
her. Tom, in turn, was not making love to Myra because
since the kids came she had been a disappointment to him.
She did not conform to his definition of a "good mother."
What turned him off completely was her tattling because this
aroused a strong memory of ugly, angry emotions from his
past. His mother used to tattle to his father about his own
misdeeds, and his father used to beat discipline into him
every Saturday morning after his mother, behind the boy's
back, had presented the father with a list of misdeeds!

Myra is also bitter because, since the kids came, the
husband turned off loving her. She thinks that he thinks that
she thinks: "I love my kids more than him. I only used the
man to have a father for my kids, who are my joy and pride
and who fulfill me." She therefore thinks: "He is jealous of
my love for the kids and punishes me by withholding his love
from me. He does not want to share me with anybody."

In our training group this spiral of misconceptions collapsed as the facts were exposed. By using techniques to be
discussed in the next chapters, the Robinsons learned to level
about their real feelings, wants, and expectations. The issue
of disciplining the children never came up again. It was
spontaneously handled by one partner or the other, as the
situation demanded.

Another popular way to divert aggressive feelings is to
repress them as "irrational" in one's personal life but to
express them by directing (displacing) them onto such *symbols* as President John F. Kennedy, Senator Robert F.
Kennedy, the Reverend Dr. Martin Luther King—or onto
the anonymity of large, faceless groups: perhaps "kooks" or
the Cosa Nostra or other criminals, or the Viet Cong and
other "enemies." This displacement of hostility ultimately
enables political leaders to engage in the most catastrophic
form of aggression: war.

Not that politicians are the only ones who are busy manipulating human aggression. Spokesmen for the Judeo-Christian religions have urged people to pray it away. Psychiatrists have tried to analyze it or rationalize it away. The late Emily Post and other etiquette devotees would have liked to smile it away. Nothing has worked, and for the most logical reason. Anger is part of the personality, like the sex drive. It can be displaced, channeled, modified, or repressed. But it cannot go away. This is why our efforts are designed to make people face it and decontaminate it as sensibly as human fallibility permits.

We believe that the inability to manage personal conflicts is at the root of the crisis that threatens the structure of the American family. Communications between children and parents are breaking down. More and more young people are "tuning out" by escaping into the world of drugs and other short-lived emotional kicks. One out of every three marriages ends in divorce. In our largest and most "advanced" state, California, the figure is approaching an almost incredible one out of every two.

Millions of other couples continue to live together physically and legally, yet emotionally apart. Atrophy, boredom, casual infidelities, and false-front façades "for the children's sake" are no longer exceptional. No one knows how many couples are emotionally divorced. We do know that millions of husbands and wives live in card houses held together by fantasy; by social, religious, economic, or legal pressures—or by the fear of change.

The philosophers say modern man is alienated, trapped by loneliness, yet hostile to those who might come too close. They blame this sense of alienation for the anxieties of most people, for humanity's daily failures of heart and nerve. But the philosophers have stated the problem backward. It is not alienation that is becoming unbearable. It is intimacy.

We have entered a psychological ice age. Except for occasional bursts of warmth, often fueled by sex after a few cocktails, truly intimate encounter has begun to disappear from civilized Western life. Closeness has become a paradox: longed for, but increasingly intolerable. Without the sweet anesthesias of role playing, libido, or liquor many people can no longer find each other or stand each other. Sustained closeness between man and wife, parents and child, and friend with friend, is in danger of becoming extinct. We believe that this quiet private threat endangers civilization as severely as the public threats of nuclear incineration, automation, urbanization and others that are constantly talked about.

Why should this be happening today, of all times? Again, the answers are so close that it is easy to overlook them. Not so long ago, the family was not a small unit but a tribe. Tribal people rubbed shoulders constantly. Everybody used to know everybody else's business. There was less privacy but more opportunity for sharing failures and unhappiness, to get attention and help from friendly souls. The things that matter in life were more visible and understandable. Today, as everybody knows, the family is segmented. We no longer witness many happenings; we merely talk *about* them. And much of the talk has become specialist's talk that only other specialists can grasp. Who can readily share the joys and ulcers of a husband who comes home from his work as a missile expert?

These trends have turned individuals into faces within a "lonely crowd," who worship privacy and autonomy as the supposedly ideal way of coping with intimate problems. Marriage, therefore, is more of a closed-circuit affair than ever. The burden on mates and lovers is heavier; they must fulfill vital functions (reacting, sharing, etc.) that used to be the job of more than one other person. No wonder that the circuits of so many marriages are becoming overloaded, and that mates are tuning each other out and playing games with each other.

When Dr. Eric Berne's book, *Games People Play,* became a runaway bestseller, publishing experts were surprised. They shouldn't have been. America's living rooms and bedrooms are full of partners who are too weak or frightened or not sufficiently knowledgeable to tolerate authentic encounters with their supposed intimates. They recognized their own camouflaging rituals in Dr. Berne's somewhat cynical and overly flip but essentially accurate descriptions. Remember "Uproar," the pointless fight that is provoked by a husband or wife early in the evening merely to avoid sex later? It is all but a national pastime. So are such marital games as "If it weren't for you" and "Look how hard I've tried."

Dr. Berne performed a valuable service because he made game-players aware of what they are doing. However, we believe he was too pessimistic in appraising their potential capacity to drop their masks and become authentic persons capable of intimacy.

Our own clinical experience indicates that most couples would dearly like to stop playing games. They often realize that the camouflaged life is needlessly tiring and anxiety-arousing. Game-players never really know "where they're at." The more skillful they are, the less they know, because their objective is to cover up motives and try to trick their partners into doing things. The game-player's life is loaded with uncertainties, and human beings are poorly equipped to withstand uncertainty.

Unfortunately, one can't simply command game-players: "Stop Playing Games!" Something better must fill the void. People have to manage their emotions somehow, especially their aggressions. (Games are actually aggression that camouflage the desire to exploit a partner, manipulate or weaken him, do him in, etc.)

Constructive fighting makes for game-free living. It is a liberating, creative alternative that works. Since we introduced fight training, the rate of reconciliation among our Institutes problem couples has increased sharply. Follow-up studies indicate that most of our graduates are living much more satisfying (if perhaps noisier) lives than before. And for the most tragic victims of our psychological ice age, the children, the benefits are incalculable. For them, a sense of genuine family closeness is as important as food and drink. When a "nest" cools or disintegrates, children can grow only amid enormous handicaps. Young children especially thrive on intimacy and starve emotionally when they cannot share and learn it. We regard the neglect of intimacy and the absence of intimate models within many families as principally responsible for the current "generation gap." Those who are deprived of an intimate nest may never care to build or to protect one for themselves.

For intimate partners, perhaps the richest payoff of well-managed conflict comes with yielding after a fight. Any intimate relationship implies some readiness to yield one's own self-interest when it clashes with that of the partner. Everybody knows that the give-and-take of trying to get along with someone often means bending one's own will to the wishes of the other. This is never easy because the psychological price of yielding to another is a loss (however temporary and partial) of one's own identity. Realistic intimates find that this is a small price as long as it is part of an equitable, mutual process and leads to an improved relationship.

The final benefit of yielding is the tremendous feeling of well-being that comes from making a beloved person happy. This is why it feels so delicious to make one's wife or husband laugh. It also explains why "It is better to give than to receive." In true intimacy, it really is. Which is one more reason why intimacy is worth fighting for.

2. Fighting For (and Against) Intimacy

When they first consult us, most people are in a skeptical frame of mind. Neither fighting *nor* intimacy seems especially attractive or useful to them. Indeed, some of them find our ideas revolting and one caller wouldn't even stay for her first training session.

We recognized her immediately. She was an attractive, wealthy young woman, the mother of three children, and her picture often appeared in the newspaper society pages. She had been divorced twice and was about to embark on a third marriage, but she was beginning to doubt whether she would ever succeed in maintaining an intimate relationship.

When we told her that our counseling leads to intimacy by teaching clients how to manage conflicts, she became indignant. "I came here to learn how to love," she said, "not to fight." And she flounced out of the office.

Most of our clients are not as prominent or as insensitive. They are housewives, secretaries, business and professional men—just about anybody. They are referred to us by family physicians, psychiatrists, thoughtful divorce lawyers, the famous Los Angeles Reconciliation Court, or by friends. Yet when we suggest that a couple join one of our fight-training groups, their initial reaction is usually scoffing or worse.

"What do you think?" the wife will ask her husband as they leave the Institute after their first interview.

"I think they're nuts," the husband often replies. Couples laugh at the notion that they, of all people, should learn to argue with each other. At the same time, they are intrigued, and they are likely to be motivated to give the idea a try. After all, when a couple comes to us for help this is an indication that they are ready to make at least some changes.

When they do show up, they have usually made a secret pact not to mention certain important but embarrassing facts, instead of being completely frank as our rules demand. We have learned to ignore these deals. Group pressure almost invariably smokes out such secrets and, besides, this pact-making is often a couple's first act of true intimacy in years.

34

People think it incongruous that intimacy needs to be taught. We point out to them that it is not a birthright or a talent, like a musical ear. It is probably the most civilized relationship within the capability of mankind. Furthermore, it is a conscious choice. Man must want to be intimate; the choice is up to him and intimacy can be achieved only when intimates rub the rough edges of their personalities against one another.

It would be a mistake to interpret the fantastic U.S. divorce rate as a flight from intimacy. Actually, it reflects a hunger *for* intimacy. Most couples split up because they failed to find the intimacy that they longed for; or because they cannot endure the pain of living without the intimacy that they once felt they possessed.

Divorce and the remarriage which usually follows show that people are ambivalent about the stresses of intimate living, but determined to try again and again. "Determination" is not too strong a word. The proportion of single adults in the population continues to dwindle into an ever smaller fringe group of hard-core loners. Fifty years ago almost one-fifth of the population never married. Now, all but 6½% of women and 7% of men have married at least once. The fact is that divorcees are marrying-type people.

Mostly they are misguided idealists who yearn for sweet but empty harmony instead of an honest relationship where the normal hostilities of each partner are aired so there will be more love and understanding, rather than less, as the years go by. Ironically, the very idea of intimacy, just like the concept of aggression, is suspect, even repugnant, and our trainee couples have shown us why.

Many consider intimacy dull and predictable and cite the saying, "Familiarity breeds contempt." This notion reflects the modern *Ersatz* age. Along with substitutes for sugar, rubber, and practically everything else, intimacy substitutes have become popular. Pseudo-intimates wear masks and play games. Their marriages become predictable and boring. They can even predict how their partners will react before cocktails, after one drink and after two.

True familiarity, on the other hand, is forever fascinating because the human brain can, and does, meet any situation in an endless variety of ways. Children tend to display this wonderful creative responsiveness before parents teach them to be on guard against openness and transparency. No wonder we must teach adults to learn to let their guard down, at least when they are dealing with loved ones.

Intimacy is confusing for other reasons as well. People are likely to equate it with sexual intercourse, even though the two can be entirely unrelated. Or they confuse intimacy with being swallowed up. Engulfment *is* a real threat for intimates, but only when they don't know how to fight right. Nonfighters can easily be overwhelmed by their partners. Constructive fighters can't be overrun. Their aggressions act as their defenses. And aggression has still another useful function. Paradoxical as it may seem, we discovered that hostility is the very emotion that makes intimacy possible and bearable!

Here is how this process works:

Intelligent fighting regulates the intensity of intimate involvement by occasionally creating relief from it. It makes intimacy controllable. It enables partners to locate what we call the "optimal distance" from each other—the range where each is close enough not to feel "left out," yet free to engage in his own thoughts and autonomous activities, uncontaminated by the other's encroachments.

Almost nobody realizes that some fights have no issue except: "Keep your distance!" These seemingly mysterious encounters often occur after sex.

Many couples tell us that the morning after their lovemaking was particularly and mutually satisfying, a fight will break out over "nothing." Perhaps the husband gets up and can't find any clean underwear. Or the coffee is too weak. Or the kids are too noisy. Or the wife complains that the husband didn't put the car in the garage. Or she wishes out loud that he would say a pleasant word at breakfast, for once. Anyway, he gets furious. The wife becomes enraged. He growls. She blows up and reminds him that she not only made a special effort to make love nicely the night before; she had also lately done *this* for him and *that* for him and why does he have to be such an ungrateful, ill-tempered bastard?

This is one of a never-ending series of fights that helps partners to find and to reset their optimal range—the psychological distance from each other that makes them most comfortable. Unconsciously they designed the fight to find out how close an intimate can come without making the partner feel engulfed; and how far he can move away without making the partner feel rejected.

Once we had learned to interpret these fights correctly, we advised our trainees not to be too vexed by them. We also cautioned clients not to be envious when somebody said of another couple, "They're very close, you know." Optimal distance or, if you prefer, optimal closeness, is the ideal goal—not extreme closeness. Of course what's optimal for one partner may be uncomfortable for the other. But this difference can be adjusted and we teach trainees how to measure—and how to make up for—such a natural disparity.

One amusing but useful at-home exercise begins with the partners conversing while they face each other about 15 feet apart. As they continue to talk, Partner A walks up to Partner B until they make physical contact. Then Partner A slowly backs away until he reaches the right distance to make conversation comfortable for A. At that point A stops and the partners measure the distance between each other with a tape measure. The experiment is repeated with Partner B doing the walking and backing up. Almost invariably, the partners' distance preferences differ. These measurements, although inexact, suggest each partner's tolerance for closeness. The partner who requires more distance in order to be comfortable is the one who will be more likely to start fights for optimal distance.

"Don't come too close to me" is the message he is signaling.

Every intimate sends such a signal from time to time because true intimacy is a state of entwinement that occasionally proves exhausting. We advise couples to take this fatigue seriously and to study each other's limits. It is not wise to kid oneself about depth of a partner's reservoir for milk of human kindness.

We tell trainees to develop their own distancing techniques. If they are having a lot of optimal distance fights they may find it advisable to take a vacation with another couple to dilute intimate contacts; or they might try vacationing separately, with each partner taking along one or more of the children.

Usually, however, optimal-distance problems subside after periodic solitary self-confinement at home. We call these pauses "refueling." Some people establish a private music corner where they listen to Beethoven or to the Beatles while they allow their recuperative forces to take hold. Others meditate over a book or a stamp collection. Our trainees know that when a partner puts up a sign (either figuratively or sometimes, literally) that says, "Do not disturb—Refueling!", nobody needs to feel guilty or angry. The refueling partner is only taking a break to make intimacy work better in the long run. According to the outmoded romantic model of marriage, it may not be "nice" to pull up one's drawbridge and withdraw into Fortress Me. In realistic intimacy, it is necessary and desirable as long as it is not misused as a cover-up for habitual withdrawal.

One of our trainees, an executive in a scientific-research corporation, used to drive his wife crazy because he almost never talked to her. This made her feel all the more rejected because he constantly talked to strangers all over the world on his ham radio set. We suggested that the couple play golf together, but this wife had a better idea. She displayed a natural genius for short-circuiting her husband's withdrawal maneuvers and decided to take a course in ham radio operating. The husband still does not like the eye-balling of physical confrontation, but he now chatters happily and intimately with the wife from the ham radio in his car. He is also becoming receptive to intimate conversation at home because he was so impressed by her ingenuity and persistence. He thinks, "If I am that important to her..."

We would be fooling ourselves and our readers if we were to suggest that anything ever stays the same in intimacy. Nothing in life ever does. A husband's life may not change materially when the last child goes off to college; but his wife's life changes a great deal, and so their life as a couple should be intimately renegotiated. Perhaps the husband should agree to refuel less often. Perhaps he should encourage the wife's ambitions to take a job or go back to college or get involved in politics. The point is that changing situations are best met with aggressive give-and-take. There is no better way to spot problems and come up with new solutions.

Until somewhat more than ten years ago, marriage counseling at our Institute was vastly less sophisticated. We worked along conventional lines and with conventional results. Aggression was considered an outgrowth of elemental frustration and self-hate and therefore "bad." We emphasized acceptance, warmth, and positive regard for the partner. We tried to achieve reconciliations by concentrating on salvaging conflict-free areas of a relationship and by-passing the "nasty" battlegrounds.

Then, one day in the wild, lonely California mountains, the senior author of this book had a searing personal experience.

He and his wife Peggy were on a camping vacation in the High Sierras with Jim and Nancy McDonald, old college friends. After a day's hard climb, they were relaxing in front of the fire near their tents, playing pinochle and enjoying an after-dinner drink. Jim and Peggy were losing. Suddenly Nancy looked up at her husband and said, "Jim, you're cheating!"

Jim threw down his cards on the improvised table. He

shouted, "You're a stupid bitch!" and stamped into the McDonalds' tent. Nancy made no move to go after him. She was as furious as he was and the fun had gone out of the evening. Later on, the Bachs could not avoid overhearing their friends next door.

NANCY: Why did you run off in the middle of the game? What's the matter with you? Are you drunk or something? Are you trying to ruin our vacation? Now you go apologize to Peggy and George. You're a spoiled little boy and a bad loser.

JIM: Don't be so tough with me, kiddo! If they didn't like what I did, so what? Why should that bother *you* . . . ?

NANCY: Because I don't like it either. And don't you call me "stupid" in front of them ever again!

JIM: Hell, stop bitching and come here and let's make love.

NANCY: Sh! You had too much to drink and you're talking too loud.

JIM: For Crissakes! There's only bears out here. I don't know what's the matter with you. Why don't you come over here?

NANCY: I don't feel like touching you tonight, Jim! You're not acting very lovable.

JIM: This is one hell of a time to tell me! It's my vacation, you know. (*Some scuffling was heard.*)

NANCY: Sh! Leave me alone and don't make a scene! Let's go to sleep. It's very late! Leave me alone! No! No! Don't!

In the morning the Bachs found Nancy curled up under a coat in the back of the McDonalds' station wagon. Even in sleep her face looked tense and she had locked herself in.

Dr. Bach went to fetch Jim, and on the way back to the station wagon Jim explained what had happened.

JIM (*embarrassed*): You have to help me. I feel so rotten. I'm afraid Nancy is really through with me.

DR. B: How come?

JIM: She said my behavior in front of you and Peggy was disgusting—which it was, of course. She said she couldn't feel sexy with a man who couldn't hold his liquor and who was a card cheat and rude and crude. All she wanted was to be left alone and go to sleep.

DR. B: We heard you and then we fell asleep. You let her be, didn't you?

JIM (*speaking rapidly*): Yes, but I couldn't sleep. I got madder and madder, and also sadder about the whole mess . . . on the second day of our vacation! Finally, I fell asleep, but not for long. I woke up and wanted to make up with her. I went to her cot and tried to caress her. This made her furious. She pushed me away and this time I got really mad. It frightened me how much I hated her. I actually kicked her off the cot and slapped her face! I cursed her and told her what a lousy wife she was! She cried and then she yelled: "It's all ruined," took her clothes and rushed out. I cooled down immediately and felt terrible—guilty, stupid, ashamed. I started to look for her, but I'd left the flashlight in your tent and didn't want to disturb you. I couldn't see anything. I was shaking and praying for the dawn to hurry up. When it finally came, it occurred to me she might have gone to the car. I ran down there and found her, thank God. But she wouldn't answer my knocks on the windows. I'm afraid something snapped last night.

Jim's excitement had died down. Now his face was grave.

DR. B: You're right. This is a crisis for Nancy. But there is something much more fundamental on her mind than your card playing and your manners.

JIM (*resigned*): What?

DR. B: I don't know. You have to listen to her. Let her tell you what's really bothering her. Let her spill her guts, everything she has on her mind. Don't chase her off any more! OK?

JIM (*interested*): OK, I'll try to take all she has to dish out. You know, I really do love her.

Mrs. Bach had persuaded Nancy to unlock herself and climb out of the car. But as soon as Nancy sighted Jim, she grabbed his mountaineer's stick out of his hand and began to flail away at him, aiming at his head and face and yelling: "You bastard, you bastard, I hate you! I hate you!"

Her face was distorted with tears and pain. Jim didn't try to stop her. He just protected his head and face with his arms as best he could until the Bachs took the stick away from Nancy. Nancy said she wanted to take the bus home by herself, but the area was too remote. Finally, Dr. Bach took her by the hand and said, "Let's hit the trail."

Nancy started at a furious pace as if to try and get away. After almost an hour of fast, silent hiking uphill, Dr. Bach begged her to slow down. She snapped, "You rest! Just leave me alone!" and she vanished. A few minutes later Jim rushed by almost at a trot. Dr. Bach waved to him and said, "Good luck! Stick with her. Let her talk!"

When the Bachs finally encountered Jim and Nancy ten hours later at a higher camp the McDonalds had obviously made up and were in excellent spirits. Next morning, both couples resumed their hike, but Nancy slowed down to talk about Jim.

NANCY: I really love him.

DR B: But yesterday you screamed at him "I hate you, I hate you!"

NANCY (*blushing*): That was very bad, very embarrassing. But I just couldn't help it. He infuriates me so when he behaves like a jerk! He's such a gifted and wonderful man! I can't stand being around him when he makes an ass of himself.

DR B: You mean when we were playing cards or when the two of you are at home?

NANCY: Oh, I don't care what he does here. He works so hard all year. If he wants to be a little boy out here, fine. But at home with the kids, I can't take it. He calls them filthy names and has absolutely no respect for them. They love him so much, but now they're beginning to be afraid. They're afraid to open up to their own father, because he'll call them "stupid" or "nuts" or make fun of their feelings.

DR B: I assume that the two of you talked about these things this morning. (*Nancy nodded*). But did you ever bring them up with him before?

NANCY (*agitated*): No, that's just it. You can't ever fight with Jim. I don't think we ever had a real fight until now. It's all one-way. He just calls me "castrating bitch" or he'll accuse me of being a "lousy mother" or a "lousy lay." Then he starts drinking and never stops yelling. When he's through with me, he starts picking on the kids. He knows that gets me ... like a knife! I try to control myself. But I'm so desperate! I want this marriage to work!

DR. B: Can't you accept him the way he is?

NANCY: Not a chance ... how can I go on like this? Oh,

George, can't you see the fix I'm in? I've thrown my life into this marriage and I don't want to waste it! If I didn't think he could change and live up to what I know he really can be, I guess I'd lose my love for him.

DR. B: Well, Nancy, I guess that you and Jim—and Peggy and I, too—have terrible fights just because we care where we stand with one another! If we didn't care, you wouldn't fight back. And what about Jim? He'd just say, "Oh, that hysterical female!" and let it go at that . . . or else he'd just leave. . . .

Over the next several years, we carefully studied and restudied the hostilities between Jim and Nancy and reconsidered many of the fights between couples who came to us for counseling. We were struck by the enormous variety of issues that lay repressed behind such fights as we had witnessed between Jim and Nancy. The reservoirs of hate within them were too vast to be ignored. And surely it wasn't wise to stand by and watch one partner react to a minor offense, such as Jim's alleged cheating at cards, with such bomblike punishment as Nancy had meted out in return. Jim and Nancy entered training with us and we helped them to negotiate other lingering issues that they had not disclosed on vacation. Yet they, as well as most of the other couples who turned to us for help, could not be considered "sick."

Neither could most of the people we call "loners." The term does not refer to left-out celibates but to the "in-group" of "cool heads" whose wariness of "entanglements" has turned them into autonomy-worshipers for whom intimacy is at best a quaint, old-fashioned word.

There are good reasons why intimacy is, among so many other things, sadly unfashionable these days. Few models exist for it. Children rarely see it at home. Many of today's heroes are not intimate types but free-roamers, unencumbered wheeler-dealers, self-made, self-propelled, self-sufficient operators of the James Bond mold—supposedly free to maneuver and become winners in the market place where nobody cares about the whole person but only about making *quid-pro-quo*—"deals."

Movies, novels, and TV emphasize broken homes, broken dreams, and cynicism—the failures of intimacy. Organization life, whether as a den mother or a corporation pyramid-climber, offers status, group identity and usually also money, and such rewards seem more attractive than the dimly perceived benefits of intimacy. No wonder people become emotional conservatives. They ask: why take an unnecessary risk? Intimacy looks to them like an investment in a high-risk stock: nice if you win, disastrous if you lose, and therefore best left alone.

So some loners turn themselves into "playboys" who leave intimacy to the "squares" and frolic around in a sexual Disneyland. Others find substitutes by becoming excessively preoccupied with cars, playing cards, tennis, power tools, record collections, the racing form; or they take refuge by submerging themselves in a group, perhaps the P.T.A., the N.A.A.C.P., the John Birch Society, or the local ski club.

Some are intimacy sufferers: college professors, missile engineers, and organization men who go through the motions of pseudo-intimacy at home but get their real kicks in the work hierarchy outside. Finally there are the truly alienated who "make out" with fantasy connections—perhaps via the TV tube or the bottle or drugs—or whose frustrations find outlets in rioting, murder or political assassinations.

It is no coincidence that the three young men accused in the most appalling murders of the Kennedy-Johnson era were, perhaps above all else, loners.

Lee Harvey Oswald, who shot President Kennedy, was a "withdrawn and evasive boy who intensely disliked talking about himself and his feelings." At 13, according to the Warren Commission, a psychiatrist noted that "Lee liked to give the impression that he did not care for other people but preferred to keep to himself, so that he was not bothered and did not have to make the effort of communicating." Lee himself then said, "I don't want a friend and I don't like to talk to people." After rejecting capitalism as well as Communism, he married a Russian girl six weeks after another girl had rejected him. He lived apart from his wife except on weekends, frequently struck her and told her to go back to the Soviet Union. The Warren Commission concluded: "His life was characterized by isolation, frustration and failure."

Sirhan B. Sirhan, who shot Senator Kennedy, was the least outgoing of six children in a family whose members rarely spoke to each other. He shunned girls, made no friends and kept his name out of the school yearbook. A schoolmate described him as "kind of secretive." A local priest remembered him as "humble and aloof." His most intense emotions were directed at the Jews. He hated them for humiliating his Middle Eastern homeland during the six-day war against Israel and envisioned Senator Kennedy as the arch-foe of his private cause: the violent dreams of Arab nationalism.

James Earl Ray, who was indicted in the murder of the

Reverend Dr. King, was the oldest of nine children who were either placed in foster homes or just drifted away from the family. In grade school he once pierced his brother's ear with a knife. He would flinch when a teacher merely reached out to touch him gently. Imprisoned for a series of petty, lonely crimes, he became a self-isolate known as "The Mole." When he escaped, he found company in cheap bars and prostitutes and ran an ad in an underground newspaper for a "passionate married female." A girl instructor at a commercial dancing class remembered him as "clumsy" and another recalled that he trembled when she came close to him. When he was on the run after the Dr. King killing, he shopped for pornography in Toronto. Again he sought out prostitutes and one said he came close to crying when she showed him photographs of her fatherless children.

All loners are grappling with the same private dilemma. They are trying to exist psychologically alone and bear the stress of isolation rather than live as authentic twosomes and bear the stress of intimacy. Most loners are nominally attached to someone. They may go steady or be married. But they cannot abide being emotionally dependent. They don't get truly involved. They detest tension and personal hostilities. The true loner would rather split than fight.

We have rarely met a happy loner. Most are cynically flip or sadly resigned; losers or refugees from false paradises. And they don't know that being a loner is downright dangerous. No one is close enough to him to protect him from irrational fantasies or ideals. Instead of intimates, he has acquaintances. These contacts are so superficial that they usually just humor him along; they lack authority to offer the loner sensible criticism and the perspective of reality. No one knows him well enough to judge, praise, or condemn him. Tragically, the loner who does not come into serious conflict with society and the law, tends to become a vicious self-critic. His self-attacks can become lethal to the point of suicide. A buffer-buddy could step in and say, "Stop that self-castration! You can fight it out by fighting me. Fighting with yourself is a depressing and dangerously self-splitting business." But loners have no buddies.

A temporary solution for people who cannot come to terms with their problems of human closeness is to buy synthetic intimacy in the form of psychotherapy. Many emotionally needy people deny themselves even this form of *Ersatz* friendship because folklore insists that one has to be "sick" or a "nut" to reach out for the aid of a psychotherapist. How unfair these labels are! At our Institute, we do see a few "psychiatrically sick" people; we treat them individually and as patients. But our typical caller is only emotionally hungry, starved for intimacy, searching for the solution to the dilemma of finding a way to become entwined without becoming engulfed.

When would-be intimates do seek help from psychiatrists, psychologists, and marriage counselors, they often fail to find it. The patients may be exposed to fuzzy notions about the "art of loving" or mechanistic physical suggestions about the techniques of love-making. Even the privileged few who have the money, time and inclination to delve into themselves through psychoanalysis may learn little about how to live with a mate. Many partners, indeed, grow farther apart during analysis and become more self-oriented as they pursue the sophisticated psychoanalytic game of self-contemplation through which a patient often becomes his own selfish pet.

Part of the problem may be the therapist's, not the patient's. Many psychotherapists are themselves loners at heart. They write books about the art of loving and creative marriage, but the personal lives of many of these experts are models of the psychologically "sophisticated" loner striving only for individual growth. The fashionable term for this selfish effort is "self-actualization." Many therapists worship autonomy so fiercely that they are unsuited for the role of helping to keep people together. And the divorce rate among these doctors is uncomfortably high.

An even more serious trouble with many therapists is their basic misunderstanding of husbands and wives who complain that they "can't live with and can't live without" their partners. Traditionally, psychiatrists have believed that when couples experience difficulties in the intimacy department these complaints are superficial symptoms and reflect deep-rooted problems *within each partner*. In marriage, according to this theory, the partner displaces his self-hate on his mate. A problem couple is therefore diagnosed as two sick, incompatible individuals who are traditionally treated separately by two psychiatrists.

In effect, the partners are told: "This is not a marital problem because your troubles as a couple derive from underlying causes. One or both of you, inside, as individuals, are too emotionally disturbed, too immature and perhaps too narcissistic to manage the stresses and strains, the give-and-take, of intimacy."

Then begins the weary archaeological process of digging out within each partner his reservoir of past and present resentments. In the end, according to this tradition, calm mutual understanding should replace aggression, which is regarded not as natural but as irrational and therefore capable of being purged. This is how traditional psychiatry often colludes with a couple's favorite way out of a marriage: the use of "blamesmanship." Each partner simply calls the other too "sick" to live with.

Many marriages that might have been salvaged receive the *coup de grâce* in this way because all too often partners who enter individual psychiatric treatment become more intimate with their respective psychiatrists (and sometimes with certain divorce lawyers) than with each other.

As we studied the stresses of intimacy among our clients, however, we discovered that most of their problems were not within themselves but were inherent in the complexities of an intimate relationship. It was the intimate system that was out of balance. We therefore work with such people as couples and in groups in order to restore their "swing" and we do not treat them as "patients."

3. Training Lovers to be Fighters

To confirm our suspicion that intimacy problems are common and not confined to "problem couples" who come to our Institute, we conducted an experiment. We asked people whom we knew through our business consulting, research, graduate teaching, and through social contacts, to help us recruit "normally happy" couples for detailed study. Our contacts were instructed: "Think of all the married couples you know. Then select the happiest of them for nomination to a 'Marriage Elite', the imaginary Phi Beta Kappa of true intimacy."

We selected 50 "elite" couples and asked them, among other things, how they handled conflict situations. One question was: "On the few occasions when your husband is angry with you, what does he do?" Then we asked: "What do you think he would like to do?"

When such questions were put to these "happy" husbands and wives separately, the result was distressing: almost none had any notion of what was going on in the inner world of the other. Typically, the wife said: "When he does get miffed about something, he is very forgiving and thinks nothing of it"; yet the husband told us that he fought an appalling fight within himself in order to control his annoyance; and he maintained control mostly because he feared his wife might reject him for breaking their unspoken taboo against conflict.

Three groups emerged from our experiment: card-house marriages, game-playing marriages, and true intimates. The card-house partners were the largest group. They put on a fake front. They were almost totally lacking in intimacy and were held together largely by the partners' neurotic concern for appearances, social success, status, and "respectability."

The partners in the second (and smaller) group were somewhat more intimate. But essentially they had resigned themselves to game-playing and other ritualized routines. Many of these unions were held together by such outside pressures as economic advantage and fear of change. They were mutual protective associations who looked on their

47

marriage as pretty much of a lost cause but felt that it would be disloyal and ill-mannered to complain about it, especially since the loneliness of being unmarried would probably be worse.

The third group consisted of only two couples. They checked out as natural geniuses at maintaining realistic intimacy. But when we asked them for the secret of their marital success, they said they had no idea what it was. All we discovered was that these marriage champions—unlike the other couples in our experiment but like successfully married pairs whom everybody occasionally encounters— argued constantly. They thought conflict was as natural as eating.

"Of course," they said, "we argue about practically everything!" Their special characteristic was that they had learned to live with aggression comfortably.

As we continued to study our clients' fights, evidence began to accumulate that couples who can't display their hostilities are not polite but phony. Gradually we started to distinguish between constructive and destructive aggression and learned that anger is manageable—not a dark, uncontrollable "mean streak." And we recognized that aggressive leveling and bonding behavior can't be learned in cozy chats between patient and doctor. It takes practice and is best learned by doing, preferably with a therapist as guide.

Our Institute is not limited to the training of marital fighters. We conduct therapy and research for many purposes and use a wide variety of methods. But for our fight trainees we offer, first of all, the self-development program for such individual problem spouses as Harold Jacobson, the fight-phobic husband who left his wife wordlessly after 20 years of ostensibly peaceful marriage. Like Mr. Jacobson, the majority of clients in this program are smarting from the hurt and exhaustion of a recent failure in their love life. They can't— or don't want to—be intimate with anybody for a while. Their morale may be so low that we see them by themselves before we place them, along with eight to ten individuals who face similar problems, in a self-development group—the same kind of group where Mr. Jacobson learned to stand up to a woman "worse" than his wife.

Then, as soon as advisable, we ask each self-developer and his own partner to join one of our groups that are reserved for couples only. These meet in series of 13 four-hour evening sessions, usually with four to ten couples, plus Dr. Bach or a member of the Institute's staff which consists of two

full-time and five part-time co-therapists and marriage counselors.*

In recent years we have also trained couples in nonstop
"marathons lasting 24 hours or more." The therapist may
leave these sessions for periodic short naps, but trainees must
nap and eat in the meeting room and may only leave to go to
the bathroom. Their fatigue breaks down embarrassment and
reticence and helps to make sure that the cardinal rule of
frankness will prevail.

Sometimes even therapists who have become convinced
that our methods are sound find it difficult to apply this rule.
Some years ago the senior author of this book agreed to
serve as consultant to a psychiatrist in another city who
wanted to conduct a fight-training marathon.

When the visiting therapist arrived, the host psychiatrist
said that among the seven married couples who would attend
the session one husband was a doctor and another a minister.
The psychiatrist said that he did not wish to embarrass these
professional men and had therefore declared a taboo on all
mentions of professions during the marathon. Dr. Bach disagreed. He argued that anybody's profession is an integral
part of his person, that it could not be ignored and that he
would take the disagreement to the group for discussion.

The group was shocked. It troubled these well-mannered
people to see their psychiatrist so personally embattled, and
they were bothered at the prospect of facing themselves and
each other with every vestige of their personal masks removed. After considerable debate, Dr. Bach persuaded one
of the wives to confess that she had made a pact with her
husband not to discuss certain particularly ugly rows that
had, on more than one occasion, deteriorated into physical
maulings when they were on their boat. Eventually it developed that several other couples had made similar secret
deals.

By the time Dr. Bach left for his first nap, the marathon
had made almost no progress. The couples, in fact, accused
him of increasing the tensions between them and stirring up
new and unnecessary trouble. At the same time, they did not
want to seem uncooperative with a respected visiting therapist who had come all the way from California. And one
ice-breaking reality overshadowed all other considerations:

* The Institute has trained more than 200 other therapists and counselors. It has held workshops all over the United States, Canada, and
Europe. A training tape explaining the program is available to professionals from the American Association of Marriage Counsellors, Logan,
Utah.

each of these couples was on the brink of a breakup. Something had to be done. Slowly, group opinion came around to the reluctant conclusion that perhaps frankness ought to be tried after all.

When Dr. Bach returned, the devotion to old-fashioned etiquette that had kept this group in chains had broken open. Accounts of truly dreadful fights poured out of every couple. In each marriage physical violence had been committed and several of these intimates had more than fleetingly considered killing their partners! Toward the end of the session the pressure to air their feelings about their fights became so intense that Dr. Bach was reminded of jet landing jams at New York's Kennedy airport. These couples had finally convinced themselves that it is "nastier" to try living with a phobia of aggression than to accept and air hostile feelings and negotiate realistic settlements. In the end they were even willing to concede something else that our trainees have taught us: the more an intimate resists the concept of aggressive frankness, the more deeply troubled his marriage is likely to be.

The relief felt by these marathoners at the end of this traumatic session was immense. They continued to meet under the new rule with their own therapist and ultimately not one of these marriages broke up.

At our Institute group sessions convene either in the therapist's home or in our cheerful, modern suite of penthouse offices atop one of Beverly Hills' principal medical buildings. There is plenty of light, plenty of fresh air, and plenty of room to maneuver during fighting. Our modern black leather swivel armchairs are equipped with casters and can be tipped in any direction. This allows combatants to move toward—or away from—each other as their moods and optimal distance needs dictate, or as they perceive cues from their partners. One room is wired for sound and we often play back fights so that the protagonists can study their techniques after the heat of battle has died down. We also run feedbacks by videotape over closed-circuit television, which enables fighters to watch every nuance of how they handle their conflicts and how their opponents listen, dodge, and counterattack.

The training of groups, rather than individuals or couples, has considerable advantages. Group work is less expensive, faster, and more effective. Couples quickly become less dependent on the therapist. The group milieu stimulates growth in a natural way. Trainees live out, for everyone to see, the patterns and postures that would only be talked about in individual sessions. And as group members question each other about their problems, they don't only weigh the then-and-there of what happened in the past; instead they demonstrate to everybody in the room the here-and-now of how they feel and what they're really all about.

Candid challenges thrive in this atmosphere. Faking, blamesmanship, and digging into ancient psychiatric museums are reduced to a minimum.

The group setting brings out within each couple an appreciation of how they differ from the others, as well as feelings of resemblance. Both feelings are helpful and bonding. When a couple learns that one of their own fight issues, which appeared unique to them, is a common feature of what we call pairing behavior, they are relieved. They say, "Oh, you fight about that, too?" and suddenly their problem no longer seems hopeless. Obviously, too, a wife may understand her own man better when she hears somebody else's husband exclaim, "It drives me nuts when my wife insists that I'm supposed to be cheerful every goddamned minute of the day!"

As mates compare their own headaches with those reported by others, they almost always find couples who are worse off. This, too, is reassuring and often results in a couple's discovery that they have intimate resources—a sense of humor, for instance—that others lack. The group makes the participants aware of their blessings, and one can hardly count one's blessings until one knows what they are.

Even when this process of differentiation is distressing, it can be constructive. In each group there is usually one couple that is really through. These partners come principally to wean, rather than tear, themselves away from each other, usually for the sake of the children. Later, they get what we call a creative divorce. When others in the group witness the process of two people leaving each other, they are likely to be frightened. The potential of their own situation becomes more dramatic. Perhaps after six sessions the divorcing partners say good-by to each other and, for the first time, leave in separate cars. Their empty chairs remind the others that they, too, are living in crisis.

When troubled husbands and wives are seen jointly or in groups, at least their alienation won't be escalated. If they share a sense of mutual failure and try working on their problems as a pair, this proves that their commitment for intimate communion is still alive. If it develops that their incompatibility is irreconcilable, separation and divorce become less painful and expensive. Children and other relatives benefit. Vicious court battles can be avoided. Guilt feelings and blamesmanship become unnecessary because both partners know they tried hard to work things out.

Some professional circles shrug off our methods as superficial. Mere "manipulation of surface symptoms" cannot induce true behavior changes, according to this school of thought. For people surfeited with psychiatric jargon this may sound persuasive, but our successfully retrained couples prove this argument wrong each day, and other therapists trained by us have reported similar heartening results.

We also hear the contention that the "programming" of aggression has robotizing Orwellian overtones or that it implies an over-training of emotions or burdening them with artificial new gadgetry. This sounds much like objecting to toilet training or even to the toilet itself (which no doubt was once called a gimmick). We believe we are disposing of dangerous, potentially contaminating material which, when it breaks out in its ultimate epidemic form, leads to war. Yes, it is machinery of sorts—much like learning to eat with knives and forks, instead of ripping into food with one's hands; or perhaps like learning to drive a car through traffic. It is learning survival in the world as it really is. It is progress.

Just how urgently this kind of progress is needed became obvious to us one Saturday afternoon in the early days of our fight-training program. From fight-evaders like Harold Jacobson and his 20 years of silence we had learned how a dove can become mired in an intolerable stalemate when he is married to a hawk. But now we faced a different situation: a pair of hawks and a pair of doves confronted each other in one of our group sessions and described how they, too, were deadlocked.

Before the hawks and the doves compared notes with each other, we briefed the group on a fight that Mr. and Mrs. Hawk had discussed with us previously. The fight had taken place in their car. These hawks had been married for 14 years. He was 42, she was 33. They had a son and a daughter and Mr. Hawk was a credit manager for a furniture manufacturer. They were coming home from a party as this fight began:

HAWK WIFE (*angry but sober*): I am not going with you to another party ever again. You danced with everybody but me. You hung around that silly girl with the pink dress until you made an ass of yourself. You know how terrible that makes me feel! Don't you realize that people make fun of you behind

your back? You and your balding charms! I wish
you'd stop it, but I guess you can't. You're too weak.
It's disgusting! (*She cries.*)

HAWK HUSBAND: Stop crying! You always cry when you
try to get your way! No wonder the kids still cry
like babies all the time!

HAWK WIFE (*drying tears*): It's a helluva lot better to
cry than to drink all the time like you! Why can't
you do something constructive, like taking up a
hobby? Why tranquilize your brain with booze?

HAWK HUSBAND (*warming up*): You should talk! You
spend more at the hairdresser than I spend on
whiskey. You look awful after those fags try to
make you look younger! Why can't you be your own
age?

HAWK WIFE (*crying again*): At least my hairdresser pays
attention to me! That's more than I can say for you,
you louse! You promised me a weekend away from
the house and the kids. Do we ever go? No! You
never keep your word!

HAWK HUSBAND (*trying to keep his eye on the road*):
You're sure in a good mood tonight! All I want to
do is drive home quietly, but it's always yack, yack,
yack. I'm trying to drive and you distract me. Well,
if we get a ticket or have an accident it'll be all
your fault. . . .

The group discussed this chain of futile complaints and
agreed that its outbursts were designed by both mates to inflict as much injury and punishment as possible. Mr. and Mrs.
Hawk listened to the discussion, and finally the husband spoke
up:

"All right, all right. We know we're in trouble. But what
are we going to do? My wife tells me she loves me. I believe
her and I certainly love her! But why do we have these awful
fights? Why can't we live in peace? We must be terribly immature or something. She thinks I'm weak and nuts. I think
she's oversensitive and insecure. But we do love each other. It
makes no sense! All I know is it's no good this way. We've
simply got to do something."

At that point the two doves spoke up.

DOVE HUSBAND: We're quiet, but I can't say it's comfortable.

DOVE WIFE: Actually it's scary. We know it means we
can't share our true feelings. We're afraid to face

unpleasantness, so we play it safe and say nothing! But it feels very tense. In a way I envy you people (*nodding toward hawk couple*) for being able to get things off your chests. We two (*pointing to her husband*) have never been able to do this in seven years of marriage and we're about ready to break up. We just can't communicate at all—at least nothing negative.

HAWK HUSBAND: What on earth do you talk about?

DOVE WIFE: Oh, chitchat: "What did you do at the office today?" "How are the kids?" "What's for dinner?"

HAWK HUSBAND: Do you have sexual problems?

DOVE WIFE: Oh, no, not that I know of . . . do we, darling (*turns to husband*)?

DOVE HUSBAND: No, my wife is the greatest sex partner a man could want!

HAWK WIFE: I sure envy you! When we have our fights I can't be sexy. Anyway, he doesn't want me unless I indicate first that I want to. So we don't do anything. The fighting has about ruined our sex life. By bedtime we hate each other! You two don't fight and you make it in bed . . . I'll take your situation, anytime!

DOVE WIFE: No, you wouldn't! Because when you don't have any conversation in the living room, the bedroom scene becomes meaningless. It sounds great, but I'm beginning to lose interest in sex. That's all we have and it's not worth it . . . there's no meeting of minds. You two at least yell at each other. That's more contact than we have!

Clearly, the hawk and the dove couple both yearned for a state of intimacy where lovers feel a vested interest in the fulfillment of the partner and actively help to bring out the best in the other. Only when partners are disenchanted and not truly intimate is there truth in the saying that "marriage brings out the worst in people." Real intimates enjoy increasing their liking for each other. They like to reduce their tensions by airing their problems. They care deeply about what the partner is or perhaps ought to become; about the way he looks, feels, thinks, and even dreams.

By now it must be obvious that intimacy without conflict is impossible. Interestingly, some groups display more skill at conflict management than others. Jews, for example, tend to be transparent and vocal. They often "wear their feelings on their sleeves." They are comfortable with the process of handling conflicts verbally. Negroes tend to be relatively uncommunicative and undemonstrative in their family lives. True, there are vast differences in the backgrounds, the psychology, and the sources of anger of these two minorities. But we believe that the differences in their tribal customs for handling intimate conflict explain at least in part why the crime rate is exceptionally low among Jews and why there is an enormous incidence of violence among Negroes, particularly among Negro intimates.

We do not mean to imply that an inept intimate fighter necessarily runs the risk of becoming a murderer or a rapist. For approximately 15% of our own clients the route of aggressive leveling is just too rough. It makes them too acutely uncomfortable. They are too frightened by the truth and prefer a life of cover-up. These genuine fight phobics are much like flight phobics; they have to take the bus. We regret our inability to help them and we take comfort in the many others who are spurred on to learn our methods.

4. Getting a Good Fight Started

Most marriages are chronic complaint societies. The husband always leaves his socks on the living-room floor. The wife always turns the bathroom into a laundry. He always forgets to put gas in the car. She always messes up the newspaper before he's through with it. He always hogs the conversation at parties. She's always too tired to make love. And so on and on. It doesn't much matter which of the partners complains for the umpteenth time about which source of perpetual annoyance; if the couple is untrained, the ensuing fight drags on approximately as follows:

PARTNER A (*wearily*): I know, I know. God, how many times have we been through all this before? I know you hate it.

PARTNER B (*exasperated*): So why in hell don't you quit?

A: I've told you and told you! That's just the way I am. Don't you know that by now?

B: Sure, but I'll never get used to it and it's driving me up the wall!

A: Why don't you get off my back about the same old stuff? What's the use? You know I can't change.

B: Well, neither can I . . .

We call such stalemates round-robin fights. Untrained couples can't get off these depressing merry-go-rounds because they subscribe to the notion that "you can't change people." This defeatist attitude couldn't be more unfortunate; it inhibits the enterprise and imagination that partners need to come up with new solutions.

To dislodge trainees from such an impasse we point out that in these fast-changing times the willingness to change oneself, and to be changed by others, is as important as growing to adulthood in the first place. It is a vital sign of maturity and mental health. A noted psychoanalyst, Dr. L. S. Kubie, has explained it like this: "The measure of health is flexibility, the freedom to learn through experience, the freedom to change with changing internal and external circumstances, to be influenced by reasonable argument, admonitions, exhortations, and the appeal to emotions; the freedom to respond appropriately to the stimulus of reward and punishment, and especially the freedom to cease when sated."

Making changes is easier than most people think because the alternatives are just about endless. One can change one's self. Or one's partner. Or one's way of dealing with the other. Or one's environment (perhaps by making new friends, moving to a new neighborhood, or visiting the in-laws less often).

Perhaps the partner who is annoying his spouse simply needs to be more careful to go into action at times when the spouse is in a good mood and better able to "take it." Or the annoyed partner should demand some improvement in living conditions or some other compensation for putting up with the annoyance. Or the annoying partner might try to persuade the other to join in the very activity that's considered annoying (drinking, golf, swearing, smoking, going to church, making love in a certain way, or whatever).

There are times when round-robin rituals can be inoffensive or even useful. If partners decide, after candid negotiations, that a particular chronic fight issue is, in fact, unimportant as long as they are getting along otherwise, they may choose to adopt such an annoyance as a family pet and trot it out for a quick fight round whenever they feel the urge to uncork some pent-up hostile feelings. But in our experience the best way to handle a chain of round robins is to break it up.

To stop the music of the round-robin merry-go-round may require a moratorium on all repetitive fighting. Here is how that system worked for Tom Condon, a 34-year-old attorney, and his wife, Lisa, 29. The Condons had been married for eight years. Ever since they emerged from the romantic glow of their post-courtship years, they found their relationship deteriorating because of constant fights about money. Typically, the fights occurred at the end of the month when the bank statement arrived. This is the way it went:

LISA (*hurt*): I've told you 'til I'm blue in the face, why don't you let me know what I can spend?

TOM (*furious*): You've got some goddamned nerve! You *know* when you're spending too much. You just don't give a damn.

LISA: Is that a fact? You just love to leave me in the dark so you can catch me. I'm not your lousy bookkeeper! You're supposed to handle the finances around here.

TOM: That's a laugh! You wouldn't do anything I tell you.

LISA (*mocking*): Why don't you try me?

TOM (*resigned*): Hell, it's no use with you.

LISA: Here we go again. . . .

We told the Condons that this ritual was their mutual punishment for being unlovable. She felt unloved because he was stingy. He felt unloved because she castrated him by spending more money than he had. Then we showed them how to break their impasse in three stages.

First, we advised them to declare a moratorium and to engage in no money fight unless they used it to introduce fresh information on how they really felt about this issue.

Second, we asked them to introduce a specific change so the exact situation that led to their last money fight couldn't occur again. Tom thereupon opened a separate checking account for Lisa.

Third, we asked them to flush out, with the help of fight techniques to be discussed here, the real issues behind their round robins. In the case of the Condons, mutual probing brought out that Lisa felt bad because Tom wouldn't ask for a raise at the office; Tom resented that Lisa wouldn't help accumulate some cash toward emergencies.

Few couples respond to our fight treatment as readily as Tom and Lisa. As our earlier explorations into the psychology of loners and other aggression-evaders showed, there are powerful reasons why it can be difficult to persuade intimates to enter the fight ring at all. Their fears make these nonfighters notoriously resourceful in the art of ducking. They hide behind newspapers or in front of television. They change the subject or become strangely hard of hearing. They're too tired, or they sigh and say, "I just don't want to talk about it now."

"Whenever my husband senses that I want something from him or that I'm upset about something in our relationship, he clams up," one fight-evader's wife told us. "And if I get too aggressive about it, he leaves the house." A husband who is married to a dove wife said: "She gets terribly upset and cries if I get angry about something—like when she puts my socks in the wrong place. She just looks at me all sad as if to say, 'You poor thing, Mama should take better care of you!' That makes me feel like a crab and I get even madder at her."

Husbands and wives can be equally adept at dishing out the "silent treatment"—and equally inept in responding to it.

Some partners interpret the other's silence as contentment and kid themselves that "no news is good news." Other people admire a "strong silent type" for his strength and feel inferior and guilty because they are less controlled themselves. Still others resort to systematic needling that only triggers uninformative explosions from the silent partner. These nonfighters may get sadistic kicks by seducing an exasperated mate into the kind of ugly eruption that makes the exploding partner look silly or "nutty" compared with the outwardly calm spouse who may enjoy the spectacle.

Another brand of unguided hostility that can lead to dreadful trouble is the volcanic eruption that we call the Vesuvius. This is just blowing off steam—a spontaneous irrelevant sounding-off of free-floating hostility. It is an adult temper tantrum that does not involve a partner directly, although it is advisable to have an intimate on hand as an audience. A Vesuvius unleashed against no one and on the open street would lead to curious glances and conceivably to arrest on charges of disturbing the peace.

A beautiful Vesuvius was delivered by one husband who came home from work and yelled at his wife, à propos of nothing in particular, "If that S. O. B. Jones does it just once more, I'll punch him in the nose and that goes for your Uncle Max, too!" (Nobody had mentioned Uncle Max for weeks; he functioned here only as a free-floating kitchen sink handy for throwing into the Vesuvius.)

The Vesuvius is never directed at anybody who is at the scene of the explosion or nearby. It never involves issues that are pending between partners. It doesn't deal with anything that the partner who is witnessing the Vesuvius could be expected to do anything about. And it evaporates as quickly as a puff of smoke. The best way to make certain that a Vesuvius is not, in fact, a bugle call to a serious fight about some brand-new issue is to listen sympathetically to a partner's outburst and to wait a bit for what happens next. In an authentic Vesuvius, nothing does.

One of our trainee husbands came home from work and found a written Vesuvius posted to the door. It was from his wife. It simply said, "I've had it." The husband became quite upset. He started searching for his wife and found her almost immediately at her girlfriend's house next door. The women were having some drinks in the kitchen. When the husband appeared, his wife brightened up and said, "Hey, look who's here!" Her Vesuvius had blown up—and over.

The worst way to handle the Vesuvius is to take it at face value and "hook in." Suppose a husband suddenly shouts,

"I'm going to take this lousy goddamn lawn mower and throw it in the swimming pool!" The trained wife would never say, "Yeah? You and who else, you pip-squeak?" She would wait for the squall to subside.

There are, on the other hand, clues that crop up in the most peaceful marriages and should never be ignored (although they usually are). They may just signal minor annoyances. More likely, they are flashing yellow danger signals indicating that the partner who is doing the clue-dropping is toting a dangerously ballooning gunny sack full of grievances. At any rate, these clues should be investigated for what's behind them. Here are some examples of clues that should never be met by silence or indifference:

"I wish you wouldn't *do* that!" Or: "You've got to stop ignoring me!" Or: "Don't push me too far!" Or: "I wish you'd take a stand!" Or: "It drives me batty when you feed the dog after I've already fed him!"

Unlike the Vesuvius, such a danger signal is intensely personal. It is a direct demand upon a loved one to stop being unlovable. It is smoke before a fire; and it deals with something that the signal's recipient is equipped to do something about.

This is the time to start the process we call leveling. Its superficial meaning is clear enough. It means that one should be transparent in communicating where one stands and candid in signaling where one wants to go. It is a special preserve of intimates and should run like a red thread through all their conflicts. With a casual acquaintance or a business associate, leveling is rarely worth the trouble. It may even be unwise. With a loved one, the art of aggressive leveling calls for careful cultivation. By "hooking in" to a partner's complaints or his hurt looks or stony silence intimates can find out "where they're at," and can then go on to fight for better mutual understanding.

On the surface, this sounds absurdly easy, and for some lucky people it is. When two natural fighters are married to each other, one of them need only say, "Come on, now, what's really eating you?" in order to get a fair, problem-solving fight going. Sometimes one partner may have to boost the leveling process by delivering a strong admonitory "Dutch Uncle" talk, knowing that when a good talking-to is directed at an intimate, it becomes an act of love. But one way or another, true intimates have little trouble starting up a fighting exchange of views.

For our many fight-resistant clients, we recommend that

they start leveling by warming up with deutero-fighting: that is, fights about fighting. Once students have had some training, they don't find this hard. One partner only has to say, "Hey, I've got a bone to pick with you!" Then the couple can level aggressively with each other about such preliminary issues as whether the bone is worth picking; and when, where, and how it should be picked.

Too often these fights are short-circuited like this:

HE: Why don't you ever tell me what you think about things?
SHE: What's the use? Who could argue with you?
HE: What in the world are you talking about?
SHE: I mean nobody can win with you.
HE: You're just chicken!
SHE: Yeah, and you're a Hitler! Nobody could argue with him without getting his head blown off!
HE: Here we go again!

This halfhearted husbandly fishing expedition was doomed from the start. A conflict-resistant spouse might be prompted to level with her husband if she is asked pointblank for her views about a particular problem, but not if he only wonders vaguely what she thinks "about things." At least this encounter did little damage. Other partners who try to place a beef may be specific enough about their complaint and still wind up worse off.

Joyce and Alfred Hayes had been wrangling for weeks about what to do next summer. Although they were only in their late twenties, they lived in a $55,000 house in suburban Los Angeles, where Al was a hard-driving insurance salesman. His mother lived in upstate New York. Year after year, she complained that she didn't see enough of her grandchildren and recently she had announced her next visit for mid-August. Joyce had long felt that Al was entirely too dependent on his mother, that he allowed her to interfere in their affairs and that he spent too much money on his weekly long-distance calls to the old lady. Joyce had never leveled with Al about her feelings. Instead, she by-passed the true fight issue by nagging him about their own vacation plans. Finally she persuaded him to agree that his mother should not come in August; instead, Joyce and Al would take a trip to San Francisco.

One evening in late June, after the children were in bed, they had this fight:

JOYCE: Have you told your mother she can't come in August?

AL: No, not yet.

JOYCE (*agitated*): But you promised!

AL: Take it easy, will you? I just haven't gotten around to it.

JOYCE (*red-faced and very angry*): I think that stinks!

AL (*controlled*): Don't raise your voice!

JOYCE: I can't ever discuss *anything* with you!

AL: Well, you always get so hysterical. The way I feel right now, I don't even want to go on that trip with you.

JOYCE (*on the verge of tears*): Dammit, why can't I ever depend on you for anything that might be fun for me?

AL (*smug and still very calm*): It's your own fault. You started it all!

If Joyce had come clean with Al from the start, he would have known that there was a lot at stake for her in this row and that she wasn't being "hysterical." Perhaps he wouldn't then have punished Joyce for trying to engage him in a legitimate argument. He punished her by withdrawing a privilege that he had already granted: the trip that Joyce was looking forward to. In effect, he rejected her in favor of his mother and made her twice as miserable as she had been before the fight. He went even further: He punished Joyce for bringing up *any* conflict and thereby seriously mistrained her for realistic future fights.

Al's parting shot in this unfortunate encounter, the almost proverbial accusation "You started it all!", was the clearest tip-off that he and Joyce were uninformed and crude marital fighters. A wise spouse welcomes the occasion when his partner is ready to "start something." With real intimates, the start of a fight is a signal that "there ought to be some changes made," and they know that if the fight is fought properly, chances are that it will clear the air and hopefully result in improvements for both.

Unlike Joyce Hayes, however, a truly intimate aggressor will try not to start a fight until she has conducted a warm-up encounter within herself to clarify in her own mind what's at stake and how far she should go to press her point, for the truth is that one cannot competently level with one's partner until one has leveled with oneself.

An inner dialogue can expose crucial information—nuggets of intelligence which untrained fighters, much to their disadvantage, rarely develop for themselves before opening up on a spouse. Here are some questions that we recommend our trainees ask themselves before doing battle:

"Is this really my fight or somebody else's? Maybe my mother's? Or the President's?"

"Do I really have a legitimate bone to pick with my partner? Or do I just want to put him down and hurt him for the sake of a sadistic kick?"

"Am I really convinced that my partner's action or attitude is bad for our relationship?"

"What's at stake here? What does this fight really mean to me? Am I approaching it with realistic arguments and weapons or am I overreacting and getting ready to 'drop the bomb on Luxembourg'?"

"How will my partner react? What price will I have to pay to gain my point? What will it take to win it? Is this cause really worth my partner's possible retaliation or ill will?"

We always caution trainees that in intimate relationships "winning" can be more costly than "losing." In a boxing match between strangers, there is only a short-term goal: quick victory, preferably a knockout. For battles between intimates, totally different rules apply. After all, a constructive verbal fight should be (even though it often isn't) just one link in a chain of steps to help intimates arrive at solutions for their inevitable conflicts. The goal is anything but a knockout. It is, instead, an attempt to improve an over-all relationship for the long-run give-and-take of marriage.

We counsel, therefore, that to "win" an engagement with an intimate enemy may turn out to be downright dangerous. It may discourage the loser from leveling in future fights. It may make him needlessly pessimistic or even despairing about the prospects of his marriage. It may turn him into a more devious, camouflaged fighter. It may give him an exaggerated idea about the importance of a particular fight issue in the mind of the "winning" partner. It sounds paradoxical, but if a "win" results in such after-effects, then both partners wind up losers.

It follows that the only way to win intimate encounters is for both partners to win. This sounds illogical, if not impossible. It isn't. Sometimes it's only a matter of sensible and good-willed negotiation. In the classic vacation fight about whether to go to the mountains or the seashore, for example, both partners can win by either agreeing to alternate destinations and flipping a coin to see whose favorite place gets the first turn; or by seeking a new third possibility, such as staying home. Even sexual problems can sometimes be solved by letting both partners have their way—in relays.

Most issues, of course, are not nearly so clear-cut. This is why we have designed an entirely original fight-scoring system that determines neither "losers" nor "winners." It gauges with considerable precision just how any fight affects the state of the union for a particular couple. Was the union's balance and its state of swing tipped in a constructive direction or in a destructive direction? This is what counts in intimate fighting—and little else. If the net outcome of the fight is predominantly destructive, both partners lose. If it's predominantly constructive, both win. This is perhaps the best way to illustrate why learning how to fight is like learning how to dance, not how to box.

Good inner dialogues show a prospective aggressor what he is getting into. Sometimes these inside conversations even become full-fledged substitutes for destructive fight rituals. One of our trainees told us how, after we briefed him, he literally talked himself out of an endless running battle that accomplished nothing, but drove his wife to distraction. He said:

"There are times when I make a routine of stopping at intervals to look back and ask: What have I just done? Why did I do it? What am I about to do and why am I doing that? If it doesn't measure up to what I am trying to do with myself, I change it on the spot.

"It was difficult for me to train myself not to impose my perfectionism on Nel and the children. I had to make it an explicit and conscious thing. I used to go to the kitchen and tell Nel how to cook and how to turn the pancakes on the griddle; or I'd just stick around and maybe turn the pancakes myself behind her back. Now when I get up and start to drift toward the kitchen, I say to myself, 'Am I going in there for a legitimate reason or to spy on her?' Then I carefully examine the answer I give myself. If I don't have business in the kitchen, I go back and sit down or go out and do something else. Over a period of time my perfectionist pattern has diminished enormously because I made myself be aware that I was doing it—and in time to head it off."

Trainees often tell us that their fights begin with Pearl Harbor-type surprise attacks that leave no time for inner dialogues. "How can I go around talking to myself?" one hawk said. "When I get angry, I just blow up."

This is just another price of gunny-sacking one's grievances. True intimates who have real beefs against their partners don't wait for provocations and risk no Pearl Harbors. They balance their books on their aggressions as soon as practical.

Whether or not there is time for an inner dialogue before a fight, a wise aggressor will make sure that his opponent knows the real nature of the fight they're fighting. The steps to convey this intelligence are a vital part of leveling. We suggest that, as a fight proceeds, the aggressor make as clear a statement as possible of his demands or expectations; of the rational basis for his goals; and of realistic ways for his opponent to meet these demands. The aggressor should specify precisely what's at stake, what it would mean to him to lose the fight, and how the changes that he seeks will benefit both fighters.

When a wife says, "You'll really ruin my whole vacation if we don't go to the antique stores at least one afternoon," she places her husband on notice that he'd better give in if he doesn't want his own vacation ruined by her grousing.

When aims and proposed solutions are logically presented, most intimates can be gradually induced to absorb far more aggression than people usually think. But everybody maintains limits of tolerance—inner fortresses that one will not give up and whose inviolability is nonnegotiable. We suggest that partners acquaint themselves with their own non-negotiable limits, preferably by way of an inner dialogue on each fight issue as it comes up. Once a partner is sure what his own limits are, he should level with the other and tell him the point beyond which there is no room for negotiation—at least not until further notice.

All these training methods are cumbersome to explain. Once they're understood and accepted, however, they're very simple to apply. Ralph and Betsy Snyder, both of whom had jobs as courtroom reporters, found this out after they had the following fight about their identical twins, who were in the eighth grade:

RALPH: I don't like the way the kids handle money.
BETSY: What's the matter with it? They're good kids.
RALPH: Yes, but they haven't learned the value of money.
BETSY: They're just kids. Why not let them have their fun? They'll learn soon enough.
RALPH: No, I think you're spoiling them.
BETSY: How in the world am I doing that?
RALPH: By giving them the idea that money grows on trees.
BETSY: Well, why don't *you* set a better example? You

might start by spending less on your pipe collection.

RALPH: What's that got to do with it?

BETSY: Plenty. When the kids see you waste money on nonessentials, they feel they have the same rights.

RALPH: I shop for my pipes. They're very carefully selected.

BETSY: Maybe, but whenever I send you to the market, you always spend more than I would. You're always dragging in stuff we don't really need.

RALPH: OK, OK. I know you're a better shopper at the market, but that's your job, you know, not mine.

BETSY: Well, then, don't blame me for the kids.

After several training sessions, we asked the Snyders to refight the same fight before one of our training groups. Here is how it went the second time around:

RALPH (*starting with a specific objective, not a general observation*): I want you to stop slipping the kids extra money beyond the allowances I give them.

BETSY (*showing Ralph why his idea may be difficult to accomplish*): But you're not around. You don't know their needs.

RALPH (*spelling out his objective further*): I want to know their needs. I want them to come to me with their money needs.

BETSY (*justifying her past practices*): Well, you know what goes on. I tell you everything. You know where the money goes.

RALPH (*specifying the real issue that this fight is all about*): That's fine, but it's not the point. I believe the children should learn more about responsibility—having to justify getting the money from me and spending it wisely.

BETSY (*making sure he's serious*): You really want to supervise all this piffle?

RALPH (*reconfirming the stakes as he sees them*): Don't you see the importance of teaching them early responsibility for money matters?

BETSY (*specifying the reasons for her opposition*): Frankly, no. They are good kids and they're having a good time. I like to give them a little extra now and then. I enjoy it when they have fun. They'll learn responsibility soon enough.

RALPH (*sizing up the results of the fight thus far and*

rechecking his wife for more feedback): I can see we really differ on this issue. Do you understand my position?

BETSY (*reconfirming her understanding of Ralph's real objective*): Yes, you want us to teach the kids responsibility.

RALPH (*seeking a meeting ground, at least in principle*): Yes, don't you?

BETSY (*agreeing to his principle but dissenting from his method*): Yes, but your method would deprive me of something I enjoy doing, and I don't believe I am overdoing it. You know I'm careful with my money.

RALPH (*hardening his stand*): Yes, you're a careful shopper and all that—I have no complaints about that—but I must ask you to stop slipping the kids extra money. That's the only way to control careless spending.

BETSY (*realizing that she'll probably have to give some ground*): I see you really are hung up on this specific issue.

RALPH (*elaborating on the reasons for his firm stand*): I love the children as much as you do and I don't want to see them develop into carelsss adults.

BETSY (*offering a proposal for a compromise*): I don't think they will, but since this seems to mean so much to you, let me suggest something. Why don't you tell me how much you think would be reasonable to give them "extra" and for what occasions, and I'll stick to it.

RALPH (*checking out that Betsy isn't likely to compromise further*): You still want to keep giving them extra money?

BETSY (*reconfirming her stand*): Yes, I do. I enjoy it, as I told you.

RALPH (*accepting Betsy's compromise, proposing details on how to make it work and offering another compromise as a conciliatory gesture*): Well, let's sit down and budget how much money they should get from us altogether, for everything every week, how much for extras, and so on. It's not so terribly important to me who gives them the money, as how much and what for.

BETSY (*confirming Ralph's acceptance and offering a further implementing proposal showing that she too is now trying to accomplish his objective*): OK. Let's figure it out; then, every weekend, you can sit down with the kids and me and see that we didn't go over the limit.

RALPH (*confirming that he understands and approves her latest idea*): Yes, I could vary the regular pocket money, depending on how much you've slipped them.

BETSY (*offering another suggestion to make sure their new plan will work and maybe show Ralph that she was right about the kids' sense of responsibility after all*): Certainly, you can also ask them how much they've spent and what for. Then you would find out all about their needs and learn how responsible they can be.

RALPH (*nails down the deal and specifies the date it goes into effect*): OK. Let's try it this Saturday.

5. When and Where to Fight

The best way to get constructive results from intimate hostilities is to fight by appointment only. This may sound silly, but the more calmly and deliberately an aggressor can organize his thoughts before an engagement, the more likely it is that his arguments will be persuasive; that the fight will confine itself to one issue instead of ricocheting all over the intimate landscape; and that the opponent will feel compelled to come up with calm, constructive counterproposals. It's like negotiating a labor dispute well before the deadline, not after the union has voted to strike.

Surprisingly few couples realize this. Most of them resemble Emily and Sam Bates, who were in their thirties, had been married for eight years, and had two small sons. Sam, a building contractor, loved his cabin cruiser. Emily didn't care much for boating. One weekend, however, she delighted Sam by agreeing enthusiastically to spend two days alone with him on their boat, which happened to be named *Carefree.*

Carefully, Sam and Emily kept their expectations for this weekend secret from each other. Sam thought Emily's enthusiasm meant that at last they were going to have a love feast away from the children, just as they did in their courtship and post-courtship days. He couldn't have been more cheerful about the whole thing. Emily had quite different expectations. She was planning to use their quiet time together, away from their sons and other distractions, to air several grievances that she had been keeping from Sam, especially about how he treated the children and also about money matters.

Their first day was heavenly. They went snorkeling and spear fishing. They made love, and Emily had one of her rare orgasms. At the dock the next morning both were in a marvelous mood. Emily said to herself, "I've done everything he likes. Now is the time!"

Out loud she said, "You know, we never really talk!" and she proceeded to empty out her gunny sack of complaints all over the shiny deck.

He became uncontrollably furious. So did she.

They promptly sailed home in agonized silence and learned only during fight training later that they could have eliminated this shipboard explosion if they had leveled with each other in advance about their weekend expectations.

Coordinating the partners' basic expectations is critical in timing a fight, and while agreement on a definite time for a "gripe hour" may be difficult, it can be negotiated. Here, by way of illustration, is a deutero-fight conducted by Sam and Emily Bates after they had had some fight training.

They were still trying to arrive at ways to run their financial affairs better. It was almost 6 P.M. one Tuesday when Sam called from his office.

SAM: I've just been going over the bank statement, and I sure need a gripe hour.

EMILY (*cheerful*): But not tonight! I'm in a great mood and I just want to have a good time.

SAM (*snarling*): To hell with that! We've really got to talk about the money situation. How about having fun afterwards?

EMILY: No, that would spoil the whole thing for me. If you're in such a rotten mood, why don't you stop at the club and play handball with your pal Bob?

SAM: OK, OK. I'll be home later, but we've got to set up a time tomorrow or the next day so we can go over the financial picture.

EMILY: I'll tell you what: Let's go over the whole thing after dinner tomorrow. But tonight let's just have a good time!

Sam and Emily had learned that fights can be legitimately postponed by common consent, if only temporarily. But the griper's anger must be acknowledged and he should be promised a specific engagement so his gunny sack won't blow up if it is jarred while he is waiting.

Far too many fights become needlessly aggravated because the complainant opens fire when his partner really is in an inappropriate frame of mind or is trying to dash off to work or trying to concentrate on some long-delayed chore that he has finally buckled down to. Indeed, there are times when failure to delay—or to advance—the timing of a fight can have cataclysmic consequences.

Julius and Barbara Mayor had been invited to dinner at the home of Julius' boss, the president of a savings and loan association where Julius was assistant treasurer. As always,

Julius was nervous about the command performance, but on the day of the dinner he had become resigned to the idea of suffering through a somewhat strained evening. Barbara, who detested the boss's snooty wife and always worried for weeks beforehand whether she would make a good impression, had an unusually severe case of jitters. It was almost dinnertime when Julius came home and noticed that she was still wearing a blouse and slacks. She lowered the boom:

BARBARA (*strained and firm*): I don't want to go!
JULIUS (*incredulous*): You can't do that to me!
BARBARA (*miserable*): Oh yes I can! I don't like to go to parties with you. You drink too much and then we always look like fools.

The Mayors were able to work things out. Julius pleaded with Barbara. He pointed out that his upcoming promotion might be threatened if they didn't appear together at his very conservative boss's house. Julius promised not to drink too much and he did watch his liquor intake. There was no damage except that he resented his wife for having been guilty of overkill; she had used a sledge hammer to drive in a thumbtack.

Such tactics are dangerous. Julius might have overreacted and canceled the dinner at the last minute, thereby jeopardizing his delicate relations with his boss and the boss's wife. There might even have been a nuclear explosion: Julius might have gone to the party alone, gotten drunk, spilled the whole story about the fight he had just had with his wife and wound up with Mr. and Mrs. Boss thinking he couldn't handle anything properly, including his wife and himself.

The sensible way for Barbara to handle her problem would have been to make an engagement with Julius at a less harassing time for a fair fight about a subject that was of serious and legitimate concern to her; to spell this out for him and not to expect him to be an expert cryptographer. As this couple discovered when they learned how to level with each other, the key fact was that Barbara was unusually sensitive about social matters. She was concerned about her husband's drinking, but not overly so. She mostly wanted to tell him how important it was for her to see the two of them display themselves as an upstanding unit, a popular, wholesome American couple. Once she had spelled out these feelings for Julius, he gained an important incentive for minding his manners when he and Barbara were with others.

Making an advance appointment for a fight is particularly

useful because mutually favored fight times are rare. There are morning fighters and evening fighters; partners who prefer to fight at cocktail time or bedtime or dinnertime, or only with (or only without) the children or others present.

People favor the time that favors them. Is the partner embarrassed to fight in front of the children? Is he more likely to give in because he wants sex or because he has just had sex and has been unusually well satisfied? Is the wife's morale extra high because she is wearing a new dress? Does the husband feel extra potent because he has just brought home a particularly fat paycheck—or is he unusually worried because it's bill-paying time and he has just discovered that his wife violated the family financial limits by charging too many purchases on her charge accounts?

Then these are the aggressor's favorite fight times.

Such differences are among the many natural disparities that exist between fighters, but couples can learn to compensate for them as we shall demonstrate later.

Often, fight times are only negotiable by way of deutero-fights. Many of these skirmishes take place at the dinner table because many partners no longer do much talking at other times. Some people can fight while they eat, some can't. We offer no firm rules for the timing of fights, except these: (1) times that are truly intolerable for a partner should be identified, if necessary through a deutero-fight, and should be respected, but (2) partners should always keep in mind that postponement can be dangerous; if the gunny sack of the partner who is itching to fight keeps bulging too long, the bickering of today can escalate into a kitchen-sink battle tomorrow.

Many people find it hard to believe, but the best time to fight is when others are present. Intimate combat in front of children presents special opportunities and problems that will be discussed separately. Fighting in front of good-willed adults can bring about excellent results because such witnesses tend to become constructive allies or referees. Usually the fighters gang up on the referee, which is also an important function of marriage counselors because it draws the combatants together.

Modern etiquette, unfortunately, is so neurotically preoccupied with privacy that people can rarely bring themselves to interfere in the intimate problems of others.

The Sylvester Colemans learned that a couple whose company they particularly enjoyed, Henry and Susan Harvester, were breaking up. The word was not out as yet, but the Colemans knew that Henry Harvester had just moved out of the family home. With the best intentions, the Colemans managed to persuade the Harvesters to spend a weekend as a foursome on the Colemans' boat. Several times Mr. and Mrs. Coleman were on the verge of leveling about the real reason for this get-together: to offer the Harvesters some help in discussing their problems. Each time, the Colemans' nerve failed them. All four spent a quiet, strained weekend and shortly afterward it became generally known that the Harvesters were getting divorced.

This breakup may have been unavoidable or even constructive, but there was no need for the Colemans to be so tongue-tied about their excellent intentions. They could have said:

"Look, we've heard what's happening with you two. You may not think it's any of our business, but we think it is. You're important members of our circle and you're breaking our hearts. We want to know how come. We think you're pulling a dirty trick on the people who care about both of you."

Like most couples, the Colemans clung to the medieval "their-home-is-their-castle" ideology—the same state of mind that also allows people to remain idle onlookers while others get killed or maimed in front of their eyes. It is the same isolation that has created the professions of friends-for-hire, psychology and psychiatry, which, in our view, ought to devote themselves principally to research and teaching.

The effects of alcohol on intimate battles are more difficult to assess. Many—possibly most—marital fights are cocktail-contaminated, at least to some extent. So are many stale-mates involving nonfighters. No statistics exist, but for every alcoholic couple that is buffeted by blasts in the *Virginia Woolf* manner, there are many more alliances between fight-phobic doves who anesthetize their hostile feelings with liquor. They quietly get stewed together and never reach each other. Most common is the pattern of one partner drinking more heavily (or being more readily affected by alcohol) than the other. This is one of the more critical disparities between partners who shrink away from leveling. Usually it is the more fight-phobic, yet angry, partner who tries to drink conflicts away. But there are also "mean" mates who exploit their partners' increased tolerance for meanness while "under the influence."

Sometimes the results of such an inequality are beneficial. Liquor may relax a milquetoastish fight-evader so he can unburden himself and maybe even yell a little to show the depth of his frustrations. A chronically angry and explosive personality (we call these people "rageolics") may turn maudlin after a few drinks and give his weaker, and usually overwhelmed, partner a fighting chance for a change. But neither situation makes for ideal fight conditions, and, generally speaking, drinking is bad for fighting.

It allows the more sober partner, who may be fight-phobic anyhow, to withdraw and evade with the excuse that "Only a fool fights with a drunk."

It can weaken the drunker partner to an unfair degree because he may display himself in a socially inappropriate way and become too easy to dismiss as a "nut."

It can lead to such unending round-robin rituals as the following: She: You drink too much. He: You're a drag. Who can have fun around you? When I need a cop, I'll let you know. (Some couples argue exclusively, and always destructively, about drinking.)

People mix drinking and fighting because they think it takes courage to fight and assume that alcohol will reduce their inhibitions. In our experience, no unusual courage is required when partners know they face a fair and constructive fight; the only inhibition that is usually reduced by liquor is the inhibition to be ridiculous. We sometimes ask a group of couples who have drinking problems to come in for a 30-hour marathon at 2 A.M. At that hour several marathoners are likely to show up inebriated. After 18 hours, when they are sober, we show them movies of themselves that were made by a hidden TV camera. They are usually shocked to see how ridiculously they carry on while drunk and then the remaining hours of the marathon tend to be unusually productive.

Good fighting, like good driving, should be preceded by no more than one or two cocktails. Partners who feel they must have more liquor to be able to fight are usually people who drink for more basic reasons that require investigation and possibly treatment.

The predinner cocktail hour is a popular fight time for some partners, but it brings up an unwelcome disparity for people who like to preserve this interlude exclusively for stomach-settling socializing. Again, this is a difference that calls for good-willed negotiation, and so is the decision on a location where a fight is to be aired.

People tend to place fights where they feel territorially at home. The wife may fight most comfortably in the kitchen, the husband from behind his big desk in his office-fortress, the young man in his brand-new car.

A boat is a superb place for an intimate encounter, especially if one of the partners is fight-phobic, because fighting goes best where the combatants are isolated and find it hard to get away from each other. A car is another popular battle site, although we do not consider it safe unless the combatants pull over to the side of the road and stop before they get a fight going. Since an unusually large number of fights break out · on vacations, it is also worth mentioning that results are excellent in American Plan resorts where a decamped or "defeated" fighter is likely to return for meals because he knows he must pay for them whether he eats them or not.

Once partners are better informed about the why, when, and where of fighting, they are ready to consider what to fight about. It would be useful if they could view their relationship with sufficient detachment to be able to ask themselves: "What are the most important issues pending between us?" or "What issues are most likely to benefit from an application of constructive fight techniques?" Needless to say, few people are all that methodical, but once they liberate themselves from any fight-evasion tendencies that may have inhibited them, they usually find a rich and ready array of issues to pick from: sex, money, children, in-laws, to name a few of the most obvious.

At this point we would like to mention only two issues that are, like the fight for optimal distance mentioned earlier, less obvious than most. Moreover, they may emerge early during a couple's experience in constructive fighting; while they may appear again and again, they are not pointless round-robin rituals.

The first is the age-old, seemingly preposterous lovers' quarrel over who loves whom the most. This may sound like childish and romantic nonsense, but it usually isn't. It begins when one partner says, either to himself or to the other, "I love you, but you don't know what love is. You don't love anybody except maybe yourself, and I doubt even that!" Or, "I give you a more central position in my heart than you're willing to give me." Or, "You only take; you never give!"

Such a centricity fight is likely to start during courtship and may last a lifetime. It can easily escalate. Partner A may say, "You've got to do more to earn a central spot in my heart." If Partner B replies, "That kind of probation status turns me off!" they may be in for trouble. "A" may be hinting through such a fight that he thinks "B" is having affairs ("you have more open space in your heart than I have in mine"). Or "A" may be using this fight to show "B" he is suffering from separation anxiety—"You can walk out on me without hurting yourself too much."

Usually, however, partners tend to read too much into these exchanges. People are rarely aware of it, but one partner is almost always more in love at a particular moment than the other. This is yet another natural disparity and it operates just as in sex, where one partner is usually more "turned on" than the other. Beyond these constant temporary fluctuations, there may be permanent differences. The reality is that individual capacities for loving vary greatly. The partner with a high capacity for loving will not be overly worried about distances prevailing between himself and his intimate. The partner with a low capacity is more likely to become nervous about these issues. We suggest that partners accept these disparities as inevitable and learn to relax about them as best they can. Certainly they are not grounds for panic.

The other chronic battle that deserves to be approached with extra care is the therapeutic fight. It is a partner's legitimate goal to change a specific characteristic of the other if such a change is incontrovertibly for the other's own good. Therapeutic fights have much in common with other fights that will be discussed later, such as the fight for a couple's greater growth and the fight for a change of their life style. But the latter fights involve changes for both partners. The therapeutic fight is a one-way fight. This makes it more dangerous.

A good mate thinks of himself as his partner's counterweight; he does not want to collude with the partner's bad habits, but he may find it hard to keep the partner in the ring; to apply constant pressure, but not to push too far or too fast. Therefore, when fights such as the following keep coming up again and again, they had best be supervised by a therapist.

HUSBAND: You smoke too much.
WIFE: But I've got those new filters.
HUSBAND: You're just kidding yourself.
WIFE: You know it's impossible for me to stop!
HUSBAND: Yeah, but I don't like it. It gives you bad breath.
WIFE: Why don't you do something about your beer belly?
HUSBAND: Why don't you stop feeding me all those fattening things?
WIFE: Because you love them so much, you idiot. . . .

This fight, as so many others, is bogged down in the romantic notion that people can't be changed ("Love me as I am!"). While this is a false premise, it is a firmly rooted one, especially when a partner demands a one-way concession. Truly therapeutic fights are healthy and bonding. Even if they don't lead to change, they can at least prevent further excesses, and it is a legitimate function of intimate partners to limit each other's self-destructive tendencies. The difficulty is that these "for-your-own-good" fights are easily carried too far and can lead to alienation, a mutual "rubbing in" of weaknesses, punitive "Mr. District Attorney" or other destructive fight styles.

The best way to decide the when, where, and what of fighting is to invoke the rule of banks that require same-day clearance for checks: in other words, to engage the intimate enemy just as soon as possible after an issue presents itself.

One husband described to his fight-training group what happened when he had learned to apply the rule of instant leveling. He was a physician who had been referred to us by a constructive divorce lawyer after the doctor had had numerous affairs during 14 years of marriage, had finally left his wife, and had only recently rejoined her for an all-out reconciliation attempt.

The doctor said: "Before, I don't think we were really aware of what we were fighting about. The issues were too confused. In some cases we never had a confrontation for a year or more after an issue was first brought up. Now, when one of us does something that the other doesn't think is right, we immediately confront each other with it, settle it, and then forget it. There is no hangup, no festering. It's above board, and we get it out, and that's it, period! So now there's a lot less tension between us. We do fight more often, but on a much cleaner, much more honest basis. Our fights are much shorter because we get to the point and then forget about it. If it happens to be the right time, we make love, which is always very enjoyable."

The same husband then related how his leveling prevented an apparently trivial incident from growing into a long-term secret marriage malaise:

"When my wife and I went to bed the other night, I noticed she seemed rather distant. After some questioning on my part, she finally told me that she had found a handkerchief on my bureau with lipstick on it. She said that after she saw it, it bothered her for a time, and then she forgot about it.

"I said to her, 'You did not forget about it because you just brought it up, so obviously it was inside you.'

"So I said, 'Let's talk about it.'

"So she said, 'Well, I guess it did bother me because of our previous experiences.'

"I said to her, 'The funny part is that it's your own lipstick! If you'll recall, you kissed me on the cheek when I came home last night and I wiped it off with the handkerchief. I noticed it this morning, took another one, and left the stained one on the bureau.'

"She said, 'Come to think of it I do remember that now!'

"So she accepted what I told her as the truth, which it was. She said, 'You know, I'm glad we can talk about things this way.'

"Being able to talk about it, made it one of those things that no longer stayed inside of her and festered and annoyed her to the point where she would argue with me about something else—something that had no bearing at all on this particular incident."

Now that the doctor knew how and when to level, this potentially devastating fight was not only short and fair, but it was easy to settle because it was uncontaminated by other issues (which this couple fought out separately as problems presented themselves). It was a spontaneous fight, and it was kept that way because it did not delve into past issues. Neither partner added to his gunny sack of grievances and neither was an injustice collector—the kind of combatant who secretly keeps books on marital complaints.

This husband and wife were also helped by the knowledge, acquired as their leveling became proficient, that *they need not be afraid of losing*. In a good fight both intimates win as they did here. Even if they have a bad fight and both lose, there is no cause for alarm. With acquaintances, clients, or "dates," a bad fight can be final. But true intimates want to maintain their continuing relationship and rarely enjoy seeing their partners miserable for any length of time. They realize that the last word between intimates is never said, and that they'll live to fight another day.

6. How to Fight a Fair Fight

Frank Herman felt frustrated to the point of despair. Year after year, his gunny sack of marital grievances kept filling up. His sex life was highly unsatisfactory and so was his social life. He also felt he had more than his share of trouble in managing his money, his in-laws, and his children. Frank was a hawk at heart, but he had been domesticated by his wife Maureen, a shapely but exceedingly introverted little brunette to whom he had been married for eleven years. Frank loved her dearly, but he could never get her to hold still for a searching discussion of their important differences. While she was outwardly a "charmer," Maureen was a fight-phobic dove, forever wiggling out of "ugly" confrontations.

While the children were awake she was too embarrassed to argue at home. She wouldn't level in front of friends because she was too afraid of gossip. In the car she couldn't "mix it" because she felt it would be dangerous. She wouldn't argue with Frank while they walked the dog because it made the dog nervous, and he started barking like crazy. At bedtime she refused to fight because it would cool her sexually, a form of frigidity that sometimes lasted for two weeks or more.

Finally Frank couldn't stand it any more. His neighbor in the scenic hills above Sherman Oaks, in suburban Los Angeles, was an engineer who was aware of Frank's problem. Together they rigged up a public-address system so anything that was said in Frank's living room could be heard in the neighbor's bedroom. Whenever Frank staged unsuccessful attempts to persuade Maureen to level with him, he experienced an emotional release of sorts: he knew that his good will and her cowardice were being broadcast before witnesses; and he was so angry at Maureen that he no longer cared how unfairly he fought her fight-evasion tendencies.

Eventually Frank sought help through fight training and confessed his trickery to his self-development group. The therapy group put Frank on the "hot seat" and attacked his undercover methods. Later he and Maureen attended a group

79

together and this group pressured him into confessing to Maureen. At first she refused to believe the story, but the engineer/neighbor confirmed it. Maureen flew into a rage not only because she felt she had been spied upon, but also because she had failed to recognize how desperate Frank had felt. She never quite forgave Frank for having "bugged" her own living room, but his extreme tactics (which we would *not* recommend) did have one result that is salutary for constructive fighting: it lowered Maureen's unfairly high "belt line."

Everyone has such a belt line—a point above which blows can be absorbed, thereby making them tolerable and fair; and below which blows are intolerable and therefore unfair. Some "chickens" like Maureen Herman keep their belt lines tucked around their ears and cry "foul" at every attempted blow. Chickens therefore must be persuaded one way or another to lower their unrealistically high belt lines in order to make themselves accessible to healthy aggressive approaches by their partners. But disparities in belt lines are universal—just like disparities in optimal distance needs or in the ability to make sense while under the influence of liquor or in the case of other inequalities already mentioned. These inequalities must be compensated for, and often that isn't easy.

There are limits of tolerance in every fight—points beyond which a partner feels he can make no concessions and will no longer negotiate, at least not for the time being. Belt lines are similar limits. They apply to a partner's over-all fighting stance or "weight."

Intimates can live with a partner's belt line only if it is openly and honestly displayed, like the honest weight of a boxer before he steps into the ring. The vagaries of mate selection dictate, however, that lightweight spouses are frequently pitched against middleweight or heavyweight partners, *i.e.*, a shy husband versus an articulate wife. It's a good thing, therefore, that real intimates realize they fight for better understanding, not for knockouts. If they didn't, the murder statistics would be infinitely more shocking than they are.

Mutual good will is particularly important in the long-term fight for better understanding because the power to inflict major psychological and social or economic damage is always in the hands of intimates. Inevitably, they come to know so much about each other's weaknesses that they can pinpoint quite precisely where to hurt the partner if they care to. We call such a weak spot the Achilles' heel. Just as the belt line is not necessarily located around the waist, so an Achilles' heel need not be part of the foot. The belt line protects the Achilles' heel, and this is no mixed metaphor. Strategic weak spots and their protective shields may be located almost anywhere.

Many people are so concerned about their Achilles' heels that they make elaborate efforts to camouflage their vulnerable spots, especially when they first meet a potential new intimate. A girl may tell her lover she is sensitive about her small breasts. Actually she isn't. In her inner dialogue she is asking herself, "How central is my position in his heart? How far can I trust him?"

Then she replies, "I'll watch what he does with my fake Achilles' heel. If he handles it with tact and support, I'll show him my true vulnerable spots."

Faking an Achilles' heel can produce valuable information on how far intimates can trust each other and to what extent they can count on support for their weaknesses. An attack on an Achilles' heel also indicates that the heel-stabbing partner harbors a high level of resentment. In general, such an attack is provoked either by great concern on the part of the stabber; or because he feels he has been pushed against the wall; or he senses imminent defeat; or because the victim is wearing an armor too thick to be penetrated except at one or two spots.

Fake Achilles' heels and fake belt lines sometimes survive through years of marriage. Marco Polletti and his wife Sylvia already had three small children when this exchange took place between them:

MARCO (*confidentially*): I don't think you can really appreciate how sensitive I am about my Italian background.

SYLVIA (*sympathetically*): Sure I do! I've felt it ever since I met you.

MARCO (*seemingly relieved*): OK, then, just make sure you never call me a "wop," not even as a joke!

SYLVIA: OK, I understand.

More than a year later the Pollettis were at a party, and Marco thought that Sylvia was dancing entirely too much with a friend of his. When they got home, he was terribly angry. Both had had too much to drink. A *Virginia Woolf* free-for-all ensued during which Marco, quite unjustly, called Sylvia a "whore." Sylvia, understandably provoked, hit below the belt, or so she thought. She called him a "stupid wop."

But the belt line had been fake—the last remnant of

Marco's premarital reservations about the wisdom of entrusting his future happiness to Sylvia, whom he married after only a few weeks of courtship. Now he realized that when he called his wife a whore he had given her adequate cause to disregard his belt line. He broke up their *Virginia Woolf* stalemate with a loud guffaw and said:

"Hey, I guess that's sort of funny. I know I told you never to call me a 'wop,' but I was only testing you. I don't really mind. I guess it's about time I told you what I'm really sensitive about. What bugs me more than anything is here I am 34 years old and I ought to be getting ahead much faster at the office. I don't think I'll ever make it there and it worries the hell out of me."

Sylvia, greatly relieved, said, "Oh, I don't care! I love you anyway. If things get tough, I can always go back to work."

Many untrained marital fighters think that only suckers give away the location of an Achilles' heel. They believe that a spouse will take advantage of such a weakness whenever possible and that the aggressive partner may yell extra loudly if the sensitive one says, "You know that whenever you yell at me, my stomach acts up!"

In an intimate, leveling relationship, however, the danger of attack on an Achilles' heel is minimized. We encourage trainees to make their area of nonnegotiability and supervulnerability known simply by shouting "Foul!" whenever a partner hits below the belt. This is the surest way to find out how far one can trust the other. One of the most love-inspiring experiences is to watch a partner treat one's sensitivities with care. If he fails to be careful and a below-the-belt blow is struck, this is not likely to do mortal damage. It may even be a good thing; at least the unfairly attacked partner has now established a basis for a legitimate deutero-fight about the choice of weaponry for future fights.

Setting one's belt line too low is masochistic and invites needless injury. Setting it too high is self-pampering and cowardly. Pulling one's belt line way up (like Maureen Herman in the first fight of this chapter) is common because high-belters feel smug and justified when they complain about low blows; they may even feel sufficiently "provoked" to justify resorting to vicious measures in "self-defense." Actually, such high-belters are not being unfairly treated. They are themselves unfair; when even a fair blow lands "below the belt" it is obviously impossible to conduct a constructive fight.

A fair and openly displayed belt line is the one that is most likely to be convincing. As intimates get to know each other better and better, a fake belt line is almost sure to be exposed sooner or later and it will not be respected. When such fakery persists, it isn't likely to do much good to keep shouting "Foul!"—just as it doesn't work to meet nonexistent dangers by crying "Wolf!" too often. Belt-line fakers are helped in their phoniness when Partner A insists he knows the location of "B's" belt line instead of letting "B" tell where it is. People who level about their belt lines, on the other hand, can save themselves a lot of trouble. If a girl knows, for instance, that her lover likes having sex with her, she no longer has to go through the pretense of a fake orgasm; chances are that his masculinity is not as vulnerable as she may have feared.

In a word, it pays to fight fairly, and a fair fight is an open encounter where both partners' "weights" and weapons are equalized as much as possible.

Once a partner's true belt line is known, a heavyweight must generally lower his. He can shout "Ouch!" when the weaker opponent hits him where even a weak blow can hurt; but he shouldn't cry "Foul!" Where great discrepancies exist between partners, it may be wise for them to fight only in front of selected good-willed friends or before a therapy group—at least not until the heavyweight has been pressured into some self-disarmament. Again, the motto is "Don't drop the bomb on Luxembourg!" If you do, you can only lose.

Not every heavyweight will allow himself to be handicapped, but usually even a bully can learn to step into the ring with one hand figuratively tied behind his back; or to permit himself to be attacked under conditions when his aggressive drives are inhibited, perhaps just before making love or in front of important company. Above all, he will have to learn to avoid maneuvering his opponent into a corner where the other may become so desperate that he feels he is fighting for his integrity or even his life.

Elegant fighters—and we like to think that *elegance* in fighting is what we teach—never, never drive an opponent against the wall. It's not only unfair; it's also dangerous because it may trigger a needlessly vicious counterattack if the cornered partner panics.

We also recommend that a lightweight fighter be allowed to pick a fight at almost any time and place, but that a heavyweight be restricted to times when the lightweight partner is "loaded" and full of confidence.

This technique isn't hard to master. Dr. Jack Holt, a busy internist, was depressed because his wife, Corinne, no longer wanted to tell him what she did with her time while he was off on his busy daily (and sometimes nightly) routine of caring for his patients. He was earning over $60,000 a year, but neither Jack nor Corinne enjoyed their money. They were living parallel lives and rarely shared their feelings except about inconsequential matters. Jack was beginning to suspect that Corinne was having an affair.

The doctor was the heavyweight in the family. He was more intelligent, more verbal, more logical, and enjoyed more social status than Corinne. When he issued a ruling in his family, his announcement carried the weight of law. Before they entered fight training, Corinne tried to compensate for her "weight" deficiencies by using alienating hit-and-run tactics against Jack. She knew, for instance, that he felt guilty because he treated relatively few nonpaying clinic patients. So she needled him by calling him "money mad." Yet she refused to listen when he tried to level with her. He attempted to find out how she might feel about living on a reduced income, but she would not discuss it.

When Jack found that Corinne could not be engaged on this issue, he got mad and accused his wife of hitting him below the belt and being a sneak fighter. His accusations only made Corinne madder. Before their fight-training group, she explained why she had resorted to her dirty tactics.

CORINNE (*toward Jack*): That's all I could do. Sure I fought dirty! But only when you overwhelmed me and had me in a corner. I got tired of losing practically all the time. Anybody would! So the only way I knew how to slow you down was to get at you with a sort of fifth-column approach.

DR. BACH: In other words, you're telling your husband: "I have to fight dirty when you corner me!" But you shouldn't have to let yourself be cornered. Has there been any improvement?

JACK: Yes, I think so—don't you, sugar?

CORINNE (*toward Jack*): Oh, yes. You're a hundred per cent better.

DR. BACH: What does he do now that he didn't do before?

CORINNE: Well, he gives me a chance to score a point or so now and then and I no longer allow myself to be cornered. I don't wait to fight until my back is against the wall, and so I don't have to fight dirty any more.

JACK (*toward Corinne*): I just follow the fair-fight exercises. I wait until *you* feel really good and *then* I

place my beef, and it works. Whenever I see you're
"down" and not up to it, I initiate a fight pause.

DR. BACH: Could you both talk about an experience that
illustrates your new fight styles?

CORINNE: Well, a while back I was asked to be maid of
honor at the wedding of the daughter of the most
important family in the little town where I come
from. It was a socially important, high-class affair.
When I got to my home town I was so thrilled and
involved in preparing for the event that I didn't tell
Jack for four days.

JACK (*toward Corinne*): Yeah! What really got me good
and sore was that I tried to reach you several times
by long distance and left messages all over the
place for you, and you never returned my calls. Of
course I felt rejected and like a goddamn fool.

CORINNE: Well, you were right to tell me off when I got
back from Michigan feeling really important and in
the swing of things. That's when you made a real
good point. I liked that.

DR. BACH: What was that point?

CORRINE (*toward Dr. Bach*): Oh, he was very angry with
my excuse that I'd been too involved in the social
affairs of the wedding. But he really got fit to be
tied when I said that he wouldn't have been interested anyway.

JACK (*smiling at the recollection*): Yeah, I caught you
attributing to me what you thought I thought—all
that stuff about "spirals" that we've talked about
here in the group. Anyway (*turning toward the
group now*): I told her to cut it out, that the
important point was not my interest or lack of it in
the wedding, but that I'm interested in anything
involving Corinne; and the way she can be involved with me is to share her other involvements
with me.

CORINNE (*toward Jack*): When you said, "You're having
your fun; all I ask is that you cut me in on it," that
made sense to me. It made me think I can learn to
share.

JACK (*toward Corinne*): So why haven't you done anything about that since you got back from Michigan?

CORINNE (*agitated*): Because I'm afraid to share activities
with you! I know that you'll belittle them and

resent them because I'm not concerning myself every minute with your fate.

JACK (*red-faced and shouting*): Foul! Stop! There you go again, telling me how I think and feel. Stop attributing things to me! Why don't you ask me? I'll tell you how I feel. Actually I'm thrilled when you go into something on your own and that it interests you. I love you for it; but I want you to share it with me. . . .

Jack "scored" a point in this fight because he hit Corinne when she was "Up" and felt strong and important because she had been invited to play a central role in a socially significant occasion. He waited until Corinne felt independent and strong enough to entertain the idea of "sharing," without feeling she might be acting like a child who is reporting to an overwhelming heavyweight. When she felt strong, she was not only able to consider his demand to share her interests with him. She was glad to let him win!

In a constructive fight such as this, there are no losers. Corinne was able to "buy" Jack's point because she gained some fresh information from this fight. She found out that he was not belittling her social interests (which *she*, not he, compared unfavorably with his important medical work); that he really meant it when he said he wanted to be included in her world but did not wish to take it over.

People often underestimate the usefulness of constructive fighting as a tool for developing new information about the way an opponent feels. Such fresh intelligence can always be put to good use. Often, as in the above fight between Jack and Corinne, it is the key to the ultimate goal of fighting: to bring about a change for the better.

For real intimates, the process of eliciting information about a partner's feelings never ends because their relationship is forever evolving. One spouse or both may read a stimulating new book; or make new friends; or take an eye-opening adult education course; or undergo psychotherapy; or experience an improvement or deterioration of the sexual relationship. All such events can set off changes in a partner's feelings, and the wise spouse will try to keep up to date on developments.

There is only one area of intimacy where something less than total candor is often indicated, and this applies to partners who probe for information about outside sexual interests as well as partners responding to such probes. When it comes to intelligence about erotic stimulation outside of marriage, whether by fantasies or actual affairs, the sensitivities of most husbands and wives tend to be so great that common-sensical couples are prone to temper the rule of frankness by applying infinite tact. Total honesty is not always a virtue and discretion can still be the better part of valor. In this case, discretion may amount to respect for a partner's previously stated nonnegotiable intolerance for certain topics, e.g., past love affairs. On the other hand, partners who greatly value total, unconditional, and reciprocal transparency, must learn to like or tolerate the other's feelings, fantasies, and actions in response to erotic stimulation away from home. Intimates should remember that the limits of a partner's tolerance are usually reached faster over this issue than any other.

Even when extramarital sex is not at issue, and a fight is scrupulously fair, it can be extremely difficult to retrieve new information from intimate hostilities. Almost everybody becomes blinded in the heat of battle, which is another reason why fighting is best done in a cool state, by appointment, at least during the early stages of training. Fighting in an atmosphere of rationality sheds more light and less heat. It conditions fighters to tolerate conflict better. Like ball players, they benefit from practice and coaching. Ball players, too, get heated up in battle and the ones who have been well coached, are the ones most likely to do the rational thing under pressure. The better trained they are, the better they will be able to blend spontaneous action with tactics that were "programmed" into them in advance.

Marital fighters can train themselves to maximize the information yield from aggressive encounters. They can reduce their anger and become better listeners during a fight by telling themselves a single word: "Tough!" We employ the word here in the sense of "It's tough all over!" It is a reminder for combatants not to become oversensitive even in the heat of battle. It is the same kind of self-warning that overweight people are sometimes urged to adopt; for them the slogan is, "Think slim!"

Other information-retrieving methods for marital combatants are discussed throughout this book. At this point we would merely like to assure beginners that they are not alone if their minds retain little of what a fight was all about.

We discovered this amnesia during the early experimental phase of our training program when we began to ask couples to record their fights on tape and bring them in for scoring by their fight-training group. Typically they made their recording over a weekend and brought them to our Institute on

Monday evening. When the couples arrived, we asked them to recall what issues their weekend fights had been about. We then replayed their tape. It developed that even so short a time after a fight the partners had forgotten all but about 10% of what the shouting had been about.

They did remember the inflicted hurts, the insults, the pain, the ego damage of their Sunday punches. They vividly recalled process, style, and form: "we had a terrible fight"; "we were very mean to each other"; "I got terribly upset"; "he hit below the belt." What they could rarely recall was the substance—the point of it all. When a couple reported "We had a good fight," they rarely referred to a change and improvement in their lives. More likely. the "goodness" of their fight reflected just its style: it was fought fairly, above the belt.

What happens is that the intensity of rage itself beclouds mind and memory. In the heat of battle, when intimates are angry, tense, and perhaps fearful, it is impossible for them to think as clearly as they usually do. They should therefore make a special effort to listen to everything that's being said during a fight, not just to the things they want to hear; and they should pause frequently for feedbacks by asking such questions as, "What are you trying to tell me? What do you mean by that?" or by volunteering, "Let me tell you how *I* heard it." Feedbacks help to sort out any controversial points at issue.

7. Male and Female Fight Styles

When it comes to airing their differences, men and women often act as if they belong to altogether different species. Many wives and sweethearts enter our fight training because, they say, they ought to learn "how to understand men." The men in turn want to know "what makes women tick." These mysteries are symptomatic of the supposedly inevitable "battle of the sexes." But as it happens, this so-called battle is largely based on cultural stereotypes, which is a polite term for illusion.

We don't wish to be misunderstood. We cheerfully associate ourselves with the French when they celebrate the anatomical differences between males and females with the dictum *"Vive la différence."* We also agree with the modern research that shows women to be hardier lovers than men. But the psychological differences between the sexes have been exaggerated in our culture, especially the male and female reactions toward hostility. As a result, the intimate warfare between men and women tends to become needlessly confused and inflamed.

The trouble starts because everybody thinks he "knows" exactly what men and women are supposed to be like. According to rules laid down by social customs, women shouldn't be aggressive and should always be sweet and neat and efficient housekeeper-hostesses. Men should always be leaders. They should always be strong and protective and be the ones to fix things around the house.

Such stereotypes of femininity and masculinity can be helpful to a young person as he goes through the process of shaping his identity. But the acceptance of culturally prescribed sex roles after adolescence tends to create shallow, synthetic people who are too preoccupied with their masculine or feminine "identities." In adult male-female relationships, rigid sex-role notions create unnecessary barriers to intimacy. Real intimacy implies freedom from routine attitudes. It allows for the joyful privilege of occasional role reversal. We always remind trainees that beyond femininity and masculinity there is humanity—one's personal identity beyond the sex role.

When partners shout, "You're not being a man!" or "You're not feminine!" they are rarely accusing each other of deviant sexual tendencies. Almost always they are just using grossly inflated stereotypes to exaggerate nonsexual differences that fester between them. These labels are favorite and unfair weapons of marital fighters. They are particularly popular with wives who need an excuse for dirty fight tactics and husbands who are fight-evaders.

One of the most pervasive marital stereotypes is the male who thinks he is displaying an "unmanly" weakness when he allows himself to "fight with a woman." After all, doesn't society insist that it's silly to fight with women? Aren't they all supposed to be "hysterical"?

Again and again we have seen these males slump into inaction when their wives complain loudly and for the umpteenth time about something that the men could or should have done but didn't. Maybe the lady's beef is that her husband didn't help feed the baby at night, or that he didn't paint the kitchen, or that he came home too late from the office, or that he didn't take her out, or that he wasn't making love enough or not in the right way for her, or that he didn't take the children to church. It doesn't really matter. The sex-stereotyping males all react about the same way: they listen passively and with seemingly bottomless patience. Their attitude suggests that they are waiting for a storm to pass. Then . . .

WIFE (*visibly frustrated*): Why don't you ever *say* anything to me when I'm upset?

HUSBAND (*calm and pleasant*): I'm sorry you're upsetting yourself so. Really I am.

WIFE (*furiously*): Don't treat me like a child. I have a right to get sore at you! If you'd only show some interest in your chores around the house, I wouldn't have to get upset like this.

HUSBAND (*sweetly*): Honey, you're just tired and upset, that's all. You'll get over it. (*To himself he says:* "*She must be getting her period.*" *He moves closer and tries to put his arms around his wife. She starts to sob.*) Truly, I'm sorry you upset yourself like this all the time.

WIFE: Oh, God, you don't understand!

At this point she pushes her husband away and leaves the room. The husband approaches his hi-fi set, or picks up a book, or goes to his hobby corner. He shakes his head and says to himself, "Poor girl, she sure is in a bad mood tonight. It's got to be her period. Or maybe her mother was here today and they were bickering again. I'll leave her alone now. After a while, I'll drive down to the drug store and get her some ice cream. That will cheer her up." But he notices that he has become too tense to enjoy his hobbies. He is irritated at himself for being irritated at her. He withdraws farther from her, forgets to go to the store and drops by the neighborhood bar instead.

The husband in such a fight is clearly untrained. Instead of declaring himself available to discuss his wife's long-repeated complaint on its merits, he leaves the trouble-fermenting issue unresolved, thereby further inflating her gunny sack of grievances and nudging it toward the bursting point. He doesn't realize that he is setting himself up for an explosion. Quite the contrary: he is patting himself on the head for being so strong, tolerant, and gentlemanly, and is resenting his wife for using her "feminine ways" as a weapon against him.

Three differences in male-female fight styles are detectable in this encounter: (1) The relatively patient attitude of males toward so-called "feminine wiles," which found such heartfelt expression in the play My Fair Lady when the vexed Professor Higgins sang, "Why can't a woman be like a man?"; (2) the relatively patient attitude of females toward noncommunicative males of the "strong, silent type"; (3) the use of tears as a female fight tactic.

All three differences are culturally induced. They have little or no psychological significance and certainly don't deserve to be such common barriers to communication in the "battle of the sexes." All three notions are drummed into children early in life ("boys don't cry") and wind up being exploited by spouses. They become excuses for tiptoeing around the partner's hostilities and frustrations so couples can avoid bringing conflicts out into the open for disposal.

True, women cry more readily than men. Usually tears during intimate battle are a signal that women feel frustrated, abused, defeated, or too scared or too hurt to continue the fight round and therefore want to call off hostilities for the moment. Men tend to handle the same situation somewhat differently. They may just put on a stiff upper lip and hang their heads in a sad-sack attitude, always making sure to display these signals clearly to their opponents. Or they may give women the "silent treatment." Or they may erupt in a fulminating rage with the express or implied message, "I'm at my wits' end with you!"

Men, when they feel too hurt to continue a confrontation, are more likely to leave the scene because they are not as "nest-bound" as women. Enraged males are also more likely to threaten or use physical force. But such minor variations between the sexes are no evidence of intrinsic differences between male and female fight styles.

Gunny-sacking and injustice-collecting also are supposed to be predominantly feminine tactics. However, in decades of interviewing husbands, we found that they, too, invariably carry mental lists of grievances against their spouses. A man may claim, "My list is fairer!" (or shorter), and his wife may charge, "A man should be big enough to absorb these things!" But again these are reversible nuances. Gender has nothing to do with gunny-sacking or injustice-collecting. The culprit is whoever fails to air his complaints currently.

The fact is that male and female fight styles are largely interchangeable. As long as spouses don't know this, however, they are tempted to drag in the masculinity-femininity issue as a red herring to aggravate disparities that do linger between them, though for entirely different reasons.

For Jim and Mary Irwin, Sunday afternoon was the time of their worst fights. He was a theatrical agent and she worked as a librarian. Sunday was the one time when their respective careers did not preoccupy them. Their children were married or in college, and for the first time in their married life, their personalities were exposed to each other in full, uncamouflaged force.

One typical Sunday, Jim had collapsed unshaven in front of the TV after two beers. Mary was working in the garden. Jim was having trouble getting good reception for his ball game.

JIM (*yelling*): Mary! Mary!

MARY (*coming into the house, annoyed*): You don't have to yell so loud. You know how I hate to be yelled at. It's one of your vulgar male things. Why didn't you come out in the yard and talk to me like a gentleman?

JIM (*still sprawled across his favorite chair and truculent*): Because I'm mad at you. Why didn't you have the TV fixed for the ball game? You sure don't give a damn about this house or anything, do you?

MARY (*primly brushing dirt off herself*): Mostly I don't care for you to spend our Sunday afternoons in front of that idiot box!

JIM (*opening another can of beer*): But you could have had the TV fixed if you cared about me. You just don't care, you just don't care.

MARY (*getting angry*): I do so care! I certainly care enough to want to do something more interesting on our Sunday afternoons.

JIM: What, for instance? (*Pause.*)

MARY (*thoroughly exasperated*): You mean to sit there and tell me you don't know what to do with me on Sunday afternoon? You call that being a man? Maybe that's why I'm always in the garden rooting around in my avocados and asparagus!

JIM (*resigned*): Well, let's do something then. (*Long silence.*) Well?

MARY: Oh, for God's sake! Can't you show some leadership? (*Long silence.*) You're always saying you know everything. Well, plan something!

JIM (*fiddling with the TV*): Frankly, honey, all I want to do is watch the ball game and have a little beer.

MARY (*turning to go back to the yard*): You're disgusting!

The Irwins had any number of problems that cried out to be aired. When their last child left home, the central focus of their lives had disappeared and they had failed to substitute friends or joint activities to fill the void. Their sex life had been deteriorating for years, but each had been unable to make his preferences frankly clear to the other. Mary happened to be the partnership's natural leader and Jim, whose ability to submerge his own desires made him so valuable to his business clients, was a born follower. But neither had ever become reconciled to his own inevitable basic role in the marriage.

In fight training they learned that they would have to make adjustments to allow for their newly childless life style. Their love life improved after each leveled with the other about his hangups, so that both could begin to accommodate the partner's preferences. Finally they were persuaded to recognize that Jim's habit of rude yelling and his tendency to be submissive were not "male" shortcomings and that Mary's taste for manual labor in the yard and her relative disinterest in household perfection did not stem from any lack of "femininity."

Their mutually annoying ways were simply expressions of their basic personality patterns, aggravated by inept conflict management.

In the heat of battle the asexuality of aggression becomes particularly noticeable. Detailed observations required by our fight-scoring system reveal that husbands and wives alike look for whatever advantages they can marshal. They are equally vulnerable to fears, threats, and injuries. If a fight gets out of hand, a man is more likely to use his fist and a woman is more apt to employ her fingernails, but the act of resorting to violence is not dictated by the aggressor's sex. In short, a genuinely angry woman is little different from a genuinely angry man, and the sooner husbands and wives accept this psychological truth, the better they will be able to level with each other for constructive intimate warfare.

8. Ending a Good Fight

Many people duck fights because they don't know how to end them. "Don't start anything you can't finish" is a favorite motto of fight-evaders. In addition to this ignorance, *fear* of fight-endings is also common. Fight-evaders worry greatly that they might be worse off after a fight than they were in the first place. What if they "lose"? What if a fight gets out of control and ends in violence or separation? Many people avoid aggressive encounters because they can't face the possibility of a disastrous fight-ending.

For inefficient, sick, and dirty fighters, the ending of a fight often becomes a disaster for the same reasons. These people are motivated to hit below the belt or to press for a clear-cut "win," preferably by knockout, either because they simply don't know how to end a fight any other way, or because they too are afraid to face the consequences.

Fortunately, good-willed intimates can train themselves to walk around all the booby traps of fight-endings. What this requires, most of all, is the recognition that in creative marriage there really is no *end* to fighting. There can only be *pauses* of varying duration. This realization is no burden. It's a relief because it removes all fear of fight-endings.

What is really feared by husbands and wives is not the cessation of hostilities, it's the possibility of getting blamed for a battle and the finality of its results. But in true intimacy, nothing is final! And when fighting is conducted fairly and constructively, neither partner needs to push for a "kill" or a drop-the-bomb-on-Luxembourg "overkill." Why should he? There will always be another chance to bring about changes.

Constructive fights fall into a natural rhythm of rounds. How to begin and end each round is easily learned through practice. Either partner may call for a pause between a round, but not in the middle of one. Each pause must be negotiated and is subject to mutual agreement (as for instance, an evening's truce when the boss comes to dinner).

There are times when partners can profit by extending a fight and other times when it is best to let a fight die down for a short pause, or perhaps for an intermission of a week, depending on progress and on the amount of heat generated.

Experienced fighters can sense which tactic is likely to work best at various stages of a fight. In general it is best to assess every fight like a campfire. There are times when the fire is so hot that it needs no fuel or fanning; times when the glowing embers are best allowed to burn down; and times when flames need fanning to keep them alive. But at no time will civilized campers generate so much heat that the forest will catch fire and force them to flee.

Ideally, a fight ends when there has been a total (or at least satisfactory) airing of each partner's views. Partners should question each other to be sure when this stage has been reached. The exchange can be simple:

"Have you gotten everything off your chest about this?"

"Yes, I have."

"Well, I did too."

Before they reach this stage, partners are advised to try to make sure that the fire of their fight is really extinguished and that no burning bits are left behind before they leave the scene. Like good Boy Scouts, they had best look around carefully to be sure that their campfire isn't smoldering.

Many fights don't lend themselves to such clear-cut resolutions. When partners become exhausted or lose interest or bog down in the "Here we go again" redundancy of round-robin rituals, they should negotiate a pause and stoke the fire of their fight until they are ready to resume hostilities at another mutually agreeable time.

It is also essential to start no intimate fighting until after the partners have agreed on a mutually accessible emergency brake; an unconditional red-light stop signal by which either partner can bring a fight to an end or at least to a temporary halt. Researchers have discovered that dogs use certain "I give up" gestures that stop even overwhelmingly victorious attackers from going on. Unhappily, this lifesaving ritual does not work too well when it is left to the instinct of humans. This is why men, in war, sometimes continue to shoot at enemies whose hands are raised in surrender.

In intimate fighting partners should arrive at an advance understanding about an "emergency brake" that will be honored by both. The signal can be almost anything, including the words "Please stop!", "Cool it!", or "You win!" Trained fighters know that if they abuse this signal, they will almost certainly find themselves—just like fighters who cry, "Foul!" when no blow was struck below the belt line—in a brand-new fight about their unfair fight methods.

No fight can be considered at an end until after the combatants have made up. Making up is sometimes a lengthy process, especially for partners who cannot bring themselves to patch things up until the opponent has spent some time in the marital jail (doghouse). Jailers mete out such sentences as "no cocktails" or "no smoking" or "no sex" for certain periods of time, or they may simply sulk or act cool.

Doghouse inmates tend to fare best if they serve their sentences cheerfully. Some lovable rascals are blessed with a natural gift for reconciliation. These are the people who know when to pop out a bottle of champagne or a pair of tickets to a show or some other welcome surprise that clears the air and, in effect, suggests that the time of penance is over and a happy time has begun.

Successful reconciliators do not make the mistake of sniveling, pouting, or running around with hang-dog expressions on their faces. The bully who turns maudlin or the shrew who acts as if she is suddenly tamed is rarely believable in the eyes of an offended partner; in fact, they may strike the offended spouse as so incongruous that such exaggerated penance attempts only make the doghouse inmates even more unlikable.

Partners who are talented at making up are careful not to do anything "extra" that might look phony, such as taking out the garbage if they normally don't. They remain in character, but display the best of themselves and thereby indicate a determination to make up. We suggest to spouses who are painters, for instance, that they paint a picture and present it to their partner. By whatever means seem most natural, the offending partner should reduce existing tension and transmit signals that his opponent can decode to read approximately as follows:

"I made a mistake and I promise I'll learn from it. I'm not a rigid fool, an unchangeable person. Now that you know me better, please forgive me, but don't forget what you've learned about my weaknesses. And please cue me in when the same thing threatens to come up again."

Only a pathological partner is likely to respond to this approach by demanding an extended incarceration in the doghouse.

Humor is another valuable tool for making up and restoring good will. One of our trainee husbands bought his wife a toy skunk and presented it as a peace offering with the comment: "I'm not going to say who made the stink: you, me, or him." They kissed and made up and then made love, which is the best making-up gesture of all. They were able to bury the hatchet for a while because they had learned that there are safe ways to start, to conduct, and to end fights; and that the continuing process of constructive leveling between true intimates leaves few, if any, unhealed wounds.

As we have cautioned previously, there are no rigid cookbook rules for intimate fighting. Each couple can find its own creative way through the issues that need airing between them. The following 17 exercises are offered only as a general guide for intimates who wish to acquire a more elegant and constructive fight style. They don't need to be learned like battles in a history class. Many people become excellent fighters without practicing them at all. Trainees do often find these workouts helpful, though, because the exercises identify the key elements of constructive fighting; they place these elements in the most useful sequence; and they give partners a chance to flex their fight muscles in a rehearsal situation. Using these exercises, partners can practice with a minor bone of contention before placing a fight about a major issue.

The first five exercises comprise the warm-up.

Exercise No. 1 is a solo affair. A partner holds an inner dialogue. Here are some questions he can ask and answer for himself:

Am I merely annoyed with my partner or am I really angry?

At what point will my frustrations boil up in the form of open hostility?

Do I have real evidence that something is seriously wrong in my relationship with my partner?

Exercise No. 2 is another solo function. Assuming that a partner has found something worth fighting about, he holds a second inner dialogue. Some questions he should now ask and answer for himself:

Should I really fight about this or not?

How afraid am I of this fight?

How afraid am I of being rejected by my partner?

How well will I tolerate the tensions of this fight?

Am I ready to be honest as well as tactful in this encounter?

Is there a danger that I might collude with my partner and duck this fight if he tries to evade it?

Am I sure that I have identified the true issue and am not about to do battle about a trivial matter that actually camouflages another, deeper grievance?

Am I ready to follow up my anger with a specific demand for a change in the status quo?

Exercise No. 3 begins the duet. The aggressor announces his intention to fight ("I have a bone to pick with you"). He pins down a time and place for the fight and engages his opponent, making certain not to hit the partner in ambush or with a hit-and-run attack. He states the issue and makes certain that his anger cannot be misinterpreted as a Vesuvius outburst, and he clearly limits his fight goals. If the partnership consists of a heavyweight-hawk and a lightweight-dove, both partners should take extra care to insure that the fight does not escalate beyond the limit announced in this exercise.

Exercise No. 4 is a review of arms-control ground rules.

Are both partners prepared to outlaw physical violence?

Are they ready to respect belt lines and observe peace between rounds?

Do both realize that their fight can yield no output of settlements unless there is adequate input of information from each partner?

Are both aware that there can be no response from one partner without adequate stimulus from the other?

Are both ready to listen as well as talk?

Are they prepared to accept no "understanding" unless each double-checks his interpretation of the understanding with the partner by feedbacks?

Are both prepared to confine themselves to the here-and-now and not to delve into the past?

Have they considered the advantages of fighting before an audience or referee?

Exercise No. 5 consists of a discussion wherein both partners assess the results of the previous four exercises and conducts a deutero-fight, if necessary, before going on to place the substantive issue in contention. This ends the first phase of the exercises.

The second phase consists of seven exercises that encompass the heat of battle.

Exercise No. 6 is the time when partners should be sure that any Vesuvius outbursts and *Virginia Woolf* insult rituals have been properly recognized as "nonfights" and gotten out of the way. Only thereafter should an issue be stated and developed through clear assertions from both partners. Both should be certain they are transmitting how they feel about the emergence of the matter.

Exercise No. 7 consists of the first feedback by the nonaggressor, who articulates what he believes the aggressor is after, and, if necessary, a correctional checkout by the aggressor to bring the issue into sharper focus.

Exercise No. 8 is the signal for the nonaggressor to respond to the aggressor's demand and to launch a counteroffensive if he considers it appropriate.

Exercise No. 9 gives both partners an opportunity to correct false or irrelevant echoes of the previous exercise.

Exercise No. 10 is a quiet time. It is an intermission that can last an hour or a week or more, depending on agreement. It is also the time for a third inner dialogue. Each partner can repeat the first and second exercises and meditate about ways to advance his own cause.

Exercise No. 11 resumes the duet. At this point exercises No. 6 through No. 10 can be repeated as often as mutually acceptable.

Exercise No. 12 is the time for mutual disengagement and attempts to articulate what changes the fight has brought about and what each partner has agreed to do to implement the changes. This ends the second phase of the exercises.

The third phase consists of five exercises to help partners deal with the outcome of a fight and to cool off pending resumption of combat.

Exercise No. 13 is another solo affair. Each partner should hold a fourth inner dialogue. Here are some questions that each can ask and answer for himself:

What have I learned from this fight?

How badly was I hurt?

How was my partner hurt?

How valuable was this fight for me and my partner in letting off steam?

How useful was it in revealing new information about myself, my partner and the issue in contention?

What do I think about the new positions we arrived at?

What did I find out about my own—and my partner's—fight style, strategy, and weapons?

Exercise No. 14 consists of making up, resuming peaceful relations, and enjoying respite from fighting.

Exercise No. 15 consists of scoring the second phase of the fight by using techniques described in Chapter 14 and comparing "wins," "losses," and fight styles.

Exercise No. 16 is the time to establish any penalties and additional changes that the partners can agree upon after judging their fight.

Exercise No. 17 consists of both partners zeroing in on leftover tensions and unresolved issues. They can stand by for (or express readiness for) the next fight which may focus on a new issue and may be fought with newly modified arms, limitations, strategies, taboos, and freedoms.

Now the partners should be ready to return to Exercise

No. 1. After adequate practice, all of these processes become "second nature." Couples adapt them so they will yield maximum comfort and productivity to themselves. Normally, a fight fought under the rules described here and in the preceding chapters will not only relieve and refresh spouses because it clears the air; it will exhilarate them because the effect of gaining new information about oneself and one's partner is much like the feeling experienced by mountain climbers when they reach the top of a new peak. Their muscles may ache the next day, but the triumph of gaining access to new sights makes the pain worth-while.

Some couples report that they feel neither relief nor exhilaration, but continuing frustration and perhaps battle fatigue. Usually these are partners who are victims of conflict evasion or bad or dirty fight styles. They should ask themselves whether they are doing enough to eliminate these depressing techniques; and here are some other questions they might find helpful:

Do we fight at optimum times and places?

Do we fight too much without observing pauses and refueling requirements?

Are we scoring our fights fairly?

Are we extracting enough new information from our fights and making intelligent use of this fresh intelligence?

Are we victims of here-we-go-again round-robin rituals?

For most trainees these test questions lead to better fight techniques which, in turn, produce the good feelings that normally follow a thorough airing of differences. If frustration and fatigue persist, partners are well advised to consult a therapist qualified to counsel them in these matters.

Sometimes even the most sensitive therapist's progress with such a couple may be agonizingly slow. This does not necessarily mean that one or both partners are psychiatrically "sick." It may just mean that their patterns for dealing with aggression are so exceptionally far apart as to constitute a super-disparity.

Some desirable behavior changes are unrealistic expectations, at least for some time, and we have learned not to push for "impossible" changes. Through trial and error, we teach far-apart partners to find out what is changeable, and to put up temporarily with what isn't.

During the period when our training was still being designed, we worked with one highly intelligent, articulate wife who could never merely state and explain a complaint to her husband. She went into rages and sometimes cursed him for hours. She agreed to let her husband attempt to limit her vituperation. Yet when he did, the wife developed headaches, stomach-aches, and other persistent psychosomatic symptoms. The husband's rage-control efforts had to be stopped. Instead, the state of this union had to be respected and so we bolstered the husband's tolerance for the wife's rages.

This wasn't difficult—just as it is feasible to increase the tolerance of spouses toward such habits as a partner's untidiness, morning grouchiness, talking-or-eating mannerisms, and other annoyances.

Partners who are faced with such trials can be taught that their opponent's idiosyncrasies are usually not directed against them; the bad habits are probably just "other-annoying," not "other-directed." When the offended partner succeeds in accepting this distinction, the explosiveness of their encounters can usually be defused.

In a word: good fighting should reduce marital frustration, but it does not work invariably and immediately. To live with frustration is part of the price of intimacy, at least until new events in the life of the partnership open the way to opportunities for new approaches at new solutions.

9. Bad Fighters and How to Reform Them

The list of ways to discourage intimacy is almost inexhaustible, and some love-killing fight styles require no words at all. Consider the spouse-watchers. They are watching, watching, watching their partners all the time. They are not participating observers who are accumulating impressions preliminary to opening a dialogue. They are like Peeping Toms or uncommunicative FBI agents gathering evidence, perhaps to be unloaded at the moment that would be most embarrassing to their partners, perhaps just to be tucked away as ammunition for a future "trial."

They are full of silent questions: How clumsy is the partner? How does he handle the children? How does he drive the car? How is he with the in-laws and the neighbors? How does he behave during intercourse? This peeping process, if chronic, can lead to titanic blow-ups or to irreversible loss of trust.

Privacy-invaders run similar risks. These people are anxious to share everything with their partners and expect them to reciprocate. This is not a poor idea in principle, but it only works if there is mutual agreement. Partners vary greatly in their need for privacy (this is another intimate disparity). A privacy-invader may become embroiled in constant difficulties because he lacks respect for his partner's optimal distance and refueling needs.

Spouses often make the mistake of thinking that a spouse-watcher, a privacy-invader, or some other type of wretched, untrained fighter is an evil—even satanic—character. These ugly personalities do exist and they are inflamed by despicable intentions. This book, however, is almost completely devoted to Mr. and Mrs. Everyman, the generally nice people who only need to learn more about managing their hostilities. And *their* intentions are usually good, or at least defensible.

Even a partner who opens his spouse's mail should not be condemned out of hand. He is not necessarily collecting evidence of possible skulduggery. Chances are he is merely expressing his curiosity about the recipient's relations with the outside world. Or perhaps he is expressing concern about the recipient's popularity; or his own need to compete more actively for the recipient's affections; or he may just be impressed that his partner is so popular. Curiosity about one's partner is universal. No true intimate should care so little about his spouse's feelings that he becomes indifferent to the partner's relationships with others.

Most spouse-watchers and privacy-invaders can be contained if their opponents say, "Look, it bugs me when you do that! Please stop." If that doesn't work, the opponent-target can become more aggressive and say, "I still don't think you realize how much that bothers me! Why won't you stop? Let's have it out!"

The same strategy works against the more hostile and articulate types we call spouse-probers. Often these are people who happen to have read a few books about psychoanalysis and whose amateur expertise went to their heads. Here is a typical example of how such misguided fans of Dr. Freud operate:

HUSBAND: Your father must have been a real son of a
    bitch!
WIFE: Why?
HUSBAND: Because you never trust me.

And here is a female spouse-prober digging away at her husband's integrity:

WIFE: I'm telling you, you're just kidding yourself.
HUSBAND: That's ridiculous! I know what I'm doing.
WIFE: No, you don't! You're totally unaware. I know you
    inside out....

Uninvited character analyses and interpretations of a spouse's motives are among the most anger-provoking tactics that husbands and wives unleash upon one another, even when, by improbable chance, they happen to be accurate. An attitude of "I know more about yourself than you do" is sometimes tolerable when it comes from a skilled psychologist or psychiatrist. It is presumptuous coming from anybody else.

Character analysis can become a global assault on the entire personality of an opponent and, if the opponent reciprocates, the engagement may escalate until the spouses find themselves engaged in the deadly sport of mutual character assassination. More likely, such an attack will be limited to minor interpretations of an opponent's specific sins. These sins may be incredibly petty, but their interpretations can ignite very damaging fights. This is what happened to Jerry Hardy, a 27-year-old office manager, and his wife Lorraine, 26, when they were having breakfast one morning. Both had slight hangovers and were more than normally grouchy. Jerry was the son of a prosperous attorney. Lorraine was raised in more modest circumstances. They had been married for six months.

JERRY (*opening his soft-boiled egg*): Why in hell don't you ever put out napkins for breakfast?

LORRAINE (*pouring coffee for Jerry*): Because it isn't necessary. I never spill anything on myself.

JERRY (*growling*): I'm not talking about napkins for you. I'm talking about napkins for *us*.

LORRAINE (*primly*): I hadn't noticed that *you* spill anything either.

JERRY (*getting madder*): So what? I like to wipe my mouth after I eat.

LORRAINE (*superior*): No, sir! That's not it at all. I know what it is. You just like to nag me!

JERRY (*stops eating*): That's ridiculous! You *want* to be nagged. That's why I can't get a goddamned napkin unless I yell about it.

LORRAINE (*coyly*): But don't you really like it?

JERRY: What, to wipe my mouth?

LORRAINE (*losing her temper*): No, you jerk, I mean yell at me!

JERRY (*getting up from the table, furious*): Oh, to hell with it! I'm going to have breakfast at the drug-store. (*He grabs his brief case and leaves.*)

LORRAINE (*yelling after him*): You're a nut and a bully!

If the Hardys had been trained fighters, this encounter might have developed approximately as follows:

JERRY (*annoyed, but mostly just inquisitive*): Honey, tell me, why don't you put out napkins unless I ask?

LORRAINE (*primly*): I don't think we need napkins. We're both neat.

JERRY (*patient but firm*): I disagree. I consider them necessary for both of us.

LORRAINE: You do? What in the world for?

JERRY: Because a well-laid table has napkins on it. That's why!

LORRAINE: Maybe so, but I'm not used to it. In my family nobody ever needed "wipes." (*She laughs.*)

JERRY (*also laughing*): Yeah, I bet! Not even in the bathroom?

LORRAINE: Now really! Don't tell me you want to have a fight about this.

JERRY: Not especially. I'd just like to tell you to put out napkins.

LORRAINE: In other words, you want to wipe your mouth, but you don't want to rub it in. . . .

JERRY (*laughing*): What are you talking about? Rub what in?

LORRAINE: My background.

JERRY (*kisses her on the cheek*): Darling, I've told you and told you! I *love* your family. They produced you, didn't they?

LORRAINE: So why do you mind asking me for a napkin?

JERRY: Every time we sit down to eat?

LORRAINE: I guess that *is* kind of silly. Well, if it means that much to you, I'll put out napkins. But you've got to do something for me, too.

JERRY: OK, try me!

LORRAINE: I wish you'd try not to be so unpleasant in the mornings.

JERRY: OK, I'll do my best. . . .

In the first of these two fights, the partners flailed wildly and attributed all sorts of motives to each other. Their relationship was alienated by this encounter, their intimacy was reduced and both wound up losers. In the trained version of the same fight, they stuck to the facts and did not try to reduce each other's egos. They employed humor to make a gloomy breakfast scene more bearable and to help keep a relatively minor issue in perspective. They exchanged some substantive information about each other and thereby increased their feeling of intimacy. A lingering misunderstanding was resolved and both partners emerged winners.

A particularly alienating form of character analysis is the technique of stereotyping. To stereotype a husband or wife is to begin to give up trying to understand a partner as a person. It is the beginning of true alienation and depersonalization, the first step in a process that can lead to emotional and even physical destruction.

To label one's partner as a type or as a thing ("I know you

have homosexual tendencies even if you don't") is inevitably ego-reducing. Again, it is the so-called "psychiatrically sophisticated" people who are most likely to turn a partner into an example of a diagnostic category. Some common labels are "alcoholic," "sadist," "game player," "con man," "dependent," "mother-fixated," "narcissist," and "voyeur." These stereotypes can only lead to insult exchanges or worse, because no healthy person can tolerate the idea of being an impersonal category.

Another popular way to depersonalize a spouse is to view him as an alleged representative of a race or kind of people, using culturally popular stereotypes to render the partner's metamorphosis—from a person to a symbol—more believable. Sometimes an attempt to understand a person in terms of a stereotype can lead to a falsely secure illusion: "Oh, I know his Irish temper; it doesn't mean a thing." More often, the categorizing of an intimate leads to negative illusions that are expressed in such cynical statements as, "Yeah, I know his kind," or, "I've got his number."

Stereotyping confuses the issue. One unhappy, confused fight trainee, a widow in her late thirties, had recently married an inveterate bachelor whose family had a vague Arabic background dating back several generations. This wife was a large, physically not too attractive woman who had been dreadfully worried that she might never get married again. Her new husband treated her like a sexy little girl, which she adored, but she also discovered that he was less than sincere and that his elaborate lies were masterpieces of deception.

These undesirable character traits she attributed to her husband's "Arabic background," and when she found a novel that described a talkative, wily villain who happened to be an Arab, she seized upon the book as conclusive proof of her hypothesis.

It developed that this husband was rejecting her because he had finally arrived at the conclusion that he was not the marrying type, after all. His behavior was a signal that he wanted to leave his wife. When these facts were exposed in fight training, the couple decided on a trial separation. The wife resumed her career as an advertising copy writer and eventually got a divorce. These, then, were people who were incompatible, but their difficulties had nothing to do with his "Arabic background."

When stereotyping becomes a way of life and a spouse's definition of the partner changes from "my wife" or "my husband" to "that one!" this transition may be the prelude to the worst possible disaster of all: spouse murder. Before one spouse can bring himself to kill the other, and not just think about it, which everyone fleetingly does at some time, he *must* transform the victim from a person into a symbol, an impersonal thing. We are therefore careful to warn trainees to escape stereotype traps either by breaking the mold through aggressive leveling or, in hopeless cases like that of the "Arab," by removing themselves from the stereotyper.

A more benign form of destructive aggression, but one which threatens intimacy, is the technique of letting down the partner's expectations. The execution of this maneuver can be deceptively mild, as demonstrated by a wife who reassures her husband as he leaves for the office on the morning of a scorching hot day. He is late for a breakfast conference:

WIFE: Don't worry about the yard, dear. I know you've got to run.

HUSBAND: But you hate to water the lawn!

WIFE: Never mind, darling! I'll take care of it.

But she "forgets," and since she forgets her promises chronically, his let-down expectation triggered a ferocious kitchen-sink fight when he came back from work late and limp that evening and found his carefully trimmed lawn parched and studded with brown sunburn spots. The lesson is obvious: a partner's reasonable expectations should not be frustrated too often.

For some spouses, letting down the partner's expectations is a way of life. They are friendly folks who love the world, hate to hurt people overtly and therefore adopt a passively aggressive fight style to vent their aggressions. Their opening gambit is likely to be irresistibly disarming.

"Let me help you," they say.

One dove-wife who fought her rather overwhelming hawk-husband with this passively aggressive technique volunteered to buy him some socks and underwear. They were leaving for Europe the following day and the husband was so busy finishing last-minute chores at his office that he couldn't go shopping for himself. Naturally, he accepted her offer with relief.

His delight was short-lived. All afternoon the telephone kept ringing. The wife called. A salesman called. A friend of the wife, who was accompanying her, called. They couldn't find this or that. They wanted to double-check on sizes and colors. Ostensibly, they were trying to make sure they would not displease the husband. In fact, they were driving him crazy. He finally became furious and told his wife to forget the whole thing. Whereupon she interrupted him still one more time to apologize for getting him upset.

When this husband returned from Europe, he proposed to his fight-training group that he spoil his wife's "Let me help you" strategy by inventing fake needs for her to fill; then allowing her to let him down; but robbing her of her aggression pay-off by acting smug and showing her that he was emotionally unaffected.

He was advised to desist because his proposed solution was not a genuine strategy; it was a phony game. Moreover, since he was the heavyweight-hawk in the family and she was the less well-armed lightweight-dove, he should permit his wife to enjoy some aggression release in the style that made her comfortable, even if he didn't consider it ideal. He was therefore encouraged to make a pact in his inner dialogue to go along with his wife's emotional needs—but only to the point where he would let her help him with things that he could do without, never with things he considered crucial to his well-being.

True, this compromise did not constitute immediate 100% leveling. However, the husband was counseled that humoring the partner along is not always a bad idea when a couple stands in the shadow of a mushroom radioactive cloud (such as the wife's possible threat to match his fury, perhaps by refusing to go along to Europe, for instance). He was also advised that later, when negotiating with his wife about unfinished business, he could reveal that he had been humoring her along and add for future reference:

"Please don't get the wrong idea. I really don't want you to offer your help unless you can deliver!"

It is tempting for spouses whose expectations have been let down to interpret these letdowns as signs that their partners are satans who are trying to drive them crazy. Actually, most passively aggressive fighters don't intend to make their mates suffer. These aggressors resort to infuriating tactics quite unconsciously. Spouses who are targets of these supposedly vicious maneuvers can always check what intention lies behind them. They need only train themselves not to become a patsy. Does the "villain" look unhappy because his mate isn't suffering? Only if he does is he likely to be a satan.

The "Let me help you" school of fighters are part of a breed whom we call crisis-makers. These people can often be reformed just by being made aware of the destructive effect they are having upon partners whom they are supposedly helping.

Unfortunately, crisis-making is absurdly easy. Suppose the

wife has forgotten for the umpteenth time to put towels in
the bathroom. The husband has just finished a shower. Wet
and cold, he is yelling for a towel. The wife brings one:

HUSBAND: Goddamnit, can't you *ever* have a goddamned
towel in this goddamned bathroom?
WIFE: Gee, honey, I've just had *so* much to do!

This husband needs to sit his wife down and spell out in
unmistakable terms just how deeply the towel crisis annoys
him and how this sort of camouflaged attack eats away his
love for her. He should also question her to find out whether
her crisis-making is a hidden signal that he has too long
ignored. Perhaps the wife is signaling: "I'm not your servant!" Or, "I'm starving for an opportunity to be needed!"
Or, "Why can't you be a big boy and bring your own damned
towel!" Or, "You're taking me for granted these days—I'll
show you how to appreciate me!" Open two-way communication can flush out such wifely feelings and the husband should
pay attention to them.

A popular type of crisis-making is "disorder." Arthur
Hamilton, a painting contractor whose wife Edith ran his
business affairs, reported such a case to his fight-training
group:

ARTHUR (*waving a bank slip for a $5-charge under
Edith's nose*): See? Here's another charge because
the bank paid a check on our account. Didn't you
know we were overdrawn? How can you be so
unbelievably stupid?
EDITH (*calm and reasonable*): But darling, you know the
bank always makes mistakes.
ARTHUR (*incensed*): Sure they make a mistake once in a
while. But you make 'em *all* the time! You're a
damned bank menace! I just don't know what to
do! The bank called me this afternoon and said
they refused payment on two more checks and one
of those checks is going to ruin a whole deal for
me!
EDITH (*starts to cry*): Why are you always blaming me
just because we're in a financial mess? I haven't
even dared to buy that new baby carriage. All I'm
trying to do is help you!
ARTHUR (*red-faced and pounding both fists on his desk*):
I always fall for that crap of yours. I really hate to

depend on you and then see you make a damn fool out of me. I've really had it!

EDITH (*sobbing*): I'm so sorry you're so upset. What can I do to help?

ARTHUR (*somewhat calmer*): I'm telling you for the last time: you can't write checks without making deposits! Can't you get that through your head?

EDITH: But I always do! This time you just didn't bring enough home for me to deposit!

ARTHUR (*jumps up from his desk, wildly angry*): But I did, I did! Come on, look in your silly purse! I'll bet those four checks I gave you a week ago are still right in there, damn you!

EDITH (*searches through one purse; then another; in the third purse, lying on the floor of her disheveled clothes closet, she finds checks that would have more than covered the checks that had been drawn against their account*): Gosh, darling! I'm so sorry!

ARTHUR (*still incensed, mocks her*): Yeah! So sorry, so sorry! A fat lot of good that'll do me with the bank and with my suppliers!

EDITH (*pats him on the arm and tries to kiss him as he dodges*): But I *am* sorry, dear. Believe me, I'll take those checks down to the bank today and I'll straighten everything out.

Discussion in the fight-training group brought out that Arthur really believed Edith was deliberately trying to drive him out of his mind. Edith was shocked when she heard this. She agreed with the suggestion that she was temperamentally unsuited to be a bookkeeper. The Hamilton marriage improved markedly as soon as he began to deposit his checks himself.

The tyranny of disorder can be imposed in innumerable ways by wives who have no shirts ironed when their husbands are leaving for the office; or by husbands who misplace so many shoes, tools, dog leashes, and household bills that their homes become paralyzed; and by teen-agers who seem constitutionally unable to pick up anything they drop.

Disorder is a favorite form of crisis-making because it doesn't require the commission of a "crime." Indeed, it doesn't require the commission of anything. It is a tactic of omission and affords three superb cover-ups for the crisis-maker: (1) "Look how hard I try to help!" (2) "I don't like it any better than you; I can't find anything either"; (3)

"How can anybody get so upset about a lot of silly little things unless they just want to be miserable and nag?"

Disorder is part of a pattern of resisting cooperation with others, especially those who are viewed as overwhelmingly powerful figures and want to push a less powerful partner around. The "victim" defends himself against the alleged dominance by what used to be called "gold-bricking" in the army. It is a form of bugging one's superiors and is often practiced by hospitalized psychiatric patients against indifferent or cruel attendants.

Frequently, the only antidotes to disorder are (1) to stash away minimal needs in hideaways that are unlikely to be found by disorder-makers; or (2) to learn to live with chaos.

Partners who delegate duties to their spouses, but then do not respect the spouse's new role, are also likely to be effective crisis-makers. Suppose a husband delegates his wife to pay the household bills and run the family accounts. Suppose he then finds that the wife's bookkeeping is not so meticulously up to date that she can reel off a precise run-down on their finances whenever he happens to ask for it, which he does all too often. Suppose he then becomes critical of her stewardship.

This wife has a right to blow her top and demand that her mate stop his nagging—unless, of course, she really is inefficient and habitually overdraws their account. This husband is a pseudo-delegator. Instead of giving his wife the autonomy she was led to expect, he only positioned her as a target for his nagging and scapegoating.

An all too common tactic is for a spouse to belabor the other's Achilles' heel. An intimate opponent's Achilles' heel is almost always disclosed after a while, and untrained husbands and wives will stab it often, especially in self-defense or counterattack. Successful intimates attack an Achilles' heel only upon irresistible provocation, but many unfair fighters display much malicious skill when they zero in on a below-the-belt target.

It is tempting and easy. Does a husband feel demeaned because he thinks he isn't making enough money? Then his wife need only go on a little spending spree to rub salt into his wound. Is a wife worried because she thinks she ought to be more creative? Then her husband need only ignore her latest writing, perhaps even after he explicitly asks to see it. These Achilles'-heel fights can result in irreversible loss of trust.

Some people feign anger to find out more about the partner's fangs and fight style. A husband can do this by nagging his wife about dinner when he isn't really hungry. Or a wife might make a fuss about a child's misbehavior even though she doesn't really much care about it; she only wants to find out whether her husband will protect the child or use the occasion to undermine her wifely authority. Playful fighting—the kind that involves no major stakes—can serve the same reconnaissance purposes, so fake anger is not a recommended fight tactic.

A few partners go so far as to make fake confessions of infidelities, or other more or less intolerable behavior, in order to probe how tolerant or punitive their intimates will turn out to be. A husband or a wife may try to test an opponent with such untruths as "I splurged"; or, "I banged up the car"; or, "I threw your manuscript in the incinerator by mistake." Such a probe can boomerang badly. It is the kind of "Wolf! Wolf!" cry that leads to overkill counterattacks or loss of intimate credibility.

Other people, in effect, emit helpless little cries of "peep, peep!" These are "Come help me!" signals for attention. They entice the opponent because they make him feel strong and appeal to his hero-rescuer fantasies. This tactic can be legitimate on occasion, but quite a few partners use it not only to gain attention but to maintain it. If the cries keep up—as, for example, if a husband keeps yammering year after year about his job—the would-be rescuer only becomes weary. "Spoiled" wives are another example of "peep, peep!" criers who eventually alienate their opponents and kill their love.

Finally, there are passively aggressive styles that have the effect of isolating partners from each other so they can no longer "mix it." Partner A may treat Partner B like a stranger so that "B" complains, "He talks right through me!" Or "A" may persuade a friend to form an alliance against "B." Or he may resort to the *"Nyet!"* technique, made famous by the Soviets at the United Nations, and invariably take a negative stance. Or he may deny that a fact is a fact and say, "It ain't so!" Or he may go on a sit-down strike and proclaim, "I ain't gonna change!"

If such an attitude reflects a true unwillingness to negotiate, no amount of fight training is likely to make much difference. The striking partner is saying, "You've got to love me as I am. After all, you took me for better or for worse, and I'm doing the best I can. If that's not good enough, you must get somebody else." Unhappily, etiquette suggests that this type of defeatism is acceptable, and so it usually leads to a more or less amicable divorce.

10. When Words Fail: Fighting with Fists and Fingernails

It was Sunday brunch time in the home of Henry Talbott, 47, a prosperous leather-goods manufacturer, and his second wife, Ingeborg, a 28-year-old Scandinavian beauty. It was a brilliantly beautiful day outside, but in the Talbotts' $130,000 home the storm clouds were hanging low. Henry and Ingeborg had started on their scrambled eggs and Canadian bacon, but they had hardly exchanged a word within the past hour. They had been suspecting each other (with ample justification in both cases) of carrying on extramarital affairs.

The phone rang. Ingeborg seized it, listened, and put the receiver down with a shrug. The same thing happened twice again. Each time Ingeborg reported, "There's nobody on the line." The last time Henry snapped, "I don't believe it!" and put the phone near his place at the breakfast table.

INGEBORG (*caustic*): I know how to answer the phone.

HENRY (*pre-emptory*): You let me handle this, do you hear? (*The phone rings and he talks into it.*) Sorry, you've got the wrong number.

INGEBORG (*suspiciously*): Who're you trying to kid?

HENRY (*face reddening*): What are you talking about? (At this point the phone rang again. Both reached for it and the receiver fell to the floor. A female voice was heard to shout, "Henry! Henry!" HENRY and INGEBORG were both pulling at the phone receiver. Neither would let go. Suddenly, he grabbed her arm and twisted. She bit his hand.)

HENRY (*losing control*): *You bitch!*

He cracked a hard blow at her cheek. She screamed and ran out of the room sobbing. He picked up the dead telephone, shook his head, sighed and went to the master bathroom to help Ingeborg put a cold wet towel against her cheek. He mumbled a perfunctory, "I'm sorry." Ingeborg

114

said nothing. In the afternoon, as if by agreement, they pursued separate activities. Henry sneaked away to phone his mistress just to be sure it had not been she who made the call that started his fight with Ingeborg. His mistress, who had been badgering Henry to get a divorce, assured him that she knew better than to call him at home. Henry was not convinced. He thought he had recognized her voice when he and Ingeborg were fighting for possession of the telephone.

At dinner, after a few drinks, Henry and Ingeborg agreed that their fight had been "silly" and that they should make up. Not long afterward they were in their bedroom with its two vast double beds. But the issues behind their telephone fight had never been aired and their mistrust lingered.

HENRY *(taking off shoes and socks)*: OK, now what?

INGEBORG *(fussing with her hair at her dresser)*: If you want to take that attitude, I've got plenty to keep me busy around the house.

HENRY *(taking off necktie and shirt)*: What do you mean? What attitude?

INGEBORG *(shrugs, removes her brassiere)*: All right, all right. We might as well get it over with.

HENRY *(annoyed, stops undressing)*: For crying out loud, you know damned well I don't like to make love when you don't have a good time. That just turns me off every time, and you know it!

INGEBORG *(puts on a robe)*: OK, let's do what Dr. Bach says. Let's stop 'contaminating the sheets.' Let's talk it out in the living room, not here.

(Now both were seated in the living room.)

HENRY *(blandly)*: OK, let's talk. What's your beef?

INGEBORG *(with a deep resignation)*: Don't you know?

HENRY *(feigning naïveté)*: No!

INGEBORG *(totally exasperated)*: I give up!

The issues festering in this marriage were manifestly so numerous that the couple's mutual sexual rejection at the end of their black Sunday added only a small amount of insult to a great deal of stockpiled injury. As this was being written, the Talbotts were still in fight training. They had made some progress, but they still had a long uphill trail to climb. Henry's success as a wheeler-dealer in business made it difficult for him to practice candor at home. Ingeborg's undemonstrative Nordic parents had never shown her how to display emotions to advantage. The Talbotts' communications problem (which also made it difficult to disclose their sex preferences to each other) was so frustrating that it was bound eventually to spill over the track of spoken words and to explode—as it did during their Sunday telephone fight—in physical violence.

As pointed out previously, our fight training outlaws physical violence, although we recognize that there are times when roughness can be pleasurable and sexually stimulating. On the other hand, we believe that the exchange of spanks, blows, and slaps between consenting adults is more civilized than the camouflaged or silent hostilities of ostensibly well-behaved fight-evaders who are "above it all."

The point is that, whether we approve or not, physical violence is far more common in adult intimacy than people like to think. Fists, fangs, and fingernails come into play quite naturally for many (and perhaps most) spouses and lovers when their tongues fail them and the switch can become a matter of life-and-death concern to anyone finding himself involved in a violent encounter.

Everybody is against mate beating. Legal and moral authority encourage the righteous protests of its victims. "How dare you hit me!" they shout. Or, "You must be insane!" Or, "Only a coward would beat a woman!" Or, "No real lady would attack a man!" And even though a tongue lashing may hurt more than physical violence, a physical fight between adults constitutes criminal assault and places anyone who switches from verbal to physical blows at a great disadvantage. He becomes a target of shame and condemnation and may even provide the victim with an excuse to exit and "win" a divorce.

Unfortunately, society's judgment does not help people understand why many perfectly "civilized" partners occasionally blow their cool and turn to violence. The fact is that such violence may not be irrational. Like the violence perpetrated by the American colonists against the British crown in revolutionary times, it may be a desperate bid to be taken seriously when nonviolent measures failed. It may be a cornered mate's last stand, a final attempt to show deep concern. Often, too, some provocation—the proverbial straw that breaks the camel's back—momentarily breaks conscious controls and releases a long-repressed sadistic urge to punish a partner and produce an "ouch!" from him, especially if he has been fighting unfairly too often.

Intimate fighters should also understand the psychoanalytic discovery that people sometimes unconsciously desire to get hurt. Everyone's dreams contain some masochistic elements. A common fantasy is being beaten up, which is a relic of being disciplined in one's youth. In adults, this psychic museum piece frequently instigates behavior that provokes aggression. There are people who all but specialize in getting beaten, exploited, robbed. or raped.

Masochistic provocations—that is, words and deeds that incite one's partner to hit or spit—are routine in childhood fights with siblings and peers when no adult is around. Thus, very early in life, almost everybody starts to enjoy jostling and fighting, which—let's not kid anyone—involves hurting and getting hurt. And most children react against the parental admonitions of "Don't fight!" just as they react against admonitions about sex play; they go underground. In this way *sub rosa* fighting becomes an exciting demonstration of freedom, just like early sex explorations with siblings and friends.

It is not so surprising, then, if later in life adults re-create some of the intimacy that was intrinsic in early peership sex and early fight-playing.

Adults, whose parents and teachers had the right to punish children by beating them up, also unconsciously associate the act of beating with those times (and perhaps these were the only times) when they were sure as children that their parents or teachers showed authentic interest in them. Traditionally, the relationship between beaters and the beaten can be extremely intimate and, therefore, reassuring.

At the same time, the act of beating someone and getting away with it is also evidence of power and privilege. Since only parents could beat with impunity, many adults savor the beating-back privilege that they never enjoyed as children. A hostile, aggressive spouse-beater usually becomes identified with the person who beat the partner "for the sake of discipline" when the partner was a child.

We train students to understand these situations so they will not be too surprised if they find themselves involved in a violent encounter that was not preceded by a major crisis. Most couples are as amazed as Gene and Eva Watson were one evening after they had been married four years. Gene came home from the office feeling irritated and achey, and here is how it went:

GENE (*grimacing and blowing his nose*): Honey, I think I'm catching a lousy cold. I'll just go right to bed, OK?

EVA (*worried and solicitous*): Gee, that's too bad! Why don't I fix you some hot lemonade and put a little rum in it.

GENE (*heading for the bedroom*): Oh, I don't want to put you to that much trouble.

EVA (*beaming maternally*): Come on! I love to do it for you!

A few minutes later Eva entered the bedroom with the promised hot drink and two aspirin tablets. Gene was sitting on the bed, half undressed, reading the afternoon paper.

EVA (*bossy*): Why aren't you in bed?

GENE (*miserable*): Nag, nag, nag.

EVA (*indignant*): Well, you don't have to be such an old grouch. I'm just trying to take good care of you! (*She puts down the drink, the tablets, and leaves in a huff*).

By about 10:30 P.M. Gene and Eva had both retired to bed. Gene was reading a murder mystery. Eva felt like talking.

EVA: Why don't we go skiing this weekend?

GENE: Umph.

EVA: I mean, we could both use a weekend without the kids.

GENE (*still not looking up from his book*): Damn! Can't you stop yakking?

EVA (*still determinedly cheerful*): Look, I think we can do the whole thing for $100 and I've already sent them a check for $50.

GENE (*sitting up in bed, angry*): You know something? You have absolutely no sense of reality. I told you last month that we can't afford any more ski trips this season!

EVA: Oh, why don't you go back to your book! By the way, how does it end?

GENE: I don't cheat and look at endings in advance!

EVA (*concerned*): Honey, what's the matter? Is it something at the office? Why are you so worried? (*She snuggles up to Gene, who continues to read*.) Guess I'll go to sleep. (*A few minutes pass*.) Honey, I can't get to sleep with your light on.

GENE: Want me to go to the other room?

EVA (*playing the martyr*): Oh, no, no. I'll just take a sleeping pill.

At this point, Gene's patience, at a fairly low point to

begin with because he wasn't feeling well, snapped. He jumped out of bed, grabbed their blanket, and tried to march off to the next room. Eva managed to snatch the blanket away, whereupon Gene seized her by the throat.

GENE (*red-faced and shouting*): Bitch! Bitch!
EVA (*hits and scratches his abdomen*): You're horrible! Horrible! I hate you!

Gene took possession of the blanket and went to sleep in the next room. In the morning, both were in a surprisingly good-natured, conciliatory frame of mind. Gene did not have a bad cold, after all. He still resented that Eva had reneged on their agreement and sent $50 to the ski resort, but actually he was anxious to go skiing himself. They agreed that if Gene had felt just a little bit better the night before, and Eva had been just a little bit less determinedly cheerful and talkative, words would not have failed them. As matters stood, this marriage was not adversely affected merely because the partners had resorted to violence in a moment of weakness.

In other cases, violence becomes the last resort of intimates who are unable to muster words to fight out urgent hostilities. Such situations were reported again and again when we began to ask mate beaters to answer the following five questions about each time when they employed physical force:

1. Report clearly and in some detail just what happened.
2. Elaborate on the "moment of truth"—the actual act of violence.
3. Describe how you felt inside just before, during, and after the violence and how you feel now.
4. Report your explanation and rationalizations for what occurred.
5. Describe what you learned from this fight.

A fairly typical report came from Annette Mains, an attractive, if somewhat sullen, divorcée of 32. At the time, she had been having an affair for two years with Phil Hale, 38, an electronics engineer who had long been separated from the wife he had married when he was only 19 years old. About a year before the following fight, Phil had given Annette to understand he would soon ask for a divorce and marry her. But he had never followed through. Annette had been too proud and inhibited to bring up the subject again. She was also somewhat fearful that her insistence on marriage might drive him away altogether. This couple almost never fought, but Phil frequently dwelled on what a dreadful mistake his first marriage had been. Obviously, he was not eager to gamble a second time with what he now considered his precious independence.

This was Annette's report:

1. I hit Phil and fractured the little finger of my right hand at about 5 P.M. last Saturday. We had gone out for lunch, but we couldn't get served, so we left the restaurant. On the way back to the parking lot I got sore at Phil because he'd made a scene with the waiter who wouldn't wait on us. I hate scenes. Phil said he had a right to get sore at the waiter. He yelled at me when we got in the car. People stared at us, and I was very embarrassed. In the car I discovered I had torn my dress slightly. I got upset and scared. We went to my house, and Phil said I should calm down and then we'd go to eat someplace else. I got hysterical, I guess. I screamed at him about why he didn't write for his divorce papers and that I'd told my parents ages ago we would get married.

2. I was sitting on the bed and screaming at him. He was trying to get me to be quiet and to think about going out to dinner. I said I wouldn't go anywhere with him. He said something about not wanting to get married. That made me feel wild. I wanted to rip and tear at something, to break things or tear them. I grabbed his shirt sleeves, and somehow my little finger hit his arm muscles the wrong way. I knew it was broken. I grabbed it and said, "Oh! It's broken!"

3. *Before* I grabbed, I felt like a hurricane inside. The whole world was inside of me and it was stormy. I couldn't see or hear or think.

During the time I felt like a big spout of water leaping out of the sea.

Afterward I only thought about my broken finger. I wasn't glad or sorry or anything.

Now I'm not sure how I feel about it. I know it was important. It mustn't keep happening. I guess I'm afraid, but I'm also happy.

4. My explanation for what happened is that when an irresistible force meets an immovable object, the force is dissipated at least for a while and you can rest a little. But I hate living a lie and my relationship with Phil, I now realize, is a lie. It has no future unless we marry and he doesn't seem to be able to decide. Or maybe he's trying to put off the inevitable, which is either to split up or marry. Sometimes I don't care any more which way it's going to be. I do know parting is negative and marriage is positive, so I guess I do

care. I want to be positive. Most of all, I don't want to keep
on being trapped in limbo.

5. I learned from this fight that it's no good to be
passive for such a long time and let pressures build up so you
feel you absolutely must fight as hard as I finally did. But I'm
not sure I could have faced the issue before this. Maybe we
both needed these years together to test out our feelings. But
now I know I must have an answer from him, for his sake as
well as mine. I want to start building a real life, and that's
impossible if we go on living the way we did. I have to
destroy his opposition, one way or the other. I guess the fight
made me feel awful and better at the same time. But mostly
awful because it didn't resolve anything.

Within three weeks after this fight, Phil applied for his
divorce and eventually married Annette. Both were basically
doves and continued to have problems because their fight-
evasion tendencies caused them to gunny-sack grievances.
But they did not again neglect any issue for so long a time
that one of them had to break up the inevitable crisis by
resorting to violence.

This chapter was designed to explain the use of force, not
to excuse it. Among true intimates, there is no excuse for it
because force is proof of a communications breakdown.
Violence among spouses (and among nations) is a rare and
freakish occurrence when communications between the parties are in reasonably good working order. Unhappily, they
often are not.

11. The Language of Love: Communications Fights

It is fashionable nowadays for intimates to complain about their "communications." The very word has acquired a certain cachet as if it were something ultramodern. Husbands and wives accuse each other: "You never talk to me" or "You never listen to me." More honest couples take pride in confiding to each other, "We just can't communicate." Whatever the wording, these grievances are likely to be aired in a tone of acute frustration or resignation, much as if the partners were innocent victims of two electronic circuits that went haywire.

Executives know that communications are the life line of business; when the line becomes clogged or breaks down, two things occur: either (1) whatever shouldn't or (2) nothing. Intimates, on the other hand, usually just blame themselves or their mates for communications failures or wallow in lamentations of the "ain't-it-awful" variety. They rarely realize that intimate communication is an art that requires considerable imagination and creativity. They are almost never aware that only a conscious, resolute decision on the part of both partners to work at the problem—continually and for the rest of their lives—can produce good communications. And even if partners are ready to go to work to make their language of love serve them better, they don't know how to go about it.

The job is big because intimate communication involves a lot more than transmitting and receiving signals. Its purpose is to make explicit everything that partners expect of each other—what is most agreeable and least agreeable, what is relevant and irrelevant; to monitor continually what they experience as bonding or alienating; to synchronize interests, habits and "hangups"; and to effect the fusion that achieves the *we* without demolishing the *you* or the *me*.

Intimates usually fail to understand that the language of love does not confine itself to matters of loving and other intimate concerns. It permeates *all* communications between lovers. For example, if one business acquaintance says to another, "I'm hungry," this message almost certainly needn't be weighed for emotional implications. It can be taken at face value and acted upon accordingly. However, if an intimate sends the same message to another intimate, he may be engaging in several activities:

1. expressing a private sentiment, perhaps "feeling out loud" just to gauge whether the partner's reaction is sympathetic or indifferent;

2. appealing emotionally to the partner in order to persuade him to do or say something (perhaps, "Come on, let's go to the coffee shop");

3. transmitting meaningful information (perhaps, "I'm starved, but I can't stop to eat now").

Partner A, then, might well be putting his foot in his mouth if Partner B is saying, "You don't understand how busy I am" and "A" only shrugs and replies, "Why don't you go and have something to eat?" Maybe "B" wants "A" to bring him something to eat from the coffee shop so he can work and eat at the same time. Unfortunately, "A" can't divine this request—which "B" would never expect him to do if he were talking to a business colleague.

Many intimates stubbornly insist that there shouldn't be any communications problems between them. The folklore of romantic love leads lovers to believe that some sort of intuitive click or sensitivity links all intimates; that this should suffice to convey their deep mutual understanding; and that this miracle occurs simply because the partners love one another. So they demand to be divined. In effect, they say, "He ought to know how I feel" or, "You'll decode me correctly if you love me." This permits spouses to think they can afford to be sloppier in their intimate communications than they are in their nonintimate contacts.

Another reason why communications are such a problem is a psychological laziness that has many people in its grip. Encouraged by the romantic fallacy that the language of love falls into place as if by magic, they find it easy to shirk the task and shrug it off.

The third reason is that the popularity of game-playing and the role-taking in today's society has encouraged the suspicion that transparency, even at home, may not be a good idea. This belief is usually grounded in the fear that candor would cause an intimate to reveal something about himself that might cool the partner. It creates still another temptation for partners to try to enjoy a free ride on the vague and often wrong presumption that they understand each other.

The easiest way to create communications problems is to withhold information from one's spouse. When partners don't confide in each other, they are likely to find themselves trying to tap their way through a vacuum, like blind people with white canes. The resulting fights can pop up at any time and place. For Herb and Lonnie Cartwright the place happened to be their kitchen. The time was the evening before they planned to give a big party:

LONNIE: I need another $30 for food for the party.

HERB: That's a lot of money for food.

LONNIE (*exasperated*): People have to eat!

HERB (*reasonable*): I know that.

LONNIE (*taking a deep breath before plunging into unaccustomed territory*): Ever since you bought that new insurance policy we're always strapped for cash.

HERB (*startled*): But it's in your name!

LONNIE (*vehemently*): I don't want you to die! Let's live a little now!

HERB (*shaken*): I resent that! After all, I was trying to do the right thing by you.

LONNIE (*with finality*): Then you shouldn't have bought the policy until after you get your next raise. I don't like to come to you like a beggar.

What happened here? These partners had kept each other in such ignorance over the years that they inevitably wound up poles apart on family financial policy. This wife, like so many others, thought of her husband as a money tree. One reason why she loved him was that he was such a good provider. She believed that, within reason, she could buy anything she wanted. But she carefully avoided a test of her notions by never expressing an interest in the family bank balance. To her, money was to spend, just like a child's pocket money. To her husband, on the other hand, money was the equivalent of security. He had told his wife that he had bought a big new insurance policy, but not how expensive it had been. The lesson of this case is that husbands would do well not to leave wives ignorant about personal finances or other basic realities of their life together.

When intimates refuse to impart strategic information that they possess, or when they refuse to react to information that is offered to them, they are asking for trouble. Sometimes a partner withholds information in the name of tact. This is especially true when it comes to sharing information about sexual preferences. As previously noted, there are times when the state of the union demands that transparency be tempered by tact. But much so-called tact is cowardice or deception—a cover-up to avoid confrontations and feedback from the opponent. The withholding of information only leads to worse explosions later.

Some husbands, for instance, don't tell their wives how broke they are. They "don't want her to worry." Suddenly a man from the loan company appears at home to repossess the wife's car. Not only is this crisis often unnecessary ("Honey, why didn't you tell me? I could have borrowed the money from Dad!"). Often it leads to irreversible damage because it erodes the wife's trust in her spouse. In true intimacy stress is shared by partners.

There are partners, however, who, without knowing it, *cause* their spouses to withhold information. One such husband tended to get excited and be in the way when things went wrong at home. Then he lectured his wife that she should have managed better. When he went on business trips he called home daily and his wife always reassured him that things were fine. Usually they were, but one day the husband returned from a week's absence and was extremely upset to find that his wife had broken her ankle and hadn't said a word about it on the telephone. In her inner dialogue, the wife had said to herself, "He's no help in a crisis." The husband had brought this lack of trust upon himself.

When intimates are frustrated by their inability to communicate clearly and straightforwardly, they tend to confuse matters further by sending messages full of sarcasms, hyperboles, caricatures and exaggerations that befog or overdramatize. The list of these statics is almost endless, but here are some random examples:

"I'd just as soon talk to a blank wall." "You've got diarrhea of the mouth." "You did *not* say *that;* if you did, I didn't hear it!" "We have nothing to say to each other any more." "You always talk in riddles." "I've learned to keep my mouth shut." "You never say what you mean." "Why do you always interrupt me?" "You just like to hear the sound of your own voice." "You never stand up for yourself." "If I've told you once, I've told you a thousand times . . ."

When fight trainees are faced with these statics as they try to communicate feelings and wishes to their partners, we sometimes tell them the ancient yarn about the Texas mule who was too stubborn to respond to commands. The owner decided to hire a famous mule trainer to cure the trouble. The trainer took one look at the mule and cracked him over the head with a two-by-four. The owner was appalled.

"That's dreadful," he said. "I thought you were going to train him!"

"Sure," said the trainer. "But first I have to get his attention."

Partners who must deal with statics need to review the techniques for getting a good fight started. The same goes for spouses who find themselves confronted with opponents who blanket out communications with jamming noises, the way the Communists used to jam Western radio broadcasts.

Some intimate jammers can be infuriatingly effective. Suppose a husband knows his wife wants to talk to him about his overspending. But the husband also knows his spouse loves to listen to gossip about his boss's sex life. The husband therefore rattles on interminably about fresh gossip he has just heard on the office grapevine and then dashes to the car to leave for work.

"Hey," shouts his wife. "We've got to talk about those bills!"

"Will do!" shouts the husband—and drives off.

Even partners who seem to appreciate the importance of open, unjammed communications rarely realize just how unambiguous their signals should be and how meticulously a message sender should solicit feedback from the recipient to check out whether his signal was understood as it was intended. Here is what often happens in the three stages of message sending: (1) the intention of the message, (2) the framing of the message, and (3) the interpretation of the message at the other end of the line.

Case No. 1: The wife tells the kids not to bother Dad. He is listening.

How Meant	How Sent	How Received
"I'm protecting you"	"Don't bother him."	"She's fencing me in."

Case No. 2: The husband doesn't bring any of his buddies home from his club. She asks him about it.

How Meant	How Received	How Sent
'It's too much work for you."	"He's ashamed of me."	"Oh, let's skip it."

Husbands and wives who wish to extricate themselves from a jungle of unclear signals find it helpful to fix within their minds the seemingly simple fundamentals of communication:

Obtain the attention of your receiver. Prepare him to receive your message. Send out your message clearly and with a minimum of extraneous static. Make sure your information is beamed toward the receiver's wave length. Stake out your own area of interest and stick to its limits. Keep yourself and your receiver focused on the joint interest area. Stimulate your receiver to respond by acknowledging reception. Obtain feedback to check how your message was received.

These principles are known to anyone who ever placed an important long-distance phone call. Yet intimates, especially while under the emotional stress of conflict and aggression, tend to ignore the basics even though they "know better." Their resistance against forging a clear connection is a sign that they find conflict stressful and don't like to accept the fact that they are involved in one.

This is why noncommunicators lead each other around the mulberry bush with such round-robin jabs as these:

SHE: You never talk to me.
HE: What's on your mind?
SHE: It's not what's on *my* mind; it's that I never know what's on *your* mind.
HE (*slightly panicky*): What do you want to know?
SHE (*jubilantly*): Everything!
HE (*thoroughly vexed*): That's crazy!
SHE: Here we go again.

This game of hide-and-seek may also go like this:

HE: You talk too much!
SHE: About what?
HE: About everything.
SHE: One of us has to talk!
HE: You talk, but you never say anything.
SHE: That's crazy.
HE: You're darned right!
SHE (*thoughtfully*): What do you mean?
HE (*wearily*): You make a lot of noise, but that makes it impossible for us to have a real talk.
SHE: Here we go again. . . .

Here's what happened after the latter fight, between two unmarried young people:

DR. BACH (*to the girl*): What was he really telling you?
GIRL: That he doesn't like me.

DR. B (*to the boy*): Is that what you wanted to convey?

BOY: No! I love her!

DR. B You two are starving for real communication. You're using words like fog to hide your true feelings.

A partner who keeps his own vested interest hidden often enjoys focusing a one-way radar upon his opponent. This kind of spouse-watching may be part of a noble effort to "understand" the partner who is being watched. But it, too, leads only to more frustration, as in the following dialogue:

SHE: You never talk to me.

HE: Why should I? You know all about me.

SHE: What do you mean?

HE (*heatedly*): *You watch every move I make. You're reading me! And whenever I open my mouth, I'm wrong. You've already figured out what I'm supposedly thinking.*

SHE: You're just saying that because you don't want to talk to me.

While the marital woods are full of couples who profess "we never talk," the truth is that many intimates—possibly the majority—talk a great deal, even about personal matters. But their virtuosity at camouflaging (and the coy kind of testing that is really inquiring, "Will he get the hint?") is remarkable. Here is a couple driving home after a party:

HE: That was a nice dinner Peggy fixed.

SHE: Yes, those baked potatoes with sour cream were terrific.

When this nebulous exchange was investigated during fight training it turned out that this husband was trying to convey that he thought he and his wife weren't popular and didn't have enough friends. The wife got the message and signaled back: "I know you're critical about our social ineptness, but I don't think Peggy is so much better." The object of this bit of shadowboxing was to reconnoiter a real problem but to avoid facing it openly in constructive talks about possible solutions. Neither spouse was ready to face a showdown about the inadequacies of their social life.

Few people are aware that routine daily conversations afford limitless opportunities to explore the treasury of feelings that reposes in the private emotional world of their partners. Here, for example, is a wife who just finished reading a magazine article about dangerous side effects of the birth-control pill.

SHE: Did you see this article about the pill?
HE: Yes, the secretaries in the office were talking about it. It made them pretty nervous.

This exchange may cover up an amazing variety of messages. Some of hers might be: "Sex is a dangerous business." Or "You don't pursue me like you used to." Or "You should take more responsibility for what our daughter does on her dates." Or "Are you sleeping with your secretary?" Or "Sex isn't exciting with you any more; it's just sort of a health exercise." Or "I wish you'd stop pressuring me to have another baby; I really don't want it." Or "I hope you understand what I'm going through now that I'm in the menopause." Or the wife may just be focusing on one of the pill's side effects, weight gain, that was reported in the article. She may be testing her husband with an implied question: "I think I've been gaining too much weight."

Some of the husband's camouflaged signals in this same exchange might be: "You always try to make your problems look unique when actually all girls have them." Or "I think she thinks that I think I'm sexually too demanding; I guess I should be more considerate." Or "I wish she wouldn't bring up sex tonight; I'm tired." Or "I think that she thinks that I think the girls at the office turn me on more than she does." Or "She should be more careful to remember to take her pill every day."

But these particular spouses were poor communicators. They immediately dropped the subject of the pill and threw away the chance to air their feelings about an important issue. They preferred fog to sunshine because they were not trained to perceive the advantages of authenticity.

Even casual conversation about topics that are less emotion-charged than sex can set off incredible confusion if partners don't ask follow-up questions. Suppose the husband asks his wife: "Have you noticed the car brakes are on the blink again?" This could be a straight expression of exasperation at the garage where the brakes were supposedly fixed only the week before. In that event, it is perfectly adequate for the wife to say no more than, "I sure did!"

But this husband's complaint could also mean, "I wish you'd be more careful with our things." Or "I don't want to show her how lonely I get, but I wish she'd come along on more of my dreary business trips." Or "You're spending so much money on yourself that there's never enough left for necessities like car brakes." Among true intimates, therefore, such a complaint about car brakes is at least briefly explored for possible emotional implications.

A failure to expose issues fully, once they have come up, may lead to a depressing communications impasse. This was the situation that lingered at the bottom of the following far from routine early morning household argument:

HE: I don't mind you not making me breakfast, but why do I have to clear away last night's dishes, too?

SHE: I'm sorry, dear. I know it annoys you.

HE: Then why do it?

SHE: I'm just so tired at night.

HE: You're not too tired to look at TV!

SHE: That's relaxing. Dishes aren't.

HE: You just don't give a damn about me.

SHE: You mean to tell me that a little thing like a few dirty dishes and my enjoying TV proves that? That's ridiculous. Why don't you go on to work— you'll be late!

When this couple came into fight training she started doing the dishes at night, but they were no happier. They had to come to grips with their underlying feelings: (1) "He thinks I don't love him any more" and (2) "She thinks I'm unreasonable in my request for love."

They were in a state of withdrawal prior to a new, more realistic fight engagement. They knew neither cared all that much about the dirty dishes. What was wrong?

It developed that he was trying to say, "Sometimes I think you love the idiot box more than me." She was trying to tell him he was being inconsiderate by forgetting to run an occasional errand for her and that she resented his stopping off to have drinks with the fellows from the office on the way home. Only an air-clearing, head-on fight with free-flowing communications finally yielded these answers and a basis for further discussion.

Intimate stalemates can also be caused by attention-seeking signals that are either too strong or too weak to "turn on" the partner in the desired direction. One strategic object of certain fights is to provoke the partner into the right amount and kind of aggressive behavior—the kind that "turns on" without going over the permissible threshold and thereby "turns off" the partner. This subtle, intimate provocation can be calibrated. Very often, however, it isn't.

John and Jill Strong were quiet, fight-evading types. When they did argue, they attacked each other's Achilles' heels too much. One source of constant annoyance to them was John's income. He earned $89,000 a year as an architect, but Jill thought he would do even better if he didn't let his partners take advantage of him. One more or less typical evening he was anxious to talk to her about her overspending. She was much more interested in sex. Whenever she was in this mood she would indicate it by wearing a sheer negligee. On that particular evening she put on one of her sexy gowns. He, still wanting to talk about important money matters, was annoyed and said, "I have some work to do." And so the scene ended in their usual cold-war stalemate. If their communications had been in good repair, they could have talked about money first and enjoyed sex later. Instead, there was no talk and no sex, either.

At the other end of the aggression scale were Art and Sally Greene, who were sexually most attracted to each other but who nevertheless were constantly embroiled in almost incredibly intense kitchen-sink fights, some of them as long as eight hours with only minor intermissions. (Their sexual attraction was by no means inconsistent with their fighting. As discussed in Chapter 18, it is inept conflict management rather than inept sex that causes most marriage troubles.)

Art was an engineering executive. He and Sally were both slim, tanned tennis players, outwardly the very picture of a happy couple. One Friday, she got a massage in her health club, sent the children to stay overnight with her sister, and put fresh flowers in the bedroom. Friday night they usually had a date for sex. Art drove home wondering whether Sally would keep their date. But he was really less interested in sex than he was in finding fault with his wife. He was a gunny-sacker who tucked away his complaints instead of arguing them out. When he got a into a certain mood, he placed her into a lethal "double bind" where she could do no right: if she didn't keep the sex dates, she caught hell ("I thought we'd have a good time"); if she did, he ignored her.

Sally had drinks ready and the hi-fi turned on to appropriate mood music, but after dinner he withdrew into his study saying: "I haven't been able to catch up with my reading all week."

At this point Sally should have invited Art to clean out his gunny sack of complaints. Instead she got furious. She followed him and interrupted his reading with recitations of what had been going wrong on the domestic front. Their boy hurt his ankle in football practice. The maid forgot to put out the garbage for the weekly collection. One of his favorite shirts had been burned with the new iron.

He tried to display disinterest. She turned up the hi-fi. He turned it off and exploded: "If you do just one more thing to interrupt me, I'll ..."

She was delighted. She had gotten a rise out of him. Out loud she said, "You rude S.O.B. There goes another weekend!"

She stamped upstairs into the bathroom, which was located right over the study, slammed the door and made a lot of noise. After a while, when he failed to respond, her fury made her resort to what we call Provocation to the Nth Degree. She barged into his study with the vacuum cleaner and began cleaning up.

ART (*incensed*): You bitch! You've got some nerve trying to stop me from keeping up with things! How am I going to train my staff if I'm going to be an ignoramus?

SALLY (*shouting over the noise of the vacuum cleaner*): You *are* an ignoramus ...

A *Virginia Woolf* type of insult ritual followed. During it, she made him feel guilty for spoiling their Friday night sex date. Finally she ran into the bedroom. Her robe had come open. She sobbed on the bed. He was still trying to read, but now he was in a state of guilt-induced turmoil. He went to the bedroom, determined to make up.

SALLY (*in tears*): Get away from me! Don't you dare touch me!

Eventually Art seduced his wife, but ultimately these hostility exchanges proved too much even for these conflict-habituated adversaries. They entered fight training and learned how to trade views about their feelings while avoiding the injuries of uncontrolled warfare.

A most dangerous time for intimate communications is the moment when the husband comes home from work at night. It is the time when the husband's world, the wife's world, and the family's world are joined for presumably realistic co-existence. Unless the differing expectations are sensitively calibrated, the result is collusion, rather than merger.

We advise not to initiate the homecoming ceremonies with

the customary "How was your day?" At best this invites the unproductive response, "So-so. How was yours?" More likely, these one-way signals are opening guns for each partner to use the marriage as a garbage can. Sometimes they hit. Sometimes they miss. In any event, it's not an edifying or fruitful exercise and it will not ease the task of merging the partners' necessarily separate daytime roles into an intimate duet.

Homecoming is a favorite time for camouflaging in many households. If the husband groans and says, "I had a terrible day, simply terrible!" he may be telling his spouse, "I think that you think I have a ball at the office, but that's not what I'd like you to think." (If he is a good communicator he sends his message directly: "Sometimes you don't give me enough release for my tensions.")

All too frequently, homecoming time also becomes displacement time. Suppose the husband does manage to tear himself away from his own troubles and asks, "What did the kids do today?" This may be just the opening the wife waited for. Her recital of sad tales begins: "Well, Johnny missed the school bus again. He would have been very late for class if I hadn't borrowed Janie's car and rushed him down there . . ." Which is the wife's way of telling her husband, "Nobody knows the trouble I've seen. Certainly *you* don't appreciate what it takes to run a house, raise the children, manage things without a second car and . . . and . . . and . . ."

Curiously enough, most people who become involved in such exchanges are convinced that this type of conversation constitutes intimate communication. This is rarely the case. Intimate communications start after the day's routine business is checked out. In the normal run of daily life, each partner should be able to handle his own usual activities in his own more or less independent way. The real subject of intimate communication is the state of the union; the relationship between the couple; the *us*.

We suggest to our trainees that they start homecoming conversations not with a perfunctory "How are you?" but with a genuinely intimate "How are we doing?" This may sound weird according to conventional etiquette, but it points intimates toward more rewarding directions, helps clear up some communications statics, and prevents the accumulation of secret reservations.

If an exchange of complaints is infected with the here-we-go-again pessimism of chronic, redundant round-robin fights, someone must eventually muster enough common sense to take the needle off the broken record and demand, "Will the real partnership problem please rise?" The weariness signal is often the phrase, "I've told you for the umpteenth time . . ."

Excessive patience does not serve the cause of realistic intimacy; neither does lack of patience. In fact, the point when to take "no" for an answer is one of the most important things that intimates should learn about each other. Here is the first round of one illustrative case:

HE: Hey, honey, guess what! I got a bonus!
SHE: How much?
HE: Enough for us to spend two weeks at the shore.

And here is Round No. 2 of the same fight:

SHE: You really want to spend all that money going to the beach?
HE: I sure do.
SHE: I don't think we should.
HE: Well, I think we should!

If this merry-go-round were to continue for 10 or 20 or more rounds, the partnership probably would only gain, not lose. The issue is fresh. The controversy is legitimate. Both partners are demonstrating that they care about how to spend their mutual leisure time and their co-owned money. They are also showing that their minds are not closed to each other, or to persuasion. This kind of ritual, uncontaminated by weary pessimism, helps partners to probe how strongly each really feels. It may not sound overly intelligent or "adult," but it is a legitimate method of finding the point where each is convinced that the other "really means it."

Some people can tolerate only one or two "no's" for an answer. The third "no" may provoke them into raising a social gun (the threat of marital exit); or an economic gun (a spiteful money splurge); or possibly even a real gun (murder). Among successful intimates, there will always be enough opportunities to say "no" often enough so each partner can re-evaluate his feelings, weigh the possibility of giving in, or work out a compromise.

Couples who enjoy good communications can signal their partner through a system of "pats," "slaps," and "kicks."

Pats are obviously signals of attraction, approval, affection, or reward. They mean "Yes," "Good," "I dig," "This turns me on," and so forth. No words are necessary. Everybody recognizes the condescending quality of a pat on the head; the more peerlike pat on the back (which may also be a phony "slap on the back"); the amorous, perhaps sex-initiating pat on the rump; or the recognition and reassurance of stroking the partner's hand.

Slaps (meaning "No," "Cut it out," "Let go," "I don't like," etc.) are useful intimate punishments or warnings that can range from the nonverbal "dirty look" to highly verbal, abusive name calling.

Kicks (meaning "Get a move on!" "Get with it!" etc.) serve as reminders, appeals, incentive and aggressive stimulation to get a sluggish or confused partner moving in a desired reaction. They can be administered by a persuasive lecture, a subtle bit of seduction, a pinch in the arm or (hopefully not) a literal kick in the pants.

In the fight for better mutual understanding, as in all fights, it is profitable to give clear cues, to avoid obscurities and, in case of a near miss, to emphasize the nearness rather than the miss. Pats are helpful in these situations.

The following fight all but carried the label, "Danger! Bad communications" in neon letters:

HE: You're pretty nervous about your mother coming, aren't you?

SHE: What makes you think so?

HE: Well, you don't usually spend so much time cleaning house.

SHE: Oh, so you think I'm a lousy housekeeper! Boy, you just don't understand me!

HE (*shrugging*): Here we go again.

After training, the same fight should go like this:

HE: You're pretty nervous about your mother coming, aren't you?

SHE: I'm not nervous about her. I'm nervous about how you're going to get along with her. By the way, what made you think I'm nervous about it?

HE: Because of the way you've been cleaning and cleaning around here.

SHE: You're pretty sharp!

As soon as partners stop putting up with silence, camouflaging, or static and learn to fight for clearer communications, tensions tend to clear up. This represents no "cure." When communications channels become unclogged, couples normally find that they are considerably further apart in their ideas for a livable marriage than they want to be.

But at least they are no longer kidding each other about their communications gap. Now they can start going to work on the process of coming as close together as they want to be in order to enjoy a smooth state of swing.

It is worth noting again that it is unnecessary to analyze the historical-motivational causes for communications failures in most marriages. Instead of wasting time and money to excavate the causes of behavior, which get them nowhere, couples can learn to appreciate that the function of noncommunication generally is to cover up something that partners are afraid to face openly: hostility of the sadistic variety, perhaps; or exploitative attitudes; or overdependency; or, more frequently, fear of rejection. These factors, too, rarely require detailed analysis. What is important is that the partners catch each other in the use of anticommunications tactics, make an open demand for discontinuance and then practice how to replace them with straightforward types of communication.

Some alienating forms of communication are difficult to recognize for what they really are. The fine art of "bugging" is a good example.

Suppose the wife is in the kitchen cooking a special gourmet dinner. The husband enters, sniffs the delightful aroma that pervades the kitchen and admires the complexity of the culinary operation that his wife has set in motion for their mutual pleasure. He is touched. He may also become aroused. The smelling of delicious food and the fussing over food were sources of his affection for his first love: his mother. Now here is his true love, his own wife, immersed in the act of being lovable. By taking special pains with her cooking, she is showing that she cares about him, about them.

He pinches her playfully. Or he tries to kiss her. Or fondle her lovingly.

She may respond just as lovingly. She may stop cooking, burn the roast, or even let herself be taken to the bedroom to make love. But not if she is like most wives. Most likely, she will be annoyed. If he fails to heed her protests, she will get mad. She is busy. She is busy doing something for him, something he likes! She is involved with her cookbooks and her seasonings. At this moment she does not see herself as a sex object but as a master chef and an efficient executive. She cannot readily desert the scene of her ministrations. Her husband's sexy behavior is incongruent with her definition of the situation and her role in it. It threatens to derail her plans and her personality. It is overloading her tension system. It is bugging her.

Almost everybody has had the disturbing experience of feeling "bugged" during contacts with another person. A relative stranger can do no major bugging because it is unlikely that one cares enough about what he does or how he feels. But if the bugging is being done by an intimate, one does care. Also, the intimate is more likely to know what bugs his partner most. His bugging, therefore, can quickly assume the proportions of a minor torture, especially when it interferes with an offer of love, as in the above example.

If an intimate's bugging is extreme and becomes chronic, it is a technique of dirty fighting and crazy-making. Here we will deal only with the more common and minor forms of bugging between relatively normal intimates who love each other but whose communications are distorted by advanced types of statics.

Complaints about routine bugging are very common indeed. "My husband bugs me," a wife says. "I can't stand being around him." Or "My wife is driving me crazy; anything I say or do seems to annoy her." Or "We can't stay in the same room together." Or "The only way I can stand it is by getting loaded; it immunizes me." Or "We can't put our finger on it, but it's so uncomfortable that we've about given up talking to each other."

Sometimes derailing remarks will do the same job as an act of bugging ("You never . . ."). Frequent reneging on commitments also has a bugging effect (agreeing to make love and then backing out). Or changing ground rules for common activities without previous discussion. Or plain incessant nagging. Children and passively hostile intimates are especially expert at these bugging techniques.

Partner A begins to feel bugged when he senses that Partner B does not really acknowledge "A's" existence unless "A" behaves in a certain way. The desired behavior is probably not clearly defined except that "A" knows it isn't natural to him. When "A" insists on being himself he may be told by "B": "You're mistaken. You're not the way you think you are. I know you: deep inside you are such-and-such."

Prolonged intimate living with such a secretive fighter exacts a heavy emotional price. It is exhausting to accommodate a partner whose ideas of what is lovable are alien to one's ego.

It is tempting to remove bugging by accommodating. It is also uncomfortable. Many an intimate slides into the unpleasant double bind of not knowing whether to be himself and alienate the partner; or accommodate the partner and alienate his own ego.

It is easy to become somebody's psychological patsy. It may do no damage to assume this role in an office by humoring along a boss or someone else with whom one is not emotionally involved. However, in relationships with intimates (especially if, like a dependent child, one cannot get away) accommodation to bugging can be dangerous. It leads not only to alienation but to a threat of the accommodator's emotional well-being; it can distort his natural sense of self and prevent his emotional growth.

Un-bugging an intimate relationship is difficult, but sometimes it may be easier than it seems. Suppose a son wants to borrow a car. If he does his borrowing from Hertz Rent-A-Car and fails to bring it back as promised, he will get "punished" by having to pay an additional charge. But there will be no emotional problems. He can't bug Hertz. If he borrows his father's car, matters will be more complicated:

FATHER: OK, but be sure to have it back by 4 o'clock. I'll need it then.

SON: Sure, Dad.

(*Now it's 6 o'clock. The son has just come home.*)

FATHER: Where in hell have you been? I *told* you I had to have the car at 4.

SON: But Dad, I had to give Amy a ride home. I couldn't leave her stranded!

Now the father is very bugged indeed. He understands the facts. He likes his son's girl Amy and certainly wouldn't want to see her stranded. But reality must be dealt with: the father was greatly inconvenienced by his son. He must do more than regret that he let the son have the car. His inner dialogue will go somewhat like this: "I feel good as a father for letting my child have a good time. That's love. But I don't want to be exploited. That would shut my love off." This is the root of the conflict aroused by bugging. Intimates who bug other intimates are shutting love off and on, off and on. This is what leads to the charge, "You bug me." It means that love-releasers and love-stoppers are scrambled together.

We usually advise trainees to try one of two techniques for unscrambling the bugging mixup. One way is to throw oneself at the mercy of the bugger and see what happens. ("You *know* this bugs me. When you get your hands on the car keys you have *me* in your hands and I won't tolerate that. I'm a busy man and when I need the car for business I just have to have it.") The other technique is to search for the function of the bugging. What is the son really bugging his father for? Does he understand what he's doing to the father? Or does he understand this *too* well and is he bugging the old man to get sadistic mileage out of it? Or is it simply that he can't ever get the father's attention—or can't influence the father—in any way except by bugging? Once the function of the bugging is determined, it becomes easier to deal with this nagging form of communications stalemate.

Good communications, in sum, are the life line of successful intimacy, and are invariably the result of hard work of dedicated partners working in pairs.

Here are some exercises that help:

1. Diagnose how efficient or inefficient your present level of communication is. Is each partner candid and transparent? Does each get a chance to tell the other what's "eating him"? Does each partner really understand what the other is after? Once shortcomings are identified, the fight techniques outlined in previous chapters should be used to negotiate settlements.

2. Locate some of the causes of poor communication by owning up to yourself and to each other that you occasionally or habitually use one of the statics discussed in this and the next two chapters. Try to catch each other in the use of static and aggressively eliminate its use. Calls of "Static!" or "Foul!" may help.

3. Stop blocking communication by explicitly renouncing the use of static maneuvers.

4. Start making communication flow more freely by deliberately making yourselves accessible, open, and crystal-clear. From time to time, take new readings of the quality of your communications. Has improvement taken place?

5. Respond with full resonance. Be sure you are sharing your private view of yourself and the world with your partner. Expressive cmmunication enhances intimacy; reflective communication is useful but secondary. The more intimate two people are, the more they take turns expressing their views freely.

12. Fighting by Mail and Telephone

In our ultramobile society, where intimates are more and more frequently separated, if usually only for short periods, it is helpful to keep in mind that distance tends to distort intimate communications. It is far easier to fall in or out of love with a symbol—such as the Beatles, or perhaps a saint—than with a real person. A telephone-person or a letter-person becomes such a symbol, which is why one folk saying about intimacy is true at least some of the time: distance does tend to make the heart grow fonder. It also explains why some people can fall in love with each other's letters. Pen pals need no personal touch; person-to-person contact might even spoil the idealized frames in which they behold their loved ones.

When eyeball-to-eyeball contact is removed, some people feel safer and therefore become more aggressive or more effective or dirtier fighters. It is this feeling of safety that makes hate, like love, easier to express from far away. It also explains why final exits are often executed by phone or by letters ("Dear John . . .").

Suicide, physical violence, and murder are more likely to be threatened by letter or telephone than eye to eye. At the same time, friendly and reconciliatory gestures may also come more easily when distance minimizes inhibitions and embarrassments.

Letters are the favorite medium of poor or pseudo-intimate communicators. Paper plus pen plus distance from the partner conspire to shape the perfect environment to sit down and build a unilateral dream world. The communicator-by-letter is free to paint himself in any light he chooses. He can bask in his own independent, unchecked interpretation of the state of swing that exists between himself and the partner. And since there can be no immediate checking-out by feedback, he can sit back and luxuriate in his self-made Utopia. Sometimes he writes a love poem and thinks of it as approximating real life.

The implication—and often the flat, naïve assumption—

is: "Since I wrote you how I feel and what I want, I assume you will understand and go along."

When such letters are sent to a partner in a business deal, lawyers call them "self-serving declarations"; they are in no way binding upon the recipient. In intimate communications they can lead to grotesque misunderstandings, simply because the partner is not available to respond to the unchecked expectations voiced in one-way messages.

Letters are excellent devices for exaggerating emotional states. This applies to healthy people who portray themselves as excessively jubilant or despondent in correspondence; or inmates of psychiatric hospitals and prisons who write bizarre letters to their loved ones to punish those on the outside for "desertion." Again, lack of feedback is the fantasy-including element in these one-way transactions.

The telephone does permit feedback, so we sometimes encourage partners who shy away from face-to-face leveling to begin learning how to level on the phone; they may feel less threatened when only their voices are making contact. Unfortunately, the phone also lends itself to pestering and tyrannizing a partner. We discourage the use of the phone as a checking-up device ("What are you doing now? Who are you with?") This only invites deception. Until two-way television-telephones come into widespread use, a partner talking on the telephone remains free from effective kibitzing. Not infrequently, we even find an intimate using the phone to support his harem fantasies by talking to his wife while in the presence of his mistress.

The telephone encourages all sorts of other communications mischief among intimates. It can become an instrument of hit-and-run aggression when a partner calls up, delivers a one-way blast and hangs up. Or a partner may use it to ignore, or thumb his nose at, his opponent by failing to listen; he may just doodle on his desk pad or make faces at someone in the room without running the risk of getting caught.

We teach our trainees, then, that long-distance communication tends to encourage deception and misunderstandings; it can free an intimate by allowing him to say some things that he might otherwise censor; it can dilute the impact of words because he doesn't have to prove it when he says, "I miss you so much, darling." In short, it can never be as real as what happens between people when they are face to face. In intimate communications, to paraphrase Marshall McLuhan, the medium is never the message.

13. Dirty and Sick Fighters and How to Stop Them

The hostilities of intimate enemies can usually be dealt with by spouses who apply the heuristic rules that have already been discussed. The husbands, wives, and lovers whom readers will encounter in the present chapter also çan, with skill, understanding, and some luck, be reformed by their own mates. But these dirty and sick fighters are often so resistant to change that the help of competent psychotherapists may be required to lift them out of the groove of their alienating ways.

Transforming a monologuer into a dialoguer, for instance, can be a delicate undertaking. The monologuer may pretend to invite a dialogue with his mate, but he reveals himself when he tolerates no substantial feedback. His "communications" are like TV commercials. He indulges in relay speech-making. He wants to maintain dominance over, and distance from, his spouse. He insists on having the last word; he won't subject himself to being corrected; and he won't tolerate the challenge of a partner's demands for changes in his supposedly intimate duet. He is usually highly competitive and loves to show off like a bright youngster trying to monopolize the teacher's attention in class. He "knows it all."

He is probably not aware of it, but he is doing his cause little good. Monologuers are enormously resented. Few spouses enjoy being chronically overwhelmed, and victims of filibusters are likely to become progressively less cooperative with husbands or wives who monopolize communications circuits. Monologuers whose declamations are intrinsically interesting run a particularly high risk of finding themselves isolated and ignored because their words are so response-stimulating. A stupid monologue can be shrugged off. A clever one cries out for response. If the response is throttled, the potential respondent is all but forced to lose interest in order to protect his own sanity.

A mate who wants to reform a monologuer would be well

142

advised to proceed with caution and to try making headway through a series of deutero-fights. If a reformer unleashes a sudden all-out frontal attack and presents the monologuer with a long list of stockpiled grievances, the result will be alienating. The monologuer may panic and say, "Gee, you must hate me!" On the other hand, if a good-willed friend or a doctor helps to present the victim's complaints and intially confines the engagement to the filibuster issue, the monologuer may see the light and respond, "God, I must be a bore."

Victims of filibusters can train themselves to silence a monologuer by walking out in the middle of a one-way speech. Victims can also try to put their hands on their ears. They can try using "slaps," "kicks," and "pats" to bring the monologuer in line. They should reward him when he does respond to the victim's corrective signals ("Gee, I got through to you! I love you!"). But nothing works better on monologuers than an opportunity to watch themselves and their victims via closed-circuit video feedback.

When the camera first focuses on the victim, the monologuer who is watching the film in our office usually sees his target listening carefully, perhaps even with such intense concentration that the victim forgets to smoke his or her cigarette. Such rapt attention is likely to impress monologuers because they usually claim: "He [or she] never listens to me." As the film of the monologue continues, the monologuer watches how his victim tries again and again to interrupt and get a word in edgewise. Eventually, of course, the victim becomes discouraged, loses interest, and begins to display indifference. At this point the monologuer can literally see his words falling on deaf ears—a most educational experience.

Sometimes the same defensive strategies work effectively against the people we call rageolics—spouses who are prone to engage in more or less chronic growling one-way rages. Some of these frightening-sounding people may also calm down when they recognize the importance of cleaning out their gunny sacks of grievances more regularly.

"I don't like my wife to run to her mother every time something really goes wrong," one of them said. "I guess the trouble is that I never say anything to her until the time comes when she actually leaves the house. Then I blow up! Then she not only flees to mother but stays there and I have a helluva time getting her to come back."

This husband ceased being a rageolic when he learned to negotiate with his wife before their problems reached a crisis point. Other spouses, whose rages are more difficult to cool down, find additional relief by blowing off steam at bystanders—waiters, cab drivers, phone operators, secretaries, and other innocents who happen to be on hand when a rageolic erupts. It is, of course, irrational to use innocent people as targets in order to achieve aggression release, but it happens often and is somewhat less destructive than striking out against one's intimates. Strangers can shrug off such attacks more easily.

Hardest to cure, perhaps, are fight-phobic couples who displace just about all their aggressions upon persons, events, ideas, or environments outside their intimate system. A vivid illustration is the case of an Air Force colonel and his wife who showed up at our fight clinic for brief periods over more than 10 years. They almost never fought. When they did engage in hostilities they were extremely disturbed. They couldn't figure out what brought on these rare but turbulent periods, although both agreed it was the husband's "fault" because he was normally polite and then, suddenly, turned so "mean."

It finally became clear in group therapy that the periods of turbulence and peacefulness in the colonel's marriage seesawed back and forth in direct relation to the state of world tensions! He flared up at home when fighting stopped in Korea. He never fought with his wife when his aggressive excitement found patriotic outlet in crises over the Berlin Wall or Cuba or the Dominican Republic. His fervor on behalf of the escalation in the Vietnam war made him something of an angel in his own house and the prospect of peace turned him once again into a vicious hawk at home.

When this was pointed out to the colonel he said, "Maybe there's something to it," but he was never able to bring himself to become an open, leveling fighter on his own home front. The same holds true for other people who cannot accept aggressive feelings in themselves and prefer to see, instead, aggression all around them. Their view of the world enables them to say, "It's not us; *they* are the bastards!" Typically, these couples become members of hate-groups who practice collective scapegoating. In extreme cases, they may even band together and commit crimes against their own neighborhood or society at large.

It is somewhat easier to reach people who resort to the indirect but dirty style of what we call "carom-fighting." They may jab at a spouse by attacking a target that is especially dear to the other—perhaps a child, particularly if it is the partner's child by a former marriage. Or they may make fun of a mate's religious beliefs. Or they go to the home of a friend who is a movie producer and argue that movies can never be a legitimate art form. It often helps to appeal to a carom-fighter's sense of fair play and urge his victim to boycott fights that are precipitated by such sneak provocations.

Similar defensive steps can be effective against the treachery of an intimate ambush. Some dirty fighters are expert at staying in hiding while they attack an intimate's Achilles' heel. If their spouse is allergic to flowers, they may put a bouquet on the victim's desk. If his wife is allergic to dirty jokes, the ambusher may quietly persuade a friend to "regale" her with a few.

The jamming of a couple's communications, discussed previously, can also be escalated in a malignant way when one partner adopts hit-and-run tactics. Suppose a husband tells his wife with a great show of sincerity that he is prepared to discuss an issue that is bothering them both. Suppose he then launches into a monologue and never lets her state her views. This sequence of warm-up-and-freeze-up, if repeated often enough, is more than a mere crisis-maker. It can become a crazy-maker (see below). Hit-and-run tactics may be applied any time and anywhere: between the sheets (as, for example, when one partner habitually has an orgasm while the other is still in the warm-up phase) as well as at the dinner table ("You made me lose my appetite.").

Other poor fight styles also are often escalated to such a degree that they become dirty tactics. A partner who displays ambivalence about the amount of authority he wants to delegate to his spouse is just a poor soul torn between desires. But the mate who constantly passes the responsibility buck to his opponent is being deliberately unfair.

Here, by way of illustration, is a couple getting ready for an evening on the town:

HE *(enthusiastic)*: Let's really have a good time tonight, honey!

SHE *(joining in the spirit of the occasion)*: Boy, am I glad you're in a great mood!

HE: I sure am. Let's do something *you* like.

SHE: You really mean it?

HE: Sure I do! What do you want to do, baby?

SHE: Well, you know I've always wanted to go down to the beach and eat at that crazy boat restaurant.

HE *(fervently)*: Hey, that's a great idea!

So much for Round No. 1. The next fight round took place at the boat restaurant, which turned out to have been a severe mistake. There had been a long wait for a table. There was practically nothing but fish on the menu, and this husband hated fish. The prices were high:

HE (*indignant*): You and your ideas!
SHE (*insulted*): But you asked me!
HE: Just because I asked you doesn't mean you have to pull a stupid stunt like this! Why didn't you at least call for a reservation? . . .

This husband was so sensitive to failure that he resorted to dirty tricks to duck out from under even such a small disaster. He and his wife had to be trained to make as many decisions as possible jointly so that neither partner could blame failures on the other.

A more devious but not uncommon device to manipulate a partner sneakily is the setup operation. It is designed by Partner A to insinuate himself into "B's" love by playing a role that "A" has decided he likes. And this is not nearly as complicated as it sounds.

A number of years ago we found that members of psychotherapy groups are not as much interested in getting to know each other as they are in impressing each other. We believe that, on a more subtle level, this is also true for intimate pairs. The strategy is for "A" to communicate with "B" not in a spontaneous way but selectively. The idea is to draw "B" into displaying himself so that "B's" behavior will complement "A's" thinking. "A" wants to have his thinking confirmed and so he will set up "B" to see him in "A's" own way. "A" will even try to persuade "B" to collude in the behavior chosen by "A."

Suppose "A," the wife, pictures herself as an ever-selfless Red Cross nurse. She wants "B," the husband, not only to see her in the same way. She actually wants him to behave as if she were, in fact, a Red Cross nurse. So she looks for plausible grounds to act out the role she has chosen for herself. Here is what may happen when the husband comes home from work:

SHE (*appraising him*): You look tired, dear.
HE (*surprised*): Do I?
SHE (*solicitous*): Yes, you do. What's the matter?
HE (*casually*): Oh, I had a bad day.

An experienced setup operator may then feel the husband's head; cluck worriedly; get out the thermometer; discover just a shade of above-normal temperature. She'll then be in the Red Cross business, having set up her husband as a weak, servile patient. Her intentions will not necessarily be sinister. The effects of her ministrations may be beneficial: her husband probably did have a terrible day. But her tactics were manipulative, basically unilateral and, in the long run, a disservice to the cause of intimacy.

This wife had succeeded where all dirty and sick fighters must begin their campaigns. She had made her victim cooperative. She had made sure that he became a patsy, just like the victims of monologuers, rageolics, ambushers, hit-and-run fighters, and buck-passers. She had enticed him into colluding with her. And cooperation obtained by collusion is not cooperation at all. It may look and feel friendly, but it is based on falsehood—the denial of the colluder's very identity—and therefore highly destructive of real intimacy.

Many colluders lie in order to evade conflict and avoid rocking the boat of a relationship. They even go along with a partner's beliefs, attitudes, and actions when these are clearly inconsistent with observable facts.

This collusive lying in an ostensibly good cause was demonstrated in an ingenious psychological experiment with newly married couples. Newlyweds are often particularly anxious to prolong the relatively peaceful idyll of their courtship. The couples were shown patches of colored paper. The color differences were minor, but the experiment was rigged to encourage husbands and wives to disagree about their perception of the colors. Yet many of the participants (more males than females, incidentally) denied seeing things differently from their spouses. As the experiments were followed up over the ensuing four years it became apparent that the couples who were most skillful at conflict resolution were the ones who were less inclined to resort to faking and colluding.

In the heat of battle, collusive lying is to be expected. It is not unusual to find a conservative Republican husband *temporarily* changing his political colors during an argument with his liberal Democratic wife if the widening gulf between them is causing him separation anxieties. While intimates are in the throes of acute conflict, as we have shown before, the content of an argument is secondary; the style—its bonding and alienating elements—is far more important.

Some husbands and wives persist in colluding through thick and thin, peace and conflict, year after year, until the resulting unreality leads to a crisis. Dottie Long had always liked to think of her husband Ralph as a big shot. Ralph owned a small discount store, but he fancied himself a big merchandising king. During their 12 years of marriage the Longs kept living higher and higher on the hog. Their home, their cars, the lavish parties that they liked to give, the private schools where they sent their children—everything was out of proportion to Ralph's income which ranged between $22,000 and $28,000 a year. After 12 years of splurging financed by innumerable bank loans, for which Dottie was a willing co-signer, the Longs had piled up debts amounting to $137,-000.

In her heart Dottie had known what was happening, but she did not know enough about true intimacy to level with Ralph about his illusions of grandeur; to help him find his financial bearings; and to call a halt to his wild spending. Instead, she colluded with his big-shot fantasies. As she became increasingly worried about the outcome of their financial problems, Dottie gradually grew frigid toward Ralph. Eventually he moved into an apartment of his own.

Alarmed friends of the Longs persuaded them to go into fight training before they filed for divorce. Within six months they had learned how to live in noncolluding style. Dottie's frigidity vanished and the family was sticking to an austerity budget to pay off their debts.

Other common collusions that can lead to intimacy crises are:

Drinking with a problem drinker; pretending passion with a frigid partner; watching boring TV programs with a partner for the sake of avoiding authentic communication; riding as a passenger in a crazily driven car; serving rich foods to overweight food addicts; finding obnoxious children cute (including one's own); being sloppy in the company of an excessively sloppy partner; patiently looking for lost items in a disordered household; pretending interest in a partner's redundant fulminations; keeping an inefficient secretary because she is your spouse.

Collusion is easy to rationalize. Here are some frequently heard explanations:

"He enjoyed these things so much, I just wanted him to have a good time."

"I loved him so much that I'd have jumped out the window if he'd asked me to."

"Sure, I didn't like what she was doing! But I wanted her to love me, so I put up with it."

"I said to myself: 'You can't fight City Hall or change the spots on a leopard, so I might as well go along.'"

"I was stuck with him/her, so I went along to keep things peaceful."

Considerable camouflaged hostility festers behind such attempts to whitewash collusion. To egg on a partner in his dishonest behavior is a form of passive cruelty because it prevents him from being himself. Then when Partner A colludes, "B" gets a false idea of where he stands; "B" is entitled to believe that "A" approves of something when "A" actually doesn't. "B" stands in lower respect in "A's" eyes than "B" believes he does. "B" may therefore be tempted to draw on a credit of good will that he actually doesn't have and eventually pull the partnership into emotional bankruptcy.

When a spouse colludes he also inhibits the emotional growth of both partners and lowers his own self-respect. Eventually he may begin to hate himself because it is demoralizing to live a life of pretense with an intimate with whom one had hoped to be able to level. Furthermore, failure to own up to what one believes, can lead to psychic nihilism and depression.

A partner who induces his intimate enemy to collude may do this as part of a strategy of hate and as an attempt to increase his distance from the colluder. The collusion-inducer's inner dialogue goes like this: "There, you see? He's doing it again, the fool! I can't wait to get rid of him." This explains why collusion frequently increases before a separation. Partner A, who is about to exit anyway, may go along with a foolish plan concocted by "B," but he is being cooperative solely to be able to cite the plan's foolishness later as "the last straw" that broke his tolerance for "B's" stupidity.

Collusion begets collusion. Its secretiveness requires energy and places the colluder in a double bind: if he keeps his secret reservations secret, he feels (and actually is) isolated; if he shares his secret with an outsider, he is being disloyal to his partner.

Many a disloyal alliance begins when a married colluder shares his reservations with a buddy or a lover ("My wife/husband doesn't understand me!" is the classic theme). The pseudo-intimacies that take place in such alliances are sometimes based entirely on the exchange of secret reservations which the two colluders have stored up against their respective mates.

While our fight trainees are taught the value of good-willed outsiders in resolving intimate conflicts, they are also cautioned that third parties in a dispute, unless selected with great care, frequently turn out to be evil meddlers.

Joe Barnes told his pal Al Higgins that he was secretly worried about going ahead with his projected marriage to his fiancée Sally. A good buddy would have said, "Let's all three sit down and talk about it." But Al said, "Yeah, I know what you mean. I saw her at the club the other night, dancing with Jim, and she was snuggling mighty close to him." The next day Al saw Sally in a downtown restaurant and said, "Say, I guess things aren't going so hot with you and Joe."

Joe and Sally happened to be lucky. They had established sufficient intimacy so Sally was able to say to her fiancé: "You know, I ran into Al today and he said something about you and me breaking up. What in the world was he talking about?" Joe picked up the cue and concluded that Al was not the kind of buddy to be trusted with intimate secrets. Quickly, Joe turned impending disaster to his advantage. He used it as an opportunity to level with Sally about some of his pre-wedding worries and both entered marriage with their eyes wider open and, therefore, with greatly enhanced chances of success.

The best way to avoid trouble when third parties become involved in an intimate two-way conflict is to make sure that no secret pacts or alliances and no classified information are allowed to mushroom within the triangle. The third party should deal with the fighters face to face. If something is said behind one fighter's back, it should be subject to later confrontation.

Suppose a wife seeks solace from a neighbor's wife. Suppose the neighbor makes a helpful suggestion. The help-seeking wife might say, "Would you come over tonight and tell this to Jim yourself? I don't think it would help the relationship between our two families if I accept help. You'd feel guilty next time you see us."

Husbands and wives should always be on the lookout for sadistic third parties who like to have fun by setting themselves up as judges and say, in effect, "Let's you two fight." These overactive citizens start out as voyeurs who listen to a couple's differences and interpret them as "personality clashes"; then they fan the flames of these clashes by appropriate remarks to egg the fighters on. When they have had their fill of enjoying themselves as spectators, they step in as referees. They call the low blows. They prolong the fight by suggesting intermissions, not so much to give the fighters a recuperative pause but to enable the referee to remind combatants of the gulf that separates them. When arguments resume, these referees "helpfully" sum up the issues. They not only keep score but, in the last stage of hostilities, finally appoint themselves judges and announce who won what and why.

For such helpers there is an old saying: "With friends like this, who needs enemies?" The only way to deal with these buddies is to eject them from the ring and never to collude with their sadistic tastes.

Collusion can make intimates particularly miserable when one partner goes so far as to offer himself openly as the captive of the other. When a wife says, "If I had any place to go, I'd have left you long ago," she is toying with one of the most hate-provoking weapons in the arsenal of intimate warfare. It is an invitation to dirty fighting on the part of the male who now thinks he has his wife in his firm grasp.

A male equivalent of this captive enemy is the husband who is sexually imprinted by his wife: he is so used to her that he can't have satisfactory sex with another woman. If his wife finds this out and he then throws himself at the mercy of her court and labels himself as her captive, he will probably be in for an unpleasant surprise. He may think that his collusion is inviting her to be especially fair when they get into arguments. In point of fact, she, too, is likely to be provoked into dirty fighting because people who cringe (i.e., the "Uncle Tom" stereotype Negro) are invariably the ones most likely to get kicked. Nobody wants a mate who hangs around only because he has no place else to go.

We have previously warned against attributing opinions and traits to a partner instead of encouraging him to level how he really feels. This kind of attribution, if continued long and intensively enough, can become an extremely dirty tactic akin to brainwashing; the partner actually comes to believe that he possesses the attribute that his opponent claims to have discovered.

A creative but badly disorganized economics professor wrote technical papers and books that made him a leader in his field. But his working methods were so chaotic that in the closing months of his writing and research projects he became appallingly difficult to live with. His wife, to whom he had been married for 22 years and who was devoted to him, was a pseudo-intellectual and of a divided mind about her husband's fame and creativity.

She was more proud than jealous during his between-crisis periods and more jealous than proud when the professor was under great stress. During these critical periods the wife zeroed in on anything that betrayed her husband's disorganization or his penchant for making things difficult for himself. If he made an unnecessary phone call she concluded, "You really don't want to finish this book." If he was despondent about his slow progress, she carped, "I'm not surprised! I know there are lots of things you'd rather be doing instead!" If he showed signs of weariness she might say, "Look, dear, don't you think you're too tired to do so much outside work? Why don't you just teach and read a paper at a convention now and then, like the other men in your department?"

If the professor's wife had leveled, she would have said, "Look, I don't want you to write any more books. It's too hard on you and you make everybody around you too nervous. It's too much for me." Instead of issuing such an open challenge for her husband to change his neurotic work habits, she castrated him with a broadscale nuclear attack. In effect, she told him, "You're too weak to finish what you start."

The professor managed to torture his way through four books, largely by withdrawing further and further away from his wife. During the final weeks of his projects he ate all his meals on a tray in his study. He took leaves of absence from his job and emerged only to sleep. Paradoxically, it was this defensive, self-imposed isolation that brought on a crucial impasse during the writing of his fifth book. Since he had cut himself off from associates and others who normally encouraged his work, his wife's negative comments reinforced his own self-doubts until he finally said to himself:

"I guess she's right. I can't write. If I really had something to say, I'd be saying it more effectively. I'll give it up."

The wife's brainwashing had succeeded.

During the three unproductive years that followed, the professor began to drink until liver damage sent him into psychotherapy. From there he went into fight training and learned the self-defensive tactics outlined later in this chapter. These enabled him to counteract his wife's efforts to make him feel something that he didn't feel at all. Once he was rid of this burden, he wrote his sixth and seventh books without interference. After a period of depression, the wife regrouped her own interests. She went back to the university and later began teaching junior high school. She even wrote a booklet on "The Creative Home."

How had her brainwashing effort succeeded?

First, she attributed a character role to her husband, *i.e.*, weakling. Second, she drove him into psychological isolation. Third, she carefully collected bits of evidence on a highly selective basis and used these fragments against him as "proof" of her type casting. Fourth, she limited her contact with her victim except to reinforce the type casting still further. It's easy to see why the same tactics are also employed by parents and teachers against young adolescents who are experimenting with a still wobbly identity.

With some exceptions, the fighters discussed up to now, no matter how dirty their tactics, do not set out with the determination to make their mates miserable. Undeniably, however, some intimates are not only dirty but despicable. Their tactics are not only unfair, but deliberate. They are not clumsy hitters who land an occasional foul blow. They are slick and sick. They don't just provoke crises; they systematically plan chaos. They are the satanic fighters who derive pleasure from destroying the morale and self-worth of their intimate enemies.

These satans induce despair by systematically undermining the intimate system. They are like firemen who start fires, policemen who rob banks, and psychiatrists who drive patients crazy. They get a kick out of the tensions of their loved ones and enjoy seeing them panic. It's easy for them to play out their sadistic games because they are virtuosos at the art of nonstop "bugging." They go along cheerfully to a big dance but then refuse to dance. They trot along to church only to look excruciatingly bored during the service. They agree to have a nice, quiet weekend and then invite a gang of friends.

Whether intimates like it or not, they are tragically vulnerable to the process of driving each other crazy. A paradox is at work: they would not be vulnerable if they weren't deeply involved emotionally; but if they are not deeply involved, they don't enjoy much intimacy.

One of the hidden dangers of intimacy, in fact, is the risk that Partner A may regress to an excessively dependent, childlike status. This gives "B" approximately the same power over "A" that was once wielded by "A's" parents. Overdependency is why spouses sometimes call each other "Mom" or "Dad"—which is a poor practice because it is unhealthy to think of a partner as a symbol or a thing; it also tends to confuse children.

All intimates are dependent on each other to some extent, but a satan exploits this dependency and turns it into a trap, usually by giving his victim the idea that he is an indispensable "protector"; that only the satan understands the victim and his problems; and that only he can keep the victim going—perhaps by catering to the victim's weaknesses (vanity, alcohol) or his specialized tastes (friends, sex).

Victims rarely understand that a satan is totally dependent on a target's masochistic servitude. There can be no satan without a cooperative patsy. Some victims are children, iso-lates, and others whose actual or imagined dependency and incompetence are so overwhelming that they feel uncondi-tionally bound to stick with satanic intimates. But a surpris-ing number of unfortunate targets go meekly along and keep themselves needlessly in bondage by denying that their de-structive opponents are, indeed, crazy. Which is precisely what the crazy satans want!

Frequently, victims will not recognize a satanic pattern of aggression until a relationship has deteriorated too far to be saved, even if the satan were to be disarmed. Satans are never transparent, for example, even when they say they are and when they appear to be. They are adept at putting on masks and playing such roles as the Good Mother Figure (which covers up for the Hansel-and-Gretel type of witch); the supportive Good Father Figure (which covers up tyranni-cal interference with independence and self-identity); the Best Friend (who exploits his intimate knowledge of the partner's weaknesses); and the Good Samaritan (who drags the relationship's anchor, splits the sails, enlarges the leak, sinks the ship and then poses as the "rescuer"). They are expert, chronic users of all statics, derailing tactics, am-bushes, attributions, crazy-making, and every other dirty tac-tic already discussed.

They are also skilled at taking things out of natural con-text. Suppose a wife is about to recognize her husband's satanic influence on herself and the children. The husband then complains loudly of one small, unwise or destructive bit of his wife's behavior that caused him minor inconvenience. The wife, being a fair and square fighter, admits her error. This may well arouse just enough guilt and shame within her to derail her from diagnosing her husband's satanic tactics.

In her inner dialogue she tells herself: "Since I'm destruc-tive, too, he can't be much worse than me. After all, he took my mistake nicely and only mentioned it when I put him on the defensive."

Another way for this husband to keep his wife from verifying his satanic tendencies is constantly to exaggerate even the slightest bit of evidence that runs counter to the wife's budding hypothesis. This technique may cause her to say to herself: "It's true that he is generally a rotten bastard, but how can I get very mad at him when he can be such an angel, too? Didn't he just buy me that beautiful Mother's Day gift and didn't he take the kids to church when I was sick?"

What with a victim's masochistic tendencies, it may require

only the smallest bit of occasional nice behavior by a satan to support the one force that is keeping the victim going. That force is hope—specifically, the hope that things will somehow get better, plus the illusion that living with a satan is better than having nobody at all. Without outside help, victims can rarely bring themselves to admit that their satan-partners' very purpose is to destroy.

Hans Spiegel was Martha's third husband. He was a suave and glamorous theatrical producer. It had been easy for Martha to fall for his sparkling conversation and his continental charm. By the time they had been married for two years it was evident that he was a rageolic at home and reserved his charm for his many extracurricular girlfriends. He did enjoy using Martha as his housekeeper and as his front of respectability. As the tensions in her marriage grew taut, Martha, who had always liked to drink, became an alcoholic. Hans seized upon this weakness with a vengeance and berated his wife about it at every opportunity.

When this couple joined a fight-training group, Hans quickly displayed himself as a finger-pointing district attorney. In effect, he brought his wife into court handcuffed and tried to use the other couples as a jury. Painstakingly he presented the evidence he had collected against his wife. He cited how many drinks she had before dinner; how many drinks after dinner; how often she fell asleep in a stupor during the course of an evening at home; how she had begun to neglect her own daughters by a previous marriage; how her drinking embarrassed him before his business associates; and how she was generally unworthy of him.

It soon became obvious that Martha could only stand to be around this man when she was anesthetized with liquor; and that she stuck to him only because she was a two-time loser who was mortally afraid that another divorce would confirm her worst fear about her own identity: "I can't hold any man." Eventually, this overpowering, sadistic husband and this meek, masochistic wife wound up in the divorce court. They had lost the good will and the patience to fight fairly with each other; perhaps it had never been in them in the first place.

A few sick husbands and wives actually seduce their partners into driving them crazy in order to punish them and to be able to tell them, "See what you have done to me!" But a more popular strategy of crazy-making is to chip away at a lover's perception of himself and his surroundings. We named this strategy "gaslighting," after the old movie *Gaslight*, starring Charles Boyer and Ingrid Bergman. In this film, the wife

(Bergman) correctly perceives that the gaslight in her home is becoming progressively dimmer. The husband (Boyer) wants to have his wife put away in an asylum and is secretly and slowly turning down the lights over a period of time. But he denies that they are changing. The effects on the wife are disastrous as she vacillates between accepting her husband's perceptions and her own.

The best self-protection against the chronic bugging of gaslighting and other crazy-making strategies is to open warfare on two fronts: (1) defensively, by resisting one's lazy dependency and the temptation to let a satan get away with defining one's identity; and (2) aggressively, by fighting for one's sane real image. When a satan steps on one's identity toes it is never enough to say, "Ouch!" One has to step right back on his toes with an affirmation of one's true self.

If Miss Bergman had played her role in *Gaslight* as a trained marital fighter she would, first of all, have withdrawn from the senseless round-robin argument of whether she or her satanic husband was perceiving the lights correctly. She would have held an intensive inner dialogue to question and then affirm her own independent perception of the observable facts. She might have consulted a friend for additional confirmation and perspective. Perhaps she might have had her eyesight checked out. Finally, she would have aggressively confronted her husband. At this point she should have been able to say, "I've figured this out! You're trying to drive me crazy! I know what I know and in this case I know that these lights aren't as bright as they used to be. So please stop your nonsense!"

The key antidote against satanic tactics is not to play masochistic victim and not to hook in and go along with a satan's bag of tricks. Some victims, fortunately, are able to spot a crazy-maker simply by trusting their own instincts. When victims are tough enough to stand up to identity-pressure that feels false to them ("That isn't me!") and resist the temptation to become overdependent, they can affirm their true selves. Intensive marathon fight-training sessions are especially valuable in helping mates to rebuild their egos so they can stand up against low-blow attacks.

Group pressure can also force some satans to own up to their aggressive pattern; to quit using it; to use aggression as a means to a beneficial end, not as an end in itself. This reform is difficult, but a satan who listens intently to the interactions within a marathon group may begin to sense that the satisfactions that can be gained from constructive aggression are superior to the rewards he has been collecting through his satanic methods.

Fight training or psychotherapy is helpful when intimates encounter sadism or masochism. In the privacy of an intimate relationship, it is relatively easy to be drawn into undesirable practices that are inconsistent with one's real self.

"I'm going with this crazy girl," one of our trainees reported, "who likes to have her nipples bitten—really bitten hard! I can't bring myself to do it and she's upset about it." This girlfriend had plenty to be upset about. She was under the misapprehension that the way to please the world was to have people hurt her. Obviously, she needed intensive psychotherapy. Her boyfriend correctly refrained from suspending his better judgment, permitting himself to be debauched, or tampering with his own good sense of what's right and wrong. He sensed that the identities of two people, and not only morals, were involved.

His girlfriend eventually experienced a complete breakdown and had to be hospitalized but, with her boyfriend's help, she came to recognize that only a considerable change within herself would enable her ever to maintain a reasonably healthy intimate relationship. At that, this couple was better off than the hard-shelled game players who sometimes find their way into fight training. Some of their experiences, no matter how well documented, border on the unbelievable.

Mr. Clark was a married man who pretended to be single. He was a loan officer in a bank. Miss Wright was a model. She was single but pretended to be a divorcée whose tragic marriage had left her distrustful of men. One afternoon Mr. Clark's wife appeared in Miss Wright's apartment. She had followed her husband to one of his dates. The two women had a long talk. Mrs. Clark wanted to save her marriage. Miss Wright was scheming to break it up. To attain her goal, Miss Wright arranged for Mrs. Clark to drop in the next time Mr. Clark came to call. Miss Wright thought that if husband and wife met in such a trap the marriage would surely not survive. But Mr. Clark, a poker-faced game player with extensive extramarital experience, outbluffed his girlfriend's bluff. When his wife burst into Miss Wright's apartment, he coldly demanded, "Who's she?" Incredible as it may seem, he managed to convince Miss Wright that he really was not married to the indignant visitor or to anyone else and that his wife was a deranged stranger.

Eventually, Miss Wright fell seriously in love with Mr. Clark. Then she learned he was seeing other girls, too. His marriage broke up, but he had no intention of marrying Miss

Wright. When she threatened to commit suicide he did agree to come with her to several fight-training sessions. There, group pressure forced him to come clean and she was able to wean herself away from him. It seemed that neither had ever been intimate with anyone and that each would probably be condemned to a game-playing life until they became too old or jaded. Many of these people wind up as psychotics, alcoholics, or suicides. They would rather die than change.

There are extreme cases who need professional help. The vast majority of husbands and wives can draw on better credits to straighten out the accounts of their relationships. And while they try leveling aggressively with their partners, they can also learn to keep up their intimate defenses and avoid unnecessary injury. Here are further tips on the art of marital self-defense:

1. A partner's tendency to engage in attribution can be short-circuited if the opponent refuses to behave with the passivity of a projection screen, such as acting sleepy or uncommitted, being silent or stone-faced.

2. A partner who mystifies his opponent by ascribing reality to unrealities can be disarmed if the mystifier is confronted with the reality of a situation pedantically, again and again.

3. A partner's scheme to entrap his opponent can be avoided by demanding that both partners be absolutely and fully explicit about their respective expectations in a given situation.

4. A partner's tendency to be sadistic or masochistic can be foiled if all intimate punishments, whether dished out or absorbed, are consistent with the importance of the issue at stake.

5. A partner's tendency to overload the intimate system with too many demands can be met by the counterdemand, "Enough!" and by temporary exits for refueling.

6. A partner's tendency to underload the system with insufficient stimulation and communication can be foiled by setting off fights and deutero-fights about current and valid mutual problems.

7. Sick and dirty fighters of all types can be foiled by methods discussed throughout this chapter.

14. How to Score Intimate Fights

The pay-off of a truly intimate fight, as we have emphasized before, is not to chalk up a win or loss for one partner or the other. Only a joint win or loss is possible: either the partnership gains and emerges in an improved state as a result of an aggressive encounter or the unit loses and its relationship deteriorates. Although a great many "plus" and "minus" factors enter into the movement of a couple toward a better or worse relationship, we have been able to design a self-scoring system that assigns the proper weight to all elements of intimate fighting.

The reaction of fighters to this system varies greatly. Some partners like to pin things down in a graphic way. They come to fight training with an attitude of "Show me!" They are the kind of people who like to peek into the inside of mechanisms and see how they work. They also like to know precisely where they stand with their partners after one fight and before going on to the next one. For such people, the scoring system with its two charts is ideal.

Others, frankly, find it tedious. They are the more intuitive types who become impatient with precise definitions and like to discuss the swing of their relationship with their partners in a more general way. These people can feel free to skip this chapter; or to return to it after they have read the rest of this book; or merely to acquaint themselves with the system, especially with our demonstration of how it functioned for one couple in the course of an engagement actually fought out and scored at our Institute.

It is not essential, then, to master the scoring system in order to learn constructive fight techniques and to benefit fully from them.

Before going into scoring sessions we remind trainees that if they are going to be intimate and open, they are going to display themselves as they really are. This also means that they are going to be biased and subjective; that, initially, they are going to hear only what they prefer to hear; that what's constructive for one may be experienced as destructive by the other. So we tell them:

"Please don't confuse your good intentions with your overt actions or words. Try to score what you actually said or did, not what you meant to convey. Let your partner correct your score, and vice versa. This is the best way to learn that it's the *effects* of a communication that really count. What matters is not the intent of the sender but the way it was received."

The opposite page shows what the fight elements chart looks like.

Here are explanations of the nine dimensions that make up the fight elements profile:

1. *Reality*. This category is designed to measure the authenticity of the fight. The fight may be labeled "realistic" if the fighter's aggression is based on justifiable, rational considerations that also *feel* real and authentic. The fight should be styled "imaginary" if the aggression is based on nonauthentic reasons or if it contains elements of phoniness or game-playing.

2. *Injury*. With this dimension we measure the fairness, unfairness, or meanness of the fight. The fight may be styled "fair" (above the belt) if the fighter keeps injuries within the opponent's capacity to absorb them. The fight is "dirty" (below the belt) if the aggression is aimed below the belt with blows that are hurtful and intolerable to the opponent.

3. *Involvement*. This measures how seriously the fighter becomes involved in the aggression. The fight is "active" (reciprocal) if there is plenty of give and take. It is "passive" (or one-way) if the fighter displays an attitude of disengagement, if he is evading and avoiding or rolling with the punch; and/or, if the fight is not reciprocal but shows an attitude of, "Let the other fellow fight."

4. *Responsibility*. In this column we measure how the subject meets or declines responsibility for participating in the fight. The fighter is rated as "owning up" if he accepts his responsibility for placing (or responding in) the fight without enlisting support of others. The fighter is rated "minus" (Anonymous or Group) if he hides responsibility for his aggression or parcels it out onto others ("Dr. Bach says ..." or "Your mother says ...").

5. *Humor*. If one or both partners laugh, giggle, or joke during the fight, this dimension measures the purpose of the humor. The fighter rates a "plus" if humorous behavior brings some joyous relief to one or both partners, as for example when they laugh benevolently at each other, simultaneously

THE FIGHT ELEMENTS PROFILE

	1	2	3	4	5	6	7	8	9
	REALITY	INJURY	INVOLVEMENT	RESPONSIBILITY	HUMOR	EXPRESSION	COMMUNICATION	DIRECTNESS	SPECIFICITY
+	Authentic, Realistic	Fair, Above Belt	Active, Reciprocal	Owning up	Laugh with relief	Open, Leveling	High, Clear, Reciprocal feedback	Direct focus	Specific
o									
—	Imaginary	Dirty, Below the belt	Passive, or One-way	Anonymous or Group	Ridicule, Clowning or Laugh-at	Hidden or Camouflaged	Static, One-way; No Feedback	Displaced focus	General "Analysis"

The "plus" (+) positions on the profile represent good (or "bonding") styles of aggression.

The "minus" (—) positions represent poor (or "alienating") styles of aggression.

The middle (O) positions indicate styles rated as neutral, irrelevant, or unobservable.

The profile is complete when one line is drawn to connect all nine dimensions, intersecting each dimension at the appropriate level (+ or — or O). When the line stays predominantly above the "O" level, the fight was fought in a predominantly bonding style. When the line stays predominantly below the "O" level, the fight was fought in predominantly alienating style.

or in relays. The fighter rates "minus" if he gets sarcastic enjoyment out of watching the opponent when he is down; if he ridicules the other or enjoys his suffering or embarrassment; if he clowns or is flip when the other is serious or disturbed; or if he tried to derail the other's concern by joking, etc.

6. *Expression.* This item evaluates the way the fighter's aggression is expressed. He rates "plus" (open, leveling) if his expression is overt, transparent, and not disguised; if he means what he says and the meaning is obvious. He is rated "minus" (hidden or camouflaged) if his manner of expression is covert, subtle, or open to considerable interpretation.

7. *Communication.* In this item we measure the amount and clarity of verbal or physical communication that takes place in the fight. The fighter rates "plus" if communication is transparent, flowing openly, in quantity, freely, reciprocally; if it is effectively received with little misunderstanding; if the "noise level" of any interfering "static" is low; and if reception of the communication is acknowledged through feedback. The fighter rates "minus" if there is relatively little open communication, much interfering static, poor listening and receptivity, much redundancy or misunderstanding.

8. *Directness.* With this item we measure to what degree the aggression is focused on the *here-and-now* opponent and his current actions—with no references to older or irrelevant situations. The fighter rates "plus" if his aggression is primarily directed to the present opponent and his current actions. The fighter rates "minus" if his aggression *is* related to the opponent but toward the past, or is displaced toward objects that the opponent holds dear, such as children, other persons or things or values.

9. *Specificity.* This item measures how much the attacks and counterattacks refer to the fighters' specific, observable actions, feelings, or attitudes as contrasted with fight tactics that generalize, interpret, or, for example, label certain of the opponent's behavior as "typical" of a broader personality trait. The fighter rates "plus" if his attacks and counterattacks are limited to directly observable behavior. He rates "minus" if by his actions the opponent is "analyzed" as belonging in a large category or pattern.

The scoring process is designed to determine how a particular fight or fight round affected the mutual "swing" of the partners; whether the fighting was relatively constructive or destructive. We therefore instruct trainees that fight scoring may be done in one of four ways, whichever the fighters prefer: (1) they may independently assign ratings to each other and then compare notes; (2) they may collaborate in determining the ratings; (3) they may ask a reasonably objective observer to rate them; (4) they may both work together with an objective outsider.

Once we have used this profile to rate the fight elements—bonding vs. alienating—that were present during a particular fight we go on to obtain a fight *effects* profile. This second profile does not simply record the level of a fight process. It registers impact. In particular, it measures the degree of change that has taken place as a result of a fight. It breaks down these changes into 12 categories. Just as the fight elements profile, so does this second scoring sheet allow a scorer to construct a curve to determine how many dimensions of intimacy were affected by a fight in a positive, bonding (+) manner; how many items were affected in a negative, alienating (−) manner; and how many categories remained unchanged (0) in the course of aggressive encounter.

Here is what the fight effects profile looks like:

To use the fight effects profile, the following rules should be observed:

The "plus" (+) positions on the profile represent good (or "bonding") results of the fight.

The "minus" (−) positions represent destructive (or "alienating") results of the fight.

The middle (0) positions represent areas where the fight has brought about no change.

The profile is complete when one line is drawn to connect all 12 dimensions, intersecting each dimension at the appropriate level (+ or − or 0). When the line stays predominantly on the "plus" side, the fight effects were predominantly constructive or bonding. When the line stays predominantly on the "minus" side, the fight effects were predominantly destructive or alienating.

For those categories where partners disagree, broken lines may be used to indicate the difference of opinion.

And here are explanations of the 12 categories that make up the fight effects profile:

1. *Hurt.* This item measures the hurt experienced by a fighter, either as a result of hostile action or because of lack of response from the opponent. The fight is rated "hurt decreased" if a fighter feels less injured after the fight than he did beforehand. It is rated "hurt increased" if the person feels more hurt, offended, weakened, reduced, lowered, or humiliated than before.

2. *Information.* In this category we measure the knowledge

THE FIGHT ELEMENTS PROFILE
for the first round of Mr. and Mrs. Myles' Loyalty Fight

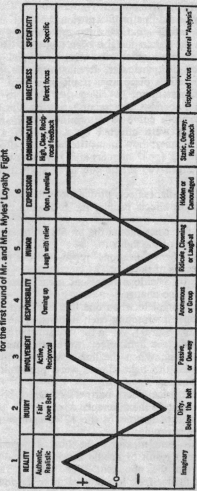

	1 REALITY	2 INJURY	3 INVOLVEMENT	4 RESPONSIBILITY	5 HUMOR	6 EXPRESSION	7 COMMUNICATION	8 DIRECTNESS	9 SPECIFICITY
+	Authentic, Realistic	Fair, Above Belt	Active, Reciprocal	Owning up	Laugh with relief	Open, Leveling	High, Clear, Reciprocal feedback	Direct focus	Specific
O									
−	Imaginary	Dirty, Below the belt	Passive, or One-way	Anonymous or Group	Ridicule, Clowning or Laugh-at	Hidden or Camouflaged	Static, One-way, No Feedback	Displaced focus	General "Analysis"

The "plus" (✦) positions on the profile represent good (or "bonding") styles of aggression.

The "minus" (—) positions represent poor (or "alienating") styles of aggression.

The middle (O) positions indicate styles rated as neutral, irrelevant, or unobservable.

The profile is complete when one line is drawn to connect all nine dimensions. Intersecting each dimension at the appropriate level (− or -- or O). When the line stays predominantly above the "O" level, the fight was fought in a predominantly bonding style. When the line stays predominantly below the "O" level, the fight was fought in predominantly alienating style.

that a fighter gained about where he stands with the other or about what turns the partner off or on. The fight is rated "new" if a fighter learns something significant that he did not know before. It is rated "old (redundant)" if a person learned nothing he didn't already know.

3. *Positional movement.* This item measures how much a fighter believes the fight issue has been advanced by the fight in the direction of conflict resolution. The fight is rated "ground gained" if it yielded a new, clearer, more hopeful position. It is rated "ground lost" if the position of the fight issue has deteriorated because it is now less clear or less hopeful of eventual solution.

4. *Control.* In this column we rate how much sanctioned (permissible) power or influence the fighter can exert over the opponent's behavior as a result of the current conflict. The fight is rated "control increased" if the fighter has gained more effective, acceptable power or influence over his opponent's behavior. It is rated "control decreased" if the fighter winds up with less accepted, sanctioned power than he had before the fight.

5. *Fear.* This category measures how a fighter's fear of the fight situation (or simply his fear of the other participant) has been affected by the fight. The fight is rated "fear decreased" if the fighter's fear has been reduced and he feels he can drop his guard. It is rated "fear increased" if his fear has been heightened and he pulls his guard (belt line) up.

6. *Trust.* In this column we measure changes that have taken place in the fighter's confidence that he can trust the opponent to deal with him in good faith, with good will, and with positive regard; that the opponent will fight fairly and fulfill his agreed-upon "contracts." The fight is rated "trust increased (dependable)" if the fighter has experienced the opponent as worthy of more trust than before the fight. It is rated "trust decreased (undependable)" if, as a result of the fight, the fighter becomes more cautious, less trusting and feels that the opponent is less dependable, more "ill-willed," or less understanding and respectful of his interests and sensitivities.

7. *Revenge.* This category rates what happened to any retaliatory or grudge feelings; or feelings of resentment with intent to seek future revenge; or any interest in retribution. The fight is rated "revenge forgiven" if it did not instigate or enhance vengeful or vindictive feelings; if hurts are forgiven or forgotten. It is rated "revenge stimulated" if the fighter who harbors vengeful feelings is now more likely to seek opportunities for retribution in the future.

8. *Reparation.* In this category we rate any move designed to undo or repair injuries or to extend apologies or forgiveness. The fight is rated "reparation active" if the fighter makes active efforts to undo or repair damage he has done and/or welcomes the opponent's attempts to relieve guilt through reparation. It is rated "reparation none" if the fight makes no attempt to encourage reconciliation or repairs; or rejects the opponent's reparation attempts; or refuses to let the guilt-feeling partner off the hook.

9. *Centricity.* In this column we record any changes that have taken place in the fighter's central significance (and value) within the opponent's heart and private world. We assign a "more central" rating if, after the encounter, the fighter feels that he "counts more" with the other and has gained more central significance in his heart. We mark this category "less central" if the fighter feels he "counts less" than he did before the fight and now occupies a more peripheral position in the other's heart.

10. *Self-count (autonomy).* This item measures any change in the fighter's feeling of self-worth—how much he values himself or, for example, how justified or guilty he feels after the fight. The fight is rated "more self-value" if the fighter feels good about the way he fought; has gained in self-esteem; and accepts his role in the fight. It is rated "less self-value" if the fighter feels a loss of self-esteem or blames himself for the way he handled himself in the fight.

11. *Catharsis.* In this category we record to what extent the fighter came out of the fight with a "purged" or "cleansed" feeling because of the release of aggressive tensions. We mark this item "released" if the fighter experienced a release of tensions that lowered his reservoir of stored-up aggressions and this caused him to feel good. We mark it "inhibited" if no tension release occurred or if the fight actually increased the fighter's frustrations and tensions and inhibited him more than he was before.

12. *Cohesion-Affection.* In this column we record what the fight did to the fighter's feeling of "optimal distance" from his opponent, *i.e.,* the degree of closeness to the partner that the fighter prefers. The fight is rated "closer" if cohesiveness and attraction to the opponent has increased. It is marked "more distant" if closeness and attraction have decreased.

We can now demonstrate how the scoring system and charts are used by couples in fight training. We'll start out by recording Round No. 1 of a "loyalty fight" between Gerald and Barbara Myles. The Myleses have been married for four years. They are a good-looking, rather articulate couple.

Gerry is a college graduate, aged 32. Barbara has had two
years of college and is 30 years old. They have one child,
Gerald, Jr., aged three. Mr. Myles is a partner in a small but
flourishing electronics research company. His annual income
is $26,000. At the time of this fight round, the M.'s had
already participated in two of our marathon training groups.
They had also had some experience observing how other
couples act out their problems in psycho-drama groups.

Here they are now, ready to do battle at our office.

DR. BACH: What's your beef? I see you're not getting
along. I understand both of you have been dissatisfied with your relationship for some time. I want
you to level with each other and confront one
another directly, eyeball-to-eyeball, with your differences, no holds barred. Our purpose here is, of
course, to find a road to agreement. But we have to
start with the disagreements.

HE: She likes to bitch.

DR. B: Please tell this directly to your wife.

SHE: Oh, that won't be necessary, Dr. Bach. He has told
me far too often that I am a bitch.

DR. B: I believe you. But neither of you has learned very
much from these repetitious harangues. I want to
see how you two can learn to fight more constructively. So please address one another directly and
don't complain about each other to me. Even if you
say nothing new to each other, it's new to me and
the fact that you are airing your differences in
front of me is a new experience for you. Now
please tell your wife again what your beef is.

HE: Honey, you just bitch too much. I'm tired of it.

SHE: If I bitch, there must be a good reason.

HE: I don't care whether you have reason to bitch or not.
I just don't like to hear it any more. Besides, I
don't think you have real cause to be so angry all
the time.

SHE: Well, I listen to your anger and your criticism of
me. And even though I don't like it, I accept it as
part of you.

HE: That's different. My criticisms are constructive.
They're certainly not irrational.

SHE (heatedly): And mine are crazy, are they? Is that
what you're saying, that when you criticize me it's
"constructive" but when I criticize you it's "irrational," intolerable "bitching"? Well, are you ever a

pompous ass! That's just plain funny! (*She laughs at him.*)

HE (*firm*): It's not funny to me! Let's be realistic, shall we? Does my criticism of you interfere with your pursuing your interests? I dare say it doesn't.

SHE (*exasperated*): You ask and answer your own questions, so how can we get anywhere? You see, Doctor, he makes it impossible to communicate with him!

DR. B: Yes, in fact I see several difficulties that the two of you have. But please leave me out of this for a while. Try to communicate directly with each other, even though you now find it difficult. You simply must practice direct contact with each other!

HE: OK. Yes, I believe I was right: my criticism doesn't stop you from doing exactly as you please even though your bitching seriously interferes with my work! And I've had just about enough of it.

SHE (*angry*): I've never interfered with your work! I know it's important to you, that you're anxious about it and very involved and ambitious. I accept all this. I love you for it and I'm proud of your work and your ambition. So how in the world can you ever say such a stupid thing, that I interfere with your work? I'm all for you, you idiot! I love you!

HE (*smug*): I know you love me, but you show it in a most aggravating manner.

SHE: You mean I protect you from making a fool of yourself . . . like, for instance, with Charles?

DR. B: Who is Charles?

SHE: Charles is my husband's business partner.

HE: He is my senior partner and we get along very well.

SHE: Yes, as long as you kiss-up to him. You always try to ingratiate yourself with the powers that be. You are kind of a sycophant. Yes, that what you are, a sycophant.

HE: Syco—what? I see you've found a new label for me!

SHE: Yes, sycophant—like elephant—only "syco" means "a kiss-up" . . .

HE (*laughs*): That's funny! How do you figure that I "kiss-up" to Charles?

SHE: Oh, you make him think he's a genius and that everything he says and thinks is pure gold.

HE: Well, it is, most of the time. The man is more often right than wrong and he has been very good to us, not only me but especially to you. You seem to forget that we met through him when both of us were working in his organization.

SHE: Now you're being silly. Of course I remember. I also remember that marrying me brought you closer to Charles and to becoming his full partner. You see, I've been very good for your career.

HE: Yes, you used to be very cooperative and helped Charles and me to get along. Lately, though, you've turned against Charles. What do you want from him? He owes you nothing. If anything, you owe him a lot. You seem to forget how much help he was to you before I ever joined the company.

SHE: Well, I helped him, too. I worked my fanny off for him. And anyhow, that's all in the past; I'm no longer working there. I don't owe Charles or his organization anything!

HE: Well, that's ingratitude for you! (*Angrily.*) You were a divorced, semialcoholic "nothing" before he put you to work! He educated you on the job and promoted you and helped you dry out.

SHE: Sure, he provided a good environment and a good opportunity. But don't forget this part, Buster (*she is very mad now*): I made good use of it! I was tired of my earlier disappointments and I helped myself! Hear? I helped myself! (*She screams.*) And I worked my way up in the organization by my own efforts! You always bring this up: how Charles (*mockingly*) made "a silk purse out of a sow's ear." That's supposed to be me, and I resent it! You're damn right: I'll bitch about that till the cows come home! Why the hell do you bring up my past all the time? Do you like to rub it in, or something?

HE (*Now very disturbed and red in the face, stands up and paces*): Yes, as a matter of fact, when you constantly undermine Charles it makes my working with him very difficult. It's good for you to be reminded where your real support came from when you were down and out.

SHE (*still very upset*): Are you kidding? I'm not denying that Charles helped me. But how long should I be eating humble pie? He got his pound of flesh out of me! And now, I don't think he does anything for me at all. He likes you, all right. He uses you! But he pays absolutely no attention to me any more. In fact, he sort of behaves insultingly toward me.

When we visited over at his house last Sunday it was the same old story again: he's glad to see you but can hardly stand my presence! And that inhibits me. I can't feel free to express myself in such a rejecting atmosphere. Why should I be pleasant about it?

HE: Why should Charles bother you? You're too "other-directed"! What the hell do you want from him? Why should he be interested in you? Why do you want his approval so much? Face it, you're not important to him. *I* am. I know how to create good public relations for his firm, not you. In fact, you knock our image with your hostile attitude toward Charles. That's so stupid of you! After all, he is important to us. For instance, are you forgetting that our new Cadillac came from him?

SHE: It's a good thing I selected the car. If I'd left it up to you we wouldn't have a Cadillac. You would have gotten a Lincoln . . . the same one Charles drives.

HE (*Sarcastically, he imitates and mocks her argument*): I love steaks, so does Charles. The only reason I love juicy, rare steaks is because Charles does. Isn't that what you're trying to say? It's all too ridiculous!

A long silence ensued. The couple had run out of arguments. The first round of this fight was over. Nothing had been settled. This is typical for early rounds of most marital fights. What happens is that the couple senses that the point of contention has been made sufficiently clear for the purpose of the first round. And that purpose is: to feel each other out and size each other up as to the open-mindedness or closed-mindedness toward any change of respective positions.

Typically, each partner tends to be more pessimistic than optimistic about his chances for bringing the other around. This pessimism may even increase until it becomes a painful feeling of despair that "things will never change." This despair is reinforced by the widespread, false belief that one should not try to change an intimate partner; that intimacy is synonymous with unconditional, positive acceptance of each other; and that, in any case, human nature, being resistant to change, is best accepted "as is"! Intimate fighters thus find themselves in an incongruous dilemma. It may be hard for them to extricate themselves without outside help. That is why many fights do not go the full distance even after pauses between rounds. They evaporate in a hopeless fizzle. The painful paradox is: if the partners accept things as they are, both are miserable; if they demand change, they supposedly don't love or accept each other!

One of the first steps in constructive fight training is to get a couple out of this trap by elevating the desire for change into a human virtue and relegating the notion of "unconditional acceptance" onto the junk heap of unworkable, romantic stereotypes.

To come back to the Myles family's loyalty fight, let us score this first round to see how constructive it was. After that, this couple will get additional fight training to improve their fight style so the next fight round will be more constructive.

The couple and the counselor filled out the fight profiles. The fight elements profile looked as shown on the opposite page.

Here is how we arrived at a rating for each numbered fight element:

1. The "reality" dimension of this round rated "two plus." Gerry felt he had a justifiable, rational complaint against Barbara because her "bitching" about his senior partner, Charles, interfered with his business. Mrs. Myles felt she expressed a real rather than an imaginary point in her self-defense. Both felt they were more realistic than imaginary about their differences. This agreed with the counselor's observation that the fight issue was real and authentic to them. There was no phony game-playing.

2. The "injury" dimension rated "one minus." He felt the round was fair. She differed. She felt that he had used below-the-belt, dirty tactics when he referred to personal failures in her past, especially since she had overcome these problems by her own efforts, an achievement for which he gave her no recognition. Instead, he gave Charles most of the credit for her own growth; she felt that was unfair, too.

3. The "involvement" dimension rated "two plus." Clearly, neither partner was passive or evasive. Both were actively involved in the engagement.

4. We also rated this round "two plus" for the "responsibility" category. Both partners owned up to carrying a gripe. They displayed their "beef" openly, taking responsibility for engaging each other in a fight round. They did not call front men into play. They didn't quote any outsider. They did not even ask the counselor to back them up, which is unusually good style for a couple just starting out in fight training.

5. In the "humor" category, this round was rated "two minus." Each partner ridiculed and mocked the other. Their

THE FIGHT EFFECTS PROFILE

	+	0	−
1 **HURT**	hurt decreased		hurt increased
2 **INFORMATION**	new		old (redundant)
3 **POSITIONAL MOVEMENT**	ground gained		ground lost
4 **CONTROL**	increased		decreased
5 **FEAR**	decreased		increased
6 **TRUST**	increased (dependable)		decreased (undependable)
7 **REVENGE**	forgiven		stimulated
8 **REPARATION**	active		none
9 **CENTRICITY**	more central		less central
10 **SELF-COUNT** **(autonomy)**	more self-value		less self-value
11 **CATHARSIS**	released		inhibited
12 **COHESION-AFFECTION**	closer		more distant

humor was sarcastic and hurtful. It increased—rather than relieved—the tensions between them.

6. Next, we rated this round "two plus" in the "expression" category. Both partners were fairly open with each other. They were not aware of holding back any feelings to make an impression or to manipulate one another.

7. The couple was also rated "two plus" in the "communication" category. Both spoke out freely and clearly. They understood what the other was saying, even when they violently disagreed. The counselor felt that they failed to understand all the feelings behind their overly expressed words but it would have been too much to expect full understanding in a first round and without further training.

8. In the "directness" category this round was rated "two minus." Even though both partners were open in their expression and free-flowing in their communication, they both failed to focus directly on alternatives for change. Both seemed hung up on old, rather than current, here-and-now concerns. They also tended to attack or defend Charles, to fight over Charles, the third person. They criticized or praised the way he treated them. They failed to deal directly with the way Charles affected their swing with one another and with the way they use Charles to get at each other. They had never faced the crucial loyalty issue head-on.

9. For specificity we also rated this round "two minus." Both partners failed to specify sufficiently what turned them on and what turned them off. Both displayed a tendency to pin labels on each other. In fact, when we discussed this fight round they freely admitted that they had seized upon specific actions of their partner—actions they had found disagreeable—and broadened them into generalized character traits which they attributed to the partner. For example, Barbara's "bitching" about Charles's supposed interference with her marriage was generalized by her husband when he claimed that she had a generally "bitching" nature. Gerry's admiration of his senior partner was interpreted by his wife as "sycophancy." And her sensitivity to social approval was escalated by her husband when he charged that she was "other-directed."

In sum, Mr. and Mrs. Myles accumulated 11 plus (bonding) points and seven minus (alienating) points for their fight style. We consider this a good style rating that already reflects their early training, brief as it was. Both partners, however, had certainly left considerable room for improvement, especially in the categories of "directness" and "specificity." They also had a lot to learn about fighting fairly and hitting above the belt.

Like many partners who care deeply about each other, Gerry and Barbara did not clearly recognize their power of hurting each other. Just because they love each other, and say so, they assume that everything they say is good for each other and is therefore automatically good-willed and fair game. Actually, as anyone could plainly see, neither one was above playing "dirty pool." Gerry rubbed in her past. Barbara attacked his obvious attachment to Charles as a comforting fatherlike figure in his life. And their humor definitely was not funny.

So much for this couple's style, which is only half the story of constructive fighting. The outcome of a fight, as of a good meal, is not only in the eating but in the internal after-effects. And the after-effects of this fight round between the Myleses, as we found out 48 hours after the encounter, were not so good. Their fight effects profile looked as shown on the following page.

The fight effects profile for Gerry and Barbara Myles shows that both recorded negative effects in four categories (Injury, Information, Positional Movement, and Centricity). For three categories they both registered positive effects (Decreased Fear, Increased Self-Value, and Catharsis). Zero (neutral) effects—i.e., no changes—were registered by both husband and wife in three areas (Revenge, Reparation, and Cohesion). Split-effects (i.e., where the two partners registered different after-effects) resulted in the two intimacy dimensions of Trust and Control. We score split-effects as "one minus," so our total score was seven negative versus three positive.

Here is how this couple arrived at the scores for each numbered category.

1. They agreed to rate their fight "two minus" for the "Hurt" category. Both male (M) and female (F) partners felt psychologically reduced by their mutual name calling: "sycophant" vs. "other-directed," ex-alcoholic, and so on. They also felt hurt by the lack of mutual respect for their respective anxieties about the role that Charles, the third man in this loyalty battle, is playing in their relatively young marriage. From the third year on, new couples usually cannot remain totally self-sufficient. Hopefully, they will stay happy with each other. But they should reach out into the world and build an emotionally and intellectually stimulating environment, a social feeding-ground for their new family. For Gerry and Barbara the "loyalty" issue obviously concerns

THE FIGHT EFFECTS PROFILE

for the first round of Mr. and Mrs. Myles' Loyalty Fight

F = FEMALE PARTNER   M = MALE PARTNER   F.M. = BOTH PARTNERS

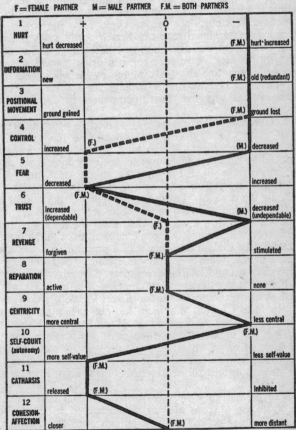

	+	O	−
1 HURT	hurt decreased		(F.M.) hurt increased
2 INFORMATION	new		(F.M.) old (redundant)
3 POSITIONAL MOVEMENT	ground gained		(F.M.) ground lost
4 CONTROL	increased (F.)		(M.) decreased
5 FEAR	decreased		increased
6 TRUST	increased (dependable) (F.M.)		(M.) decreased (undependable)
7 REVENGE	forgiven	(F.M.)	stimulated
8 REPARATION	active	(F.M.)	none
9 CENTRICITY	more central		less central
10 SELF-COUNT (autonomy)	more self-value		(F.M.) less self-value
11 CATHARSIS	(F.M.) released (F.M.)		inhibited
12 COHESION-AFFECTION	closer	(F.M.)	more distant

(Broken lines indicate female partner's views for categories where she differed with the male partner's views)

how much influence should be allotted to Charles who had earlier been of such crucial matchmaking, match-sanctioning and couple-confirming significance. Gerry is still very fond of, close to, and emotionally and economically dependent on Charles; he is hurt that his wife does not find this good and proper. When she does not respect Charles as "lovable" he tries to manipulate her into sharing and confirming his admiration of Charles by "slapping" and "kicking" his wife in that direction. This hurts her and backfires. Now Barbara is more than ever determined to wean herself away (and hopefully him, too) from the old emotional ties with Charles. She is hurt by his lack of respect for her drive toward self-value and autonomy. She also feels injured by his willingness to put her down in defense of his feelings for Charles. These are some reasons why the "hurt" component in this fight is so strong.

2. Gerry and Barbara readily agreed to score this round "two minus" for "Information" because no really solid new information emerged. If anything, Barbara was somewhat shocked to find that her husband not only looked on her in an unfavorable light but that he might treat her in the condescending way she had come to expect from Charles.

3. In the area of "Positional Movement" the couple also had no trouble agreeing on a score of "two minus." Their situation seemed to them less clear after the fight than it was previously. They are now more confused, even dumbfounded, because they did not come up with a position on how Charles should fit into their own intimate system. Their thinking has gone underground. Barbara wonders: "Doesn't he want me to become more independent, more self-reliant? He always accuses me of being too 'other-directed.' Well, *I* don't want any more of Charles! Why does he want me to be so nice to Charles? I don't understand it at all." Gerry also seems puzzled. He thinks: "Surely she must see it's important for the three of us—Charles, her, and me—to get along so I can be productive and successful in my career. She behaves as if she doesn't belong in this scheme of things. How is that possible?"

4. In the category of "Control," Gerry and Barbara could not agree on a score and so we registered a "one minus" rating. Barbara scored positive on this item for herself. She felt she had gained in control. By standing up to her husband she felt that his respect for her was increasing. She also felt she had achieved firmer control because she had successfully asserted her feelings in self-defense against his low blows. She stood her ground and was not intimidated or blackmailed by

her husband's reference to her weaknesses or by his gunny-sacked accusations concerning her past mistakes. She also let her husband know that she cannot simply order her into a new attitude toward Charles and that her husband cannot readily control her authentic distrust, even distaste, of Charles's cold, explosive ways with people, especially herself. Her husband, to the contrary, felt some loss of his usually considerable power over Barbara, especially when she refused to sanction and confirm Charles's growth-stimulating, benevolent value to her in the past. He was considerably annoyed and pained by this loss of control.

5. In the "Fear" department, Gerry and Barbara did not hesitate to rate themselves "two plus." They showed some of their "fangs" and survived. They did not scare or cower. Rather, both expressed their differences openly without any loss in closeness. Both partners reported that whatever fears they may have had, before the fight, about bringing up and facing up to the delicate "Charles-role" issue, were reduced by this encounter. It proved to them that the issue of Charles is indeed negotiable and need not be kept under phony wraps of tact and discretion.

6. In the "Trust" column, Gerry and Barbara registered a split vote, i.e., "one minus." He felt no change. She scored "minus." She felt forced to become a little more suspicious because of his "gunny-sacking" of her old guilts. She had long ago confessed everything to him and during their courtship he had been very understanding about her past. Now it turned out that he felt their courtship had had therapeutic overtones. He had assigned her the role of psychiatric "patient." In effect, he surmised that she had been saying to him: "Honey, you just watch how great my growth-potential will be if you marry me!" Under those conditions he seemed to be all for her. He was even proud of her. Now she wonders about the wisdom of exposing her "guts" to him so completely in the future.

7. In the "Revenge" category this couple agreed on a "zero" score. Neither mate felt that, in this round, there was anything to forgive or to hold a grudge against.

8. They also scored themselves "zero" in the "Reparation" column. Neither had an impulse to offer, or receive, apologies or other restitutional messages.

9. For "Centricity" Gerry and Barbara rated themselves "two minus." The opposite of occupying a place of central significance in the partner's heart is tangentiality—being pushed into a more peripheral position. This is what both felt was happening as an aftereffect of their fight. They felt a

certain depression, a sense of loss of significance. They had to infer that Charles was also of central significance to each of them. This indicates that the relationship to third parties may at times be as important or even more important than the intimate relationship to one another. In this case, Gerry clearly is not exclusively concerned with his wife's welfare. He thinks of himself *and* Charles. The very fact that the husband is so concerned with how his wife could ruin his emotionally and economically important relationship to Charles demonstrates to the wife that her private significance to him is conditional; it depends significantly on how creatively she manages their social involvement with a third person.

10. In the "Self-Count" department the couple decided to rate themselves "two plus." Both felt somewhat self-enhanced by this fight. They felt they had shown reason, justification, and healthy aggression. They felt no guilt and no need for self-reproach. The increase in their self-esteem was also related to their ability for owning up, for leveling with each other. There was no yielding, colluding, or accommodating.

11. For the "Catharsis" factor, the couple also quickly agreed on a "two plus" score. Both partners were emotionally highly involved in the fight. Both got quite hot under the collar and let go of authentic wrath. As a consequence, they felt better. They had relieved themselves of some of the frustrations that they had long secretly harbored about Charles. They felt so much better just after the fight that they were able to joke and laugh about it on the drive home. Then they stayed up late and made love. They knew nothing was really settled. The good feeling about the *process* of the fight, in spite of its not very creative *content*, was due to the relatively constructive style in which it was fought.

12. The obvious score for "Cohesion" was "zero." This is a very cohesive, well-communicating couple and this fight round did not make any significant change in their feelings of closeness or distance. The administered "slaps" and "kicks" were absorbed without increasing the distance between the partners and without creating a need for making up.

We can now piece together a fairly reliable picture of the constructive versus the destructive *elements* of Gerry and Barbara Myles's fight. While the M.'s scored 11 positive (bonding) points and seven negative (alienating) points on their fight style profile, their fight *effects* profile is far less benign. It shows three positive points and seven negative. Nevertheless, this is a reasonably respectable showing for beginner trainees because good style can absorb the bad after-effects of a fight to a surprising degree.

This is possible because intimates tend to forgive and forget almost any malign content of a fight; but they always remember crude, hurtful, or unfair fight style or process. The ancient dictum operates: "It ain't what you say, it's the way you say it." Fight training therefore concentrates strongly on the development of good style. Luckily, smooth fighting is an eminently teachable art, as Gerry and Barbara Myles continued to discover.

After they discussed the aftereffects of their first fight round with the counselor and four other couples who participated in a fight-training seminar, they were asked to return for further sessions as a couple. Before they met with the counselor for the first of these meetings they were asked to come to the Institute's playback room to witness their first fight round as recorded on video tape. An assistant instructed them:

"Please look and listen carefully for the *way* you talk to each other. Try to hear and see the communication *process* that passes back and forth between you. Get a feeling for your style of arguing with each other. Try to ignore the content of the fight as much as possible. It's best to pay no attention to *what* the fight was about, and concentrate on *how* you fought. Stop the playback any time when one of you feels like discussing the fight style with the other. When you see Dr. Bach after the playback, you and he will be able to come up with better ways to fight the next round. You may take notes if you wish, but please listen and watch very carefully."

We mention both "listening" and "watching" for two reasons. We like to encourage trainees to watch each other's reactions while they witness the tape. Seeing, as well as hearing, oneself fight with one's mate and being able to observe one's own manner and emotions while engrossed in the heat of argument is a most educational experience. We recommend that each of our trainee couples watch themselves fight at least once after their anger has cooled and they can judge their own behavior more judiciously.

Here is what happened after Gerry and Barbara Myles had witnessed their first round on tape:

DR. BACH: Do you both agree that the first fight round we had in this office last week was not very constructive in its aftereffects?

SHE: Well, Doctor, I don't know about your charts and

all, but I think that fight was pretty good for us! We haven't stopped talking about all this ever since that first session.

HE: Yeah, but we haven't settled a damned thing. You still bitch about my dealings with Charles, and that still interferes with my work. Frankly, I don't see what's good about that!

SHE (*ignoring husband and addressing the doctor*): What I meant, Doctor, is that he (*pointing an accusing finger at her husband while looking at Dr. B.*) usually stops talking long before that.

DR. B: Long before what?

SHE: Well, remember the point on the tape when he started becoming a clown?

DR. B: You mean the line about "I love steaks"?

SHE: Precisely. He always starts kidding or clowning when we get too close to the truth. And then he withdraws with some sarcastic exit remark!

DR. B: Why are you complaining about him to *me?*

SHE: Well, isn't that what I am supposed to be doing, airing my gripes?

DR. B: Sure, but not to me! What good is it to air your gripes to me? *He* is the one you're living with. Go ahead, address yourselves directly to one another— and fight it out with the purpose of locating static noises in your communication system, or other defensive strategies you use with each other. Then, after you locate them, you're supposed to negotiate a clear-cut agreement to stop using them and start leveling, zeroing in, owning up, facing and sharing what turns you on, what turns you off and what each of you can do right now and from now on to turn each other more on and less off!

SHE (*directly and heatedly toward husband*): OK, your clowning and your sarcastic exits not only turn me off; they *bug* me.

HE (*sweetly reasonable*): That's the idea, dear. It's my way of slapping you down when you persist in maintaining a position that's ridiculous and untenable.

SHE (*scoffing*): What position is that supposed to be?

HE (*superior*): Oh, come on! Don't ask! You know perfectly well what I mean.

SHE (*triumphantly pointing finger at husband*): Foul! I got you! You static-maker, you! (*Toward the doctor.*) He is not supposed to assume what I know or how much I know, but find out directly from me. Isn't that right, Dr. Bach?

DR. B: Sure, but there's something else to be considered, too. You're too delighted to be "catching" him doing something bad. Why don't you tell him how you feel right now when he does that?

SHE (*to husband*): It cools me when you don't try to learn anything here. I know what you have in mind. You want to make me "the heavy" so the doctor is going to pronounce me a nut.

HE (*red-faced and furious*): Stop! Foul! Foul! Foul! Who's telling whom what who has in mind? You not only make false assumptions. You're attributing hidden motives to me! You're trying to tell me what I supposedly have in my mind. Come on, now! Maybe you think yourself that you're the nutty one.

SHE : Don't be ridiculous! Of course you're the nut.

(*Both start to laugh at their evasive sparring for position. But after the laughter there ensued a long silence.*)

DR. B: We're laughing about something that's not really funny. But maybe you should laugh and ridicule each other even harder. Maybe that would help to get you both down to brass tacks. Have you ever satirized each other?

COUPLE: How do you mean?

DR. B: I mean you could deliberately make fun of some of the ways you have for communicating with each other. Take that exit-clowning. (*Toward wife.*) Have you ever mimicked him and given him a feedback in caricature of how that act looks to you when you see him doing it?

SHE (*startled, toward doctor*): Is that good for his ego? He'd get so sore he'd knock my block off! (*Toward husband.*) Wouldn't you, honey?

HE (*thoughtful*): No, not really—not if I can do it to you, too. I often feel like giving you a good imitation of how you sound to me when you're bitching.

SHE: Here's how *you* look when you walk out of an argument. (*She demonstrates in silent pantomime how he exits with a smirk.*)

HE (*he grins, somewhat embarrassed but acknowledging*): OK, kiddo, I got the message. You needn't rub it in any further.

SHE: Well, then, will you stop it and start staying with me when we fight the next time?

HE: OK. I agree. Now let's not waste the doctor's time. Let's get to work on ourselves. What's on my mind—and I mean it—is this: I'm afraid you won't stop interfering with my work. Just thinking about that really turns me off.

SHE: Sometimes I think you want to be turned off. . . .

Gerry and Barbara subsequently fought four more rounds of their loyalty fight. Gradually they became acquainted with the complete range of fight rules and at-home exercises. Since then, they have ,attended two Institute reunions. Once a year we rent cottages in Palm Springs for anywhere between 50 and 100 alumni who bring each other up to date on their progress and new problems. At last report Mr. and Mrs. Myles had achieved a distinctly better marriage as a result of fight training. They had broken out of their post-courtship stalemate and, for the first time, fashioned a life for themselves as a couple.

Gerry learned that he had to demonstrate greater independence from Charles, his friend and boss, in order to gain his wife's respect. When his open worship of Charles decreased, Barbara was able to stop nagging her husband about him. Yet her own sense of independence increased considerably and the couple's relationship with Charles did not deteriorate. This was largely the result of a growing friendship between Barbara and the new wife Charles married shortly after the Myleses graduated from fight training. Both wives attend adult education classes together. The couples are on friendly terms as a foursome. They also know how to keep their distance because each pair has a satisfying life of its own.

Gerry and Barbara bought a new house and had a second child. They are socially popular. At home they fight just about daily. Their fights, however, have reached new and higher ground. Neither Gerry nor Barbara has too much spare time and each has four times as many ideas as they need to fill their leisure hours. Most of their fighting is about whose ideas are better and they often bring in friends to help settle the more or less constant arguments. Best of all, the couple noticed that, with rare exceptions, they no longer hurt each other when they argue.

"I'm no longer afraid to speak up to my husband," Barbara told us. "And he no longer closes his ears. So now I no longer pick on him."

Loyalty, of course, is only one of many fight issues that boil up between intimates. Indeed, there are far more of these issues than even the most versatile intimate fighters realize.

15. Fighting Over "Trivia"

In one of their public-opinion surveys some years ago the pollsters of the Louis Harris organization asked couples across the country, "Most of the time, what is the biggest single source of friction between you and your spouse?" The two main fight issues mentioned by husbands and wives were money spending and child raising. However, as a close third they listed a variety of remarkably trivial-sounding complaints. Husbands objected to too much petty criticism from wives. Wives complained because their husbands were too sloppy around the house. One husband remarked:

"My wife is always after me over nothing: clothes, cleaning up the yard, this and that. I stopped listening years ago."

This typical fight-evader had elected to tune out on a vast amount of strategic intelligence about his marriage. But so, strangely enough, do most intimates who daily engage in epic battles about such matters as burning the toast, misplacing a car key, setting the clock, airing the dog, forgetting an errand, arriving late, arriving early, and so on and on.

There are four psychologically important reasons for this amnesia:

1. In the heat of battle, as discussed earlier, intimates cannot think as clearly as they usually do; or they may react to an angry voice like an ostrich sticking his head in the sand.

2. Shame represses memory. In the calm of dawn's early light it is easy to recognize the disproportion of the emotional stress that the partners experienced over such *apparent* trivialities. The embarrassment during the Monday morning quarterbacking goes so deep that partners frequently apologize for each other ("Oh, he was so mad he didn't know what he was saying"). They may even seek escape in after-the-fact evasion ("I didn't mean it. Don't mind me. I was so mad I don't even remember what I said.").

3. A trivial issue may be a decoy. It may be part of a broader—but usually not consciously schemed—battle plan. It may be an excuse to get angry just to scare the partner; or

to make a big impression on him; or test the limits of the bond snap line (How much anger can he take?). More likely, the trivial issue camouflages a signal that calls for sensitive decoding. Forgetting to run an errand may mean to a partner, "You don't interest me any more"; telling an off-color story at a party may be interpreted as, "You deliberately try to humiliate me." These messages are often exaggerated by injustice collectors. They lie in wait, prepared to seize upon any trivial act as proof of deeper villainy. To them, being seven minutes late to an appointment proves habitual neglect; talking to another woman at a party is taken as evidence of secret philandering.

4. The substance of the trivial issue itself really is trivial and therefore isn't worth remembering! Often it is so absurdly trivial that it would be downright embarrassing to remember having become so upset over "nothing."

Why, then, do intimates experience so much anguish when they fight over "trivia?" Why does a pair of pants turn into a "federal case?" Why do *strangers* often fight violently (perhaps even lethally) over important matters but almost never over trivial ones? There are three explanations:

1. Intimates care deeply about each other; strangers rarely do. Intimates are forever scanning each other for information about their "temper" or the "good" or "bad" nature. They hold hypotheses about where they stand with each other and, like scientists, they like to check them out. This is an intuitive technique and a constructive one as long as it is not overdone in the exaggerated, vindictive manner of the spouse-watchers.

2. The intensity of fighting over trivia is often the result of the cumulative effect of "gunny-sacking." Between intimates and non-intimates alike, a minor disappointment is an equally trivial drop in the bucket of life's frustrations. The crucial difference is that the bucket into which intimates drop a trivial grievance is often already full. Any new stress, however small, will increase the reservoir of tensions until something has to spill over. Trivial bickering, therefore, functions as a safety valve in enduring intimate relationships. If trivia are dismissed often enough as "not worth having a fight about" and all minor frustrations are suppressed in the interests of domestic peace and harmony, there is eventually bound to be a major explosion, perhaps over trivia, perhaps over something far from trivial. In either event, there is too much heat and not enough light.

3. Between intimates, as the discerning reader will have gathered, trivia often is anything but trivial. It is a kind of emotional shorthand that intimates develop in the course of

thrashing out an enduring relationship. With important exceptions, a specific fight over trivia can be a clue to a more basic underlying conflict. Only the apparent fight issue is trivial; the emotions it arouses are quite likely to be serious.

What serious message is being conveyed in the following seemingly absurd domestic tiff?

It is Friday morning. Sam Rhodes, a certified public accountant, is about to leave for work. His wife, Hope, is making the beds.

HE: I hope I can get away for a game of golf with Charlie tomorrow.

SHE: Why not? Let me help you get ready for it. Is there anything you need?

HE: Say, do you mind taking my golf pants to the cleaners this morning and have them done on the "one-day special"? I have to have them back tonight if I'm going to play tomorrow.

SHE: Sure, It'll be fun for you. You always enjoy playing with Charlie.

HE: Be sure to have the pants back! They're the only ones I'm comfortable in.

SHE (*annoyed*): Why do you alway worry about those silly things? Please leave everything like that to me. You should keep your mind free for the office.

(*Now it's Friday evening. Sam comes home after work. Hope is fixing dinner.*)

HE (*cheerful*): Hello, honey! Oh boy, am I glad this week is over! I sure look forward to a good game of golf tomorrow. Did the pants come back from the cleaners?

SHE (*shocked*): No.

HE (*more alarmed than angry*): Should I run down to get them? Maybe you better phone the cleaners so they don't close before I get there!

SHE (*devastated*): Oh, I'm so sorry, darling! I completely forgot to take them! Wasn't that stupid of me? I had to go shopping anyway and I could have done it so easily. I even went by the cleaner's this morning. I just forgot. I really am so sorry!

HE (*very angry*): That's great! In other words, you don't keep your promises. That's really irresponsible! You just don't care about me any more. You just ruined my weekend. Thanks loads!

SHE (*shouting*): How can you say that! You know how much I love you! You're cruel! You hurt me very

much by what you just said. (*She cries.*) I don't
know why I put up with a selfish, ungrateful man
like you!

Good fighters don't fan the flames of such a conflagration,
as these contenders did, thereby setting off an appalling
explosion that ruined their weekend; nor would they find it
rewarding to pour water on the fire by resignedly accepting
the wife's forgetfulness as "sloppy housekeeping." After they
learned to level with each other in fight training, Sam and
Hope took up the issue of the not-so-trivial pants once again.
Here is how it went the second time around:

HE (*stating position and making demand*): I hope you
don't mind if I play golf tomorrow with Charlie,
and if I'm going to play tomorrow I need these
pants cleaned today.

SHE (*checking out*): You really want to play golf tomorrow?

HE (*confirming*): Yes, I think it's a reasonable request,
after a week's hard work. I want the exercise and
Charlie is fun to play with.

SHE (*stating her position and making counterdemand*):
Well, it's reasonable *if* you also spent some of your
spare weekend time with me and the kids.

HE (*checking out her proposal*): Can I play golf with
Charlie tomorrow if we do something together as a
family Sunday?

SHE (*leveling about what she's really after*): Yes, I want
you to take all of us to the beach and out to
dinner. I think that's a reasonable distribution of
your leisure time, don't you?

HE (*pinpointing areas of agreement and disagreement*):
Well, to be perfectly honest, I prefer staying home
Sundays and watching the ball game on TV to
milling around on the beach or in restaurants.

SHE (*probing*): Under what conditions *would* you spend
some time in family activities? Or can't you stand
to go out with us? I know you like to stay home
but I'd like us to go out. Who is going to have his
way?

HE (*proposing conditions of agreement*): Let's alternate
between my way, your way, and then develop a
third way: a new way of spending family time that
might be fun for all of us.

SHE (*checking him out*): In other words, every third

weekend I have my way, and you'll really cooperate?

HE (*committing himself to a position for time being*): Yes, but this weekend I want to play golf with Charlie Saturday, watch baseball on Sunday . . .

SHE (*interrupting*): . . . and take us out to dinner Sunday night! That's great! I'll have your golf pants clean and ready for your game tomorrow.

When this couple made a systematic, good-willed attempt to get to the bottom of the pants issue, they found that the pants could hardly have mattered less. The real issue was a conflict between the wife's and the husband's differing notions over how to spend their leisure time. Once they recognized the true issue, they could negotiate their differences without much trouble.

On other occasions, the bone of contention may be less obvious. Suppose a husband tells his wife, "Why in hell can't you match the socks in my drawer?" This explosion may hide the dark husbandly suspicion that she is applying the strategy of deliberate "disorder" and is telling him, "You don't love me enough" or "You like to torture me" or even "I think you like me to depend on you just so you can let me down." She may also be using "disorder" to signal him, "I'm tired of you being a helpless little boy" or "I don't respect you for expecting me to do this, even if I offered to; you should be beyond this sort of thing." More likely, the fight is really trivial. She is only signaling him, "I'm damned sick and tired of being your servant."

The only way to find out whether the socks issue is trivial or not is to ask for a formal fight engagement. The husband can then flush out the underlying trouble: "What is it, darling? Are you just trying to keep me irritated?" If the answer is that the wife has a maid complex, a solution can be sensibly negotiated. Perhaps she should have paid help for a few hours a week. The husband should realize that this solution reduces the source of the wife's irritation but won't eliminate it. It is up to him to show his wife in new ways that she rates as a person with him, not just as a maid; that being a maid in the socks department doesn't make her a maid anywhere else.

Suppose the sock is on the other foot. Suppose the husband litters the house with socks, cigar stubs, newspapers, and tools and is then upset if the house is in disarray and tells his wife, "You're a lousy housekeeper!" Then it's up to the wife to do the decoding. Does it mean that he feels she doesn't love him enough or respect him enough?

Chances are the issue is not that serious: the husband is probably only signaling that coming home at night is no fun for him; that he had to take orders at the office all day and now wants to have somebody to boss around. Perhaps the wife should let him have this pleasure up to a reasonable point. At any rate, she shouldn't—as some frustrated housewives do—leave the vaccum cleaner and ironing board ostentatiously displayed in the evening to show him silently, "See, I'm doing my best!

Actually, in investigating fights that break out when husbands come home from work at night, we found that many men get plenty of aggression release through conflicts on their jobs while housewives only have the kids to yell at and usually feel guilty about getting too angry at them too often. It is rewarding for a husband in these cases to make adequate listening and sympathizing allowances for wifely carping about what a "terrible day" she had at home while he was kidding around with the fellows at the office and drinking it up at a delicious expense-account lunch.

Among major fight issues that are more serious than they appear and are therefore often erroneously downgraded as trivial are what we call nesting fights. Man is a territorial animal and the maintenance of cooperative nesting behavior is an intricate art. If a wife says, "I'm sick of apartments, I want a house in the suburbs," she is probably not talking about real estate but about her image of herself and her joint image with her husband. Furniture fights ("I don't want wall-to-wall carpeting; I don't want our house to look like a hotel lobby!") also provide admirable illustrations of why nesting is a danger zone.

Each partner usually has his own taste in furniture. He is likely to be cagey about disclosing it. If his taste turns out to be tasteless, this becomes embarrassingly visible to the partner and even outsiders. He may therefore maneuver the partner into becoming responsible for a particular purchase; or at least try to make the partner co-responsible for getting an item he himself wouldn't quite have guts enough to get. The trouble is that most people's nesting image tends to be fuzzy. Also, most people tend to be errorphobic; instead of learning from a mistake, they prefer to avoid the experience and find a scapegoat for any ensuing problems. Finally, for many people such items as tables, lamps, and (especially) pictures are really extensions of themselves. So furniture can become an adult security blanket that is sometimes more important than clothes—a fact well known to furniture salesmen.

Buying a car can also be emotion-charged. Even though people don't live in a car all the time, it visibly displays life style, tastes, and status. According to tradition, the car is a masculine symbol. The wife may select it but only subject to the husband's veto and the husband is usually deferred to in relative peace.

In the case of interior decorating at home, traditionally a feminine domain, the intimate involvement is far more amorphous. The interior of a house reflects a family's taste as well as who wears the pants. This becomes evident in the following conversation that took place when a wife called her husband at his office:

SHE: I finally found the right chair for your study.
HE: Where?
SHE: Here!
HE: Where are you?
SHE: At Macy's.
HE: Gee, I wish I could come down.
SHE: I wish you would.

This wife wanted to make her husband co-responsible for a purchase that she wasn't too sure about, or at least to protect herself against the charge that she didn't consult him about an item that mattered very much to him, and in a very personal way. Such husbands should come out leveling and say, "I care!" and their wives should admit, "I'm afraid to make a mistake."

The solution is to define the decision-making authority in advance, to establish the bargaining flexibility, the degree of freedom, and the finality of decision. If the wife is convinced that the husband has dreadful taste and he then gives her veto power, the result may be a United Nations-type stalemate. They could wind up buying nothing. Many incompletely furnished houses reflect such a responsibility stalemate rather than financial difficulties.

A complete change of nests may be symptomatic of most serious difficulty in a marriage. Quite a few troubled couples maintain unrealistic expectations of the benefits they might derive from moving. They hope that a change of scene might overcome some of their psychological problems. In point of fact, the opposite usually happens. Nesting changes are unsettling to people. Tensions increase. It's a case of *un*familiarity breeding contempt. This pattern is so common that we call it

"Realtor's Delight." We have seen many divorce cases where a change of nests was not the hoped-for salvation but the final blow to a wobbly marriage. Real estate agents and lawyers were the sole beneficiaries of these unrealistic attempts to solve serious intimacy problems by crude materialistic shortcuts.

Not infrequently, a ridiculously tiny annoyance becomes a conditional stimulus and ignites a disproportionately serious conflict. This happens when a trivial point reminds a partner of a nontrivial issue that is gnawing at him. In such a case the trivia becomes a cue to him that the partnership is out of balance.

This is what happens in the fights for optimal distance. (See Chapter 2.)

Sometimes it is fruitless to look for serious motives behind a trivial fight because such motives may simply not exist. In such cases it may be destructive to dig into a partner with investigative questions. Indeed, the word "why?" is the most overused word in marriage. Much of the time nobody could uncover the real, way deep-down answer to why a partner did something; and if anybody did find out, it might not help to know. Lively participation in the give-and-take of the here-and-now pays off best.

How can anybody know when a trivial fight doesn't need to be decoded for underlying causes? Our first suggestion is that students learn to recognize, and to ignore, the useless volcanic eruptions of the Vesuvius.

Trivia can also be dismissed as trivial when it is subject of a fun fight. This is a fight without real issues, as when two puppies tease each other aggressively but without a bone. A gesture or inflection may be the giveaway whether a fight is for real or for fun. The husband may say, for example, "You *mean* it?" If the wife says, "Sure I *mean* it" in a certain way, both are likely to recognize that there is no issue.

Most fun fights rage over pseudo-issues. Are the 1969 cars better than the 1968 cars? Did Adlai Stevenson lose the presidency in 1952 because he wasn't married? Did the husband (or wife) miss the point of last night's movie? These are fun fights because nobody has a great stake in the outcome.

Fun fights have sensible functions. They help prevent boredom. They can entertain an audience. They may serve to get others—especially children—involved in a family activity ("What do you think, Jimmy?"). They may provide vicarious exercise and release for everybody's natural aggressive proclivities; typically, such an exercise surfaces as "good-willed sadism" in a game of wits.

The bridge table is a fine place for such a game because almost everybody enjoys a hostility-releasing laugh at somebody who is losing. Incidentally, our trainee couples are always urged to play *against* each other. This allows for a healthy aggression outlet and minimizes the more cutting hostilities of a partnership situation ("What's gotten *into* you? How *often* have I told you not to . . .").

One completely unexpected pay-off of fighting over trivia became apparent as a result of a strategic error during early experiments with fight training. Originally, trainees were asked not to fight over silly, irrational nothings or, if they did, to translate the trivial into deep, underlying issues. As a result, some of our early graduates become extremely efficient at settling conflicts rationally, swiftly, and reasonably in the best logical-rational style of formal debaters. These couples found not only peace but some estrangement.

One of these couples announced proudly that they were no longer arguing at all because they negotiated all issues and came to agreements. A fascinating group discussion ensued.

GROUP MEMBER: You know, both of you sound as if you're missing the fighting.

HE: Oh no, not me! I'm tickled pink that she's become a logical and rational person. We can make sane decisions about real problems now. She doesn't pick on me for silly things . . . well, hardly at all. I like that!

SHE: Yes, we don't yell at each other any more. It's much better this way.

OTHER GROUP MEMBER: You still sound sad, almost depressed. And you look pouty, both of you. (*Silence.*)

HE (*after exchanging "checking-out" glances with his wife*): Well, since we stopped fighting we've also pretty much stopped sex (*group laughter*).

SHE: Everything is so nice and quiet and rational and nothing is happening in our sex life. I just don't feel anything. Neither does he, and that's very unusual for us.

HE: Yeah! We usually made it three or four times a week, but that was during the good old . . . bad and noisy times. (*He laughs sarcastically.*) During the last three weeks or so . . . nothing! Just peaceful coexistence!

SHE: I don't understand it! Now that we get along better, our sex life has suffered. Why is that?

DR. BACH: The group's observation was correct, you are sad. Do you miss the fighting?

BOTH HE AND SHE: Oh no! Those fights were vicious and stupid. I don't want to go back to that.

DR. B: OK. I think you're right and I don't think you need to go back to fight in your old nasty way ever again.

HE: Fine and dandy. But how're we going to get back together again in bed?

DR. B: Well, does it seem to you that some kind of fighting, perhaps playful fighting, is sexually stimulating to both of you?

We learned from this and similar discussions by other couples that the most successful intimates don't suppress but allow for trivial bickering and even major outbursts over "nothing." The pay-off comes when they make up and the mood changes from "stay away" to "come close."

Lovers and spouses who don't fight over "nothing" actually miss a great deal. Especially they miss out on the erotically rejuvenating powers of the revived courtship pattern where attraction and repulsion alternate in the familiar cycle of realistic romance: attraction-repulsion, counterattack-chasing, refusing-forgiving, calling back-resistance, and so on. In general, the redundant sameness of rituals doesn't serve the cause of realistic leveling, but this is an exception. We found out the hard way that long-term intimates can ill afford to dismiss trivial fighting as something that is beneath them.

Exactly how does trivial fighting stimulate love? The cause-and-effect process operates because the aggressive chase and the assertive claim of the partner as "mine" are themselves a strong stimulus to the arousal and release of love emotions. Conversely, attraction wanes when couples no longer chase or claim each other because they take each other for granted. The security of belonging—and being spoken for—is enjoyed by stable couples at the price of a less intensive love-releasing experience. Contrary to folklore, both sexes like to chase and to be chased at various times, to seduce and be seduced, to claim and to be claimed. And the partner who is, as intimate parlance has it, an "easy lay," always available, always accommodating, robs himself and the pursuer of considerable pleasure—although there are times in an authentic intimate relationship when an "easy lay" can become a comfortable insurance against sexual frustration.

Successful intimates know all this, just as they also know that if either the chase or the resistance is overaggressive, it is likely to boomerang and turn, at the very least, into a major fight about poor communications. It is fortunate, then, that sometimes the very absence of major fight issues makes intimates "pick" fights. They may bicker to upset the marital applecart just to be sure there are no rotten apples in the load.

Trivial fighting deserves encouragement as long as the issues are current, the style is spontaneous, and neither partner attempts to be hurtful or depreciating.

16. The Dream: Courtship Fights

It all starts with the dating-mating game, a notoriously confused and confusing time and place. The moment two strangers are attracted toward one another across the crowded room, each begins to create a set of three mental images that describe his feelings about the other. There is a *you* image of what the attractive stranger will turn out to be like upon closer acquaintance. There is a *me* self-image that determines how I decide to present myself to the new person and how I expect him or her to see me. The mutual attraction generates a *we* image of what it would be like to become emotionally involved with the stranger.

Each potential intimate enters courtship with such a set of three images. They are related like panels on a three-way tailor's mirror, but unfortunately they show not the real person but only biased, wishful reflections of him. Even more inconveniently, the pictures in each panel overlap portions of the other two. Fights over each of these disparate images—and especially over what constitutes a "fair" image—are inevitable.

The sooner these fights begin and the more realistically the courtship fighters level with each other, the better off they will be. But prospective intimates almost never see courtship in this way. As a result, they often carry along vague or distorted *you, me,* and *we* images into their marriages. Disillusionment and pain are the natural consequences.

To meet a prospective intimate is every bit as exciting as it should be. Then, slowly, the *you, me,* and *we* images are fleshed out as the new friends gather random pieces of information about each other. Some of this data is objective, like "This girl has nice legs" or "This man has been married before." But much of it is highly subjective and purely emotional, like "See what a handsome couple we make" or "At last someone appreciates the real me!" These facts and feelings combine to produce the overwhelming sense of excitement and anticipation that can be stirred by a fresh encounter with a new and interesting person.

But even among the most sincere and upright people, camouflaging and faking usually begin at once. She may say to herself, "He might not like me. If I'm going to attract him, I better not be too sexy." He may feel like telling her, "I like you." Instead, his expression of interest may be articulated as, "I don't like the way you do your hair." No wonder new acquaintances so often manage to fool—and quickly lose—each other.

Sometimes a spiral of misunderstandings begins in the most innocent way when a man asks himself, "What does she like about me?" The spiral widens when he gives himself the wrong answer and *then* decides to make the most of his supposed advantage. Listen to the following very early court-ship fight between two college students:

FIRST ROUND

SHE: What kind of wheels do you have?
HE: Why?
SHE: I just wondered.

SECOND ROUND

HE: Do you like the Beatles?
SHE: Do you?
HE: I asked you first.

THIRD ROUND

HE: I still want to know why you're so anxious to know what kind of car I have. (*Unspoken: She may not like convertibles.*)
SHE: Because I am. (*Unspoken: I hope he doesn't have a convertible. It'll ruin my hair.*)

FOURTH ROUND

HE: I'll give you a ride home.
SHE (*seeing convertible*): Oh!
HE: Don't you like convertibles?
SHE: What makes you say that?
HE: (*Unspoken: Hallelujah, she loves convertibles!*)

FIFTH ROUND (*They're in the convertible.*)

HE: Great night, isn't it?
SHE: (*Unspoken: I like him, but I don't want the top*

*down because it would spoil my hair. On the other
hand, if I don't agree it's a nice night he'll think I'm
stupid.* She says nothing, but snuggles up to him.)

This romance has barely begun and is already off on
several wrong feet all at once. The young man is now entitled
to think that she likes convertibles. The young lady is entitled
to think that he likes a display of affection in his car. The
truth is she can't abide convertibles while he relishes his
command of the convertible so much that he likes best to
drive with one hand, the top down, one arm casually leaning
against the left door, his attention focused on a discussion of
his latest athletic triumphs. He likes his snuggling later.

Two lessons can be learned from this classic convertible
fight; first, it's a lot of extra trouble to start a romance under
the cover of camouflage; second, decoding a partner's signals
is hard work. Even experts often can't unmask all the dissem-
bling that goes with the spiral of I-think-that-she-thinks-that-
I-think and the geometric escalation of misunderstandings
that follow. The couple in the convertible will be lucky if
their evening manages to end in the following frustrating
fight for optimal distance:

HE: See you tomorrow!
SHE: No, I don't think so.
HE: Why not?
SHE: Oh, I've got something on.

If he is leveling by that time, which is unlikely, he would
come right out and say, "Hey, I don't like that!" More likely,
he'll say, "But I can call you, can't I?" Or, if he is naïve, he
may try, "Can't I come along?"

The poignant truth is that it is not easy for men or women
to gain a secure place in each other's hearts. The gregariousness of people who present themselves most congenially to
each other, and are "easy to meet," can be a front that hides
fear of rejection, or getting involved, or encroachment, or
engulfment, or sexual inadequacy, or disloyalty to existing
liaisons, or fear of intruding on the world of the other.

The reservations of newly-mets tend to be of two kinds.
First, there is a serious reservation about one's own attractiveness, and not necessarily in the visual or bodily sense
alone, although this is terribly important to most people; it is
more a question of one's own worthiness to be included in
the private world of another person. Second, there is a

question about the other person's acceptability to oneself as a potential partner: "Is he my type?" "How far can I trust him?" "If I love him, will he exploit me?"

It goes without saying that people do not love everything and everybody. They *frame* in mentally what is lovable about another person and what is not. If the other person doesn't want to be loved in the way dictated by our imagery frame, he is "not my type." Human beings have an enormous capacity for pseudo-loving someone who is new and almost unknown; or to adore someone in fantasy at a far distance (like Jesus or a dead hero). But everybody is extremely limited in the capacity to love real and familiar persons, including one's own real self. The limits for giving and receiving love are determined by the love frames that are manufactured in the hearts of intimates.

The reason why "love at first sight" is always so overwhelmingly exciting is that it is an instant, emotional breakthrough, a hysterical brushing aside and an overdetermined denial of reservations about another person. Impulsive "love on sight" dramatically releases one person from the emotional stress of anxiety about being included or rejected by another. It's a delightful experience. But, as everybody knows, it doesn't last very long. With luck, it may signal the start of a genuine new relationship, but the real start and future course of any such intimacy will be determined by the way the couple copes with the first series of hurdles: the acceptance-rejection crisis.

"Falling" in love is always a form of hysteria. It is not a mutual, open exchange of mutual feelings. It is a unilateral interest in one's own feelings, fantasies, and needs for the other person. The other person then responds and calibrates his own interests with those of the "fallen" as best he can. The idea is to keep the fallen on the hook. But nobody accepts anybody unconditionally. Sartre was right when he said, "Hell is other people." And it should come as no surprise to anyone that few people fall in love gracefully. Most are "mad" or "sick" or at least insecure toward partners who have begun to mean a great deal to them. At this point, they are afraid to level and be realistic. The insecurity suffered by newly-loves makes them pose, play games, and manipulate each other in order to reinforce the still tenuous attraction. All new lovers become liars and actors. And even though they are excited, they are usually distraught, too.

As one attractive, unmarried female graduate student once put it in a seminar on intimacy:

STUDENT: Professor Bach, I hate myself most when I am in love.

DR. B: How come? Aren't you happy to love and be loved?

STUDENT: Yes! The way you put it, that would be fine: to love, feeling absolutely loving towards a guy, that would be great; also, feeling his loving me, receiving and accepting being loved. But that's not what I meant.

DR. B: That's what I heard. Correct me!

STUDENT: I meant I become very bitchy when I *fall* in love or when I have *fallen* in love. It's not a secure posture, is it?

DR. B: No, falling is definitely not secure.

STUDENT: When I really like a guy, I become aggressive, fighty, and feisty.

DR. B: Why?

STUDENT: I don't know why. I do know something happens to me. I become more critical, more aggressive ... maybe to test the fellow? (*Pause.*) Or maybe I resent being "hooked." I resent him and myself for *falling* for him. Even the idea of falling for each other is absurd when you come to think about it, and I like him less when he "falls" for me! There's that word again, "falling." It makes me angry, on guard. I don't like to be vulnerable. We can do hurtful things to each other now. I can hurt him just by not returning his calls or any other silly thing we do can be interpreted as "rejection." It's a hateful state to be in and I don't like it. So we become ornery and pick fights with each other.

DR. B: Which is ...?

STUDENT: His vulnerability, like mine, is our love for one another.

DR. B: Then why fight?

STUDENT: I guess it's because I want to play "rejection-insurance." I reject him first so that when he rejects me it will not be real. It's just his defense against my rejection of him.

This girl was reacting rationally toward the partial loss of self which is inherent in the falling-in-love process and can well be terrifying. It is somewhat like rebelling against a loss of freedom. This student was advised to be aggressive about preserving her identity, but that there was no ground for panic.

Suppose her boyfriend wanted to go to the beach. Her tendency might be to say "yes" because she is in love and "no" because she doesn't want him to have his own way. One way out of this trap is to ask the boyfriend, "Are you suggesting the beach just to please me?" Whatever the answer, the girl's follow-up question ought to be to herself: "Is this something I want to do? Is it one of my me-things or not?"

It is natural for intimate fighting to break out whenever Partner A behaves dissonant to (or outside of) the love frame of Partner B or when "A" fails to display "in-frame" behavior clearly enough. "B" will fight to keep "A" within the love frame, either by "kicking" him into it or "slapping" him when he is out of it. "A", loving to be loved by "B", may try to accommodate "B" for fear of rejection. Or he may fight "B" to broaden "B's" love frame because he recognizes that does not realistically reflect his real self. If "A" does not fight "B" for realistic framing, then "A" is guilty of collusion.

Collusion, provoked by self-doubt and fear of rejection, creates a "setup" for much more bitter fighting later on, usually around such themes as "You tricked me," "You're a phony," "You certainly aren't the person I used to love," "I'm terribly disappointed in you," or "How can anybody change so much?" Yet collusion is a common component of the early, romantic courtship phase when eager, reality-shy strangers grasp at all kinds of irrational, untested fantasies about each other.

Quite possibly, this phase, when partners use stereotypes or excessive fantasies in lieu of realistic expectations, may even be essential to get strangers together and help overcome their strangeness. But as a prelude to establishing an enduring intimacy later on, it adds a real problem. By clinging to wishful dreams, lovers subdue fears and ambivalence over new intimacies so they can make a deep commitment to the new partner. But the sooner they can give up courtship dreams and accept realities, the better off they'll be.

At any rate, courting partners should learn to check on their real selves by starting to fight shortly after they become interested in each other. The successful ones never stop. The later-to-be-unsuccessful intimates usually have quiet, courtly courtships. If they are particularly fearful of rejection, they may pretend to be unconditionally pleased with everything the partner does. Their quiet courtesy breeds unchecked assumptions and unrealistic expectations of future bliss. Courtly courters may also use ingratiation, a style of "good-impression-making" which we regard as illicit because it is a strategy of maximizing one's attractiveness by selective self-display and fakery. The ulterior purpose of nonfighting court-ship behavior, of course, is to evade transparency and to avoid authentic encounter for fear that the real self would not fit into the romantic early love frame and that the faker would not be lovable.

Most people who use these and other dishonest tactics are by no means sick or even unusually mean. They are insecure, eager, and perhaps desperate. They know that the best de-fense against the isolation of being a loner is to find a central place in the heart of one intimate partner. But they try to win that place by phony tactics. In the pursuit of centricity lovers harbor irrational ambitions. They try to become the whole world for the partner because the more central one's place is, the more one belongs, the more secure one feels in an indifferent world.

To be of central significance to a partner means to be close; to share the peak moments of a lifetime as well as the trivial ups and downs of daily existence; to be included and brought into the private world of feelings, wants, and fears of the other; to care and fuss about the other's growth, his triumphs and frustrations, his lot in life; to identify and empathize with his ways of being and growing; to be fussed over and cared about by him; to have a partner for sharing one's private concerns about oneself, about life, growing, succeeding, failing; to give and take pleasure and to facilitate in each other a sense of well-being; to enjoy the safety of a private harbor in a sea of troubles.

People are hungry for evidence that they are of central significance to an intimate partner. They don't just desire this role. They need it. Without it, a person would be "a nobody" whose very sanity might eventually become threatened by an absence of self-confirmation. For all but the most hardened loners, game-players, and the psychiatrically sick, it is intoler-able to confess, "I belong to no one."

But before a promising battle for central position in some-body's heart can even begin, one must first fight for accept-ance, for inclusion in the other's world. Almost always, "B" has granted other people important places in his or her heart before "A" ever appeared on the scene. To make a place for himself in "B's" heart, "A" must at first put up with the others. "A" may try to move out the earlier arrivals or reduce them in importance to "B" so that "A" can become No. 1 in the center spot of his partner's heart. But this is not always easy and frequently the effort is unsuccessful, as the following case illustrates.

Lou Cramer, a perpetually worried-looking 43-year-old advertising account executive, divorced two years previously, had been going with his new girl, a divorcée named Sophie Burns, for only three weeks. Desperately upset, he came to fight training and said, "I've just spent the craziest weekend of my life." He reported:

"I want to get married again and succeed the next time around. I almost got pushed into it last weekend. Sophie likes to keep our relationship secret, especially from her roommate. I dated the roommate first but only for a while. Last Saturday at 9:30 A.M. Sophie phoned and said she was going to come right over and stay the weekend. Then her roommate called and said she'd found out about us. When Sophie arrived I told her about it and said, "Now we don't have to hide any more." She looked shocked and sick. She never gets angry, never raises her voice or uses profanity. I said: "You should feel good! Now we're rid of a clandestine situation. The true story is beautiful: We love each other! There's nothing to be ashamed of!" Finally, she mumbled, "If I can't trust you in a little thing like that, how can I trust you with my life? I really loved you but you spoiled it all!" Then she left. I was very disgusted. It was so depressing, the thought of having to go out and find somebody new. The silly dating game, I am so tired of playing that! Then I felt anger: What would I really get if she is that kind of person? Then she telephoned.

SOPHIE (*mellow*): Darling, I'm sorry. I got too upset. I guess it's not that important.

LOU (*perplexed*): How can we get along if you run away every time we have a disagreement. Why can't you stay and have it out?

SOPHIE: I didn't run away. I just wanted to be alone for a few hours.

LOU: How did I know it would only be a couple of hours? I thought we were through!

SOPHIE: I drove to the harbor and sat in my boat and thought and thought. Now I want you. Please come and get me.

(At 4:15 he picked her up.)

SOPHIE: I have to be back by six.

LOU (*flabbergasted*): I thought we were going to spend the weekend!

SOPHIE: I wasn't sure you wanted me. My brother-in-law called and invited me to dinner, so I accepted.

(Lou felt very annoyed and made her drive her own

car. She followed to his place. He fixed a bourbon for her and a Scotch for himself. They started to pet. As always, she aroused him tremendously, but this time she refused intercourse.)

SOPHIE: No, darling, no. Once I have sex I'd want to stay. I can't go over to my sister's house for dinner if I make love to you. Let me go! But I tell you what I'll do. I'll be back just as fast as I can and I'll stay all night.

(At 10:00 P.M. she called. It was evident that she had had a lot to drink.)

SOPHIE (*happily*): We're still eating. There's going to be champagne with dessert. I'm so tired.

LOU (*angry*): You mean you're not coming, after all?

SOPHIE: Oh, no. I'll be over as soon as I can get away.

LOU (*furious*): You're not very dependable, are you?

SOPHIE (*surprised*): But darling, *I love you* and I'll be over. So long. (Lou said to himself: "To hell with her! She should have the guts to tell them that she had an appointment with me!")

At 11:30 P.M. when there was still no sign of Sophie, Lou went to bed. Sunday morning he called a girl in the same building and they played tennis. When he got back to his apartment at 3 P.M. Sophie called.)

SOPHIE (*anxious*): I've been trying to reach you all day!

LOU (*furious*): I simply can't understand what's going on between us. You tell me to spend the weekend with you and then you accept other engagements!

SOPHIE: I'm sorry! It'll never happen again. After this we'll be invited together *as a couple.*

LOU (*resigned*): OK. Come on over. There's a party next door and we're invited.

(At 3:30 P.M. she came over. They necked and she tried to go further, but he did not want to get excited again. He was proud of his self-control. They went next door to the party where she stuck close to Lou and whispered, "I want to be yours. I love you." As they left the party she said she had to go to the yacht club because her boat was being painted and a contract had to be signed.)

LOU: Fine. I'll drive out with you.

SOPHIE (*embarrassed*): I don't think you better. Dick, the fellow who co-owns my boat, will be there.

(Lou began to think Sophie was dating another fellow or maybe two or three. He walked her out to the car. They stood close.)

SOPHIE (*whispering*): I want to be yours. I want to give you babies. I want to cook for you, clean your house. I'll make you happy, very, very happy. I want you to take me now, marry me.

LOU: We've known each other only three weeks. It takes me longer to be sure.

(She seemed irked and drove off to see Dick. On Monday, Sophie called at 6:00 P.M.)

SOPHIE (*sweetly*): How come you didn't call me today?

LOU: Honestly, honey, you confuse me.

SOPHIE: What's so confusing? I want to be your wife.

LOU: But why do you always run off some place?

SOPHIE: I have normal obligations and must take care of them. What are you doing now?

LOU: Oh, nothing. I don't feel well.

(She came over, cooked him some soup, and massaged his back. He got excited. They started to make love. But when he tried to put on a condom, she turned away from him.)

SOPHIE: I'd only do it without that rubber. The rubber hurts.

(He refused. She cooled off, put on her clothes, and was ready to leave.)

SOPHIE (*sad*): You don't seem to really want me as I am.

LOU (*coldly*): I don't want you pregnant, no.

SOPHIE: What's the difference? We'll be married soon, anyhow!

LOU: Let's not go over the same broken record: I'm not ready to get married.

SOPHIE: Because you don't know me well enough?

LOU (*icy*): No, honey, I know you well enough. And I won't marry you because I do know you well enough!

This series of "lost weekend" battles illustrates many of the difficulties experienced by potential intimates in the process of getting together and becoming significant to one another. Here is a couple strongly attracted to one another, starved for true intimacy. Each would like to get married to somebody. During their first three weeks of courtship they thought they had made such a good start that they not only became sexually involved but began to negotiate about marrying!

What went wrong? To begin with, they simply did not give each other sufficient opportunity to be in enough situations together so they could collect adequate impressions and information about each other's lovableness. Wanting and desir-

ing a partner is obviously not enough. In fact, it can become
a blinding force. When an attraction is impulsive, new and
strong, there is a tendency to narrow the relationship to an
erotic love-bond, isolated from the realities of everyday existence. In the thrall of such overspecialized bonds not enough
information can be obtained by either party to make a
prediction of durability and maintenance of the initial attraction. Too much is left to wishful fantasies and mere hope
that the partners will stay lovable to each other.

Both partners of this "lost weekend" fight participated in a
weekend marathon group meeting for premarital, marital,
and postmarital (divorced) couples. The partners came independently to the 30-hour nonstop meeting. They participated honestly, confronted each other with their love-frames
and left separately, never to see each other again. During the
meeting it became abundantly clear to the group and to the
couple that they "were not meant for each other." He was
"not her type" and she was not his. The marathon group
experience helped them to complete the process of weaning
themselves away from each other after an abortive beginning.

The trouble was that their love-frames did not match nor
mesh. The frames did not encompass their real selves. Also,
the respective we images failed to match—which is an under-
statement because there was hardly any overlap between the
two unilateral love-frames. Her love-frame could be summarized this way: "What turns me on in a man is complete
confidence in himself combined with infinite tact and discretion." His love-frame went like this: "What arouses me in a
woman is her complete loyalty and reliability. And, of
course, she must look sexy."

She was sexy, all right, but she was far from reliable. She
sprang surprises. She constantly shifted plans. This was her
way of testing his ability to remain calm and sure of her in
spite of the runaround she gave him!

Her idea of their we image centered on independent,
autonomous interests and lots of freedom. His expectations
of enduring intimacy centered on "sharing and doing everything together." Their we image overlapped in the areas of
sex and money. But this was not enough to make the fight
for the center of each other's heart rewarding. They both
quit before they became hopelessly entangled.

This couple would have been better off never having said
"hello" to each other in the first place, but quite a few loners
are unable to take even the first tentative, probing step
toward intimacy and to attempt matching their love-frames
against those of anyone else. One good-looking, "successful"

25-year-old bachelor said, "I simply can't bring myself to dance with any girl I really like. I even have trouble talking to her unless she makes the first move toward me, and that hardly ever happens. When it did, once or twice, I never followed up. I was scared."

DR. BACH: Do you like being without a date?
HE: Of course not!
DR. B: Well, what are you doing about it?
HE: I have a pretty active fantasy life, but I never talk about it.

When this intelligent, heterosexual man later shared his inner world with a fight-training group, it developed that this otherwise productive young person preferred masturbation and imaginary intercourse (with the aid of pornography and sexy movies) to the risks of becoming involved with a real partner. He feared he would be rejected and that this would confirm his irrationally low evaluation of himself.

Once people do become emotionally involved and win their fights for acceptance, inclusion, and centricity, new questions are likely to arise: "Now that I am presumably in the center of his heart, how does he view me? What does he propose to do with me? And where do we go from here?"

Again, many partners evade these issues. They may be fight-phobic. But perhaps they just don't "know their own mind" yet. They may know that the relationship could take several turns, but they don't know which turn they prefer. Nor would they know how to embark for whatever goal they seek. For such undecided partners a good inner dialogue may set a constructive direction.

The following case of a 22-year-old girl who is having a love affair with her boyfriend, with no commitments made by either partner, shows that "talking to yourself" is far from "crazy."

SHE: My question revolves around the depth of our relationship, whether it is a fleeting affair or a serious friendship.
DR. BACH: The conventional part of you fights for marriage?
SHE: Yes, and sex has a lot to do with this. My conventional side tells me that if I press for marriage now I'll have better sex because I'll have a regular sex partner and it will be socially approved. I won't have to hide.

DR. B: Is anybody opposing your conventional side?

SHE: That would be the independent side of me. That side is saying: why hurry into marriage? Eventually yes, but not now! Now you're interested in doing things independently, learning to live by yourself, having fun. Why face the responsibility of marriage now? You can date anyone you like, and yet not tie yourself down.

DR. B (*addresses the trainee's "independent" side*): Now, Miss Independence, if I may interview this part of you: Would you care to debate the points Miss Convention made?

SHE: Yes, I would say that sex doesn't have to occur just within marriage to be good, beautiful, and meaningful.

DR. B: Does Miss Convention want to talk to Miss Independence on the subject?

SHE: Well, Miss Convention says: "I think that sex is an expression of love between husband and wife and it's not a park-bench affair between boyfriend and girlfriend. Besides, the marriage license isn't just a piece of paper, and you know it. It is a social sanction. Miss Independence's answer to this might be: "I don't need a social sanction. I don't live at home where I had this kind of conventional pressure. If he wants to come over he can stay, eat breakfast, we can make love, take a shower together, and who's going to know or even give a goddamn?"

DR. B: In other words, as a single girl you don't present your bedroom to the world. You only do that by the marriage title of "Mr. and Mrs." Now, speaking to you as a whole: Did you notice in yourself any different feeling, depending on whether you took the position of Miss Convention or Miss Independence?

SHE: That's hard to say.

DR. B: Which one felt more confident? In which role did you feel more like your own self?

SHE: I think there ought to be a compromise, with sexual relations now, and marriage in the background for later.

DR. B: So there are three parts of your inner debate: conformity, independence, and compromise. Does this mean you will press your friend for a commitment to later marriage?

SHE (*emphatic*): No! The marriage plan exists only in my fantasy. But I do want to find out what my relationship to my boyfriend really is! I think uncertainty is the one problem that even Miss Independence does not like. I want to know: Where do I stand with him? What do I mean to him? Where are we going? Because if we're not going anywhere, why not have lots of men and have real freedom and independence?

DR. B: That's being "completely free"?

SHE: That's what real independence means to me. Now when other men come on strong I feel "I should be loyal to Bob." But Miss Independence says, "Why the hell should you? Has he committed himself?" If I am only a play girl, Miss Convention gets mad and calls me bad names!

DR. B: What names? Let her speak up.

SHE: She would say I'm a fool letting myself be used by the man for his own pleasure. If I were to run around with a lot of guys she would call me *a whore!* (*Pause.*)

DR. B: Do you now want to confront your friend Bob? (*Pause.*)

SHE (*thoughtful*): Not now. I think it's my own problem. I have to think where I am as a total person; where my relationships to men fit into my life.

DR. B: This inner debate will help you. It fills in where you're going and what the implications of the various alternatives are. I think it may be helpful if you listened to the tape recording of this inner debate so far. Listen for changes in your voice and check whether your confidence, hesitation, or fluency change, depending on which part of the inner debate you're taking.

(*They listen to the tape.*)

DR. B: Which side of your inner debate sounds more confident, and more adult? Which is weaker?

SHE: Miss Independence seems to have a stronger argument than Miss Convention, but there seem to be more than two sides. Miss Independence says the relation with men should be a meaningful, close relationship whether or not one is married. Now a third side comes along and says: "What difference does it make? I can just go out and see what other guys are like!" This is a side I hadn't realized was in me before. It is a whorish side that comes out and says, "If Miss Independence isn't going to be responsible and establish a meaningful relationship with one man, I come in and let you have fun with all!"

DR. B: You let a new voice in the inner dialogue speak up, a component you call the whore in you. Is there any real chance for her to take over?

SHE: No. I think this "whore voice" brings Miss Convention and Miss Independence together. Their combined forces are saying to me: "Well, you better find out what your relationship to your boyfriend is."

DR. B: Have you then decided to explore with your boyfriend and in your own mind where you two are going?

SHE (*relaxing for the first time*): Yes, and not only in my own mind! I want to confront him and find out what he thinks of me, and where he wants to go with me.

DR. B: All right, in other words, from this debate you have learned that next time you see your boyfriend you will have a program for exploratory action. What will your program be?

SHE: I haven't decided yet, but the general idea is to say: What is our relationship? I don't think it will be done exactly in this way; it'll be more indirect. I might tell him how I feel about him and more or less leave myself wide open to bring him out to say where he stands.

DR. B: But you will probe?

SHE: Well, it's about time because I've been putting off and putting off discussing my relationship with him by saying, well, I haven't known him that long, why rush things? I may scare him off by showing that I think seriously of him, love him, and that I feel very close to him. Now I say why should I put it off? I want to know where we stand!

DR. B: You want to know what direction you're going in, so you're now ready to risk scaring him off.

SHE: That's right, it's a risk. There is a certain hesitancy. I feel I want to do it, but can I put the issue to him?

DR. B: Perhaps you need a little more inner debate about this, but certainly the debate so far has already moved you a little closer to resolving this anxiety

and toward active risking, rather than passive
floating.

Everybody is afflicted with commitment jitters when it
comes to milestone decisions about relationships with an
Intimate Other. This uneasiness tends to reach uncomfortable
peaks when society is summoned to witness the ultimate
commitment at the time of the marriage ceremony. Everything that happened before took place largely or wholly in
private conversation. It was all words. Even getting the
license was not witnessed by anybody. But now comes the
show! The guests will disperse after the wedding, but they'll
be back. In a year or so, they will ask the couple, directly or
indirectly, "How are you doing?"

Today every marriage is a horse race and every couple
knows it. The spectators all but take bets: How good will this
marriage be? How long will it last? What problems will this
couple have? Will they make an addition to our social circle
as a married couple (instead of just one unmarried friend,
the way it was before they became a unit)? It is hardly
surprising that such tensions breed exhausting prewedding
fights.

Precommitment battles may start in relative calm over
such issues as the guest list, whether to have the wedding at
home or in church, whether the ceremony should be performed by a judge or a minister. But suppose the groom then
"forgets" that they planned to keep the honeymoon destina-
tion secret and tells his mother where they are headed. The
bride could interpret this as his first serious breach of trust.
From now on his every move will be watched and weighed
with extra vigilance. Who will be his best man? That slob
bachelor who kept trying to talk him out of the marriage?
How will the groom behave at the rehearsal? Will he be late
for church? Will Daddy get along with him if he loses his
temper?

Meanwhile, as in every deep crisis, the bride will question
her own image: Am I going to be too fat for my dress? Will
my hair *ever* look right?

All this time, everyone is supposed to act overjoyed.

Comes the wedding and the reception. The couple is sched-
uled to leave, but the groom is having a few drinks and is
enjoying himself:

FATHER-IN-LAW: Weren't you supposed to leave a couple
     of hours ago?
GROOM: That's our business.

Now the couple is in the car, ready to leave. Everybody has run out of rice. But the mother of the bride is still giving her little girl last-minute instructions. Finally, Mama tears herself away. The couple is alone . . . and upset.

HE: Won't you ever be able to tell your mother off?
SHE: Don't be cross, dear.

It would be pleasant to be able to avoid such stresses at happy times. It would also be an unrealistic expectation. And unrealistic expectations are, in all likelihood, one burden which the new Mr. and Mrs. are already toting along in abundant supply in their emotional dowry as they head from the dreams of courtship into the reality of married existence. The so-called honeymoon is, contrary to the "let's make nice" tradition, a good time for partners to start weaning each other gently but firmly away from this dowry of courtship dreams.

17. Fighting for Realistic Romance

And so they were married. Unless partners are total fight-evaders or courtly lovers of Victorian dimensions, they will by now have had some lovers' quarrels. If they are lucky or trained, the fights will become more serious before too long, perhaps in a matter of six months or a year. If they are inept fighters, these serious quarrels will not break out for many years, but the delay will be no reprieve because the fights will then be much more bitter and possibly irreversibly destructive. In any event, these love fights—they can also be called frame fights or reality fights or image fights—are by no mean "sick." They are human, normal, and necessary.

Since human love flows easiest when directed at a blurred object (it becomes so much more inviting that way!), a lover can swoon and attribute to the partner all sorts of lovable characteristics; these, in turn, act as love releasers for himself. This image-making seems essential to get people together when they have been brainwashed by romantic traditions. But the psychodynamics of initial attraction and getting together are quite different from the dynamics of staying together enduringly. To stay together, partners must be able to depend on each other *for real,* and fighting fulfills the function of ridding couples of unrealistic or even fantastic expectations. For better or for worse, the correction and calibration of two differing love-frames is more than a gentle descent from the Garden of Eden. It is a battle. The goal is a state of livable reality. The issue is: whose "reality" and whose definition of "livable" shall prevail?

It is quite true that, as romantic love-doves get to know each other better, "Familiarity breeds contempt" because familiarity destroys romantic illusions. But the point is that such a bored, sterile state need never arise. The romantic school of love and marriage couldn't be more misguided as when its spokesmen admonish: "Keep your distance! Preserve the image of love!" The trouble is that this Utopian vision cannot work. In rare instances a marriage that operates on the after-you-my-dear-Alphonse principle may last a lifetime—a lifetime of fake accommodation, monotony, self-deception, and contempt. Most partners, however, can only fool themselves and their intimates for so long and then must work their way through the reality-testing phase of intimacy.

In this stage each partner tries to salvage from his cherished courtship expectations those dream segments that he has a realistic right to see fulfilled. If he is wise, he will try for no more and no less. Stressful upheavals occur when the Utopian phase is allowed to last too long. When partners tote fantastic images in their grievance gunny sacks year after year, there is likely to be a needlessly loud bang when the sack finally bursts.

Suppose an overly ambitious wife imagines her rather ordinary husband to be a mental giant or financial wizard. Suppose he tries to hide his limitations and attempts to behave in the manner she expects. Since his true capabilities cannot live up to his false image, he is sure to fail sooner or later. She will be enraged at this failure and perhaps blame him for having egged her on and colluded with her preposterous expectations. He will retaliate by accusing her of not "believing in him" and that her lack of support doomed him to defeat.

Or suppose a wife dresses up sexily for a party and dances only with other men. She is really trying to make herself attractive to her husband. She may sense that it is entirely legitimate to arouse herself and him in this indirect way. After all, in the end he is going to be the one who will take her home and go to bed with her, and sex under these circumstances can be highly stimulating. Unfortunately, the other couple in the example just described, these partners have not leveled in advance with one another. And so, instead of a sexy husband, the wife has created a suspicious and jealous one.

The transition from courtship images to post-courtship realities tends to be not only painful but downright puzzling, as the following case shows. Jack Marks felt cheated because after three years of marriage his wife no longer behaved as she did in the first flush of their romance.

JACK (*exasperated*): Whenever I want her, I can't have her, so I have to take her the way she wants to give herself to me.

HELEN (*self-righteous*): What's the matter with that? Ask the doctor here: That's the way women love. You can't make them love you. It has to come from within, doesn't it, Doctor?

DR. BACH: Love has many faces and styles. You two have the problem of calibrating, fitting your style of loving to one another. (*Toward Helen.*) You need not quote to yourself or to him generalities about love and loving to defend your particular way. Let's hear more from you two.

(*At this point, Jack, who had been sitting on a couch, was offered a comfortable swivel chair and wheeled, with him in it, right in front of his wife for better eyeball-to-eyeball contact. Helen was already seated in the same kind of chair.*)

DR. B: Now, just face each other and level with one another. Leave me out of it for a while. Let me listen. I'd like to hear and see how you talk to each other about this.

JACK (*disgusted*): Oh, Doc, we've been all over this so many times and we always wind up nowhere. It's a vicious circle. She's heard it all before and I've heard it all before.

HELEN: He's right. We've nothing to say to each other because we'll get into the same old hassle like a broken record. I'm tired of it, just plain old tired!

JACK (*getting angry and rolling closer toward Helen in his chair*): You're tired! I'm disgusted! It's driving me nuts! I've told you a thousand times I resent that it's me that has to come to you every time I want to make love, every time! You used to be so affectionate before we got married and during the first two years. Now you never come to me any more.

HELEN (*controlled and not moving her chair*): Never? Well, hardly ever, I guess. It's difficult for me to be sexually aggressive. But I always respond to you when you make the advances.

(*Silence. Jack sat angry and sullen, his facial expression saying: "See, Doc, she's not even trying to make me happy."*)

DR. B: How do you feel about each other right here and now?

JACK: Lousy. We're deadlocked again.

(*Another long silence.*)

HELEN: Why are you so depressed about a good thing?

JACK: What's good about it?

HELEN (*reasonable*): We have a good marriage, that's what's good. I really don't know what we're doing here except you always seem to be so dissatisfied with everything: not just me, the kids, your work, our income, nothing is ever enough! And speaking of premarital times, sure I was affectionate and maybe even seductive! I felt it. There was nothing phony about it. I wanted you for my husband and still do. And you played differently then, too. You were enthusiastic and stimulating, nothing like you are now.

JACK (*heatedly*): I felt that way then because *you* (*pointing strongly*) loved *me*. All I had to do was respond, and I lapped it up. I love to be loved! Now—nothing!

DR. B: Well, I can see you're stuck like a broken record that keeps saying, "Oh, where are those exciting courtship days?" They're over and you should be going through the reality-testing phase. But you're fighting it and this creates a crisis . . .

HELEN (*shocked and moving her chair slightly toward the left*): Crisis? We're in no crisis! That sounds awful!

DR. B: Yes, you're in a crisis because a decisive *change* for better or worse is imminent. The burial of the courtship phase has been overdue. Both of you have hung onto expectations that are no longer appropriate.

HELEN (*toward Dr. B*): "Crisis" sounds so dangerous and foreboding. (*Toward Jack.*) I don't feel our marriage is that bad, do you, darling?

JACK (*decisive*): What the doctor means is that there have to be some *changes* made. Isn't that right?

DR. B: Yes. A marriage crisis is an unbalanced state of affairs. If it's not straightened out there'll be stress to a point of intolerance. The imbalance requires decisive change. You can't persist in your present mood. The main problem is to channel the change into a constructive new direction. In marriage you can never go backward. The romantic doll-playing days are over. Now the question is, "Are you happy?" You no longer have to confuse what you really are with the way you want each other to be. People are so eager to mate that they instinctively behave—and even feel—like the kind of man or woman whom the lover wants! But in intimacy old phases are not renewable or relivable. It's no use dwelling on the romantic past of your relationship. The real questions are: Where do you want to go from here? What can you do with—and for—each other except to have regrets?"

(Dumbfounded silence.)

HELEN (*worried, toward Jack*): But I can't just make love exactly when you want! It's impossible! I'm what I am and if that's not good enough for you then ... (*There was a half-smile on her trembling lips.*)

DR. B: OK, you feel very deeply about this. And so does your husband here. (*Jack had moved close toward Helen, trying to comfort her as* DR. B. *addressed him.*) You told me many times how perplexed you are with the situation and that is why you invited Helen over here. (*Toward Helen.*) When you hear Jack complain: "I must take her the way she *wants* to give of herself," does that make you angry?

HELEN (*vigorous*): It sure does!

DR. B: I thought so, the way you looked when he said that earlier. Why do you allow yourself to get hung up on that bit?

HELEN (*indignant*): Well, wouldn't you?

DR. B: Not necessarily. But tell me your problem, mine can wait.

HELEN (*allowing herself to show anger, but addressing the doctor*): Well! He's making an ogre, a bitch out of me when he complains (*she mocks his expression*): "I must take her the way she wants to give of herself" as if I could be just anything I want to be, tailor-made to the peculiar tastes of my husband's à la carte menu for women! (*Finally turning toward Jack in anger.*) Do you really want me to play games and pretend to be what I'm not, just to please you?

JACK: I wouldn't mind a bit if you tried. It wouldn't hurt my feelings at all if you tried to please me!

HELEN: Well, I used to try that, but it's exhausting and I felt phony. It doesn't work, anyhow. So, I'm not going to try that game-playing with you any more. Otherwise, we'd have two unhappies instead of just one.

JACK (*anxious*): Don't you want to please me? Do *I* have to make all the changes?

HELEN: It isn't that I don't want to please you, but if it doesn't come off right and I feel false about it —and since you're so tough on yourself—I might as well at least be true to myself and comfortable with myself.

DR. B: Fine! Game-playing is a necessary evil in courtship. It's a by-product of the romantic phase. But it should be over by now for both of you! Here is what you have to understand and talk over with one another between now and our next meeting. When you first fell in love you chose each other not realistically but romantically. You were driven toward each other physiologically, sexually. In order to rationalize this sex invasion of your intelligent cortex, you invented a lot of fantasy pictures in your mind. You didn't really know one another, and it's your present job to get acquainted—to become transparent and real.

HELEN (*moving her chair slightly away from Jack's*): But I'm afraid of that. Maybe we'll find out we're too different! We actually are, you know. Take that sex bit, for example. It's just not my nature to throw myself at a man, not even one I love as much as this crazy lug over here.

DR. B (*to Jack*): Tell her something.

JACK (*stumped*): Tell her what?

DR. B: Well, you might tell her you're a man of the world and that you can stop playing that old-sex-complaint record.

JACK (*laughingly*): Honey! I'm a man of the world. And I'll stop bitching to you about sex. . . .

DR. B: You're just starting to become intimates! You see, intimacy starts where romanticism leaves off. And true intimacy starts with realistic appreciation of your differences. Never mind your similarities! They don't count because they're so comfortable. It's your differences that stimulate and present a challenge. The problem of how to fuse two people into one close relationship is not for little girls and dream boys. It's an adult problem. Try to feel each other's nature. Things will be different. You will experience the same situations very differently when you share your differences openly. It'll bring you closer together.

JACK: How's that?

DR. B: Because when you appreciate differences you're showing empathy. And respecting differences earns and deepens intimacy and gains responsive respect. We'll work on this next time, when you report to me what you've found out about how different you are and in what respect, besides your style of sexuality.

Jack and Helen wound up sitting in dumbfounded silence. They had become so accustomed to their impasse that it required two more sessions with the counselor before they could act on the notion that a new orientation was possible for them, even though intellectually they accepted this at the first meeting. Their perplexity is not unusual. Even the most intelligent marriage partners often believe that a certain rut is bound to be an immovable fixture of their relationship. They overestimate the difficulty of changing old habits, even though people change in their professional lives all the time. The truth is that many old habits can be cast off as easily as an autumn leaf that has been shaken by the wind.

Partners develop strong attachments (yes, love) for their self-made images of what their mate and marriage ought to be. They are more in love with their mental pictures of each other than they are with their authentic selves. They'd rather fight than switch from image to reality. Unhappily, this image-fighting is usually anything but constructive because the pain of dissonance is blamed on the partner who must then be punished for "ruining everything." The need to punish an image-spoiling partner often takes precedence over the realistic necessity to move the marriage on to a new phase. Disappointed partners can waste years in mutual punishment for breaking up a dream of what "ought" to have been reality, but wasn't.

Trained couples do not need to test their images of, and love for, one another. They acquire this knowledge as a by-product of continual leveling. They can balance their intimate books any time and so they always know pretty well where they stand. In untrained love-testing, each partner's love-frame is usually kept locked away like a secret formula. Instead of coming clean, the love-testers use every image-making and image-preserving method ever devised:

1. Deliberate deception: posing in one's Sunday suit in order to appear as lovable as possible;

2. Unconscious deception: same as above, but believing in it oneself.

3. Divining: expecting the partner to fathom entirely on his own just what is lovable;

4. Hinting: "Wouldn't it be fun to take the boat without the kids this weekend?";

5. Leaving clues: "I really like to watch how you handle the kids";

6. Selective validation: secretly watching for signs whether the partner fits into one's love-frame;

7. Setup operation: manipulating the partner at least partially into one's love-frame;

8. Ordering the partner to behave lovingly. (This may be combined with such threats as, "If you don't do ... I'll leave you!")

It is entirely human for each partner to want his Sunday picture of himself (his idealized self-image) to be confirmed, rather than his Monday morning picture (negative self-image). When Mr. Sunday turns out to be Mr. Monday in an intimate relationship, the disillusionment can lead to such blunt and brutal counterattacks as "You don't make enough money!" or "You're too fat!" or "No wonder you've been fired!"

Most people know their Monday image all too well and don't have to be constantly reminded of it. We tell trainees to respond with signals like these: "Stop telling me my faults and playing Mr. District Attorney. That's not what I married you for. I need that like a hole in the head."

Instead of supplying support and comfort along with post-courtship reality, intimates are more likely to lose hope and get bogged down in the exhausting rituals of round-robin fights. Here is a post-courtship fight between a husband who used to think that his wife would remain complaisant like a geisha and a wife who used to think that her husband would remain as liberal with his money as he seemed to be during their premarital dates.

HE: You've overdrawn the checking account again.
SHE: Why don't you tell me what I can spend?
HE: You have some nerve! You know damned well when you spend too much. You just don't care.
SHE: You like to leave me in the dark so you can catch me. I'm not your bookkeeper. You're supposed to handle the finances.
HE: That's a laugh. You wouldn't do anything I tell you.
SHE: Why don't you try me?
HE: Hell, it's no use with you.
SHE: Here we go again!

Or consider this encounter between a wife who met her prospective mother-in-law only three weeks before the wedding and a husband who had been managing to hide, until sometime after his marriage, that he was something of a momma's boy.

SHE: You're spending too much time with your mother.
HE: Are you starting that again?

SHE: You're the one who starts it by always running over there.

HE: I won't let you tell me what to do.

SHE: I don't care what you do as long as you'll just quit being a kid and running to Mom all the time for your security blanket.

HE: You're psychoanalyzing me again.

SHE: You can't stand the truth.

HE: This is ridiculous.

SHE: That's where we always wind up.

HE: I'm tired of it.

SHE: So am I.

Such fights, bred by postcourtship *tristesse,* should not be confused with the up-to-date, nonredundant fights over trivia which we favor. The encounters just described are rituals of conflict-habituated couples who are condemned to raking over the same trivial pseudo-issues again and again. Their moves and counter-moves are as predictable as those in an openhanded card game without jokers. Each party knows all too well what will come next. If people could learn to be less sensitive to possible rejection and start leveling with each other instead of being so intent on "making nice," they wouldn't later substitute round-robin fights for intimacy.

There is still another reason why the Utopian mold of early courtship is so hard to break. Not only are the dreams that people spin about their intimate partnerships extraordinarily rich; but, typically, they are unilateral. Partners concentrate only on their own fantasies and tend to ignore the fantasies of their mates. It is as if they were saying to themselves, "It's *my* dream, isn't it?" And so they keep their imagery secret from the partner and live in the hope that the partner will behave in accordance with it. This hope dies very hard. Usually a partner tries to turn it into a self-propelling prophecy. Directly or indirectly, Partner A will try to draw "B" into behaving in accordance with "A's" imagery or map.

As demonstrated by the cases reported on the preceding pages, this sort of shadowboxing is not likely to work well. A partner's actual alternatives are these:

1) He can change his behavior to conform with the partner's map. 2) He can demonstrate the unrealistic fantasy status of the map by chronically behaving dissonantly to it. 3) He can have the partner change *his* map. 4) He can change his own map to conform to the other person's map. 5) He can change the other person. 6) He can tear up all maps and live from moment to moment. 7) He can team up

with his partner to draw up a mutually acceptable, flexible, up-to-date, general map to take care of established and predictable occurrences and leave much of the rest map-free and open to negotiations. The last approach is the most practical, the most creative and also the most delicate.

The final reason why courtship fantasies seem so persuasive for so long is that they have been legitimized as part of the cultural heritage. The pressure on the female in our society to "get a good man" is so strong that girls become accommodating, chameleon-like actresses during the dating-mating phase. The brighter the girl, the more artful her show will be. But all girls are required to play this game of "catch" to match the boys' equally culture-conditioned game of "chase." All cultures have folkways designed to get boys and girls together by hook or crook in order to perpetuate the human race. Once a couple is mated, however, our culture loses interest in the intimate relationship and the couple is left to hammer things out as best they can.

To Lola and Frank Owens this prospect sounded hopelessly complicated, even though it wasn't. When they first came to a fight-training group they told what happened when Frank consulted Lola's psychoanalyst before they decided to get married against the doctor's advice.

LOLA: My psychoanalyst told me you were a "mother addict." He said that no matter whom you married, you'd have to hate your wife for taking you away from Mummy. Then he said: "Of course, I can't tell you how to live your life. If you insist on marrying him, go ahead. You can always get a divorce."

FRANK: I know. He told me the same thing. Here is about what he told me, as I remember it. He said: "You're a professional bachelor. At the age of 38 you've never married. I think you're sick. I suspect that unless you come to me 4 times a week for at least 3 years, your mother fixation will foul up any marital relationship you try to involve yourself in, especially with Lola. She's been in psychoanalysis for 4 years now, and I'm just beginning to free her from her father fixation—which she transferred to me, of course." (*Frank paused for a deep breath. He winced and continued his recital of his painful recollections.*) So then the analyst got kind of upset. And this is about what he told me. "Lola is just about to surrender her father fantasy and is becoming more realistic about life. Now you come along. You don't know it, of course, but you're rekindling her childlike hope that she, at the age of 29, can have a daddy after all, and that's you! What a laugh! You, the mother addict, are now supposed to take on the father-figure role!" (*Frank turned toward Lola.*) At this point your analyst laughed sardonically and made fun of our relationship. Here's what he said: "Can you imagine the mess? You're accepting and encouraging Lola's attraction for you which is based on her unconscious longing for a father. She hopes to rival successfully with your mother by taking you away from her. In the meantime, you, in your deepest unconscious, are actually psychologically incapable of giving of yourself. You're not free to give because you're still concerned with getting, taking in, getting your share of the mother's tit in a litter of pups, with your eyes still closed to reality. You're interested in Lola because you'd like to replace the two outworn tits of your old lady with two hopefully more productive, more 'understanding' ones. The fact is that Lola is not interested in nursing you. And she isn't capable of nursing you. She expects you to take care of her. You'll be hopelessly at cross purposes —until lots of psychoanalytic work, especially on your unconscious mother fixation, frees you so you can attempt to establish a realistic relationship." (*Frank paused again and then continued to direct himself earnestly at Lola.*) I violently disagreed with your analyst, of course. I said I had weaned myself away from my mother long ago. I pointed out that I'd enjoyed many years of Hollywood bachelor living. I told him in no uncertain terms that I'm now ready to commit myself to you and to raise a family. (*He gazed intently at Lola.*) I know all about the Oedipus myth. You've had over $30,000 worth of psychoanalysis! Boy, that ought to be enough for both of us! I finally told that analyst off. I told him he was long on psychiatric theory and short on human understanding. "Well," he said, "of course, you're entitled to disagree with my diagnosis. I can't tell you how to live your life. If you're set on getting married, OK. Try it, if you like. Later, you can always call me!"

LOLA: I remember how you came back from the analyst.

That was the time when you definitely proposed to me and I accepted, in spite of the doctor.

GROUP MEMBER: Well, are you in the kind of mess predicted by the analyst?

LOLA: (*to group*): Yes and no. I mean: no, we don't want a divorce. But: yes, we're at cross-purposes—too often, anyway. That's why we came to Dr. Bach.

FRANK (*to group*): Yes, that's why we're here. We keep having a few wonderful days together, but then, every fifth or sixth day, we get into a terrible hassle that lasts a day or two. Then we forget all about it and enjoy the peace and quiet until it starts all over. Frankly, I'm completely exhausted from this emotional roller coaster, and I've been trying to figure out what's really wrong. I think it's all because Lola is basically immature. She's just insecure, like a child. She doesn't have enough confidence in herself!

DR. BACH: Do you want to get off your roller coaster?

LOLA (*cutting in before Frank has a chance to reply*): Yes, Dr. Bach, that's exactly the feeling I have. He wants to get off. Deep, deep inside of him he doesn't want to be married, at least not to me.

FRANK (*waving her off and protesting laughingly*): Oh, nonsense! Why do I come to a marriage seminar with you? I'm here, aren't I?

LOLA: But you're always so irritated about everything I do . . .

FRANK (*smiling a bit smugly*): Not everything, my love.

LOLA: Of course not (*laughs*). You like me in bed. You like the way we make love. But you can't live your life in bed. You nag me about everything else—little, silly, crappy things: the way I drive, the way I comb my hair, the way I make do and prepare economy dinners, which you call "left-overs." You nag me when I don't practice my piano lessons. Then, when I do play, you criticize the way it sounds. (*She begins to cry; she turns to the counselor and the other four couples and bursts out.*) Deep, deep inside he just doesn't like to be married to me!

This protocol illustrates some common errors that intimates make when they "translate" the trivial into the significant. They second-guess motivations. They search for remote unconscious causations and veiled disguised motivations. They worry about "Why, deep inside, did he/she do this?" This interpreting and second-guessing is a professional game played by many old-fashioned psychiatrists in the scientifically unfounded belief that if people only knew the why of their actions, this knowledge would automatically help them to change and to improve their relationships.

Actually, insights into the past self do not help much. What is needed is "we-sight." Clinical experience in psychotherapy, accumulated during the last ten years of research, has shown that most people can improve their lot in life more effectively when they stop worrying why they have various troubles and start focusing on practicing new ways of being in this world. Looking forward, experimenting with new ways of dealing with old problems, learning how to live together—rather than speculating on why one can't—and then practicing effective ways of relating to others, that is the new orientation of scientific psychotherapy.

Applied to the problems of intimate living this means that one should scan for information about where a relationship is "off-balance" and then try together to straighten it out, in a mutual—not a unilateral—procedure. Translating trivial annoyances and distilling from them cues about where the partners stand vis-à-vis one another is an important step.

Lola's analyst probably would interpret Frank and Lola's marital discords as inevitable "derivatives" of unconscious motivations and fixations. He would no doubt say that their troubles, just as he had predicted, were caused by remote events in Lola's and Frank's childhoods. The couple fell into that same trap. Lola thought that the sum total of Frank's trivial complaints meant that "deep-down he wants out." She thus interpreted his stance as destructive. Frank also indulged in psychiatric speculations. He figured that Lola got so upset by his "reasonable requests" that she must be suffering from an "inferiority complex." He inferred that she had a character-defect that made her feel "insecure" at the first sign of a simple disagreement. All these "readings" translate discords into speculative interpretations of *what* they are and *why* they are there, without distilling useful cues to *how* to improve the relationship.

A more creative way of translating trivia is to focus on what the fighting between Lola and Frank tells us about the state of their relationship, and what they have to do to improve their life together. A few sessions later Lola and Frank were able to use this new information-retrieving orientation and began to make progress:

GROUP MEMBER: I think the way you nag her about being afraid to drive on the freeway and taking too long to get dressed and not playing the piano well enough—it all shows me that you don't accept her weaknesses. You don't want to protect and take care of her.

FRANK (*taken aback*): No, no! I do like to protect Lola —if she's in real trouble. (*Turns toward Lola.*) Remember when you had trouble with the land-lady? Go ahead, honey, tell them . . .

LOLA (*toward group*): Yes, when it comes to business matters, Frank is always right there and takes care of any conflict that comes up. That always makes me feel very secure.

DR. BACH (*toward Frank*): So you accept her dependency on you in certain areas—but in others it annoys you. For instance, we seem to have established that it annoys you when Lola shows some human frail-ties . . . like having difficulties driving, dressing, and piano playing. These are all things she must learn to do by herself and you're impatient with this.

LOLA (*empathetically*): Exactly! He is terribly annoyed and nags me about these things and, in fact, any-thing that I try to do or have to do on my own. It's always something where he can't have any real part in it himself, such as cooking, housekeeping, and things like that. That's when he gives me the nee-dle!

DR. B: Frank, is that how you read it?

FRANK (*pausing and thinking*): I guess so. And I guess it's pretty lousy of me. (*Pause. Then he looks at Lola*). But I am goddamned irritated at you when everything you do is such a hassle. Everything is a problem! Everything is "difficult"! Yes, that annoys me and when I tell you about it, all hell breaks loose.

GROUP MEMBER: It seems to me you don't accept her as she is. You want to change her into something she isn't.

FRANK: Are you suggesting I should accept her incompe-tence, when I don't like it? I thought we're sup-posed to "level" with each other here! I'd feel false and foolish to pretend I like her childlike, insecure side. I don't. I hate it!

(*A long silence ensued*).

LOLA: Well, if you would only leave me alone about

things that I have to do by myself anyway, I think we'd be much better off. You really could afford to stop nagging about them. You can't do anything about them anyhow. I have to set my own progress in these things. When I feel I'm doing pretty well, there's no sense in your coming along and taking the wind out of my sails, is there? Why don't you learn to shut up about these things and let me be!

FRANK: Because whenever you have to do any of these things you bitch and bitch how hard it is for you.

GROUP MEMBER (*to Frank*): She's asking for support from you.

DR. B: But why should she? (*To Lola.*) You could stop asking Frank for support in areas he can't give it right now, couldn't you? How can he honestly pamper you when you behave in a way he finds very unattractive? Frank seems a little allergic to this apparent helplessness in you. In areas where he can't really be your helpmate, why expect it of him? (*To both Lola and Frank.*) How would you two like it if you, Lola, no longer would report to you, Frank, all your personal trials with the driving problem? Would this be a small step in the right direction?

FRANK: Then she'll accuse me of not showing any interest.

GROUP MEMBER (*interrupts*): I'm sure your wife will be better off if you don't show interest that isn't sincere. When somebody learns to master something new, the last thing he looks for is being nagged about it.

LOLA (*To Frank, resolutely*): I guess I've got to get used to two new ideas: First, that I can get along without your support in matters where you are so "bugged" with my limitations that you can't help me without being phony. And God knows, I don't want to play games any more. Second, I now see for the first time that you have limitations. I mean your tolerance, understanding, and acceptance of me is not unconditional but has definite limits . . .

In a still later group session, a group member asked Frank and Lola: "How are your 'awful' fights coming along?"

LOLA: We haven't had any big ones lately—just several little ones! I guess we're beginning to learn how to share our annoyances as they come up.

FRANK: It's much more peaceful now. But I sometimes feel nostalgic. Something we once had is now gone out of our marriage. I used to supervise everything Lola did and she'd report to me about everything. Now she does many things on her own and in her own way. I'll agree that she enjoys it more this way, but I feel somewhat left out.

DR. B (*to Frank*): Do you also feel less loved?

FRANK: (*to Lola*): Do you?

LOLA: What?

FRANK: Love me less?

LOLA: I love you more, you old dope. It's just that now I love you realistically, within the limits of what you are: You're a lovable bastard!

FRANK (*to Dr. Bach*): See what you've done? I've become a "bastard" because I don't cater to her any more. And I'm not her big protector any more either.

DR. B (*to Frank*): It seems to me that your protectorate, which belittled your wife, is being emancipated into a really swinging peership. She loves you more than she did before. Neither of you suffers from big, destructive blow-up fights. And all you've given up for these gains is some of your watchdog role and that was never one of your most attractive qualities anyway.

Some of the most intelligent people cannot face the task of hammering out a realistic, joint postcourtship image until they have lived through years or even decades of despair.

This is what happened to Dr. and Mrs. Karl Bond after 21 years of generally frustrating married life. Dr. Bond was a highly successful psychoanalyst. When his 19-year-old daughter brought home a college boyfriend as a house guest one summer, both he and his wife Sue felt compelled to do something about their own relationship. They were touched to see a young couple in love. And they were particularly impressed by how freely and realistically the young people talked about what they thought of—and expected from—each other. The parents contrasted this with their own inhibited courtship ways and began to wonder how the false impressions that were born at the time had managed to endure.

This brought them to our Institute. The husband, who had often sought out simulated intimacy in sexual infidelities with call girls, strongly criticized Sue for "never" entertaining anybody, "never" going into the fabulous swimming pool of their new success-dream castle, "never" being willing to take a trip with him, "never" staying within their sizable budget, "never" assisting him with proper enthusiasm during the official socializing which his position entailed . . . never, never . . . matching her behavior with his courtship image of their "we."

It developed that this doctor—incongruous as it may seem—had always defined his wife as a born hostess with an abiding interest in outdoor sports and a great yen for traveling with him to far-off places. He also saw her as frugal and full of gratitude to him for bringing home such a good income. This was the picture of herself that she had displayed to him a generation before in order to "catch" him!

At the end of the husband's complaints, most wives would have cried out, "If you think all that, why do you stay married to me?" This usually means, "I'm not ready for the truth; let's get some more mileage out of the old false image." Sue, although in tears, was ready to level. Her marriage began to be for real when she shouted at her husband: "You're right! I'm not the girl you think I am and I never will be. I can't! But I can do other things, things we both like. Didn't we have a good time last weekend? . . ."

In a somewhat similar case, a physician and his wife had for 12 years played out a fantasy reminiscent of *Pygmalion*. He fancied himself something of a Professor Higgins, a Messiah. She teased him at first for colluding with his fantasy by paying him such compliments as "I know I have a lot to learn from you." Later she carried the farce further by playing the cute sex object at parties. He retaliated by drawing other dancing partners too close and displaying his success as a masculine seducer by kissing them on the neck and casually ignoring the stares of the ladies' husbands. When the wife caught him necking with another wife in the kitchen at a party, she became furious and later bit his lower lip bloody. To him this meant war. How could Professor Higgins tolerate public humiliation and the ruination of his public image as a queenmaker and queen-possessor who has the freedom to be as sexually popular as his wife?

When all this imagery was flushed out and inspected in the open, it turned out that the doctor did not really feel he had an immovable stake in the Professor Higgins role and that his wife did not feel comfortable playing Liza, either. Again, these were courtship images that had come home to roost . . . 12 years later. Under the threat of crisis these fake images could be erased by the partners when they were challenged to do so.

Not infrequently, the partners' fantasy-maps turn out to be hopelessly irreconcilable, and money may be the force that drives the images apart. It should be an obvious reality that intimacy tends to curtail self-indulgence. But when the freedom of a partner's spending arm is curtailed, anxiety ensues. This happens because financial restrictions run head-on into the romantic expectation that two together will be stronger than each one is separately. Financially, this is almost never so, yet people who get married frequently become more and more insistent on self-indulgence.

The problem may be to weigh a man's boat against a wife's fur coat. The objective is to convince the partner that the self-indulgence is for the common good. But all reality having to do with material possessions may be so firmly woven into webs of enticing courtship dreams that it can never be untangled and logically faced.

We tried unsuccessfully to negotiate a *modus vivendi* in the case of a football coach who had long dreamed of buying a jeep and taking a two-month trip through the rough countryside of Mexico's Baja California region. During his courtship he often mentioned this Walter Mitty fantasy of himself as an explorer. His fiancée encouraged him with enthusiasm. Secretly, she thought that once he got his jeep she would have a car of her own, which he felt was extravagant.

After they were married, he became anxious to fulfill his dream. He even wanted to buy the jeep ahead of their furniture. They fought and fought about the jeep. He kept losing. Year after year he went to the annual automobile show, inspected the new jeeps, and talked with the demonstrator girls who sometimes wore camping uniforms and talked the way his wife had talked when they were courting. One year he again went to the show and could stand it no longer. He bought not only the jeep but a lot of expensive equipment, including an electric generator.

The wife was incensed. She finally agreed to let him keep the jeep but demanded that he return the equipment. This compromise was her way to cover up her responsibility for reneging on a premarital agreement. He refused to return any of his acquisitions. He felt betrayed because her enthusiasm for his explorer dream had been an integral part of his *we* map. She had never really wanted any part of the explorer image and now the truth was out. The wife refused to come to fight training and eventually the couple was divorced. Of course they also disagreed in other areas. But his dream had helped to draw them together and it was her spoiling of the dream that triggered the breakup.

Once couples come to terms with the realities of themselves as a partnership, they usually develop—more or less consciously and yet spontaneously—a way of life that is comfortable and fairly predictable, where tastes blend together and where each can say, "That's us." This feeling is an important part of a reasonably well-functioning state of swing. Style-of-life fights break out when one partner develops new tastes and acts on them more or less on his own. A fight for a station wagon versus a sports car can be a mild example of such a conflict. So is a fight over whether to spend more time with friends ("We never do anything" versus "All we ever do is run around"). The point is that the destruction of an existing order requires only one person, as Lee Harvey Oswald was able to demonstrate with cataclysmic results. But to create something in marriage—especially a new style of life—always requires two people.

Harold and Joy Young found this out when their marriage was threatened, of all things, by their fairly recently achieved prosperity. Joy had worked hard to help Harold through graduate school. During the next few years, their finances had remained tight while he established himself as a biochemist in a major cancer research laboratory. As soon as they had acquired some savings, Harold took a major portion of them, about $1,000, invested them in a pyramid club which turned out to be crooked, and lost all his money. Joy was secretly glad because she hoped the experience might wean Harold away from foolish financial risks.

Instead, he began making himself an expert on the stock market. Some of the time he had spent reading scientific journals was now devoted to going over earnings charts of his favorite growth companies. He also went to the races, always after studying the racing form with scientific thoroughness, and occasionally he would go off to Las Vegas for a night of gambling. Joy protested, but Harold pointed out that his investment and gambling gains outstripped his losses thus far. Besides, he said, this type of risk-taking appealed to him as fun and he deserved some fun after so many years of hard work.

Joy was not satisfied with this turn of events, and soon there were developments that caused her even more concern. One Saturday she said to Harold, "If you take me to the shore I'll make love to you all weekend. See if that isn't more fun than gambling." He agreed to go, but at the last minute he insisted that they go to Las Vegas instead, so that they could make love and he could gamble, too. Since she considered herself something of a siren, she was shocked to discover that her allure had to compete with the attraction of the gambling tables. Not long after that weekend, she returned home from the supermarket and found her husband on the floor with the children, playing gin rummy for money.

At this point she blew up. Harold said, "It's my one self-indulgence, and I earned it!" She yelled, "But it's destroying us!" He shrugged, "I don't see how!"

During their subsequent fight training, Harold found out that Joy could not love him unless he was true to his pre-gambling self. Their style of life had become entrenched over the years and she was entitled to believe that he would not unilaterally change the rules. Even though he still dabbles in stocks and phones his bookie, he learned to find an outlet for his gambling urge in relatively innocent poker games with pals at his home.

This doesn't mean that there is no room for legitimate personal growth in real intimacy. On the contrary: aggressive leveling is ideal for stimulating growth and training a partner to come to terms with it. Typically, these growth fights may start like this:

SHE: I think we're growing apart.
HE: Come on!
SHE: I really think we are.
HE: How do you mean?
SHE: Well, for instance, I'm getting damned tired of playing bridge all the time.
HE: But you love bridge!
SHE: Not any more, I don't. I've got better things to do.

To face such a newly developing disparity is a crisis to be taken seriously. The growing partner could accommodate the bridge player and just keep on playing bridge, but this is potentially disastrous because it encourages the accumulating of hostility. A refusal to play bridge should encourage the change-seeking partner to offer the spouse some alternatives: perhaps chess or making new friends who don't play cards but who exchange interesting ideas instead. Such a confrontation may be brought on by self-dissatisfaction that develops within one partner during psychotherapy. Or it can be sparked by an act as simple as reading a book. A distinguished physicist, Professor Joseph Bird, discovered this in

ed one night when his wife Maria told him about new
ctivities that were taking her away from home during the
ay.

JOSEPH: I don't care if you do all these things as long as
it doesn't distract you from the "main show": me,
the house, and the kids.

MARIA: What you call "distraction" means "coming
alive" to me. I'm a better person now than I was
when I devoted myself entirely to you and your
"glory" as I did last year and the year before. You
were my whole world!

JOSEPH (*amazed*): Was that so bad? I don't see what's so
wrong with that. I loved it and you gave me every
indication that you loved it, too, or else I would've
never married you. I need a woman who's one
hundred per cent with me. I had the other kind
before and I don't need it again. In fact (*getting
angry*), I won't have it, do you hear?

MARIA (*gently placating*): Now, Joe, darling, stop that!
Stop working yourself up into an unhappiness that's
not really there. All that's happening to us is that
I'm growing up a little.

JOSEPH (*increasingly indignant*): By turning your back
on your husband? You call that growing up? I call
it regressing to selfishness!

MARIA (*dead earnest*): What's really your beef? What do
you want?

JOSEPH: You know what I want.

MARIA (*sarcastic*): You want me to be your darling-slave
and be happy to be fortunate enough to be the wife
of the exciting, interesting, and brilliant professor—
you!

JOSEPH (*incredulous*): Instead of enjoying my success,
and the benefits we both get from it, you're knock-
ing it. Are you jealous or something?

MARIA (*emphatic*): I want you to be a success. I want
you to enjoy it. But your success isn't enough for
me.

JOSEPH: Why not? Before I married you and even up to
last year everything I did professionally was interesting to you. While we're at it, you used to be
more interested in sex, too.

MARIA: There's absolutely nothing wrong with our sex
life. We make love any time you want, don't we?
Have I ever refused you?

JOSEPH: Well, no, not directly. But, indirectly, yes. I'd say you've lately refused, sort of . . .

MARIA (*insistent*): How's that? What do you want from me?

JOSEPH (*taking a deep breath*): I might as well give it to you straight: most of the time our sex is banal now. I don't think your heart is in it.

MARIA (*surprised*): Well, gee . . . what else can I do? I'm there with you.

JOSEPH: You're there in body but not in spirit. You let me have sex with you, but when you're not really with it I feel like a fool. I wish you'd get with it the way you used to. I don't want to be tempted to get it elsewhere. I wouldn't like to run around and cheat on you.

MARIA (*shaking her head*): That's silly! I love making love to you. It's just that it has a different meaning to me now than it used to, that's all. Don't make a federal case out of this. Sure, I used to be a frantic "swinger" to please you. I was so damned insecure! I had to put on the big act because I felt that I had nothing else to offer . . . just sex. So I gave you all I had. I'm glad you liked it.

JOSEPH: Just to trick me into marrying you, I suppose.

MARIA: Oh, come on! You can call it "tricky," if you like. All I knew was I loved you and wanted you for my husband and father of my children and I still do. But who can swing from the chandelier all the time? I admit my mind is on other things.

JOSEPH (*mocking*): Other men?

MARIA (*insulted*): Are you kidding? I had my share of men. You're all I want. I'm satisfied.

JOSEPH: Then what's so much on your mind that made you less interested in sex?

MARIA: Well, I'll tell you. I'm concerned with my own identity. I'm tired of just being Mrs. Big-Shot!

JOSEPH (*thoroughly furious*): Oh, now I get it! It's that damn book you've been carrying around, *The Feminine Mystique,* where that frustrated housewife tells women how to live and get "identity." Well, let me tell you, honey, the best identity you'll ever have is right here, right through me, our home, our family, you and I, we, right here! That's your real identity. "Out there" is the "jungle." And anybody that's telling girls like you that your identity is "out there" is really spinning a mystique! I think that book has been very destructive to our marriage.

MARIA (*primly*): I don't think so at all. But if you do, you should take the responsibility. It's all your fault.

JOSEPH (*laughs mirthlessly*): My fault? That's absurd.

MARIA: Well, everywhere we go *you* get all the action. You're the important person! I'm just a pretty tag-along, a nothing.

JOSEPH: But don't I include you in everything?

MARIA: Sure, as part of your audience.

JOSEPH: Well, of course. You're my wife and part of my "show." What's wrong with that?

MARIA: Nothing. I like it. But it's not enough for my own identity. That's why I've started doing outside things around town without your help. And I'm beginning to make a place for myself in the world—singing, painting, and studying. And let me tell you, it feels great, even though it's a tough struggle at times. That's what my mind is on these days, and I would love you even more if you could understand what I'm trying to do and trust me that it's for our mutual interest.

A growth fight such as this may continue through various stages for many years before the partners come to terms. It is sure to produce moments of discomfort for both, but it will yield less bitterness than the partners would face if the issues were hidden and/or the spouses were unable to communicate what really bothers them.

18. Sex as a Fighting Word

Sex rears its attractive-repulsive head again and again as a fight issue and as a weapon. We have shown the unhappy effects of sex faking and sex withholding; sex provocation; sex indifference; sex monotony; even the death of sex for lack of psychological stimulation in marriage. Are sex and all types of fighting inseparable? This is a common impression, reinforced in many minds by the increasing number of choices and conflicts offered by the new sexual freedoms: the freedom from unwanted pregnancy; the freedom from the double standard; the freedom of freedom itself, as illustrated by the increasing frequency of infidelity and divorce; and the freedom to listen to the growing horde of sex experts, many of whom offer advice that is inconsistent with human psychology and physiology.

A realistic-therapeutic approach to so-called sex problems frees many intimates who use sex as a fight strategy to enjoy it, instead, as a pleasurable experience for its own sake and to learn how to love by "fighting right." Such classic psychological sex problems as frigidity and impotence are usually substitute expressions of hostility and rejection. As soon as partners learn how to communicate hostility directly through constructive verbal fighting in the living room or on other neutral ground and not in the bedroom, their sex problems tend to vanish. When intimates learn to control the temptation to use sex as a strategic weapon, they usually find that hate need not contaminate love; that sex need not enter into fights about nonsexual issues. The only exception is the use of sex as a strategy in "making up" after any type of fight; this is recommended without qualification.

Admittedly, previous conditioning makes it difficult for most couples to reshuffle their thinking along realistic lines. We try to help them by advising, first of all, to appoint themselves the only authentic arbiters of their sex preferences. Then we suggest that they communicate with each other about their sexual difficulties and learn together through pure-sex (or sex-calibration) fights just what produces good sexual swing for them. Sexual swing is highly personal (pair-specific). It is not catalogued in sex manuals or labeled by psychiatric definitions. It is best attained by partners learning to calibrate individual differences.

Before couples can learn to do this they should be aware of seven major myths that are widely mistaken for facts about conjugal sex today. These myths are responsible for most of the irritional sex hangups suffered by reasonably healthy couples. There fictions must be disposed of before we consider the legitimate aspects of sex as a fight issue.

The first big myth about sex is that *sex and love must always go together*. In true intimacy there can be satisfactory sex without love; love without sex; and, of course, love with sex. Not everyone is capable of enjoying all three states, but many people experience all of them at different stages of a long-term relationship.

Sex without love is not usually intimate, even though lawyers like to tell courts that anybody who climbs into bed with anybody else is "being intimate." In fact, physical love is lustful rather than intimate. Both men and women possess the capacity to enjoy lusty sex with almost anybody who is physically and/or socially and/or economically attractive as a partner and is willing and able. At times, loveless sex can be very intimate; for instance, when the partners momentarily feel passion with each other and take some responsibility for making the encounter maximally enjoyable. Loveless but lustful sex can also initiate subsequent intimacy, for today sex is no longer necessarily the reward at the end of a long courtship. We pass no moral judgments here or elsewhere in this book, but it is a fact that sexual attraction can sometimes be a key that opens doors to deeper intimacy—the very doors that many people like to keep carefully locked.

Love *without* sex is a state experienced during the many hours of nonsexual emotional entwinement with a partner. For some couples, these hours may stretch into weeks or years because, as every long-married couple knows, sex can at times become a routine bore.

Colette, an astute author on intimate matters, wrote: "I fear there is not much difference between the habit of obtaining sexual satisfaction and, for instance, the cigarette habit." Researchers have described successful marriages where partners cared little or nothing about sex. On the other hand, some close but nonsexual friendships approach a level of psychological intimacy that is envied by many sexually linked but emotionally divorced pseudo-intimates.

Love *with* sex, the optimal condition for genuine intimacy

between equals, is also the state most readily contaminated by extraneous fight issues. Good sex helps mates to become good spouses, but it is no longer enough. The two need not even be correlated. Tradionally, sex was equated with intimacy because sex alone was able to create a permanent bond between mates when the male was a privileged person and the female distinctly subservient. Today the value of an intimate partner naturally goes far beyond the supplying of erotic pleasure. It is this expansion of the value of intimacy— the sex-transcending psychological needs that partners have for each other—that have caused the lusty, sexy side of intimacy to become infected. Many highly proficient, pleasure-giving bedroom partners do not enjoy psychological intimacy and find it difficult to talk to each other in the living room. Good lovers don't necessarily make good partners and poor sex partners often experience an enviable breadth of mutual understanding and share deep affection for each other. In short, true intimacy includes but transcends physical love.

The frequent withholding of sexual pleasures is, next to physical violence, the crudest and most desperate weapon in the varied arsenal of intimate warfare. Sex should never be used for blackmail and it can be kept uncontaminated as "sexy-sex" to proceed independently of other conflicts. When sex is used in a pure pleasure-giving way, it cannot escalate other problems. Instead, it is available for mending the intimate system after a fight and as a way for partners to maintain needed contact with each other during times of intimate crisis.

The second big myth about sex is that *variety is always the spice of one's sex life.* While long-term intimates often do complain that their sex lives have deteriorated into a set of dull routines, mating with the "same old" partners tends to produce a comfortable kind of habituation that may build confidence and elicit greater and more secure orgastic release than can be achieved by sex novelties—either by a variety of new techniques or new partners. Sex variety is usually very stimulating in fantasy. In reality, extracurricular sex may turn out to be satisfying and enormously exciting, at least temporarily; but it often produces practical complications that greatly reduce the excitement.

The leading experts in this field, the experienced playboys and playgirls among our trainees, discover that after a while their experiences with a variety of sex partners tend to pall. The fun wanes. Pleasure may turn to pain when habit leads to satiation or compulsion. Then, ritualized sex varietism is not so good after all, and most of the varietists eventually find themselves searching for the wholly committed form of intimacy where sexual give-and-take is only one aspect of mutual sharing, and not necessarily the central one.

Initially, love affairs provide an intriguing change of pace in the accustomed sex life of intimates. But the fun only lingers if the lovers manage to focus exclusively on sexy-sex. Unfortunately, affairs never seem to stay that way. The hunger for deeper intimacy reaches out beyond lusty physical sex. Good lovers nearly always tend to get more totally involved. Their playmates become helpmates. Then the lover becomes, in effect, a second wife or husband and the love affair turns into an additional intimate system with problems similar to those faced by the married partners.

The same problems often turn out to be more troublesome for a lover to face with his mistress or her beau than they would be for spouses to face with each other. It's only sensible that extramarital partners are usually more demanding than married intimates. The extramarital affair *has* to be more exciting than married love. If it isn't, why bother? Experienced sex varietists also tell us that—possibly because of the associated anxiety and guilt—extramarital sex is by no means automatically better than the marital variety. It should come as no surprise that good swing with one's mistress has to be achieved by fighting with her, too. To give such a relationship a chance to last, one must also pass it through the same fake-ridden courtship that the husband conducted with his wife, only this time under clandestine and more conflict-prone circumstances.

"Oh, I just love this little place," the mistress may say when she is ushered into a motel as the scene of a sex date. Actually, she hates the spot. She is wondering whether so much tawdriness is too high a price for the morale-building uplift of a love affair. A major fight may be in the making.

Marital fighting about extramarital sex—that is, actual sexual varietism as well as threatened or suspected varietism— is one of the commonly brandished weapons of intimate battles. It is equally popular with "devils" who play and "faithful angels" who don't. Both know how to make each other miserable over the sex issue, whether it is real or imaginary.

The angels have the culture-sanctioned guilt "drop" on devil spouses. The favorite strategy of angels, male or female, is to collude secretly with their devil-spouses' weakness for sex variety ("I noticed Jim really turns you on!"). After encouraging the devil indirectly to act out the foul deed of betrayal, the angel likes to catch the betrayer or hear his confession. Then, forever after, the angel can read the devil the riot act whenever a little "shamesmanship" might come in handy as a slap or kick in a conflict unrelated to sex.

When devils display betrayal behavior to incite pangs of jealousy, they may have several purposes in mind. Who knows? Maybe the devil suspects that the angel is an occasional but underground devil, too! Or maybe the angel needs to be signaled, "Wake up! Don't take me for granted!" It may be a case of plain brinkmanship; or a guilt-relieving maneuver; or tit for tat. For this strategy to be effective, however, the betrayed spouse must care enough to defend his psychological territory, his central spot in the heart of the other. Otherwise, the display of sex varietism tends, in our culture, to lead only to further alienation and divorce.

The third great sex myth is that *both partners should always be equally eager for sex*. Between intimates, aggression is often expressed by the demand of one sex partner that the other should more frequently be wholeheartedly "with it." This is never a realistic demand because sex is initially triggered as much from within as from without. For males as well as females, the sexual orgasm is a self-centered self-expression. It can never be a command performance. Neither is it a passive response. Because sexual fulfillment is basically self-regulatory, the question of how one feels within one's self will determine the quality of sexuality as much as how one feels about the sex partner.

An attempt to arouse a partner who is internally not receptive can be a repulsive, rather than an attractive, maneuver. It often happens that when the female is most wanting, the male tends to withdraw, and vice versa. Some of these differences in sexual receptivity can be calibrated, especially if they turn out to be manifestations of hostility or fear of closeness. But many differences are simply examples of disparities in sexuality that can be tolerated and lived with, and with no embarrassment.

Because of the self-centered nature of sex, people must shape the course of a sexual event—the timing, movements, kinds and amounts of caresses—largely according to their own idiosyncratic prescription for what aids them in attaining orgasms. Rarely will the same prescription work for both partners. Both have to learn that the way to please themselves is not the same as the way to please their partners. The practical solution often is: "I will do it with you in your way now and you will do it with me in my way later." This requires sexual goodwill and skill. Instead, many couples use the occasion for rejection maneuvers by withholding orgasm, losing erections, premature ejaculations, infrequent intercourse, refusing foreplay, and generally not doing what the partner knows the other likes.

The fourth great sex myth is that *simultaneous orgasm is a major requirement for good sexual adjustment.* Certain psychiatric schools of thought hold that "the divine in human form is the ecstasy of orgasm." According to this myth, sexually mature women must be totally responsive in body and mind with a deep vaginal orgasm at the precise time when the male partner by the rhythmic nature of his pelvic thrusts signals that he is about to ejaculate. This is supposed to trigger the true feminine vaginal orgasm. Male and female must both bring each other to full genital "surrender." Both must be completely "with it" to earn mental health honors for certified masculinity and femininity.

The myth of mutual orgasm demands that a man, to be a genuinely masculine lover, be able to produce sexual fulfillment in his partner every time in order to confirm his masculinity and her femininity. This unrealistic model for healthy sexuality supplies each partner with a veritable arsenal of weapons and ammunition—and the psychoanalysts with an endless supply of patients. If partners are set up to be helplessly dependent for sexual fulfillment on the orgasm of the other, what happens when they fail to reach the simultaneous, reciprocal ecstasy required by the myth? Whose "fault" is it? If she does not reach full climax, is it because he is not masculine enough? Or is he slightly impotent? Or too clumsy? Inexperienced? Inconsiderate? Or even covertly homosexual? Or is her "frigidity" to blame? Can any woman resist resorting to the technique of not "getting with it" if she knows this will have a castrating effect on a mate she is trying to punish?

No wonder many partners would rather fake orgasms than face such attacks. The most unrealistic application of the mutual-simultaneous orgasm-myth is to use it as a "love-test." The hypothesis is, "Since we don't make it together, our marriage can't be any good!"

All these fight issues are illusory. According to the most recent authoritative research, orgastic sexual release is a highly intricate and specialized response pattern that varies greatly between individuals—in some respects even more than between the sexes. It is therefore infinitely more practical to accept some good, albeit unilateral, sex fun even when a partner is only facilitating it and is not himself orgastically passionate at that particular time.

Although the orgasm myth has been discredited among scientists, its message has brainwashed two generations of the public. As a result, intimates have created for themselves still another neurotic hangup.

We call it orgasm-watching. This is another type of spouse-watching. Tactful awareness of the quality of the partner's sexual response can enhance erotic excitement for the orgastic spouse as well as for the facilitator. But worried watching of a partner's struggle for orgasm acts like a command and is joy-inhibiting. Anxious watching is not part of considerate facilitation.

Many orgasm-watchers tend to score and rate the partner's sexual response. They secretly gather data for their own "love-test" and to support later accusations of sexual inadequacies. Watchers rarely realize that their watching inhibits the partner or causes a fake passionate response.

Closely related to the anxious watchers are the orgasm-collectors, who count the number of orgasms reached by their partners. They then compare the total with the number of their own orgasms and arrive at a love-test score of plus or minus! This scoring is usually associated with jealousy of a more orgastic partner.

What are the physiological facts about orgasm? After initial attraction, desire, receptivity, communication, warm-up, and genital excitation, sexual response tends to run its own course. The partner who is approaching orgasm will use the other partner in an aggressive way and hopefully cause him to supply the right kind of sex-release stimulus (by preferred movements, fondling, thrusts, posture, friction etc.).

It does not matter how the sex release is achieved: by genitals, manually, or orally. There need be no orgasm at all because sexual aggressiveness can be enjoyable for its own sake; intercourse without orgasm can be a highly pleasurable erotic "wrestling match."

In the moments of orgastic passion, everyone becomes a narcissist. The urge for sexual self-relief propels body and soul, demanding full concentration and focus on one's own (not the partner's) sexual excitement.

Those moments require nondistractive supportive behavior from the partner. Ideally, they are tailored to the partner's usually highly specific, idiosyncratic requirements which, then and there, should be clearly conveyed. Such aggressive signaling has the all-important function of bringing the partner into proper sexual coordination to achieve maximal fulfillment.

Aggressive sex serves a double purpose: sexual joy and emotional aggression-relief. Anger and frustration are inherent in successful intercourse—as in any attempts of partners to calibrate and coordinate differences. Angry sex is common and normal because the partners, in their concentrated self-focusing, are apt to respond "wrongly," unless very firmly and clearly cued. Fortunately, anger in love-making is more often an exciting stimulus than a turnoff.

In fulfilling sex there is a constant interplay between physical aggression and tenderness—getting a firm hold and letting go, driving, demanding, commanding alternates, following, submitting, surrendering. And in this seesaw of complementary as well as apparently paradoxical emotional states, male and female partners may reverse their traditionally assigned stereotype roles (male-aggressive; female-surrendering) several times during a single erotic encounter.

It now becomes apparent why the fiction of simultaneous orgasm is far from helpful. A partner who is momentarily but deeply involved in the approach of his own orgasm is hardly in an ideal state to select the right sex-supporting behavior for his mate with maximum intelligence and creativity, especially since the partner is also preoccupied with preparation for orgasm and is, in turn, not in optimal condition for sex cooperation. All this explains why we have found, during 25 years of psychotherapy and fight training, that for most couples mutual orgasms are more or less accidental. Orgasm in relays—with the orgasm of one partner instigating the orgasm of the other—tend to be more productive of good sexual swing. Sexual pleasure is much less likely to be spoiled this way—and the power to spoil a mate's sexual pleasure is a most lethal weapon in the battle of the sexes. To remove this power from the scene is an important help in the process of decontaminating fights about sex.

Sex myth No. 5 holds that *men and women have specific rigid roles to play in sex.* Modern man is so preoccupied with his search for identity that many people seem to be perpetually on the lookout for differences that they might label "masculine" or "feminine." We are not talking about the obvious physical sex characteristics. Some psychologists and psychiatrists have gone much further. They have decreed that certain kinds of adult *behavior* are solid evidence of masculinity or femininity. Madison Avenue, anxious to expand two markets instead of one, supports this effort to widen the gap between the sexes. "Want him to be more of a man?" asked one perfume ad. "Try being more of a woman."

Our fight training is designed not to change adults into

neuters but to reinforce their natural reversibility of intimate roles as total humans, including gentleness in men and aggressiveness in women. We find that this is a crucially important reminder for many couples because the popular emphasis on sex differences has created considerable intimate havoc.

Artificial, culturally induced stereotypes are barriers to a partner's accessibility ("You'd never understand me because you're a man."). They can be used as a shaming device ("I hate it when you baby-talk. It's so unmasculine."). They can put a partner in emotional handcuffs or keep one's self in handcuffs for purposes of withdrawal ("Women never ask for sex."). And they can be powerful barriers to desirable change —the kind of growth that may be the result of effective therapy ("Don't make this a command performance! I'm the man. We'll do it when I'm good and ready.").

Most unfortunate of all, such accusations as "You're not feminine!" or "You're not masculine!" have created new neuroses by bewildering and worrying many partners about how to be genitally more orgastic in the "right" sex-role style—how to be able to have the fullest orgasms in order to be truly feminine and how to maintain virile staying power to be authentically masculine. So now males worry about what they ought to do to be considered male enough; and women worry about what they ought to do to live up to being an ideal woman as pictured in this sex-role casting game. Each partner projects onto the other the fear that they will not live up to the stereotypes. And the accusation of not living up to these myths has become part of the use of sexuality as a strategic weapon. We teach trainees to cry "Stereotype!" or "False!" or "Foul!" whenever a partner tries to use sex-role typing during fighting, but it is remarkable how many partners are eager to play patsy to the sex identity game.

Although we have discussed the reversibility of male and female roles previously, we should caution here that reversibility does have limits, and they all seem to favor the female. There is, for example, a real difference between the sexual stamina of the sexes. Once fully aroused, the average adult female has a far greater sexual capacity than even the most proficient male lover. Therefore, contrary to the pretentious male philosophy espoused by the playboy-encouraging magazines, only the female is naturally endowed to fulfill varietistic sex dreams. In today's culture not much is heard about these female fantasies. At least not yet. But if some day enough women decide to become active sex varietists, they will revolutionize the culture by reversing the double stand ard. Meanwhile, it is at least worth noting that no one male can possibly fulfill the maximal wants that a sexually mature female is capable of enjoying; so there is always the danger that the one male of a one-male female can be made to feel sexually inadequate, castrated, or exhausted.

Physiological differences also make it obviously easier for women to engage in sex faking. But probably the most significant gap between the sexes is a psychological difference engendered by the role of the female as the producer of life. All that the male can hope for in sex is an orgastic ejaculation. The female's need for sex release is not necessarily as urgent, probably because she senses that her real day to shine is in the delivery room, not in the bedroom. Consequently, the female is freer to use the sex act for nonsexual strategic purposes.

In a fight-training seminar we once enacted a psychodramatic simulation of a bedroom scene that went as follows:

HE: With me inside you I feel alive, like a real man.
SHE: So why did you have dinner at your mother's last night?

The seminar group rocked with the laughter of ready recognition and several of the men exclaimed, "Ouch!" The wife who figured in this exchange, like so many others, had used the urgency of her husband's arousal to turn him into a captive audience for an extraneous grievance. She happened to use sex as a weapon after intercourse. Most women would strike beforehand, perhaps just to clear the decks. At any rate, women would do well not to abuse their natural advantages by contaminating the sex act in these ways. "Victories" in sex fights that do not really deal with sex itself tend to be short-lived. Usually they just inspire resentment and further needless battles. This again illustrates that a short-term "winner" in marital fighting can be the loser in the long run.

Sex myth No. 6 holds that *sex games are an innocent sport.* We are not referring to sexual playfulness (such as chasing and being chased), but to hostility rituals as in masculinity and femininity type casting and as described in the book, *Games People Play.* Sex games are notorious instruments of conflict-avoidance and sex-spoiling. They are the avocations of couples who are fearful of being hurt through involvement. The games may appear to help establish a stable and mutually agreeable-seeming routine union, but in point of fact they yield a gradually increasing anger between the players and are foolproof insurance against the emergence of spontaneous, transparent, realistic intimacy.

Earlier we discussed how many times a partner should be required to say "no" to a partner's request so that both will be certain of their true positions in a conflict. In nonsexual matters, this is a useful strategy—at least up to a point. But when applied to sex, this technique easily escalates into one of the most common and crude sex games. It begins when a partner, male or female, makes a sexual advance and the other either ignores or repulses it. Most people think of this as a primarily female ploy as described by Dr. Berne's game book in his version of "Frigid Woman." Our clinical experience has shown, however, that—either verbally or nonverbally—the game of "Come on, keep trying so I can reject you!" is played by both sexes.

The rejection may range from a continuing refusal of intercourse to an eventual perfunctory giving in—but with the passive partner, who may be male or female, displaying the fact that he or she is merely going through the motions; which is a form of accommodation that actually insults and rejects. Weak egos cannot afford this game and must accept or be accepted on the first round. But often the rejector seduces the advancer to go on making advances. Inherent in the game is a test of attractiveness: "How many times can I say 'no' to you and see you still trying?" This kind of provocation-through-seduction, followed by rejection, is a potentially lethal strategy. Some people like to test a partner's "understanding" by means of this game, but this is emphatically not recommended.

According to the seventh and final major sex myth, *sexual adjustment is a natural process that happens more or less by itself*. Nothing could be further off the factual mark. Intimates who want good, successful, fulfilling sex must be prepared to fight for it. Negative emotions, far from spoiling sex, as tradition argues, play a necessary and sex-enhancing part in the creative process of two lovers searching for their own best sex-fit.

As with other fight issues, there are always partners who would rather go without sex than fight; or who would put up with perfunctory, unpleasurable sex because they fear authentic encounter. But most cultured people not only have a very active sex drive but are willing to fight for better sex if they see they have a chance to attain it.

The necessary calibration process is best learned through the pure-sex fights mentioned early in this chapter.

Once again, physiological fact suggests why this is an

indispensable step. The only natural aspects of human sexuality are the capacity to be aroused; and, once arousal and its physiological responses exist, there is a natural interest in doing something appropriate to achieve sexual release. When the action phase is reached in normal adult men and women, however, they cannot rely on "what comes naturally" because what comes naturally in sex situations is worry and insecurity: worry about sufficient attractiveness; about how to persuade the partner to become cooperative; about being rejected; about sexual incompetence; about fulfilling the sexual expectations that were aroused during courtship.

What to do about one's sexual interest, then, is based on knowledge acquired through many trials and errors. Couples learn by gradually discarding the sex myths and accumulating authentic sex information about each other. Throughout this process, fights are helpful in achieving good sexual swing. And people who are allergic to mixing sex with constructive aggression will, in our experience, wind up with a much less satisfactory sex life than those who confront each other with their respective preferences and keep these sex calibration fights clear of other issues.

19. Fighting Before, During, and After Sex

How can couples purge nonsexual issues from sex fights? Many mates find that this is a difficult skill to acquire, but the practical way to do it is absurdly simple.

Suppose the husband is aroused but the wife says, "Oh you've been so awful. I just can't suddenly forget that and make love now. I'm not a machine!"

This stance may tempt the husband to become a con man. He may lie and say he has changed his mind about the conflict that made him appear so "awful" in his wife's eyes. He may falsely deny the importance of the controversy. Or ask forgiveness when there is really nothing to forgive. Or he may play hurt and try to shame his wife into changing her mind.

These con-man methods are not fair and they may boomerang badly during subsequent attempts to manage conflicts about nonsexual issues. Husbands who find themselves in such situations should try to accept what is often difficult at the time: that contaminated sex—*i.e.*, sex dependent on negotiations about other kinds of conflicts—is not worth having. The sensible way for the husband to cope with the above situation is to get out of bed and say, "Let's let the sheets air out. Let's go in the living room and talk."

Trained couples also learn how to buy "rejection insurance"; they know how to negotiate for sex now, with the understanding that there will be a fair fight about the pending nonsexual issue later. Couples can wean themselves away from chronic sex withholding—a technique, incidentally, that is even more popular with men than with women.

Sex withholding is not only a cruel but an unrewarding ploy, even when the withholder has no ulterior strategic motives. Suppose the wife is simply "tired." In this common situation she should consider having intercourse anyway as long as the husband does not demand that she be fully "with it." A demand for full passion is an irrational request in the face of a natural disparity ("If I'm turned on, I expect you to be turned on, too"). Such male demands for matching

246

passions turn most women off because the acts of *being* loved and *giving* love are not the same and do not have to happen simultaneously.

There is nothing wrong with saying, in effect: "I'm hungry. Can we please have dinner? Maybe you're not hungry, but surely that isn't going to prevent you from feeding me, is it?" Such an approach may not be in keeping with old-fashioned ideas of courtly romance, but it serves the relationship considerably better than an air of unhappy resignation, followed by an insulted, "Aw, let's forget it," which converts a demand for sex into something close to an obligation.

Of course there cannot be intercourse every time one mate is so inclined. A certain amount of daily physical warmth greatly helps by serving as a sex substitute. We often hear the complaint, "My husband (or wife) is never affectionate unless it's for sex." Most of these couples would not have this difficulty if they solved their bedtime snuggling problem. When we start to talk seriously of "snuggling" as a problem, most people begin to laugh. This never bothers us because couples who master the intimate art of snuggling find that this eliminates many of their sex difficulties.

Creative snuggling strengthens the intimate bond by providing helpful reassurance of love, for example during the menstrual period when women are likely to reject themselves as undesirable. We suspect that for couples who establish good snuggling habits early, the mastery of this art may prove life-prolonging in their less passionate senior years. And we have records of numerous cases of stubborn insomnia that were cured by newly learned snuggling techniques.

Creative snuggling is not feasible in twin beds. A narrow bed lacks space for adequate maneuvering. We are opposed to twin beds anyway because they encourage an attitude of "We only get together for sex." It *is* possible for mates to sleep in separate beds or even separate rooms and still maintain intimacy. Some spouses insist on this separation because one partner snores or is afflicted with light phobia or other conditions. These people must be on guard to remain ultra-communicative in their living rooms in order to compensate for their bedtime separation. Even then, however, they may be excessively interested in asserting their individuality; they may not have solved the problem of finding and maintaining optimal distance from each other so they can enjoy entwinement without engulfment; and their insistence on separate beds may represent a partner's radical protest against too much encroachment on his autonomy as an individual in his own right.

Natural snugglers usually manage to maneuver themselves silently into a position of maximum contact warmth. These tend to be the fortunate partners who enjoy back-to-stomach contact. They are also the ones who have no problem finding complementary positions for their arms so they can embrace. Others must be encouraged to experiment and apply verbal or nonverbal pats, slaps, or kicks. Back-to-back snuggling can be satisfactory, although an embrace is necessarily lacking. Two partners who are natural stomach-to-stomach snugglers must learn to snuggle in relays. In relationships where one partner is a natural snuggler and the other is a natural nonsnuggler this disparity can become a major issue for fights and negotiations.

Once the first sex issue is joined—to do it or not to do it—the next legitimate point of conflict is the matter of who chases whom. Almost every couple in fight training has complained about imbalances in this phase, and the grievances come from men as often as from women:

"I always have to be the one to make the pass," or "He never reaches out for me," etc. A typical session with a couple may begin like this:

HE: I always have to start it. You never come to me.
DR. BACH: What's wrong with that, as long as you get together?
HE: It's not fair.

Such a couple probably has an unrealistically romantic picture of the sexual relationship as a *quid pro quo*, like an exchange of presents. We may suggest: "If you have complaints about this picture, you are always at liberty to tear it up. If you really feel it would be more fun for you to be the receiver of aggression more often, then you have to change your wife's and your own attitudes and work things out. This may not be easy. We know many couples where neither partner is a good receiver, for instance. You may be starting to tinker with a delicate balance. This is perfectly all right as long as both of you know what's involved and are interested, out of a sense of love, to change things."

The point is that, ideally, a balance of stimulation can be achieved between intimates. Some supersensitive people resent all comparisons between humans and animals, but it is educational to observe how an intelligent dog calibrates the chasing problem into superb balance when he plays "come and get it." He will pick up a bone or toy and try to set up his owner to give chase and take the toy away. The dog will be far superior in agility, speed, and evasiveness. So he handicaps his master and lets him take the toy after an ideal amount of chasing. The ideal point is reached when the dog judges that the chase lasted long enough for both to have fun, but not so long that the master becomes exhausted or loses interest.

Another realistic sex fight can arise over efforts to fuse the partners' tastes for sex fun and aggression release. Many women complain that their mates are too passive. These wives often wish for more aggressive, rougher, even hurtful sex. And husbands, not theirs, frequently bemoan that wives inhibit male aggressiveness, insisting that they can make love only "if you're gentle with me."

Most couples learn on their own how to cooperate so they at least occasionally combine the best sex release with a mutually liked and safe aggression release. But in these hedonistic times sex release is easier to achieve than aggression release because so many people have been brainwashed against personal aggression in any form, natural as it is. Today's culture defines aggression as carrying obnoxious stimuli to an opponent, but this does not explain why some forms of pain yield pleasure as well as information; for example, in the sexual act when aggressive responses such as squeezing, biting, pinning the partner down, or noises of an aggressive nature, abusive language or telling dirty stories become part of pleasure. Indeed, for some so-called "sado-maso" partners, giving pain or threatening it is a necessary condition for promoting orgasm.

Sexologists have hardly touched upon this subject except with respect to extreme sadomasochistic sex behavior that is clearly deviant. In our view, normal partners should be carefully encouraged to practice the kind of carefully gauged "attacks" that we have come to call "sextacks." This requires very sensitive coordination between the two sex fighters. And it is risky: being either too meek or too rough in the search for aggression release may cool the partner or even lead to physical injury. It is therefore necessary to gauge oneself and one's partner about the level of aggression that provides the best mutual release. For this purpose we developed a *sextacks self-rating scale* with statements for the female partner to answer "yes" or "no" about herself. Here are the various possible forms of sextacks:

1. GENTLE THROUGHOUT: I never like to be handled aggressively.

2. PRIMARILY GENTLE: I like things to become occasionally, but very briefly, aggressive.

3. AGGRESSIVE GENTLE: I like things mixed, as momentary mood dictates, but never anything as in 6 and 7, below.

4. GENITALLY AGGRESSIVE: I like to be firmly handled in sex, but without extra aggression.

5. AGGRESSIVE: I like to be very firmly and very aggressively handled in sex but not hurt or threatened.

6. THREATENED VIOLENT AGGRESSIVE: I like to be threatened with physical attacks.

7. VIOLENT AGGRESSIVE: I like to be physically hurt in sex: bitten or pinched, or pinned down or hurtfully slapped, squeezed, etc. This turns me on and makes me more passionate.

To ascertain the degree of congruity or dissonance between spouses, and as a means of accurately understanding the other and not just attributing to the other a position not actually taken, the male partner should *independently check* the rating scale, trying to guess which of the seven levels his partner would check. The question is:

"In making love to your mate, how aggressively do you think she prefers to be handled by you to maximize her pleasure?"

Generally there is a tendency for the guess level to be one or two steps removed from the self-rating and this goes for both male and female guessing. The female usually guesses the male as preferring higher amounts of aggression than he himself rates. Women, especially during the uncertainties of seduction and early courtship, will accommodate to the male level of aggression assigned to them. They usually keep secret their own desire for more or less tenderness and tend to fake a step or two up or down the sextacks scale. This faked accommodation is a form of collusion designed to keep alive in the male the stereotype image of feeling masculine, using the female's response as his measure of masculinity. Similarly, women use their popularity with males to confirm their femininity and worth, even though this does not work—as the tragic case of Marilyn Monroe and the ruses of other female sex symbols demonstrate.

As partners learn how to fuse sex and aggression, their sex satisfaction gradually increases and their need to injure others verbally or physically decreases. By working with single and divorced sex varietists we also discovered that ideal levels of aggression change whenever partners change. For example, when Partner A is with Partner B-1 he prefers sextack level 5; with Partner B-2 his level of sexual aggression must be raised two levels. The optimal sextack level is always pair-specific for males as well as females: with one male a certain female prefers to be taken rape-style like Ivan the Terrible while another partner turns her off and cools her at the application of roughness beyond sextack 4. In other words, she cannot enjoy the more aggressive sex approach from everybody.

Few people like to admit it, but many men and women have very lively fantasies about aggressive sex, including raping and being raped. Producers of pornography and movies cater to these fantasies and people who harbor and enjoy such secrets are by no means psychological freaks. In women, these dreams are often started in childhood if their chief contacts with their fathers consisted of being firmly held or spanked. In men, these fantasies may hark back to fathers who liked to pin down their son in rough wrestling matches.

Marital "rape," of course, can be condoned only if it is rape by invitation or consent. As a strategy it is not usually recommended, but for some couples it is not necessarily a poor idea. Some men are most strongly stimulated if they occasionally signal their mates, "I can't stand to be near you without possessing you!" And some women like to resist and protest too much. When they say "No, not now!" they really mean "Yes if" (you really passionately want me). Then such a wife can give herself to the rapist and say "I'm overcome by you."

Women may be greatly embarrassed by their concern that it's not "nice" to seduce men to overcome female resistance by physical means; or for women to admit that this is one of their favorite ways of surrendering. But men should not simply assume that their partners don't at times feel like being raped; and that "no" can mean "yes" if the pursuit is persistent, skillful, and genuinely passionate.

We would like to re-emphasize that it may well be dangerous to toy with these techniques. No one should ever assume he has *carte blanche* to play Ivan the Terrible. It's best to be on the lookout for clues: Does the wife have to be "overcome" every time? Does the husband know how to cope with "invitations" when they are issued in the form of strenuous resistance? And it's worth remembering that in constructive fighting, aggression by one partner is constantly open to be checked by limitation from the other.

Finding the right range of acceptable sex aggression is indeed a problem. But a mismatch of sex styles may lead to less sex and then to infidelities. Experiments to discover the mutually agreeable sextack level can be fun. The preferred limits can be signaled and success in locating the right sextack level increases erotic joy. Next to physical cruelty itself, perhaps the most cruel thing that can happen between intimates is to deny a partner sex fulfillment. And one way to deny it is out of fear of hurting the other.

Another type of fight that cools partners prior to the sex act is the conflict over pregnancy. Suppose both husband and wife want a baby. This may turn sex into a command performance for the husband, especially at such times when the wife is most likely to become impregnated. Quite a few husbands resent their wives' control over their offspring and the pressure to perform at certain times may render males psychologically infertile (impotent). They tell their wives, "I won't do it on command!" And to themselves they confess, "I can't do it on command."

In such a situation the wife should remember the facts of life: Pregnancy is her responsibility and it may well depend on her skill at erotic seduction. If it cools a husband to have sex on schedule, it is up to her to use her feminine charm and persuade him to have sex as often as possible without regard to her temperature chart or his sperm count.

More frequently, the fertility fights will be contraceptive fights, and these are by no means restricted to couples worried about their fertility. The issue is a pregnancy unwanted by one of the partners. Here is a couple where the husband has cooled because his wife insists on using birth control pills:

HE: I'd like us to have another child.
SHE: I think two are enough. I can't wait to get Bobby and Mike into school so I can go back to school myself. I don't like to be tied down.
HE: You're selfish!
SHE: You're damned right I am!

This is an example of another contaminated sex fight. This couple's sex life will probably be adversely affected as long as they fail to negotiate an agreement about the obvious nonsexual aspects of their disagreement about contraception.

In a similar case, the husband is equally put off by his wife's control over their offspring, but for the opposite reason: he doesn't want another child, but he suspects that his wife does. So he checks on her supply of pills in the bathroom and finds that none has been taken.

HE: I see you haven't been taking your pills.

SHE: It isn't that time of the month yet. (*He studies the instructions on the pill container and reads them out loud.*)

SHE: I only take them because you hate condoms so much. I hate the pills. They make me fat and nervous and I keep hearing they could be dangerous.

HE: Now you're making me feel selfish. I thought we had this all settled.

SHE: You started it by snooping around my pills. . . .

This couple was advised that neither partner should ever play detective on the other. If the husband hadn't started snooping, this wife probably would have resumed taking the pills at the proper time. If there was an issue unsettled between them (Should he try condoms again? Should she change to a diaphragm?) the conflict should be argued out on the basis of the merits as the partners see them.

Most commonly, contraceptive fights involve the super-bomb of deception. The wife may pretend to take the pills, but actually omit taking them in order to have a child for the purpose of tying the husband closer to her. Some husbands insist on watching their wives take the pills with their breakfast juice each morning, just to be sure there will be no undesired pregnancy. This raises the delicate subject of sex faking—whether actual or merely suspected or threatened. Unhappily, the variety of methods for possible sex fakery is enormous and a remarkably large number of partners use at least one of the methods some of the time.

Much of this deception is based on male distrust of possible feminine trickery. In investigating the increasing number of males who ask surgeons to perform vasectomies (making orgasm possible without impregnation), researchers learned that many unmarried women want to become pregnant so they can apply "wedding pressure"; and quite a few married women swallow pills secretly to avoid having children wanted by their husbands.

Quite a few vasectomy-seeking males also have hidden motives. They suspect that their women may be unfaithful and wish to have proof of infidelity if a wife becomes pregnant. Sex varietists who want to reduce conflicts over their own promiscuous sex activities also favor vasectomies. And there are wives with tied tubes or hysterectomies whose husbands are convinced that the women use the freedom from pregnancy to get away with sexual infidelity (although, of course, the men can never know).

The more conventional forms of sex faking involve Partner A's pretending to be pleased by sex techniques which "B" is "good at," and which "B" strongly believes to be effective in producing sexual joy for "A." In fact, "A" does not find them exciting. This is another form of colluding with a partner's unrealistic fantasies.

The faking usually begins, as so many hidden intimate conflicts do, in courtship or during the honeymoon phase of marriage. At the beginning of sexual intimacy, there is an urgency about sex without bothering about the finer points of the quality of sexual experience. New sex mates are so eager to please, and to be experienced as pleasing, that they often do not know their own true feelings. And if they do know what turns them sexually on and off, they dare not tell. They may fear to reveal their inexperience or inaptitude or the limits of their sex-technical education. Or they may fear they are *too* experienced and might overwhelm or shock a less experienced partner.

Fear of rejection, eagerness to be a successful seducer or vamp, and the wish to please a new love are powerful motives for sex fakery. This is a natural tendency during the uncertainties inherent in being in love, but it can be the start of serious trouble. Joy based on faking almost never lasts, and the sooner new lovers bring themselves to level with each other about their sex preferences, the less likely it is that they will be drawn into the cycle of sex withholding, infidelities, and possible divorce.

The most common form of sex deception is the faking of orgasms. Women, obviously, can fake by play-acting. They can get away with it because most men would rather believe the fakery than face sex problems. A man cannot fake sperm ejaculations, but his sex faking can consist of such techniques as: exaggerating passion; inventing and displaying passions he does not feel; faking fatigue (rather than admitting disinterest); escalating pelvic thrust and other vigorous movements moments before he senses he will lose his erection; withdrawing and pretending that he feared impregnation and therefore preferred not to come "inside of you."

The male faker's strategy must circumvent the old adage that "The penis never lies." He cannot play-act as effectively as the female. Even this sex-role difference is being erased, however, as millions of sex-book readers become familiar with the more diffuse but nevertheless clear signs of true female orgasticity. One sure sign of fakery is a woman's report that she always comes at the precise time of male ejaculation. This wish to fake climax is based on the erroneous assumption that intercourse without climax is a total failure and always causes pain and frustration. On the other hand, an occasional exaggerated display of passion—physically and/or verbally—can be a loving act designed to maximize the sex pleasures of the partner.

Differences of orgasic release experiences are customarily attributed by Partner "A" to "B" so "B" can take the blame for a relatively poor experience. The weapon is to slap "B" down for any "performance" that is not up to par, especially if "B" is personally and/or sexually insecure.

To castrate the male and degrade and devaluate the female is extremely easy. Nobody has to say anything. A little sigh of boredom or annoyance is enough for an insecure partner to pick up the signal: "You're a lousy lover!" By the same token, not trying one's best as a lover and being careless and inconsiderate is also a weapon. This signal says: "As long as I enjoy myself and you don't mind, why not?"

Many sex partners, particularly near-frigid women who have to have conditions just right to achieve orgasm, engage in collusion. Like Tom Hurst, a 24-year-old management trainee, and his best girl Caroline Hayes, 22. First there is the fight they had one night in bed:

CAROLINE (*with real hate in her voice*): All you ever do is take care of yourself!

TOM (*sleepily*): Why not? You never objected before. It's better that one of us gets something out of it, isn't it?

CAROLINE (*frustrated*): Well, I like it too . . . I just need more attention.

TOM (*yawning*): I *am* attending to you. I make love to you any time you want.

CAROLINE (*angry*): But you don't do it right!

Now here is what happened when this fight was discussed at a group training session:

CAROLINE: He got so mad! Now he doesn't call me any more and it's my own damn fault. I let him get away with it during our first dozen or so dates. I faked. But it hangs me up, having to pretend for his sake. Now I can't pretend any more because I started to drink. I got high and he got mad and left, so we never got things straightened out.

GROUP MEMBER: Why didn't you tell him: "You don't

satisfy me the way you make love; it doesn't turn me on. Let's try something else"?

CAROLINE: If he's so stupid that he couldn't tell I was faking and I wasn't really with it, why bother?

DR. BACH: You overestimate his ability to understand the situation, and you underestimate the difficulty of understanding something negative and threatening. People don't want to see problems they are causing, and they certainly aren't searching for problems in a love affair. You may be a good actress in bed, but how can you expect anybody to disregard his pro-sex orientation and divine your reserve?

CAROLINE: Oh, I know I let him get away with it. But I was afraid he wouldn't want me any more and would get mad at me and I find him terribly attractive. So I colluded, as you say here. I can't help it. When I like somebody I guess I just collude!

DR. B: Sure, but in the long run you lose them and in the short run you kid yourself and each other. Losing and kidding, is this your way of love life?

Such collusions in bed are good for only occasional sex-fun fakery, but on a steady diet of such "sexual cooperation," intimacy would gradually starve to death.

The idea that anybody can be made to feel like a "real big man" or a "real lovely woman," just because of a partner's reactions, is not valid, at least not with people who have worth in their own eyes. If this value is only in the eyes, brain and heart of the other, and not in the self, there is no way of transferring it—at least not between adults. Only during a relatively short, impressionable phase of juvenile identity formation can a significant reference figure, who is admired by a youth, impress him with his worth to the extent that the youth can incorporate the friend's positive image.

Once this phase is passed, no transfer of worthiness from the other to the self is possible. And yet, this is the secret wish of many hopeful intimates: to increase their own self-worth, particularly in sex, through identification with the other's positive view and response.

A sexually insecure partner often believes that by serving as facilitator of the partner's orgastic experience and being a good lover in the partner's eyes the insecure partner will become a good lover in his own eyes.

This is a facet of the orgasm myth and only creates bitter disappointments in the failing partner. Instead of discarding the myth and working directly on the lack of self-worthiness, immature and insecure lovers tend to get rid of each other and hold onto the myth, looking forever for the "right" partner through whose orgastic fulfillment they can themselves be confirmed as "good lovers."

This is another example of how much more than sexual intercourse goes on between the sheets. Sex is easily used for identity validation, and lovers who depend on each other's sexual response for their own sex identity hold a more lethal weapon over each other's heads than those who enjoy sexy-sex for its own sake, uncontaminated by the identity struggle.

Except for its occasional value in heightening erotic excitement, sex faking is more than an energy waster and tension producer. Worse, it creates the kind of misplaced good will and tactfulness that stimulates counterfaking. Soon the entire intimate system may be infected by phoniness that can always be rationalized as a "concern for the feelings of others." It can also create a backlash of mistrust because even the most artful sex fakers are found out by their partners, later if not sooner. How? The faker may get tired of the burden. Or he may not care what happens and spill the secret. Or he may want to provoke the partner into extreme anger. Or he feels he can hold the partner regardless. Or he feels he can do without orgasm.

Whatever the reason for discovery, what happens? Permanent mates tend to develop a repertoire of certain sex routines. If these routines turn out to have been based on fakery rather than genuine likes and dislikes, a couple's entire sex life can become exposed as a net of white lies. Few liaisons, however prolonged, can survive such a discovery.

Sex fakery can be exposed before there is permanent damage. Mrs. Ethel Harper, a 29-year-old mother of two, had never had an orgasm. She had always faked it. Her husband Bill, the owner of two dry-cleaning stores, had remained unaware. Eventually, the faking became too much trouble for Ethel. She became sexually indifferent. She loved her husband deeply, but she told Bill, "It just isn't any fun any more."

Both partners blamed the problem on their older child. "I can always put the baby in his crib," Ethel said, "but the four-year-old just keeps barging into our bedroom. And even when he doesn't I'm always so aware of their noise." The Harpers couldn't conscientiously farm out the children because they both had neurotic parents. This had been one of their bonds during courtship.

Bill did nothing about the situation because he felt he

should be a good father and not curb the children's freedom. As a result, he had no sexual satisfaction and he was beginning to resent his little sons.

Not long after this couple began fight training their sex life had turned much more satisfactory. "You can't believe the change in my husband," Ethel told us. The privacy problem had been solved in no time at all. Bill simply put a lock on the bedroom door. But the crucial point was that they began to level with each other about what really bothered them, as shown in this exchange at our office.

DR. BACH: Did you do your homework and share your concern about your small breasts with your husband?

ETHEL: Yes. You see, my husband subscribes to *Playboy*. So I opened up the magazine to the Playmate of the Month. She was huge. To me she looked like a man's dream girl. I felt so small. I asked Bill, "How can a girl compete with this?" He just laughed and told me not to be ridiculous. The girl in the picture was much too big for his taste.

DR. B: And did you find out anything about his own sex worries?

ETHEL: I sure did. I guess the talk about my breasts brought it up. Anyway, he told me he felt his penis was very small.

DR. B: And what did you say to that?

ETHEL: I told him that now it's my turn to tell *him* he's ridiculous. I said, "It's not the size; it's what you do with it that counts."

Their mutual discovery and reassurance, without deep analysis, was sufficient for this couple to find their own way toward a better relationship.

Other orgasm conflicts develop because it is so much easier for the female to continue faking than it is for the male. Since the penis cannot usually avoid displaying whatever state the male's emotions allow it to be in, the woman possesses greater power to collude with the male's image of masculinity; she can make him feel like a great lover and carry her burden in private. The male is more vulnerable to being duped. Knowing this, he is generally more cautious about becoming involved. For the same reason, the vulnerable male also tends to be grateful to females who reliably give him a true sense of virility by the skillful use of passion-arousing strategies.

A common embarrassment occurs—and while it involves no faking, it is so great an embarrassment that it is sometimes interpreted as outright hostility—when a couple approaches climax but the male loses his erection or the female loses interest at the moment when the other is approaching climax. This may occur for several reasons. A partner may sometimes experience an overcharge, followed by a physiological short-circuiting. Psychologically, it is also possible that an element of sexual competition may be making itself felt. One of the partners may be feeling, "I won't let him/her have more fun than I have." Hostility may also play an important role in a man who resents that his partner is not displaying enough excitement. Or the wife may resent that he isn't paying enough attention to her cues ("He's supposed to serve me!").

The true explanation for this embarrassing difficulty is usually much simpler. One of the lovers may be too tired or may have had too much to drink. Or it may just be an evening when they "aren't on the same wave length" for some reason. If this doesn't happen too often, what difference does it make as long as the problem doesn't linger, undiscussed, to poison a relationship?

Fortunately, true intimates do not prolong sex faking beyond the point necessary to get together and enjoy each other. They forgive each other's fakery if it is confessed tactfully and early enough in the relationship. After all, theirs was probably a mutual game of image-making. Nevertheless, the transition from sex faking to a genuine love life represents one of the major crises of intimacy and relies heavily on the ability of partners to fight it out in the open for better, more authentic sexuality.

The ensuing experimentation calls for a fusion of "his" way and "her" way into "our" way. Each should become a facilitator for the other. As their repertoire grows, they should eventually find new ground that is mutually exciting. The acquisition of this knowledge is a very bonding event. It increases sexual confidence and makes mutual, if not simultaneous, orgasm more attainable. Feedback—about what turns each partner on or off—stimulates excitement in the other.

After a while, experimentation tends to cease because partners prefer to conserve sexual energy and to expend it only on tried-and-true ways to give and receive sex joy. Now they can relax and enjoy successful sex unless they happen to be sex varietists at heart, which most people, male and female, are not.

How to keep sex exciting and still predictably pleasurable? This is one of the main paradoxes of intimate living. It, too, can be mastered through legitimate sex fights. Sex rituals, no matter how desirable and comfortable, should be kept open for revisions, repeals, and amendments; the routines must always be kept negotiable via clear cues or commands. This is effective insurance against monotony, and we tell those women who fear that female criticism at the time of intercourse will make the male feel inferior that this is certainly thoughtful; however, if reluctance to criticize leads a woman to collude with an illusion of what is manly about her mate, he will feel far worse when he eventually discovers the truth.

Another insurance against sex monotony is the extension of sex beyond the bedroom. The bed is not necessarily the best place for the desirable daily exchange of some physical affection. Most couples have no reservations about the role of the bed in sex, but a sound psychological case can be made against it. Bed is where people go to be lazy, sick, tired, infantile, and eventually to die. People prefer the sterility of the bed for sex because of obvious convenience and we don't argue with them about it. We do encourage spouses to realize that the integration of general affection with specific sex can best be accomplished by learning to sense and share feelings of warmth, interest, and concern—even the slightest stirrings of such feelings—everywhere, and not just in the bedroom. If there is sufficient privacy for sex on the living-room couch, in the office, in the garden, or anywhere else away from home, we recommend it as a stimulating experience, especially for older couples.

Established sex mates know exactly what to expect from the first look of interest and the first touch of erotic foreplay. They cannot fool themselves or each other, and therein lies the deep value of familiar sex rituals among permanent intimates. The rituals may not always be the same, but after a while there is likely to be less variety because the old ways are deeply conditioned and imprinted. The sex partners become dependent on the nonvariety ritual, often to the point where even the most enticingly new love affair will leave them sexually cold.

We do, however, usually encourage fighting for more sex fun between established partners in order to relieve monotony and avoid possible boredom. Fortunately, mature and experienced partners do not mind some not-so-enjoyable sex activities. They consent, for example, to the intimate use of vulgar language if one of the partners finds this exciting. Doing something sexy with—and for—a partner, as long as it is tolerable and not painful or considered "disgusting," can be an important gesture of giving—a sexual favor bestowed as a goodwill offering. When partners find such gestures difficult or impossible, and this frequently occurs in fights for a greater variety of positions, the resistance may be based on sources more significant than aesthetics. To illustrate:

HE: Why don't you ever let me make love to you from the back?

SHE: Oh, honey, we've been all over that before.

HE: Yes, and that's just it! I've told you so often I like to experiment with different positions, like it says in those books I bought. Have you read them yet?

SHE: I tried to. I honestly did. But they're disgusting! I have enough trouble doing it the regular way.

HE: But can't you see? I want to help you get over that. I'd like you to feel sexually free.

SHE (*annoyed*): Now you're pushing me! You know how hard it is for me to come. I couldn't care less, but it's so important to you that I come ... no, that isn't even it; it's so important to you that you make me come. ...

HE: Well, of course, I want to be good for you. Don't you like to get all excited?

SHE: Not if it means I have to swing from the chandelier and do somersaults, for heaven's sake! I'm not the type. If you need a lot of fancy gyrations, go and get yourself one of those bunnies you keep staring at in *Playboy*. If you have the energy and the time and money, go ahead and have yourself a ball! I'm not a whore!

In this case, the husband's sexual demands actually were excessive for this partner. Her offer to let him practice his sex-varietist urges outside of marriage were the result of her desperate search for a safety valve. Rather than lose this mate, the wife reached for outside help for relief from the intolerable pressure to be sexually more competent.

Fights after love-making also tend to have a special significance that couples can learn to recognize. As noted earlier, there is a tendency for lovers, after love-making, to grope toward a return of an optimal distance between each other. For many couples the experience of orgastic surrender is frightening—to the surrenderer as well as to the agent and witness of the surrender. A wife often picks a fight "over nothing" soon after a particularly close sexual experience with her husband. The husband will be greatly puzzled by this. He may not want to face the real issue that the wife is fearful of her sexual dependency, or perhaps fearing to love "too much" and becoming too vulnerable to rejection.

The post-orgastic strategy of alienating and "cooling it" is also often needed to bring lovers out of the autistic, narcissistic frame of mind into which they were plunged by their own orgastic activity. They need time, literally, to re-enter the state of emotional intimacy after having been so strongly involved with autistic sex intimacy.

For couples who learn to understand the paradoxes and other human complexities of a long-term sexual relationship, it becomes entirely feasible to divorce themselves from non-sexual conflicts before making love; to recognize the need for pure-sex (sexual calibration) fights during the love-making phase; and to resume the fight for good, livable emotional swing a reasonable time afterward. Husbands and wives who have mastered the art of keeping their sex life dynamic in the ways described here—while keeping sex away from possible contamination by other issues—report that their marriages are more stimulating and satisfying than ever. These successful long-term lovers also say they feel more secure with their partners. This is no small achievement because, as everybody knows, the institution of marriage has never in modern times been so vulnerable to attack by the temptations of extramarital sex.

20. Marital Fights About Extramarital Sex

To be or not to be monogamous is, for most married people in today's culture, a perplexing decision, and the choice is becoming more difficult in more marriages all the time. Infidelity is on the increase. The late Dr. Alfred C. Kinsey's statistics, based largely on interviews conducted in the now so distant 1940's, revealed a remarkably high incidence. Since then, encouraged by the freedom granted by birth-control pills and by an atmosphere of growing permissiveness concerning all sexuality, sexual roaming has become considerably more prevalent. Whatever may motivate partners to live their sex lives by either the exclusive or the varied commitment is not at issue here. Neither are the complex moral and legal implications. What concerns us are the effects of infidelity on intimate partnerships.

When both partners are true loyalists and neither one "plays around," they have the formidable task of making their sex life with each other so mutually fulfilling that their suppressed varietist urges do not give them too much trouble. For whenever varietist tendencies make themselves felt, perhaps at cocktail parties, on business trips or at other opportune times, the partners are likely to nag each other about the limitations of their sex life. Inevitably most mates will be tempted—or threaten—to cheat at least on some occasions during a long-term bond.

A mutually fulfilling monogamous sex life is highly desirable and entirely attainable, especially when couples appreciate the importance of realistic fighting for better sex. Unfortunately, the loyalist life is threatened right at the inception of marriage and by the very instrument that is supposed to guarantee stability: Strangely enough, the mischief maker is the marriage contract that calls for "forsaking all others." By signing the marriage license, too many partners tend to assume that a permanent state of mutual exclusive possession is now automatically insured vis-à-vis the "one and only."

Clinical experience proves, however, that the one-time, society-chosen marriage license is more likely to be a license

to become psychologically lazy; that the official documen
turns the fine art of spousing into a routine civil service job
with supposedly perpetual tenure for both partners. Even the
bureaucracies of universities know the wisdom of not extend
ing tenure to professors until after a series of periodic
reappointments, based on continuing scrutiny, merit, and performance. We believe a marriage contract should be based
on private testing and continuing negotiations between partners.

Today there are at least five major styles of intimate
living:

1. *The Exclusive Fidelity Style.* This excludes sexual variety or autonomy and is strongly supported by tradition and
stereotype. It is the favored life style for newlyweds.

2. *The Sex Freedom Style.* Couples who live by this model
are primarily concerned with the quality of commitment and
devotion that exists between them, not with what the mate
does elsewhere. Outsiders—the "they-group"—are not regarded as particularly interesting. They are not considered
threatening to the "in-group," the "we."

3. *The Double-standard Style.* The wife lives by the fidelity
model and the husband may play around, if he does it
discreetly. Two principles apply: "What I don't know doesn't
hurt me" and "Boys will be boys." Tolerance of extramarital
activities tends to cease, however, at the slightest indication
that the marital commitment is being diluted.

4. *The Single-standard Style.* In this relatively rare model,
information about extramarital experiences can become a
source of ritual entertainment ("How is she/he in bed?"). In
such marriages both partners feel drawn to one another as
they enjoy deceiving the third and fourth outside partners,
who are usually used only fleetingly as sexual entertainers,
while the in-group marital unit sticks together.

5. *The Nesting Style.* Many couples are primarily interested in building a family, raising children, and maintaining a
nest where they can entertain themselves. Couples who are
nesting-oriented are frequently rather tolerant of extramarital involvements as long as these do not interfere with the
nesting functions. Extramarital sexual liaisons may be tolerated while children are "too young to know or to sense," but
during the sexually crucial teen years, while children are
groping for their own sex roles, this becomes intolerable and
leads to extremely vigorous fighting.

Many couples adopt one or another of these styles at
different stages of their marriage, and numerous other styles
exist. One type that is becoming less uncommon, especially

among women who harbor aggressive feelings about female rights generally, is the double standard in reverse. As noted earlier, the woman is physiologically highly capable of becoming a sex varietist. She is also presumably "sexy" and somewhat "flighty" while the male is supposed to be steady and devoted. The double standard in reverse is usually kept secret by women who believe in it. We learn about it because these women reveal their attitude in our marathon groups, where faking becomes so difficult that only an actress of almost professional caliber will stick to her illicit guns.

Double-timing women justify themselves by saying: "My extramarital affair is a necessity for me to compensate for the poor state of intimacy between my husband and myself. It saves our marriage." Here is an example of a 32-year-old attorney's wife who play-acted with her husband for years until she thought she was ready to ditch him, if necessary.

SHE: I never let my husband know that I came repeatedly.

DR. BACH: Why not?

SHE: Because he would come and then all sex would stop. He'd just go to sleep and I'd still be sexually aroused but not released. On weekend trips and after parties he'd usually want sex but if he had a golf date the next morning he'd skip sex. When he didn't, he'd be so relaxed that his golf score would be all off. He'd shoot ten or more strokes higher.

DR. B: Wasn't your husband an affectionate and loving man?

SHE: Oh yes, he was affectionate as long as there wasn't any sports activity on the golf course, in baseball, football, horse races, bowling alley, the fight arena, or on the radio or TV. If there were two or more sports events going on he'd have the radio tuned in on one station and the TV to a different sport. And he really knew what was happening in each game! He could even carry on a conversation about an entirely separate third sports event.

DR. B: That's remarkable.

SHE: It is. But, here's where I drew the line; no sex, please, while sports activity was going on. I just didn't feel like that much of a "sport."

DR. B: Didn't you set down the conditions when you could have good sex with your husband?

SHE: No, because if I told him how I really felt I couldn't

trust him. He would make fun of me or use the information to spoil sex for me.

DR. B: Well, didn't you ever have a good fight over this?

SHE: No, we never fought. I became cagey and hid my feelings. Eventually, I fell in love with my minister and we had sex regularly. He was wonderful to me.

DR. B: But you paid a high price for this: anxiety, confusion . . .

SHE: If I had a chance, I'd do it again. I wouldn't have missed it for anything. . . .

When the affair with the minister ended and increasing marital tensions brought the lawyer and his wife to training it developed that this wife had felt she could not display her sexuality to her husband without risking his becoming impotent. Every time she became passionate, he lost his erection. He was one of those partners who become jealously competitive and hostile when the other has more fun. This couple also believed in the myth that only mutual, simultaneous orgasms are fulfilling. Gradually, this husband was able to learn to fulfill his wife first and both eventually were able to enjoy orgasm in relays.

The faking of exclusive devotion is an obvious, attractive strategy for a partner who is married to an overpossessive, overly jealous, sexually insecure spouse. It can even be argued that possessive-controlling spouses invite and conceivably deserve being cheated. In any event, the energy that is spent in maintaining any sort of fakery or overpossessive posture adds strain to the intimate system.

As we noted earlier, transparency must be tempered with infinite tact in cases of sexual disloyalty, at least in most marriages. Over the years we found that only about 10% of our trainee couples are able to live with total honesty in this delicate area. The act of covering up infidelities, then, may become an act of love and save the partner from the indignity of snooping and playing district attorney. At least this strategy is necessary for partners who "know but don't want to know." For them, silence saves them from sanctioning deception ("I don't want him to know that I know"). These loyalists want to look away, and one should not argue with them. For them it is a case of too much realism being too much of a good thing.

The delicacy of this problem has manifested itself many times. In one memorable marathon session some years ago, the majority of the seven couples who were present had partners engaged in extramarital affairs. When one husband courageously opened his inner life for group inspection, he was viciously attacked by the sex loyalists in the group. None of the "infidels" came to his rescue or dared to identify themselves with him. We were about to say, "Halt! You've gotten enough mileage throwing stones at this glass house!" when the confessor's own weeping wife came to the husband's rescue.

"Leave him alone!" she screamed. "Let him be. *I* have to live with him. I *want* to live with him. He's my husband! He likes to be the sexy-stud and he's also a little boy who wants to play. I hate that in him, but I love him anyway!"

She then turned to her husband and shouted, "Go ahead! Screw all your whores! But from now on, I don't want to hear about it again—ever, ever!"

Finally came her last blast: "And to hell with your honesty principle, Dr. Bach! It's very destructive. It's just an excuse to show off. It doesn't do any good. . . ."

This wife had placed herself on record, at last, and made clear that she found the husband's behavior infantile and love-spoiling; that she was neither indifferent nor tolerant toward it. But she had found it even more distasteful to check up on the husband's outside activities and definitely did not wish to lose him.

The husband had exposed that he was a sex varietist at heart but that he also loved his wife and children and liked being married. He claimed that occasional extramarital encounters helped, rather than diluted, the primary intimacy that he shared with his wife. By indulging his playful boyish self on the motel playground, he acquired additional self-importance. Extramarital abstinence, he also reported, often made him turn nasty toward his family; he became depressed and at times even lost sexual virility with the wife. As the partners negotiated a settlement of their differences in the presence of the fight-training group, he agreed to live by the rule of infinite tact and total discretion. This is rarely an ideal solution, but sometimes it is best to accept that rain can occur simultaneously with sunshine.

There are substantial pay-offs for loyalists who are married to sex varietists. Extramarital sex can not only provide relief for the loyalist partner from the varietist spouse's pressure to become sexually more proficient. More importantly, it places the powerful, socially sanctioned weapon of self-righteous moral up-manship into the hands of loyalists. This gun can be trotted out at "angry time" to intimidate an errant partner and reduce his ego: "You chaser! How weak you are!" Or,

"You slut, how can I ever trust you again?" Or, "You poor, immature fool!", etc.

The pairing of a self-righteous loyalist with a self-indulgent varietist provides an ideal setup for the sado-masochistic hostility routines encountered in dirty fighting. The loyalist becomes prosecutor, judge, and jury. He revels in his authority and dominance. In applying punishment, he can turn sadistic, if he likes. Then, in his additional role as victim, he can feel masochistic, castrated, rejected, and sorry for himself. He may possibly be fulfilling an unconscious wish to fail and lose his love object to a sexually more proficient competitor.

The presumed hurt of the loyalist can at times actually be stimulating—even more so than the excitement of a varietist mate's love affair. The loyalist, therefore, enjoys playing his accusatory record over and over again ("See what you did? Will you do it to me again?"). It is always good for a guilty squirm or flurry of angry self-defense from the varietist spouse.

By way of compensatory pay-off, many offended loyalists fulfill their own varietist fantasies vicariously through jealous identification with a practicing varietist partner. In these cases, the varietist is acting out what the loyalist would like to do but would find excessively stressful himself. In the end, there is triumphant sexual satisfaction when the varietist comes home to roost. The loyalist is the winner, after all, and the extramarital sex partner may have served as a competitive stimulus to save a stale marriage.

In marriages that are no/longer salvageable, the existence of a third party may add reality to the bankruptcy of the marital situation. Sometimes such a third party may be necessary to clarify the state of the bankrupt union. Before the appearance of sexual competition in such cases, there were two very unhappy people. Afterward, there may be two happy people. The third, who is the sex loyalist spouse, now has at least a chance to embark on a new and better life. These are triangles that lead to "creative divorce."

Such solutions are preferable to underground warfare. An example of a commonly used strategy of underground sex fighters is the practice of infidelity by fantasy. The weapon is masturbation. It is often used when one partner feels it is too much trouble to "turn on" the other. It is an easy practice to slip into because it is usually kept secret and therefore gives no offense (in the rare cases where it is disclosed, it can become a form of blackmail). Another reason for its popularity is that it allows the straying partner to remain ostensibly faithful. It does not openly violate convention and is therefore less conflicting than extramarital involvement. In marriage, masturbation is a poor idea. It violates our rule of sharing intimate concerns, and the partner who masturbates is also diverting sexual energy that he could use to pressure the cool partner.

Frequently, trainees ask why they should risk starting trouble by disturbing the status quo of a stable marriage where one partner engages in masturbation. We point out that to disturb such an arrangement is not to start trouble; the trouble is already there. The partners' sex life is not in reasonable balance. We merely direct their attention to the likelihood that the invisibility of a taboo practice like masturbation deters them from negotiating a better settlement.

Collusion with infidelity is another common and potentially most destructive practice. Too often, Partner "A" sanctions, through indulgence, a form of "B's" behavior that is actually objectionable. It is probably the most perilous type of the communications statics because it is deceptively cooperative and sometimes even a part of loving. The partners kid themselves and each other into believing that what they are doing and thinking is sanctioned, when actually it is not. The loyalist partner is, in fact, forming an unholy alliance with his worst enemy: the "dark" varietist side of the spouse's personality.

The case of the wife, cited earlier in this chapter, who objected so strenuously to hearing about her husband's infidelities, was one example of collusion in action.

Another case follows.

Very early in her marriage, Holly Robertson, a former model, knew that her husband Howard had sex problems and therefore felt compelled to "play around." She knew that her tall, lean, hawk-faced husband, a spectacularly successful fashion photographer, had been pursued by other girls right up to the time of their wedding. Holly married him anyway, hoping to train him later to settle down after marriage. We find that many varietists do become monogamous because extramarital sex becomes too perfunctory or too much trouble, although there are others whose outside activities merely become more moderate and still others whose varietist activities increase after marriage.

Holly's strategy was to give Howard as much sex at home as he wanted. She also accepted, at least seemingly, his varietist tendencies. She hoped this would cause him to tire of his girls sooner than if she were to interfere openly.

Here is how her situation was settled in our fight-training

sessions—after the Robertsons had been married three years and had acquired three children and more material comforts than they'd ever dreamed about before their marriage:

HOLLY (*timid*): Sex is my weakest point. It's a hassle for me. I envy women who can make it easily.

DR. BACH: What other sex do you have—other than orgastic?

HOLLY: Oh, you know—just pleasing my husband.

DR. B: You mean "duty-sex"?

HOLLY (*hesitant*): Yes, sort of . . . but not really, because I love to please him, even without trying to make it for myself—because, well it's hard for me.

DR. B: Does he know this? Have you leveled with him?

HOLLY (*sighing*): Oh, I don't need to say anything about it. He is very sex-experienced and he can tell. It's quite obvious because I really have to concentrate. All kinds of conditions have to be just right. The kids have to be sound asleep, I have to be in a good mood, and so on. You know the routine. You must have heard it a thousand times.

DR. B: I still think you are selling yourself short, not working this out with him. Try to discuss this on some new level when it comes up in your group session next time.

HOLLY: Yes, I am sort of tired of our routine.

DR. B: It's a ritual, you see—he goes out and you don't try to make it. Then he goes out some more and you are hurt and try even less. It's a round robin.

HOLLY (*very quietly*): Yes, that's the way it's been for a long time.

DR. B: And you're tired of it! So why don't you break it up—the ritual, I mean, not the marriage?

Later, Holly resented the group's analysis of her behavior as collusion:

HOLLY (*defiant*): That was not collusion, that was love! You'll never understand, none of you, what a good, devoted woman will do to keep her love for her man alive!

DR. B: Precisely! She will go as far as colluding. She will go along with something she really doesn't approve of, but not out of love . . .

HOLLY: Well, what else could it be?

Group members now joined the therapist in various suggestions enumerating the possible motivations for her colluding. She eventually accepted that she colluded because of her strong feelings of separation anxiety: she feared he would abandon her.

HOLLY: Well, I had nowhere else to go. I didn't want to go back to my parents. And, by the way, you (*pointing to Howard, who had been listening and watching intently*) were most discreet . . . until the time when we had kids and I was stuck. Then you knew that I loved our home and was more concerned with your being a decent and loving father to our kids than with what you're doing about your sex thing! That's when you knew you could get away with it! You had me in your pocket!

HOWARD (*indignant*): I never thought in those cruel terms. I'm not an emotional blackmailer.

GROUP MEMBERS: So why the hell do you hurt her?

HOWARD (*blushing*): I don't see it. I think you guys are just getting a lot of mileage out of hurting me! As for my wife, I don't blame her. I love her.

GROUP MEMBER: You don't deserve her! You're mean to her. You're a triple-hitter: you hurt her once when you do it, you hurt her twice when you let her know you do it, and you hurt a third time when you let us and the whole world know that you're doing it!

HOLLY (*crying*): Yes, you rat fink! I don't mind that you're weak and fool around with those silly little girls who think you're so great. Have fun! But not at my expense!

GROUP: Hear—hear. (*Group approval of the wife is unanimous.*)

HOWARD (*gravely facing group pressure all alone*): Now look here all of you! I've got enough of this farce! I'm not the rat fink! She is! (*Pointing to Holly*). You've always gone along with me. You've entertained my mistresses and made best friends with a couple of them! I don't believe you went along with all that because you're my helpless little prisoner. Hell, any guy in this room would have you, not just for sex but as a real person! I just can't believe you're so insecure. I honestly thought you had the kind of strength and tolerance I need. Now I know differently! You're just a passive conformist like those wooden models in *Harper's Bazaar*. You don't love me! At least you don't love my being what I am ... or do you?

The group was excited at this point and the confused chatter temporarily endangered the important confrontation between husband and wife. After much agony this showdown resulted in the following dialogue:

HOLLY (*screaming at the group*): Leave him alone! I do love him! He's my man. But—from now on there is one thing I'll insist on. (*Turns to Howard*). I will never collude again with your thinking that I condone your so-called sex varietist feelings. If you have to act them out, you must keep it a dark, dark secret hidden from me and everyone else ... you understand? Everyone!

HOWARD: But that's living dishonestly. I don't believe in that. (*Sarcastic laughter and a muffled "Oh, brother!" from the group.*)

HOLLY: Who pays the price for your honesty? Now you know there are certain lines that even you shouldn't cross. Don't bring up what amounts to inadmissible evidence. Or if you have to, it ought to be you ... not me, not our kids, not our friends who'll be burdened with it and drawn into deception for your silly ego's sake!

It took about a year before Howard accepted Holly's definition of the situation. At first he was depressed, but gradually he was drawn closer to her. He later reported in a private session that his sex variety interests and activities had radically diminished.

HOWARD: Soon it'll be down to zero. I guess telling and bragging about it was half the fun. The idea of running around with my wife's license made me feel so free and privileged compared to other fellows who were being sneaky. Now that I'm a sneaker myself, the whole bit has lost a lot of its attraction. You know, Doctor, I wish she'd have kept me at home instead of colluding with me. I had a few exciting affairs, but most of it was just off-beat distraction.

A remarkable number of intimates voluntarily confess disloyalty to each other. The confession may be outright. Or it may take the form of lipstick not wiped off, letters left lying on a bedside table, or telephone calls overheard. One newly married husband invented an infidelity and then "confessed" only so he could discover what the wife would do if he ever were to trespass upon their marriage contract.

At the time, he had no interest in such a trespass. But he was intensely interested in finding out what his young wife's reaction to any future straying would be. This husband was looking for containment, and the unconscious need for containment and control seems to be the psychological basis for the amazing clumsiness of some infidel partners. They allow themselves to be discovered even while they consciously attempt to be discreet.

Usually, these containment maneuvers are set in motion in connection with harmless or relatively minor disloyalties and therefore rarely lead to major marital fights. But even when important or chronic infidelities come up for negotiation, sexual varietism in real life does not create the havoc pictured in most fictitious dramatizations. Partly, this is probably because most partners are aware that the marriage license is not psychologically binding. And partly, the previously cited pay-offs for loyalists may neutralize some of the fall-out.

To re-emphasize: our data do not indicate that extramarital activity necessarily shows a partner to be neurotic or dissatisfied; or that the marriage is in difficulty; or that outside involvement must necessarily weaken the primary marital relationship. Any or all of these causes and effects are frequently involved; but they *need* not be.

The point is that for real intimates infidelity tends to pall. True, the infidels may learn that the range of their sexual responsiveness is greater than that habitually displayed with their regular partner; and that making love with the "right" stranger stimulates new dimensions of sexual enjoyment. But they also discover that sex with a swinging new partner is usually more of an emotional hassle than the sexual fun is worth. The tried-and-true sex rituals at home tend to look attractive from the vantage point of a tryst where the consort is impotent, the *femme fatale* is frigid, and both cower undercover for fear of social ostracism. Indeed, such excursions often show a straying partner how much emotional and sexual capital he has on deposit in his marriage bank.

Finally, and to the detriment of further growth of the motel industry, our most sexually mature adults, perhaps after a period of extracurricular experimentation, do not enjoy being adulterers. It is simply not a rewarding role in the long run. This is why so many mistresses of married men lose out in the end. The men may claim they cannot leave their wives "for the children's sakes." If they were more honest with themselves and their extracurricular ladies, most of these husbands would probably confess that it is not so much the children who tie down wandering males but the comforts of making love to "the one and only."

21. Fighting With (and About) Children

Triangular family fights involving mother, father, and child are considerably more complex than battles between husbands and wives—not only because they are three-sided but because the goals of the combatants are more ambitious. Some mothers and fathers resort to remarkable efforts to misuse their children as weapons in adult combat. And children fight for nothing less than their very identities when they do battle against their parents.

Conflict can hurt youngsters as they grow up. But it can also help. We try to teach mothers and fathers how to employ aggression as a constructive technique in childrearing, and there is even more at stake than the personality development of the youngsters. For unless children learn how to fight right at an early age, they may never be able to transmit this knowledge when they have families of their own.

It goes almost without saying that true intimacy can exist only between peers who wield more or less equal power, never between parent and child. To the parent, it doesn't always seem that way. As long as a child is small and very dependent, there can be moments of blissful intimacy: the parent can pour out his protective feelings and love, and the child can openly show and give in to his own dependency needs. Necessarily, these moments become fewer and fewer because it's the child's role to overcome his dependency by fighting the parent aggressively, especially nowadays when so many mothers and fathers tend to be overprotective.

Conflicts between parents and children are traditionally viewed with discomfort or even horror. Yet fighting for growth, fighting for opportunity to explore and learn, is a vital function of growing up. Children learn nothing more important than the art of becoming an independent person. And to become independent, they must learn to fight with—and stand up to—everybody in the family and in the community until their sense of self-worth has reached a level that makes it possible for them to be adults and fight for good "swing" as equals with other grown-ups. Until then it is the natural role of children to fight adults for recognition and privilege.

The normal infant shows aggression at once. He cries when frustrated. Before long he takes things from others and sometimes hits them. Many mothers then impose a system of etiquette that defines under what conditions one may perhaps fight back. Such parental programs for controlling aggression are considerably less than realistic. They tend to fall into four categories: (1) encouraging indulgent, submissive reaction to aggression by parents and other children; (2) control by coercion, along with severe punishment; (3) a double-bind combination of indulgence and severe discipline; (4) control by irrational threats ("if you don't stop, I'll . . .").

As a child grows and assumes an individual identity, he becomes articulate. This process is partly the result of fight experiences that allow him to clarify positions and attitudes by clashing and differing with (and differentiating himself from) others. It can be most clearly observed in playful but often vicious sibling rivalry fights. This beginning of the fight for self-hood is not destructive but part of the articulation of a sense of self. Fighting experiences increase an awareness of the nature of the opponent. And the opponent's opposition increases the awareness of one's value as a person in one's own right.

Many years ago our own research demonstrated what happened even to supposedly docile little nursery-school girls when school and family etiquette made it impossible for them to fight the establishment aggressively long before they ever reached a college campus. The children asked themselves, in effect, "How is one allowed to express aggression?" Then they took out their hostilities on dolls—inanimate things— that can help no one to differentiate and grow. This is socially approved, and so they learn early in life to channel their aggressions toward symbolic targets. The children had answered their own question by saying, "Only in play, in make-believe, is aggression acceptable."

Aggression in interpersonal conflict remains taboo. Later the child is permitted an aggression outlet in sports and there, finally, learns the rules of fair play. Fair playing in sports is a step toward learning the realistic programming of aggression.

Of course we do not encourage trainees to permit mayhem among children, either for the purpose of counteracting aggression or for any other reason whatever. We do ask parents to recognize that most adults in contemporary Western culture can afford to be less squeamish about constructive education on how to deal with violence. Since the slightest display of it is now forbidden and punished by parents or other older, stronger authority, young children learn hostile words twice as fast as "nice" words; they are more likely to "blow up" in tantrums or unhealthy symptoms; and they associate aggression with the privilege and power of adults (or armies), not with creativity or constructive problem solving.

Today's culture tends to instill unrealistic and destructive ways to achieve aggression release. TV and movie violence as well as war news teach youngsters to release aggression by killing fellow humans whom we declare "enemies."

Within their own homes, children are likely to become strategic weapons of adult intimate warfare, and very few parents have the slightest idea of the resulting psychological havoc.

To begin with, the children's natural dependence on the parents is exploited, and here is an example of how this works: overprotection is experienced as comforting by children. Actually, it interferes with the weaning process and retards differentiation and independence. In extreme cases, wealthy parents keep their children financially dependent into adult life. This places the young people in a psychologically corrupt position because getting the goodies from Daddy and Mommy has become an addiction in affluent families. Even many far less coddled children tend to become excessively self-centered, often tyrannical, and if their self-development was effectively suppressed they tend to become both depressed and rebellious.

In battles between spouses, the strategy of hurting a child by interfering with his natural needs is a favorite way of getting at the partner who loves the child—which is one of many reasons why it is dangerous for a child to be the favorite of one parent. It makes the other parent jealous and invites misuse of the child as a weapon. In extreme cases this results in physical cruelties and even infanticide.

The more emotionally immature and neurotic the parents, the more they will try to gain their own self-worth through the way their youngsters respond to them and to the world.

It is common for parents to be overly stern to kids who fail to display traits that will enhance the parents' self-esteem. Parents who are clumsy often punish children for not being graceful enough. Punishing kids for not being smart enough usually means that the parents feel stupid; by punishing their "stupid" kids they deny their own feelings of inferiority. Punishing kids for low grades often means that the parents are less educated than they want to be. If teen-agers are too promiscuous, it may mean the parents are immoral or frigid.

Almost universally, among even mildly neurotic parents, mothers and fathers interfere with the natural process that draws their children to identify with peers as they grow older. One favorite parental strategy is to ridicule teen-age films and focus on dress, dancing, music, and other customs that make parents feel unneeded and ineffectual. Peer influence is viewed as "bad" simply because it is more effective than parental influence.

The antidote to all strategic uses of children is to teach them as early as practical to fight adults constructively. The best place is at home. The best partners are the parents. The best fights are fights for what the youngsters consider most significant, including the integrity of their private world.

We will shortly outline techniques parents can use to fight effectively with their children. Here we would like to show only that the battle is not nearly as one-sided as is generally assumed. While parents are physiologically superior until children reach the teen years, and society gives mothers and fathers great power (for instance, the power to restrict the movement of youngsters), children see this as a justification for using concealed weapons and other gimmicks against their elders. Most children are masters at deception. This alone can make them very effective fighters indeed.

Children have other advantages. They can absorb considerable punishment and usually don't much mind hurting or bugging adults. Having relatively little compassion for injuries inflicted on their elders, they may fear retaliation, but rarely guilt. Making adults unhappy is a form of self-defense.

They may have support from their pals. They can acceptably use such disarming infantile styles of aggression as laughing, running away, biting, harassment of all kinds, refusing to dress, refusing to eat, playing baby, playing sick, pouting, and so on and on. They can count on the parents' vulnerability to a child's reaction. Parents want to be loved, and a child therefore has the power to withdraw love or perhaps just to demonstrate that he is hurt. In today's child-centered culture the mere fact that a child is unhappy can totally disarm a parent by shamesmanship—a very potent weapon.

A child's disadvantages as a fighter are more apparent. He fears physical hurt from physical superiors. In the early years, his childish feelings of omnipotence cause him to be constantly surprised when he cannot have his way, and he therefore gets depressed easily. Restrictions on movement or privileges may be so painful to him that he may feel lost to the adult world, even its captive. He can rarely restrict his parents or correct their wrongdoings. And since logic, wit, and sarcasm are traditional adult tools for fighting with a child, the child's restricted vocabulary is a handicap. Most of all, a child has a great need to be loved and to belong. The fear of loss of love and the feeling of anxiety over possible separation severely hamper a child's fighting capabilities vis-à-vis parents. And his gunny sack of hostilities toward parents and teachers is ever ready to break out in violent fantasies and into fighting with siblings and peers.

Parents who are extremely tolerant of their children often complain that their youngsters engage in excessively intense and cruel rivalries with siblings. No wonder: since these children cannot release aggressions against parents, they fight harder with each other. Mothers and fathers who tend to overlook the capacities and handicaps of children as family fighters also are often unaware of the multiplicity of roles that youngsters may assume in intimate battles. Kids can—and often are—used as:

1. *Targets.* This is most likely to happen when parents shift the brunt of their adult battles from spouse to child.

2. *Mediators.* As when the father says, "Tell Mummy to be nice to Daddy."

3. *Spies.* The mother says, "Go and find out what mood Daddy is in."

4. *Messengers.* The mother says, "Tell your daddy that I'd like to come back to him, but make sure he thinks it's your own idea."

5. *Divorce attorneys.* The mother says, "I can't stand your father. But I'll stick with him because of you." Whereupon a child may say, "I'll help you get rid of him."

6. *Translators.* The child says, "Daddy didn't mean that. What he meant was . . ."

7. *Monitors.* The child says, "Mummy didn't say that. What she said was . . ."

8. *Referees.* The child says, "Why don't you let Mummy explain a little more? Let her talk."

9. *Cupids.* Parents, especially fathers, often cast their children as love releasers. The way to a man's heart may be through his stomach; the way to a woman's heart is often through her child.

10. *Audiences at adult fights.*

In time of marital crisis, the use of children in any or all of these roles is probably inevitable and possibly helpful. In general, however, we find that Roles No. 1 through 5 are destructive. Role No. 6 may be constructive or destructive, depending on the cast of characters and the situation. Roles No. 7 through 9 can bring about constructive results. Role No. 10, much to the surprise or shock of many of our clients, is the most important and desirable of all. It will be given separate discussion, but first we would like to dispose once and for all of the child's Role No. 1: the displacement target.

We have referred to this grossly unfair fight strategy before, but another example is in order:

> FATHER (*disgusted*): You're a lousy mother.
>
> MOTHER (*unbelieving*): You're out of your head!
>
> FATHER (*insistent*): Come on! You're never even around to *be* a mother!
>
> MOTHER (*primly*): Dr. Spock says it's important to get away from your child. At least Jimmy isn't going to be overprotected like you were.
>
> FATHER (*accusing*): How many days in the last six months were you gone and how many nights did the baby wake up and I had to take him into our bed?
>
> MOTHER (*nettled*): Don't you call a four-year-old a baby! He knows about my job. He knows I always come back. He loves to come to the airport to pick me up. And how about all the times when I took him along?
>
> FATHER (*stubborn*): I don't like it.
>
> MOTHER (*triumphant*): Now you're talking! It's *you* who resents my career. I'm not going to give up all my fun. And there's no fun around here!

This mother was the high-powered, high-salaried sales manager for a cosmetics manufacturer. She traveled a good deal and her husband resented her success. As a fight strategy against his wife, this husband began to pamper their only child. The father wanted to alienate the youngster from the mother in order to persuade her to give up her career. Eventually his strategy succeeded to the point where the child recoiled from the mother when she returned from her business trips—and the parents ultimately wound up in the divorce court.

Many of these displacement fights use the disciplining of children as an overt issue to cover up conflicts about sex and other issues that are far more importantly raging between mother and father. Even when discipline is an authentic fight issue, children are often given an unrealistic view of life and marriage because many parents insist on displaying a "united front" to their youngsters.

Here is a family in mild uproar over the children's bicycles being left in the front yard. The mother wants the bicycles in the garage whenever they are not being used. The father thinks the bicycles may be leaned against the house.

SHE: Why don't you back me up?

HE: Because I disagree with you.

SHE: Do you want them to think they can get something from you after I've said "no"?

If the couple is untrained, the father will usually allow himself to be maneuvered into backing up the mother after all. If they are trained and the father is convinced that the mother's demand on the children is silly, he'll say, "That's not the issue; I'll tell them to take it up further with you." This avoids the display of a phony agreement between husband and wife. It avoids contaminating the marriage with an issue that needn't be an issue. It promotes the children's intimacy with an individual parent, and keeps matters at the level of a duet instead of escalating it into a complicated triangle. Most of all, it teaches the children that each parent has his own quirks.

Important family decisions concerning children must, of course, be made jointly by mothers and fathers and in such special cases the showing of an authentic united front between parents makes excellent sense; it gives children a clear-cut direction to follow or to rebel against. Nevertheless, the most trivial fights between a mother and a child build up into ugly brawls involving the entire family.

Frequently, the escalation of conflicts between one parent and one child is due to an unconditional "Back me up!" policy that obligates the second parent to support the authority of the first, no matter what.

In one typical case Mrs. Stanley Johns returns from shopping late in the afternoon. Her three kids had been assigned to do the dishes in her absence. As she drives up to her home she honks the horn, but nobody comes out to bring in the groceries. Furious, she goes inside, carrying one of the heavy shopping bags. The dinner table and kitchen are untouched. Upstairs the television is blaring and the children are obviously fully absorbed. Mrs. Johns is stunned and furious. But she does not order the children to do their chores. Feeling like an exploited slave, she drags in the rest of the groceries and does the dishes. She talks to herself: "God, this is a drag! Am I just being selfish if I get mad at them? The kids are having such a good time!" Eventually she answers herself: "That's ridiculous."

Mrs. Johns thereupon charges upstairs, turns off the TV, and ferociously confronts her children, who are aged 12, 10, and 7. She yells: "You sure are an inconsiderate bunch! Clean up your rooms! Start studying! Stop loafing! Do something!"

At this moment the husband drives up, expecting the nightly "Welcome home" ceremony that he feels he richly deserves after an absolutely impossible day at the office. When he finds nobody downstairs he does not settle down with a drink and the paper to await the return of peace upstairs. Instead, he too charges upstairs and joins the free-for-all. He takes the side of the martyr-mother and applies the traditional "backup-or-bust" policy.

By plunging with his fatherly nuclear armament into a teacup tempest that was not his concern, Mr. Johns was acting out a role that Western society (and especially mothers) increasingly expect him to play: trying to make up for his protracted absences from home. Theoretically, this is a fine idea. In practice, it doesn't usually work. Johns was a computer salesman, not a nineteenth-century blacksmith who worked at home, ever available for family consultation. Even when he did not feel committed to the "backup" policy, Johns functioned, at best, like a referee who entered fights in round 10. His notions about the previous nine rounds would depend largely on the lung power and verbal skill of the highly prejudiced combatants who tried to bring him up to date.

We have tried to make fathers central to the routine daily domestic decision-making process, but have never succeeded. We therefore counsel clients that it is usually best if the father's role calls for the fullest possible moratorium on fights with children, especially on weekdays. On weekends he should be available for conferences with his children; for handling the week's unfinished business; and discussing important matters. This solution may not be ideal, but we have found that it is best to treat Daddy as president of the company; to let everybody appreciate the greater importance of the mother's role; and to stop mourning the dear dead days when father was around the house most of the time.

The mother, in particular, should realize that the essence

of family life is her marriage; that the less she burdens her man with minor problems concerning the children, the more lovable she will be to him. We usually counsel mothers to promote authentic relationships between the children and their father, uncontaminated by fall-out from mother-child conflicts, and to avoid casting daddy exclusively as bogeyman and disciplinarian-in-chief.

Next to fights about discipline and family authority, children are most likely to be misused by parents to avoid sex. We showed earlier how these adult sex fights erupt and what spouses can do about them. But what should be the parental position toward the children? We generally advise mothers and fathers to be candid with youngsters who are at least three and a half years old. They can say:

"Mummy and Daddy want to be alone to make love. This is a private thing. When you get married, you'll do it, too. Meanwhile, when our bedroom door is locked, you should respect our privacy. It doesn't mean that we don't like you."

Most couples tend to resist this approach, partly because of post-Victorian inhibitions and partly because some psychiatric experts have warned parents that exposure of children to sex at too precocious an age can be excessively stimulating. Our own data suggest that children of three and a half can be taught to understand the concept of making love and that they sense they are themselves a product of love. Sex, therefore, is not only perfectly normal to them but they generally realize that their very life depended upon it. In our own experience, the idea that sex is frightening to children is the result of parental antisex propaganda, or children witnessing bad parental sex experiences accompanied by tempers, curses, screams, slamming doors, and dashing in and out of bedrooms.

At the age of six or older we do not hesitate to have a youngster attend a conference at our Institute along with his parents so we can talk *with* the child, not *about* him. Of course we do not call a family session for the specific purpose of discussing the parents' sex life. This is a very incidental matter with most children and we treat it accordingly. Nevertheless, at this stage of the discussion there are always embarrassed snickers and usually some blushing faces. Not, however, on the part of most children. They don't much care what parents do as long as they can pursue their own normal activities and don't have to stay quietly imprisoned in their rooms. Most children are delighted to have their parents preoccupied with each other, rather than with the young set.

Quite a few mothers and fathers tell us that they nevertheless feel inhibited about making love when the youngsters are around and awake. We tell them that these feelings are generally the result of cultural brainwashing; otherwise parents who live in the cramped housing conditions of Russia or India never would make love at all.

"You don't *have* to make love when the kids are awake," we tell these parents. "But it's important that you don't kid yourself and your partner by using the kids as an excuse when you are really trying to get out of having sex." In the majority of cases among the more than 100 couples where this problem has come up, the partners revealed the true reason for wanting to turn off sex within earshot of the children. Usually it was the resistance of one partner against revealing his sexual disappointment.

In these situations we are principally concerned with the use of children as a turnoff of love. We advise parents that anything that turns a child into a frustrator of joy can be psychologically dangerous for the youngster. Partners have a tendency to reject these kids. In the parents' eyes, spoiler-children become "no good." They become more or less chronically associated with "trouble." And children quickly sense when they're in the way. They may say to themselves, "If our parents really want to have fun they shove us out." It is parental secretiveness, rather than candor, that causes children to focus on the adults' sex life.

Needless inhibitions also make it difficult for parents to let their children become witnesses of marital conflict. The very idea strikes many of our trainees as revolting and possibly dangerous to their offspring. This reaction is not necessarily unwarranted. We certainly would not recommend that young people be in the audience as their parents tear each other apart in the manner dramatized in *Who's Afraid of Virginia Woolf?*. And it is regrettably true that far too many children today get the idea from their parents' crude fighting that marriage is an excessively troublesome and hurtful estate. Yet all of this adds up to only a single *caveat:* dirty intimate fighters don't deserve child audiences.

Clean, constructive parental fighting—spontaneous encounter that is ultimately resolved by making up—is something else altogether. Witnessing a fair fight teaches children the facts of life about aggression and conflict resolution. The only alternate models are likely to come from television, movies, or gangs. Naturally, there are times and issues that make the presence of young witnesses inappropriate; intelligent decisions must be made as to when it is constructive for children to be on hand. American parents tend to be much too shy about fighting in front of youngsters. Instead of presenting themselves to their children realistically and completely, as in a full-length mirror, they like to censor part of themselves and display only what's "best." This façade-keeping tactic may bolster the parental self-esteem, but youngsters almost always see through the censorship.

Fighting in front of children does raise problems. It may inhibit one partner much more than the other. Partners who are less sensitive to children may gain such an inordinate advantage by having children as an audience that any fighting in the kids' presence may constitute a low blow ("How often have I told you that I can't keep discipline if you bring up in front of Joey that I overdrew the checking account?"). On balance, however, the point is this: to the extent that a parent can wean himself away from the romantic family ideology that peace and quiet are to be prized above all, he will welcome his children to the scene of conflict resolution. People who do manage to fight in front of their boys and girls find that children not only relish the role of spectators ("Boy, they're at it again!"); participation in these true-life situations, and watching as problems are resolved, actually increases a sense of family belonging and (by way of differentiation) youth's own self-hood. Furthermore, parents who fight in front of their children almost invariably become more efficient, fairer fighters because squabbling parents don't wish to look like brutes to their kids. Besides, some parents discover that the *only* way to get their spouses to fight fairly is to have the children present as an audience that resents foul play.

Instead of leveling with their children at least to a reasonable degree, many parents engage in camouflaged warfare with them. The battles often begin around the age of one and one-half, when babies tend to become tyrants. Typically this is what we hear from the mothers and fathers:

FATHER (*bleary-eyed*): Junior makes me so mad! He won't leave me alone. He wants me to be with him whenever he knows I'm around the house. He screams when I try to use the phone. And my wife won't help. She won't take him off my hands. I get so mad at her!

MOTHER (*exasperated*): Junior drives me crazy, too, with his whining and screaming. I know he does it because he can't say everything he feels. So when he wants something he screams and whines until he gets it. The easiest thing is to give him whatever he

wants. But I know that's the lazy way. And is it
right? Shouldn't I be breaking him of the idea that
he can have whatever he wants?

DR. BACH: Of course. Why not go ahead and level with
your baby?

MOTHER: How do you communicate with a one-year-old?
Do I tell him, "You turn me off and frustrate me"?

DR B: I'm not your Dr. Spock book. But I think
you owe it to this new little person not to mislead
him about the fact that life is going to be a little
tough and that he won't always be able to have his
way. Or even most of the time! While you're at it,
you'll also find ways to tell him: "You'll make it
anyway, honey, and I'll help you. So please stop
bullying me! You'll soon find out that you can get
along very nicely without getting everything you
scream for."

It is difficult for many mothers to handle this type of
situation with her first-born unless she can look it up in Dr.
Benjamin Spock's fine book on child care. We suspect that
this distinct deterioration of the mothering instinct—and the
popularity of the book—are rooted in a loss of confidence.
This, in turn, is the result of too many "rules" that have
changed too quickly and generated too many conflicting
signals. Many mothers look to Dr. Spock to tell them what to
do in the area of child psychology because they lack respect
for their own maternal common sense. We feel that no one
can treat such a spontaneous and complex relationship as
exists between mother or father and child as if it were a
routine, established procedure. All three parties within a
family should learn how to live together creatively, not by
looking each other up in a book but by consulting each
other; by fighting things out; by experimenting; and by learning from the hurts and laughs and the moments of happiness
what swings and what doesn't.

As a child grows older, parents unwittingly encourage
many needless battles by engaging in barter or contract-
making ("If you bring home good grades—or mow the lawn
or wash the car—I'll give you your allowance"). We discourage contract-making. To begin with, it is the parents' responsibility to help a child grow and learn. It is the child's
birthright to be brought up. And the child must learn that
people—first his parents, then others—depend on each other
for practical and emotional support. Besides, being helpful to

others, with family members enjoying priority, feels good inside.

By keeping relationships spontaneous, the child becomes sensitive to what others find truly helpful. And the chores will get done a lot better at the same time. They will be clearly defined in terms of what can be done and supervised now. When the work is contracted for, on a sustaining basis, there will be less feeling of responsibility and consequently more goofing off.

Contractual arrangements in intimate relationships generally serve only as initial and temporary measures to define broad limits of responsibility. With children in particular, the fewer areas that are rigidly covered by "role contracts" and the more room there is for spontaneous participation, the more at home the youngster will feel. The true meaning of being at home applies: that is, being more spontaneous with one's family than anywhere else, especially since most outside activities in school, on the street, and in sports are governed by role contracts of one kind or another. The intimacy of home and love life would be destroyed by chronic insistence on compensation for value received.

Many parents become destructively aggressive in fighting with their children. Teasing is a favorite tactic. Parents tend to interpret teasing as affectionate. Actually, it is a mixture of aggression and affection. If carried beyond a point where "it's not funny any more" it becomes an outright provocation or aggressive attack.

Parents fool themselves that children like to be teased. In truth, they put up with it, at best, to accommodate the parents' need for a hostility release. When children allow themselves to be teased like "good sports" they are actually just hungry for parental attention. They are accepting the teasing or other hostilities as substitutes for genuine encouragement. To be teased is better than to be ignored.

Teasing is also a form of toying with taboo satisfactions. A father who is suppressing incest feelings may tease his teen-age daughter about her "boobs" and thereby at least partially act out his incest fantasy.

The fun of teasing is deceptive. A child can't do much but "go along with the gag." If he had the strength to demand, "Cut it out—I don't like to be teased," he would probably be teased a little more and, in addition, be told he's a bad sport. ("What's the matter, can't you take a joke?")

The strategy of teasing involves, first, locating some particularly vulnerable area of the target's self—something that the self does not want to have displayed to anybody; next, to bring some incidents in this area to everybody's attention. In other words, it is the cruel use of intimate knowledge—an unfair stab at a child's Achilles' heel.

Linda Knight, aged eight, is trying to overcome her big problem in her swimming lessons. She finds it impossible to keep her face down in the water while swimming. So her mother tells her that she'd make a dreadful mermaid.

A 42-year-old client of ours is still bitter about the way his father, a baker, used teasing as a Sunday afternoon family entertainment. "As a kid I had the ambition to become an artist," said this man who had, instead, become a teacher and hated his job. "I used to sketch on Sundays and the whole family, after a few glasses of wine, passed my sketches around and poked fun at them. Everybody thought it was real funny. The whole family followed my father in the act."

Certain subtle ways of teasing are occasionally useful to bring victims to terms with some forms of anxiety. The ridiculing of destructive behavior can also be beneficial for defensive adults in fight-training groups. But on the whole we consider teasing an alienating, rather than bonding form of aggression, especially when children are the targets. Whenever we catch anybody doing it during family or marathon therapy we say: "Let's not laugh about experiences that aren't funny to the person experiencing them."

Since justifiable releases of personal hostility are hard to come by in today's etiquette-conscious society, parents sometimes seduce a child into committing an "objectionable" act solely in order to be able to let out their aggressions against the scapegoat youngster. They may tell a boy to "have a great time" when he goes out, and then condemn everything the boy does. Most children seem to sense this parental need to give expression to "disciplinary wrath." Kids usually find it easiest to accommodate these parental setup operations and later practice the same folly on children of their own.

Seduction for the purpose of scapegoating at times involves unconscious actions on the part of parents (or teachers) who actually go so far as to entrap a child into disappointing adults, perhaps by giving him too much spending money so he can later be accused of extravagance. The disappointments are then used to justify the adult's own punitive and unfair aggression against the child for being "unreliable," "disobedient," or simply "a pest."

Parents who don't spare the rod for fear of spoiling the child—the mothers and fathers who are generous with discipline but tight with encouragement and praise—expose themselves to ingenious retaliation by their children. These youngsters become experts at the fine art of frustrating and bugging parents, teachers, and adult guests. Often, bugging remains the only way to compete for attention against such adult-attention-getters as cocktail parties, TV shows, the newspaper or "grown-up talk." This is how many youngsters learn that "troublemaking" pays off psychologically; and they are good at it, as any college dean knows.

Still other parents use camouflaged ways to confuse and retard the growth of a child by infantilizing him because of their own unmet adult needs. The parental motives need not be sinister. Suppose a divorced mother clings to her teen-age son and treats him as if he were still the little boy pictured in the old family snapshots that she carries in her handbag. Chances are this mother is merely starved for companionship and fears the day when her teen-age son will move from home and leave her alone. Nevertheless, the effect of her behavior is to make the son too passive, and unless he learns to fight back constructively against the mother and for his own sense of self, he is likely to be in trouble later on.

Overly aggressive children—frequently called "hostile"— are also likely to be reacting to parental neuroses. We are fortunate in that our Institute has for many years maintained close liaison with the Carthay Nursery School in Los Angeles. Its owner-director, Mrs. Dorothy Carter Nelson, has often called us for consultation when problems arose with particularly aggressive children. We found that an overly "hostile" child's aggression was in almost every instance the evidence of fall-out from parental stimuli of the kind common in dirty fighting.

Many a nursery-school mother kept fluctuating from severely irritated overt rejection of her child to guilt-driven overindulgence. These erratic fluctuations could make no conceivable sense to a child. So, to ward off further confusion and bewilderment, the child fought back. To protect himself, he became aggressive, as if he was saying: "I must not respond to this crazy environment. I must barge ahead, assert myself and lash out against the environment. I guess I'll make myself bad, consistently bad. Then I'll be consistently attended to by being scolded for being a *bad boy!* That's better than being confused by a crazy mixture of erratic love and hate."

Another strategy in parent-versus-child crazy-making involves parental identity casting: telling children that the parents know what children think and feel and interpreting a child's behavior accordingly; in other words, imposing a parent's view on a child and thereby robbing the child of having his own feelings recognized. This is not as complex or as bizarre as it may seem at first glance. Unfortunately, it is shockingly easy, as the mother in the following dialogue illustrates:

CHILD: Mummy, I want to go and play with Frieda.
MOTHER: You know you don't like Frieda.
CHILD: Don't I? But couldn't I anyway, Mummy? Couldn't I?
MOTHER: No. You *know* the last time you came back from her house you were all tired out.
CHILD: Was I?

In some severely disturbed families the mother or father (or both in collusion) derive a sadistic, almost satanic, pleasure in controlling the "I" or "me" that a youngster should experience for himself. It is not exactly surprising that false and corrupting identity pressure ("You're a bad child!"), when continued long enough, can drive a victim literally crazy.

This happens when the natural self is slowly destroyed because its confirmation is denied. The destroyer is a "significant reference person," of the child, usually the mother. The mother accomplishes the destruction by mystifying the child and colluding with his own destructive tendencies. If this process is allowed to go on, the child's real self is slowly annihilated. At that point he only experiences his false self. The child is no longer himself! He will be in despair because he has become a nonentity, a nonperson. His real self is dead.

In family therapy we sometimes suggest one form of insurance against crazy-making when a child is being victimized by a sick, hostile mother without being taught by anybody how to fight back. The idea is to help the child recognize and contain the mother's aggression and limit it to manageable proportions. In one case a mother was severely paranoid. She lived in a private world populated by ghosts. We were able to train the children to tolerate this ghost world as if it were some temporary impersonal possession that belonged to the mother but had no significance as far as the children were concerned. The mother's ghost world was tolerated like a necklace she might wear. When she tried to persuade her children to confirm the existence of her ghosts, the other family members were trained to reject the mother's forays.

In short, family members learned how not to collude with (nor reject) a fantasy-ridden member and to assist in her therapy by fighting her crazy-making strategies. A fantasy-ridden person may be slow to improve, but effective fighting immunizes the immediate family against psycho-pathological contagion—and without committing the sick member to an institution. Often, when sick mothers and fathers see that their children do not accept a parent's crazy idea of reality, the adults will be more ready to give up unhealthy notions.

While these are extreme examples, all intimates find a way to get inside the minds of each other and determine how the self is experienced. Identity casting, then, even when conducted by parents who are not psychiatrically sick, is an active, emotionally loaded way of influencing the young and can easily become a brainwashing tactic that stunts a child's emotional growth. We observe this casting or typing process constantly as members of our fight-training groups become more intimate and induce one another to experience themselves or the therapist in some preferred way.

Parents also use setup operations to draw youngsters into behaving in accordance with the parental frame of what a youngster ought to be and how he ought to feel. Typically, mothers will practice "father typing" on male children, often with the same results that became apparent in the following case.

Richard Hart, a sexually interested, affectionate, and virile public relations counselor who had been able to achieve good sexual relationships with his first wife and with a number of women after he was divorced, became extremely frustrated when he met Mary Knoll, a young woman of whom he really was fond. There were certain things about Mary that turned Richard on. However, to his great frustration, his sexual response was entirely inadequate. He was completely impotent with her. This eventually led to her alienation and withdrawal, although she was otherwise fond of him.

At first Richard was rather flippant about his impotence since he belonged to that class of fairly successful and uneducated businessmen who become easily embarrassed by problems of a private nature. But gradually, after self-examination and a counselor's consultation with Mary, as well as through his own discussion with the counselor and with a fight-training group, Richard became reflective. After several weeks he came into the consultation room, describing very excitedly what he called an "internal discovery."

"I know you and Mary think that I don't want to have sex with her because I was rejected as a kid," he said. "But I discount this completely. I feel the fault is in myself because I'm always afraid I won't satisfy the woman that I might be with at any particular time. If a woman is unenthusiastic about my advances, I immediately get this fear of inadequacy. I now trace this in my mind back to my teen-age years with my mother, when she attempted to instruct me on how to act with women. She made a very definite point and stressed the fact that a man's important duty is to satisfy his wife or the woman he is going with. She kept making a very important point of this. At the same time, she also kept criticizing my father as an inadequate lover.

"Over the years this became a very important and strong thing in my head. Then, when Mary also stressed to me how important it was that she be sexually satisfied, it scared me out of my wits. I immediately lost my erection and stayed out of the game."

Happily, most healthy youngsters are adept at fighting back not only against these clearly neurotic and crazy-making strategies but also against the more ordinary parental encroachments on the youthful self.

22. When Kids Fight Back

We know a 15-year-old boy whose affinity for TV shows featuring Nazi villains has helped him develop a commendable technique for signaling his father whenever Daddy makes an excessive demand on the son's services or good nature. When such a situation arises, the boy answers with a snappy, *"Jawohl, Herr Kommandant!"*

This response eases tension between father and son because it lets the father laugh at himself. It allows the boy to display self-assurance and lets the father know, inoffensively, that the son thinks Daddy is being arbitrary. It also serves notice on the father that his son might become disobedient if pushed too far.

We thoroughly approve of this young man's psychological skill and also admire the many other youngsters who find their own methods to disassociate themselves from parental demands that are alien to a young person's developing ego. The parent who becomes furious when his teen-ager refuses to go to the opera with Mom and Dad does not usually realize that the youngster's obstinacy is probably a constructive act. The chances are this young person is not simply revolting against "square" music. He is taking a step in the long, long road toward establishing his own identity. In this case, he is employing Mahatma Gandhi's strategy of creative disobedience.

Few parents manage to be overjoyed when their youngsters become command-resistant or when kids decide to go on strike with a defiant, "No, I won't!" To know when and how to be insistent, and when and how to relent, is one of the most sensitive functions of constructive parenthood. It requires considerable insight for a parent to question himself and decide what is truly "for the child's own good" and deserves to become a legitimate fight issue; and what, in fact, doesn't fall within this mandatory category and had best be soft-pedaled or dropped. We try to clarify the problem for trainees by presenting them with the following wholly imaginary conversation.

PARENT: I love you and I care about your welfare.

CHILD: That's nice. I'm glad. It's good to love someone. It must be nice for you to be a mother [or father].

PARENT: Well, that all depends on you!

CHILD: What do you mean?

PARENT: You know perfectly well what I mean: I love you when you are nice and show me by your performance—like straightening your room and being polite to adults—that you care.

CHILD: Care about what?

PARENT: Care about performing the routines that I prescribe and doing them well and on time!

CHILD: Oh, those. Most of them I just do to please you— or to keep you from yelling or hitting me.

PARENT: But those routines are for your own good.

CHILD: I don't know about that. Don't you like to order me around and organize me?

PARENT: That's not the point. I hope you appreciate that I'm training you because I care and because I love you.

CHILD: That's nice for you, but don't all parents have to care for their children?

PARENT: Well—yes. But it's for your own good.

CHILD: I disagree. I think it's mostly for your own good.

PARENT: What on earth do you mean? Don't you love it here?

CHILD: Yes, where else is there a place for me? But I don't like most of your routines.

PARENT: How else are you going to learn?

CHILD: Learn what? To do what you want?

PARENT: Oh, not that so much, really! You really are upsetting me now. Don't you know I love you and you are precious to me? That's the only reason why I accept the responsibility of training and criticizing you.

CHILD: I don't believe it and don't much need it. But I guess you *have* to love me in your way. I am your "flesh and blood," as you always say. I see I can make it difficult for you by not returning your love—by not performing those routines of yours.

PARENT: They're to help you learn how to get along in life. Besides, why would you want to make my life difficult?

CHILD: Well now, that really is *our* problem. It's sort of mutual. Do you really think it's good for my development that you're the only one who can make life difficult for me? I can reciprocate, you know.

PARENT: I've lived longer than you, and you should respect me.

CHILD: That's your problem. I prefer my age, but don't get too upset—I won't be around forever. In the meantime, I appreciate your devotion to me, but please don't ask me to perform too many routines—or I must fight back. So sorry.

In a way it is fortunate that youth groups tend to assign leader status to members who demonstrate outstanding fighting abilities. Useful aggression release comes from the knowledge that players in body-contact sports, such as football or water polo, may be "mean" and simultaneously skillful without suffering unnecessary penalties for themselves or teammates. The rebel who is aggressive in his criticism of the prevailing order and authority also tends to command a following and a high reputation among his peers.

All this is part of youth's intense search for achieving self-value through each other. When this search begins to incorporate criminal activities or the use of so-called mind-expanding drugs, it almost invariably means that youngsters are trying to find substitutes for the growth-stimulus they were never given at home.

When parents are unable to curb the temptation to exploit children emotionally—usually by heaping demand overloads on the youngsters and following up the overload with punitive parental aggression release—the healthy child soon learns to defend himself. Usually, he finds a way to lull the parent into believing that the youngster can be relied upon to take on the overload ("Yes, will do, Mom!" or "Don't worry, Daddy-O!"). What he is really saying is, "Yes for now, but I really mean 'No for later when you're not watching me closely.' "

All adults know the tendency of children and youth to use this formula in order to reduce adult demands or to escape from them entirely. In most cases it is probably smarter for a youngster to adopt this approach rather than attempt to be a hero and say "no!" In a command situation the commander is not likely to accept "no's." Even when the adult-commander later becomes very angry and aggressive upon discovering that the child's "yes" really meant "no," the child is probably not too troubled about being blasted for disobedience. Never having felt committed to his "yes" in the first place, the youngster needn't feel too guilty or rejected for not having performed. This is why the technique of setting-up-and-then letting down parental or teacher expectations is the favorite fight style of children. They know that in an over-load-command situation they can wind up "the winner."

Adults naturally find this maddening, unless they learn how to decode and deal with this strategy. But even the infuriated parent is vastly better off than the parent of a child who succumbs to a demand overload and really tries to mean it when he says, "Yes now and yes for later, too." This is almost certainly an unhealthy child who will feel guilty if, after trying ever so hard, he fails to live up to the rigid expectations of the parent. After several years of such attacks on a youngster he will probably develop moods of depression that may eventually paralyze all his activities.

Only the child who fights back against unrealistic demands has a chance to emerge as a healthy adult. And this child will find a way of telling his elders: "It's not realistic for me to fulfill your expectations. Nor is it constructive for either of us when I deceive you by saying, 'Yes for now but no for later.' I will quit seducing you, dear adult, into anticipating that I will do something unless I really mean it. I am now strong enough to deal with parental pressure."

Another sensible style for outclassed and outnumbered fighters is, of course, to avoid engaging a superior enemy in the first place. Children who lose too many battles may hide in their rooms and become hippies in later life so they can gain strength in a passive peer culture where they feel they have a chance. Children who are less hopelessly beaten down usually prove highly inventive in devising evasive maneuvers that render them inaccessible and beyond injury. They feel that their influence, power, and skill never give them a chance to "win."

Wise parents intuitively try to equalize the weapons system that is in use between themselves and their children so that youngsters won't become too discouraged and will continue to come out fighting for more privilege, independence, and growth. But far too many children wind up feeling they are permanent "losers."

The loser's strategy is to try to get back at the winner, and the "Yes now, no later" formula is not the only way for children to counterpunch. They can spoil an adult victory by making the winner feel guilty, for instance.

This is why children are so expert at petulant pouting, being soreheads, and dwelling on their losses and hurts. Such guilt-making through self-suffering is a most effective child weapon, and the young ones know it. They cry and display suffering most dramatically with parents whose guilt can be most easily aroused, as Lisa Carter, aged six, demonstrates below:

LISA: Mommy, I'm going to the store to buy Shelly and me something.

MOTHER: Lisa, where did you get that nickel?

LISA: I've had it.

MOTHER: You didn't have it yesterday and I haven't given you any money.

LISA: Well, I don't remember where I got it.

MOTHER (*sternly*): Lisa, where did it come from? You asked me for some money this morning, and you haven't gone anywhere. So where did you get a nickel all of a sudden?

LISA (*upset*): I don't remember!

MOTHER (*smug*): Well, you'll just have to sit there until you do remember!

After endless probing by her mother Lisa remembered that she had found the nickel in her doll's purse. She confessed this, but only after her mother promised *not* to get mad, not to say anything more than absolutely necessary about it, ever again! But her mother couldn't resist getting mad anyhow. Lisa thereupon stared at the floor, eyes burning, and finally fled from the room. She stumbled onto her bed with her blanket and began to suck her thumb. Her mother sat stunned. After a short while, she felt rotten and mean. "Poor baby!" she thought. "I guess that's how children look when nobody loves them or listens enough to their troubles. I've been cruel and heartless. I must comfort her immediately."

The mother proceeds to Lisa's room:

MOTHER: Lisa?

LISA: What?

MOTHER: Are you all right?

LISA: Yes.

MOTHER: Are you mad at me?

LISA: No.

MOTHER: What are you doing in here?

LISA: Lying down.

MOTHER: What are you thinking about?

LISA: Nothing.

MOTHER: Do you want to talk to me about anything? Do you have anything at all to tell me or complain about?

LISA: No.

MOTHER: Do you think Mommy's mean to you or unfair? I know I make mistakes, too, and I want you to tell me when you feel I'm being unfair or wrong about something. OK?

LISA: OK.

MOTHER: Well, I guess I'll leave you now if you don't have anything special to tell me . . . OK?

LISA: OK.

Feeling confused and remorseful, the mother tried to find the eyes of her child, but Lisa looked away and sucked her thumb.

The recent emergence of psychotherapy for entire family groups has exposed the shocking fact that average families— and not just the psychiatrically sick ones—tend to mistreat the emotional dependency that one member feels for anoth- er. Teen-agers are especially affected by this type of static. Because the young want and need to be emotionally accepted and understood, they are constantly tempted to accommodate the love-frames and hate-frames that their parents cast around them. And since teen-agers are no longer an econom- ic asset to most families of this generation and therefore have no valued place in society, the confirmation of their own identity is crucially dependent on the kind of treatment they get at home.

It is doubly deplorable, therefore, that many parents bug their kids with the same kind of communications statics that spouses use to drive each other crazy. There is a tragic difference: since kids are not equally powerful fighters, they are forever pushed into dirty or fighting-fire-with-fire tech- niques. In other words, much of the bugging that is done by teen-agers is really counterbugging.

It is not always easy to persuade parents to view matters in this light. Nor can they casually accept the fact that straight- forward bugging by their children is often more than an act of paying parents back for spankings and other punishment. It may be an act of creative provocation designed to force parents into demonstrating that they *care* about their kids. Children rarely believe their parents have affection for them until they meet their mothers and fathers in occasional mo- ments of wrath. The youngsters find it difficult or impossible to equate total acceptance with love and affection.

In child raising, as in agriculture, people reap what they sow. This may not be apparent when kids are young, but by the time the teen years come around, the bad seeds usually emerge in three types of "inconsiderate" young people:

1. *Rebels without a Cause.* They were rejected when they were smaller. Their teen-age strategy is to be inconsiderate because they enjoy making parents miserable.

2. *Spoiled.* They say to themselves: "Mother did everything for me ever since I was little; why should she stop now?"

3. *Imitators.* They were taught to admire one of the parents and now they ape the privileged father or mother.

The more openly and realistically youngsters are encouraged to fight back against parental strategies that put kids off, the less likely will they later become prone to the conflicts now identified with "generation gap" problems; *i.e.,* the mutual lack of understanding and communications between parent and child.

Parents who have learned to decipher what their children are signaling sometimes return to us and describe eye-opening experiences. One father reported that he was concerned because his 16-year-old seemed unusually uncommunicative. This father was something of a monologuist who had a weakness for lecturing his son at length about whatever the father thought would be useful to the boy. The son was ostensibly encouraged to ask questions, but he usually just absorbed the flood of information stoically and rarely responded. He didn't act bored, yet the father began to recognize that the son was more passive than the boy's general alertness warranted.

One evening when his father was beginning to hold forth on the subject of social climbing he finally paused for some filial feedback. He asked, "Hey, do you know what we really mean when we say somebody is a 'social climber'?" The boy said, "Well, I guess not, really." The father was upset and inquired, "Why in the world don't you ask?" The boy said, "Well, you never give me a chance." The father then realized that the boy was signaling, "Who wants to ask *you* questions? That'll just set off another dull lecture."

This boy was finally encouraged to put up a fight for his own tastes and identity. He now had a better chance to move on to the weaning phase which so often turns into a needlessly tortuous tearing away of a youngster from his family as he becomes old enough to be on his own.

Many teen-agers are torn between desires at this point. They are frightened by the idea of independence and sex freedom and by their own experiments with their self-worth in the distinctly noncoddling outside world. Yet they are being weaned vigorously and yearn for psychological and economic security and little else.

During this transition many parents feel exploited by their teen-agers because the youngsters have no time or heart or taste for intimacy in the bosom of the family. Fathers, in particular, often have trouble understanding this phase. They may have appalling fights with their daughters. Often these conflicts are fanned by the mothers, who are delighted that the rival for their husband's love is getting in trouble with Daddy. Especially when Daddy's unhappiness with his daughter drives him closer into his wife's arms.

Elwood Saunders, the well-to-do owner of an automobile parts manufacturing plant, went to the trouble of composing a long, detailed mock "Manifesto of a Selfish Daughter" which he attributed to his 19-year-old June, a gorgeous girl who was taking Daddy for a lot of money in financial support but gave mostly heartache in return. Here are a few excerpts from this father's disillusioned document:

"You owe parents nothing." "Best way to get along with them is to stay away from them." "If parents ask you to cooperate at home as a member of the family, do not do it." "Always have the last word. This means you've won the fight." "Your life is only your business—no one else's." "If you have to make promises, OK; but remember you don't have to keep them." "Keep people waiting on you. After all, you're the heroine in your own life." And so on and on and on.

Here is what happened when Elwood, June, and her mother, Kathryn, discussed this document at our office:

JUNE (*blazing*): These aren't my thoughts! You just say they are!

KATHRYN (*smug*): But Father has your number. If you don't think these selfish thoughts, how come all your actions are selfish?

KATHRYN TO ELWOOD: Read her the list!

JUNE (*disgusted, to counselor*): Dr. Bach, do I have to listen to her list for the umpteenth time? It's ridiculous.

ELWOOD (*trying to be calm*): We're here to get help and I want Mother to read the list so the doctor can see for himself whether I'm making things up about you.

(JUNE *withdraws, looks bored, and puffs belligerently on a cigarette.*)

KATHRYN (*primly toward doctor*): Here's my list of her

daily routine, and let me tell you, doctor, she's driving us crazy:

"1. Sleeps until 10 o'clock, sometimes 2 P.M.

"2. Stays in nightgown most every day with hair a mess.

"3. If she eats anything it must always be something that is already prepared. Drinks only out of containers, bottles, or cans. Doesn't want to get a dish or glass dirty.

"4. Only time she gets up is when phone rings. Has mostly boys calling. (Most are not wholesome young people, not the kind we would hire for a job at our plant.)

"5. Leaves everything for someone else to clean or straighten up. Has her six-year-old sister take care of her room, if it gets done at all. Leaves rest of house to her parents to clean after their day's work.

"6. Says she will stay out Monday, Tuesday, Wednesday, and Thursday nights until 10 o'clock and other nights until 2 o'clock. (Her hours are usually two hours later—12 o'clock to 1:00 o'clock on 10 o'clock nights, and late nights 'til 2:30 or 3:00 A.M. This is why she then sleeps all morning or all day.)

"7. Refuses to be with family. When she does go out to dinner with us, she wants to hurry home and becomes nasty if she thinks we are not hurrying.

"8. Never ready on time; keeps people waiting ten minutes to two hours. Always starts out late for appointments.

"9. Vile temper—gets angry and starts swearing in a filthy way, possibly to shock us. Calls Father: 'You bastard.' Mother: 'You bitch.'

"10. Can't leave her with her little sister. She just sleeps and the little one has to care for herself although we live in corner house where traffic is heavy.

"11. Spends all the money she makes on herself. Her little sister had a card and a gift from every member of the family, but not from her older sister."

The reading of the list was followed by a triumphant silence on the part of the parents. They clearly expected their daughter to be criticized by the therapist. Here is what happened instead:

DR. BACH (*to Kathryn*): Tell your daughter what she can do that would make you happier with her while she still lives with you. I want all three of you to negotiate a clear-cut settlement of what you can reasonably expect from each other.

KATHRYN (*stubborn*): I knew you would try that—but agreement means nothing to her. Right now she will say "yes" to anything to get out of this therapy. But she has her tongue in cheek. (*Turning to daughter.*) I know you.

DR. B: Stop telling her where her tongue is and what she thinks. If she thinks that way and wants to share it, that's when I want to hear it.

JUNE (*eager*): No, no, I don't think that way at all! I just want to be left alone. My parents insist that I concern myself with their feelings. Frankly, I don't. But that doesn't mean I'm impossible or a freak or nut or something.

Eventually this unhappy triad agreed that in exchange for room, board, and a car, the daughter would do some regular chores, including babysitting with the much younger daughter, so that the mother could help the father more in his business. Naturally, she resented all of this, particularly doing a mother's job with her sister so that Mother could be with Daddy.

When June threatened to get married "to almost anybody—just to get away from home," Mrs. Saunders asked for a special interview. Her lament went this way:

"I just can't help her. She won't level with me. She's always found it extremely difficult to be honest, even about things where the truth would be better than a lie. Now we can't talk at all any more. She's always hedging about where she's going, what she's going to do, and everything else.

"When I suggested that we spend an afternoon together June said that when she really needed me I wasn't available, so I shouldn't try now. I don't believe this was justified although I did have to spend time at the plant when she was younger. But she had more of my time than she is willing to admit.

"She says, 'Just leave me alone!' and claims she'll get married as soon as possible to have someone for herself. She doesn't seem to realize that to have someone she must go halfway.

"The other weekend my husband and I were away at a meeting. She said she intended to have a party. I told her that we did not approve as long as we were out of town, and she replied that she wouldn't have a party in our stupid old house, anyway. We came home to find the guest house in disarray, beer cans all over the place, cigarette trays full, and the living room a sight. She didn't even have the courtesy to clean up!

"My housekeeper has been off work for three weeks, so it means that the work at home must be done by me. June simply refuses to help with anything. I suggested she make a list of what she does for us and we would make a list of what we do for her, but she wants no part of a list. She wants our room, board, food, telephone, car, gasoline, and all the rest, but she won't do anything to help us. All the money she earns, when she does work once in a rare while, she spends on herself. She also gets money from us, of course.

"Doctor, is it possible for anyone to be really happy if they aren't doing something worth-while? We've tried to explain to her that you can't play all day and night. You have to face life and reality! She claims she's too young, and has the right to have fun now before she gets tied down. All her friends are busy, though. Many of them work and also go to school, but June just does nothing! She dates seven nights a week. When she doesn't have a date she stays away from home, anyhow. She says she doesn't want to be around us. But we go to sleep early. We wouldn't bother her if she wanted to stay home and read, watch TV, write letters . . ."

June Saunders soon moved away from home and got herself a job. The parents, in effect, had forced her prematurely out of the house. They had dealt with her as if she had still been the little girl in the cuddly family snapshots that the oldsters prized. And they had failed to establish an emotional bond between themselves and the next generation.

It was too late (and therefore unrealistic) for them to try to build up nonexisting communications with their alienated daughter. When such a situation arises in the late teens, separation is the only answer, and often this painful step must be unilaterally forced by the parents or the youngster.

The travail of the Saunders triad is fairly typical. The cliché that today's youth is "alienated" from its parent generation is largely true. Contacts with parents are often disrupted by divorce—especially the contacts with fathers—and, almost invariably, by the increased professional, civic, and social preoccupations of most parents. It is of no small significance that the generations drain each other economically instead of bringing gain, as they once did. But mostly the difficulty is that the generations can no longer contribute so much to the solution of the life problems faced by each. This is at the root of most "generation gap" problems: today's oldsters can play only a relatively small role in solving the problems of the youngsters, and vice versa. For each generation the peer group is more influential than those "ahead-of-you" or "behind-you."

Conditions today change with such dramatic rapidity that the 20 or 30 years that separate the generations often render the old experience largely irrelevant to the conditions that face young people. Consequently, the transfer of learning, of skills, of wisdoms—all the gifts that shape a realistic bond between generations—no longer yields the comforting, useful old results.

Often, though by no means necessarily, the loss of educational and economic linkage encourages a drain of emotional closeness between parents and young people. This emotional alienation has serious implications for the mental health of new generations.

Contemporary Westerners have to face the fact that after their children reach junior or senior high school, most parents have few *tangibles* to offer their youngsters. They support them, true, but the relationship all too often becomes obligatory. It is dutiful rather than meaningful. Like all obligatory involvements, it triggers considerable resentment. It isn't only youth who resents the dependency on elders. The elders, too, resent having to support a generation that returns neither love nor economic benefits.

To cope with the crises inherent in this situation, parents should try to establish a meaningful bond with their children on grounds beyond economics and/or education. Otherwise, they will become obsolete like workers replaced by automation. A psychological bond of mutual understanding and intimacy is more essential than ever.

As youngsters enter the teen years parents would be well advised to temper their lectures, to soften the "ought" tone of their communications and become more the intimate friends and companions of their children. Parents are then in a position to impart an emotional education to the youngsters which the next generation cannot possibly get as comfortably anywhere but through the intimacy of family life.

We must be realistic. Many parents lack the skill to accomplish this fully. Therefore, teachers, counselors, coaches, youth leaders, any adult friend of any kind, can serve as an important bridge over the hostile gap between generations. Even a single brief session with an understanding counselor can be a turning point or a moment of truth in the mind of a youth—a moment that can freeze or unfreeze the direction in which a human being is developing. Sometimes an outsider who comes to an encounter with a young person without the encumbrances of past misunderstandings is in the best position to show that this is an exciting world but that it is moving fast and that older people do have something to teach youngsters: how to live and grow.

Youngsters must be made familiar with the guidance professions and learn how to make use of consultants in psychology and related fields. If necessary, such counselors can provide a new channel for transmission of knowledge from generation to generation and help youngsters to shape a sensible perspective on youth's place in this fast-moving world.

When parents and children learn to fight right in the first place, they can eliminate most generation-gap problems before they arise. Constructive fighting had best start early in childhood when knowledgeable parents first start setting limits on the behavior of their children. Many parents still fail to recognize that youngsters need limits as urgently as a ship needs a captain's decisions. When parents fail to volunteer limits, children find ways to ask for them. Often even the smallest children force parents to set limits for aggressive behavior. They do this by misbehaving, thereby goading mothers and fathers to set limits.

The overly permissive parent is not responding authentically either to his own role or the role of the child if he is afraid to risk a child's resistance to limits. Without limits children will go overboard again and again, until either the parent gets the "I want limits" message or the child gets his painful comeuppance from the unloving and far from permissive outside world.

To default on the matter of limit-setting and to indulge a child is actually a passive form of hostility on the part of the parent because a spoiled child will develop undesirable behavior traits for which he will then encounter rejection: first from the once so accepting parent and later from the world. In raising children, as in therapy, Dr. Bruno Bettelheim's famous dictum applies: "Love is not enough."

The act of saying "no" with love is best performed by omitting sentimental lectures about how much parents love their children or that the kids' behavior is being restrained "for their own good." It is best to be straightforward. We advise parents to go along with what they think they can and should and not to tolerate—absolutely—what they think they can't and shouldn't. To refuse children without guilt and without punishment is perfectly possible if parents level with their youngsters and let the children in on where they stand with Mom and Dad. A useful signal is: "That's the way things are as of now. Maybe later I might feel differently or have more to offer."

The last portion of this signal is of utmost importance. It should firmly convey that everybody in the family has the right to differ fairly and squarely, that even a child has a right to differ. This is more than a signal of vague hope. It means that the child has a fighting chance to have his wants and views accepted, perhaps later if not now, and that he has the opportunity to gain dominance at least some of the time. Giving a child a chance to "win," if he earns it, facilitates agreeable solutions for parent-child conflicts. Nobody can be expected to be forever a loser.

Neurotic, overprotective (and probably guilt-ridden) parents who give in to almost everything their children demand deprive their youngsters of aggression training, especially the experience of standing up to powerful parental authority. These parents unwittingly maneuver themselves and their children into a vicious double bind: first they deprive children of gaining strength through realistic experiences that involve a certain amount of risk taking; and later these same parents are angry and disappointed when their children can't or won't perform effectively.

Kids get their best fight practice if father and mother, separately as well as in a parental unit, let the kids take them on. Parents can then show children what wins with them and what loses—just as honest lovers show each other what turns them on and what turns them off.

A parent who wants to fight right with a child is well advised to consider the child a worthy opponent, a person with natural aggression in his little heart, which he needs and likes to release, particularly against those on whom he depends so much.

In marital intimacy, aggression increases whenever "over-dependency," overentwinement (too close), or overcontrol increase. Ideally, constructive fighting between adult intimate partners brings lopsided dependency into a better balance. Two peers then achieve a particular balance of dependence, optimal distance, and power-control that both like to live with. The sooner they achieve such a balanced state of swing the shorter and less bloody their fighting.

Parent and child have the same balancing job to do, but theirs tends to be a more or less continuous battle because kids axiomatically feel unequal and outclassed, and they are. Parents do not need to "rub it in" that they have the advantage because a child already feels very dependent. There is a risk that the child may become overcontrolled;

and a child lacks power to enforce limits on the parental privilege to curtail freedom from supposedly loving engulfment and smothering.

In conflicts with a child a creative mother or father knows how to gauge his superior weapon system and hold it down at par or perhaps just a little bit ahead of the child's. Such a parent will limit the child to fair weapons and will inculcate respect for reasonable belt lines. This will give the kid a chance to learn how to assert his aggression in a rational, realistic, and straightforward manner. If the parent "overkills" the child and overwhelms him by failing to adjust the cutting edge of adult claws to the skin sensitivity of the child, then kids, while apparently losing, will have to fight back underground, and they do.

A child can "win" a fight with an adult not necessarily by "defeating" the adult and watching the adult "concede" the battle but more often when the adult takes the initiative and recognizes openly how much progress the child is making toward adulthood.

Suppose a parent plays ping-pong with his child. According to adult rules, the winner is the one who gets 21 points first. But if the adult is sensitive to the child's needs, any score can yield a winner's satisfaction as long as the child's progress is recognized and applauded. ("You got eight points this time! That's more than you ever got before. Good for you!")

To cut down on needless, unfair, or destructive fighting with children, the following general guidelines help:

1. Avoid giving excessive orders. This cuts down the overload of demands.

2. Eliminate requests that are made in the name of "character building" at a time when they have no practical utility.

3. Demand only what a child can complete *now*. There is time for more demands later. Demand-making in segments makes for more cheerful, efficient performance.

4. Supervise and give follow-through help so a child can fulfill his commitment to do what he was told. Stay with it until the commitment is fulfilled. If you can't, avoid making your demand until you can see it through.

5. Show the child exactly what you expect and make sure he understands not only what he's to do but how he can do it. This arouses the child's expectancy of success and approval—and that's what fighting is mostly about.

23. Family Fights

Although goodwill is essential to constructive fighting and conflict resolution, it is difficult for most people to develop empathy for more than one intimate at a time. A group of more than two is often experienced as an abstraction. To teach all family members how to gain and maintain empathy and respect for the integrity of the entire family group is, therefore, a formidable assignment.

Anyone but a hermit knows that this isn't the only reason why family relationships are complex. Two people can only fight on two levels. The addition of third, fourth, fifth, or even more parties changes the character of fighting markedly. It's not a matter of numbers alone. Now there are allies, prosecutors, defenders, mediators, judges, jurors, and audiences. There is side-taking, applauding, booing, judging, reforming, conspiring, punishing, outcasting, scapegoating—an almost unlimited opportunity for multidimensional kitchen-sink fights that often drone on for decades and sometimes do not stop until death does them part.

Nevertheless, in our family fight-training sessions we have been able to introduce parents, grandparents, relatives—and even children as young as the age of three—to constructive, guilt-free communication of their aggressions and conflicts. Each family is encouraged to spell out fair fight rules for itself and to commit every member to use the rules much as in fight training for twosomes. The idea is not to eliminate family conflicts but to make them more emotionally productive and to reduce the hazards to mental health by making the family drama psychologically more realistic.

It *is* a drama, of course. Early in family training the therapist explains how the many disparate character actors are bound to turn family life into a production where harmony at times gives way to conflict and every member of the cast plays his very own role. In addition to feelings about one's self and one's own life and about each individual in the family, each member of the cast also has reactions to the group as a whole. Then the therapist elicits information from the cast:

"What kind of drama does your family play? Have you noticed any themes that come up often? What roles do you play when these themes are acted out? How does your family make decisions? How are you affected by these decisions?

"Do you participate in these decisions? How much do you do things together? How much do you conform? How much do you rebel? What use do you make of this group? What do you do about differences of interest? How do you handle conflicts generally? What was your last family quarrel like?

"Is your house open or closed to outsiders? Do you use your family as a source of your own reputation? Do you think of the family situation as a fun place, a fight arena, a place to eat and sleep, a prison, a department store where you get goodies? How does your family life differ from your school life, club life, from your work?

"In what respects would you like to improve the family life? Do you think everyone plays his role well? How well do you play your own role? What parts of family drama do you like best? Who and what would you like to change?"

It quickly becomes clear that the group members see things differently and have different expectations of each other. Before long they are almost certain to attack each other. Since the members function at different maturity levels, the disparities must be carefully watched so that children, especially, will have an opportunity to use family fights as a source of emotional growth.

Often one member is singled out as the "sick one," the problem member, the dark sheep of the family. Then follows an attack by the others and the "scapegoat" drama is on. Sometimes the patsy embraces the "sick" role as a source of his identity, however negative. But most people do not like to be the person about whom the others contend: "If it were not for you our family life would be bliss." So the scapegoat usually tries to throw off the blame for family dissatisfaction and make the "it" another member. He may seek the protection of the therapist and try to engage him in a defensive alliance.

At this point other roles tend to emerge for the other family members: the protective Red Cross nurse, the fair judge, the psychiatrist who analyzes the sickness of the scapegoat as reflecting a childhood trauma, the sadist who keeps rubbing it in, the clown who thinks the whole thing is silly, the escape artist who withdraws from it all, and the underground fighter who sabotages the proceedings by his camouflaged tricks.

The core role repertoire of the family is usually displayed before the therapist in the first 90 minutes of family therapy, and the drama is often dominated by the scapegoating theme. Assigning the scapegoat role to one member is the favorite method of role casting through group pressure. It is a source of group release of emotions. The task of the family group therapist is to unveil family dramas, to expose their redundancies, and to show the players how their roles prevent, rather than encourage, the solutions of family problems.

An atmosphere of "analysis" (fault finding) is to be avoided. The therapist functions as a micro-anthropologist. He helps everybody in the group to understand the micro-culture created by their emotional satisfactions and frustrations. When they recognize, even partially, the emotional gains and losses they derive from family dramas, the members can begin to make more constructive contributions to conflict resolution. At that point, new ways of dealing with lingering family problems have a chance to emerge.

A useful antidote to the scapegoat drama is for the group to restrain the "sick" role player from overplaying his part and thereby exhausting the others. The family group can also control behavior that might bring the actor to the more punitive attention of community resources for correcting deviant behavior. This drama is psychologically productive all around. Correcting and guiding a troubled soul is experienced as mastery of somewhat similar problems in oneself. Conflict, frustration, and aggression arise when one or more family members tire of this type of family drama, which we call *Reform*. But without cooperation from all actors, family dramas can't be enacted at all.

The drama *Reform* can also be played unrealistically, as for example when the family fails to bring "it" to the attention of correctional forces outside the family, such as professional psychotherapy, even though the "sick" player would clearly be better off with outside help. In fact, psychologically unrealistic enactment can intensify, rather than ameliorate, an actual "sickness" of "it." So this is hardly a drama to be taken lightly.

Another family drama is called *The Good and Evil in Word and Deed*. It deals with what's right, wrong, and fair; in and out; nice and nasty; decent and indecent; mean and kind. The family serves as a testing and clearing ground for

values-in-action by the ways in which it expresses approval
and disapproval.

In another drama, *Possession and Separation,* family members maneuver to obtain information about who possesses
whom and who would like to be possessed by whom. The
active form of the drama deals with attempts by a member
of the family to possess another. The passive form is an
effort by one to be possessed by another. Historically, the
roots of this type of drama may be traceable to the Oedipus
situation, but we do not limit ourselves to such hypothesized
remote causes. More likely, aggression in this drama is used
by a family member to determine the limits of his own
acceptability to the others, and such an effort is accompanied
by a great deal of separation anxiety.

Typically, the person who is testing his acceptability issues
a threat like "I will leave you" or "Why don't you leave
me?" or "Please do not leave me." The pay-off comes in the
relief from separation anxiety when he finds he will be
accepted regardless of his behavior.

One of our family group consultations centered on the
theme of the summer vacation: who would go with whom,
who should be left behind. When the mother said quite
seriously, "Why don't you all go without me?", the fat was in
the fire. The therapist refrained from analyzing the origins of
the drama. He facilitated communications until each family
member had made it abundantly clear why the vacation
would be spoiled for him unless the differences could be
settled so that the mother would see her way clear to coming
along.

Lively fights also accompany attempts to clarify what kind
of behavior is realistic for each family member. From a
standpoint of healthy personality development, fighting out
this drama of "Who are you?" is significant because the
outcome deeply influences the pictures that members of the
family have of themselves. We encourage everyone to make
his expectations explicit and to attempt to elicit agreement
from the others. But this, again, requires careful, sympathetic
supervision. Many a psychotic and neurotic has been the
victim of idealistic role casting; he couldn't live up to the role
of "Great White Father" or "Dr. Einstein" or whatever was
unrealistically expected of him. When such character actors
are unable to fulfill their assigned roles, they eventually face
brutal rejection on the part of the role caster.

To fight against being cast in a role that is alien to a
developing being is, as we made clear in the discussion of
parent-child conflicts, an essential aspect of healthy personali-

ty development. An interesting aspect of this "Who are you?" drama is the pressure by children for parents to behave in a certain way or to present a certain image for the children's psychological comfort. This is particularly evident during adolescence when social sensitivity is at its height. Group pressure, conformity, and rebellion have their say and play in this drama.

The authority structure within a family can also be a constant source of conflict and aggression. This power drama may be called *Who Is Boss?*. The motivation is to find leadership (to be able to indulge one's dependency) and to practice leadership (to be able to exercise one's assertiveness). Trouble starts when authority is distributed so that it does not fulfill one's expectations for dependency or leadership. An excellent example is the competition for authority to be the family disciplinarian. As customs change, tradition is no longer a reliable guide and the resulting fluidity leads to leadership fights.

By unscrambling the misuse of the need to depend and the need to lead or dominate—and by clarifying how common this drama is—the therapist can help a family to rewrite this important production so it will be more fulfilling to members of the cast. The idea is for everyone to perceive the difference between, for example, a Hitler and a constructive leader or between a loyal follower and a sniveling slave.

In the Parsons family the father, Gene, was doing all the disciplining. He only had authority to punish. His wife, Martha, always handed out the goodies to the children. Thus, in the eyes of the children, the mother had authority to love; the father only had authority to hate. Whenever the children's grandparents saw this plan in action, they applauded. This made for fairly good discipline in the early years when the children were too young to realize that Gene actually was reluctant to punish them and that he did so only in answer to reports, demands, and suggestions from Martha.

At first this earned Gene the image of a tough, even cruel, father. Later the Parsons' three children developed the impression that they had a weak mother and an accommodating father. Martha was seen by her children as a cowardly, tattling personality who was somehow able to make Gene do whatever she wanted. Such experiences with leadership roles tend to shape the attitude of youth toward what is good and bad about being a leader or a follower, a husband or a wife.

We referred to this drama previously in connection with what we believe to be the most rewarding role fathers can play in today's domestic scene. In the above case the mother violated the principle of dealing eyeball-to-eyeball with her children. She cast the father as the district attorney. She made herself unlovable not only to the children for her tattling but to the husband for her inability to handle domestic dirty work. Most unfortunate of all, she undermined herself by casting herself as just another child in need of a referee.

Other versions of the power fight drama may be simple competition for leadership in the family, *i.e.*, a fight over setting the pecking order; or it may be a production of *Follow the Leader* (or *Third Reich* or *Caine Mutiny*). In this production the whims of a nonbenevolent despot are entertained by other members of the family. Indeed, catering to the quirks of a dominant family character actor is a common way to maintain his sickness and liberate the others from feeling guilty about it.

The seemingly paradoxical fact is that the sickest member of a family is often given great authority, just as 70 million Germans, many of them intelligent and highly educated, catered to the well-recognized eccentricities of Adolf Hitler. In such a drama for authority, dominance is often confused with affection. The victims deny their masochistic, self-destructive behavior by telling themselves and each other that they are following someone who "knows best."

Follow the Leader, when played in troubled families, is no nursery game. It may be an anonymous release of excessive dependency needs or a stimulus and excuse for sporadic rebellions. In extreme cases it may cater to such overwhelming infantile guilt feelings that perfectly capable adults give up their identity and autonomy to almost any leader, and often to an incongruous one. This explains at least in part why a family leader need not necessarily be a parent. It can be a child, a dog, a relative, an outside person, or a psychotic —a Hitler.

When all parts of a person become exposed in family life, contempt and aggression follow almost inevitably. As the saying goes, "Everything seems to be everybody's business" in the family. Although this offends one's narcissistic self-image-making, which requires privacy, it is quite natural for everybody in the family to be concerned about what clothes you wear, how you do your hair, how you talk. And there is bound to be a great deal of family pressure to abolish tastes that peers may consider chic (*i.e.*, teen-age fads) but that the family considers gauche.

The fight for privacy comes up in many incarnations. All are useful because maximum privacy (without losing a sense of family belonging) is a worth-while goal for everyone. One of our trainee families consisted of four sons, one father, and a lonely mother who lacked even a place to do her toilette in privacy until she learned to level and fight for her femininity. A therapist can guide these dramas to yield information that family members can use to create greater intimacy without threatening the cohesiveness of the group.

The fight for privacy takes on particularly intense proportions during vacation times, especially when the family travels together at close quarters or camps out together.

First there may be a clash of ideas (and personalities) over where the family ought to go. Once that is settled there is a tendency to think of the vacation site as being practically around the corner; only rarely do the family tribesmen keep in mind that getting there may not be half the fun, especially if they're going in the cramped quarters of a car. Car fights are too standard in the American family's fight repertoire to warrant review here (Will the windows be open and closed? Who may smoke? When will there be a rest-room stop? What radio station should be turned on?). But the escalation of these fights deserves attention. Tempers seethe over such fights as the co-pilot's role:

SHE: We took the wrong turn, you idiot!
HE: But I'm watching the traffic and the cops! I thought you were following the map.
SHE: I'm trying to!
HE: No, you're not! You're sitting there, being driven around like Queen Victoria.
SHE: You *know* it makes me sick to read when we're driving. . . .

When the kids in the back seat hear the battle noises in the front seat, hostilities become contagious. Finally the family arrives at the vacation paradise. They're dead tired and hopping mad at each other and there is quite likely to be a major brawl over the accommodations, the sharing of facilities, or the process of settling down in strange and possibly disappointing surroundings.

Unfamiliarities and disappointments are compounded by the reactions of family members who may or may not be trying their best to adopt their relatively unaccustomed roles as vacationers. It may be difficult for laymen to believe, but in our research of murder between intimates we studied the case of a partner whose demise was almost triggered by his inability to handle a hotel reservations clerk in the masterful manner expected by his spouse.

Even among the most peaceful family groups, people generally experience greater stress during vacations and holidays than at other times. They are each other's captives. In the car they cannot get away from each other and find refuge in personal activities while they recharge their emotional batteries. At the vacation spot there may be much less privacy than the family is used to. Privacy is vital to everyone. When there is little or none, all sorts of unfamiliar habits and personality quirks may suddenly materialize among the loved ones, and these traits are rarely found pleasurable by the rest of the clan.

The concept of a "holiday" implies freedom and license to most people. Actually, when everybody has time on his hands and there is much unaccustomed and enforced togetherness, considerable discipline is required. Everyone must cope with a loss of personal autonomy and has to give up the narcissistic omnipotence ("I am the master of my own fate") that is enjoyed by most people at least some of the time. The proposition that "I can do anything I like," often followed by the assumption that "What I like is sure to be liked by others," runs counter to the realities of family life and is almost certain to lead to conflict.

Vacation-bound intimates should realize they are headed for a danger zone where they will be tempted by many invitations to violence; where they will function at considerably less than optimal distance from each other; and where they will find few exits for escape from excessively close family bonds and bondage. The best ways to reduce trouble are, first, for every member of the family to understand the nature of these problems; and, second, to prevent as much trouble as possible by hammering out family disagreements before the vacation starts and to rehearse vacation situations (drives, meals, sleeping arrangements, etc.) ahead of time on weekends during the year.

Fights with and about in-laws tend to be even more explosive. The meddling mother-in-law is a familiar fight figure. For example:

HE: You're spending too much time with your mother.

SHE: Come on! You know she doesn't have that much longer to live.

HE: I don't really mind her except that you go over there whenever we're not getting along. I hate for you to be a little girl running home to Mama.

SHE: I just like to make her happy.

HE: That's impossible.

SHE: What do you mean by that nasty crack?

HE: All you ever do over there is bitch about me.

SHE: I'm damned glad there's *somebody* around who's still listening.

HE: That's disloyal!

SHE: What do you want me to do?

HE: I want you to make clear to her that she should stop undermining me. . . .

This couple was beginning to reap the benefits of fight training. They were starting to level with each other about the true bone of contention in the mother-in-law relationship. But the basic issue in in-law problems is rarely recognized and therefore difficult for husbands and wives to cope with. Here is an illustrative consultation with a trainee couple who was having grandmother trouble:

HE: Doctor, it drives my wife and me nuts, but my mother insists on psychoanalyzing our kids all the time.

DR. BACH: What's your hangup about that? This is her way of being useful.

SHE: But she doesn't really know the children well enough and she's always spouting terrible nonsense. We can't stand listening to it.

DR. B: But why do you take nonsense seriously?

HE: Well, obviously my mother was smart enough to bring me up pretty well, and I get bothered when I start thinking that maybe she's right, after all.

DR. B: What makes you listen in the first place?

HE: Well, you've got to be tactful.

DR. B: *That's* your problem and your wife's. You prefer to treat your mother like an incompetent who's not worthy of being confronted with the fact that you disagree with her analyses of your kids.

HE: You're right, I guess, but she always says, "I've got nothing to live for," so this is her way of finding an interest in life.

DR. B: You're condemning her to the worst possible position: that she can't change. That just isn't true and you don't even give her a chance. . . .

We advised this couple that the least they could do about this grandmother is to tell her openly, "Let's talk about something else." But the issue of this fight, which is really the mother-in-law's fight for inclusion in the family, can be faced if husband and wife could give the old lady clues on how to make herself liked, how to be "in." Becoming a likable mother-in-law is a creative challenge. Unfortunately, husbands and wives rarely know how to lend a helping hand with it. They want to be "tactful" and usually don't realize that if they deprive a mother-in-law of her right to be the psychoanalyst of her grandchildren they are only depriving her of an illusion that seems hardly worth fighting for or about.

The deeper issue is that, realistically, the place of grandparents is less important today than it used to be. There is a senior generation gap: just as the experience of today's parents has less relevance for today's children, so the distance between parents and grandparents has widened. Yet grandparents still volunteer advice and directions—plus punishment and authority—on the basis of seniority alone. Few people object to grandparents just because they are old. In fact, they can be useful where parents fail. Grandparents are only objectionable when they are uninformed, uninteresting, no fun, and bossy ("You mean you *let* the children leave food on their plates?").

The problem usually is to keep the old folks at a distance without being cruel; to include them enough so they will be useful to themselves and the rest of the family; and to exclude them enough so there will be no needless, unconstructive conflict. Once this problem is faced realistically, each member of the family usually has his own idea of how it should be solved. Then there is likely to be a fight over whose plan should prevail.

We sometimes call a clan together to help mediate such a fight. The mere presence of the two or three generations for this specific purpose is helpful. Without it, members of the cast might never put all their cards on the table. This is crucial because the real villain usually is that nobody wants to take responsibility for defining the role of the grandparents. Everybody acts under the phony assumption that the old people are always welcome and that their relationship and seniority give them *inherent* authority over the rest of the family.

At our sessions, we define the grandparents' real and acceptable roles. The idea that they have to *earn* their value in the family embarrasses most people. It shouldn't. It challenges the old people to be imaginative in their show of interest toward the family. It confronts them with the need to develop more of a way of life of their own and not to live as marginal family satellites. We believe this is far less cruel than to encourage the fiction that they are always welcome— welcome to be endured and to deliver advice no one wants or heeds. This is no longer the age of ancestral privilege.

Once oldsters understand that it is not realistic for them to insist on a *carte blanche* welcome, they develop more activities of their own and become more comfortable with their contemporaries. They also become more creative in their contacts with the younger set. One psychiatrist's mother who was trained by us, used to call her son constantly and say, "I'm so lonely! What are you all doing?" Now she is more likely to say, "I'd like to take the kids to the circus. Can I come over and discuss it with them?" Oldsters thus turn into helpers who are in touch with the family's current interests. Everybody has more fun. And if the grandparents occasionally allow themselves to be impressed by the children's accomplishments, they won't only reap mutual pride and enjoyment. The oldsters will also be in a better position to exercise one of their best contemporary functions: to give children the idea that they are worthy carriers of their own ancestral line in an era where a realistic sense of continuity is a valuable and rare gift.

24. Exit Fights

Most husbands and wives occasionally blow up at each other and issue such challenges as, "I'm leaving!" or "Why don't you divorce me?" or "If you like, we can break up!" or "All right, I'm going to see a lawyer!"

Usually these are strategies of mock divorce—reminders that some changes are overdue in the relationship. An aggressive fight about the issues pending between a couple is clearly preferable to the brinkmanship of divorce or separation threats, particularly if the threatened partner suffers from high separation anxiety to begin with. But sometimes such threats serve as useful alarm clocks. They may jolt a partner awake and make him admit, "I really had no idea you felt that strongly about it!"

One wife who likes to show her husband that she is not to be taken for granted—and at the same time make sure that he is as fully committed to her as ever—sometimes throws a few clothes into a suitcase at the height of a furious argument. Then she rushes to the yellow pages of the phone book and looks up the names of some likely hotels and starts phoning for a reservation. Every time she has reached this stage, these moves have sufficed to induce the husband to offer the peace overtures that the wife was really soliciting by her maneuvers.

Partners who do storm out of the house and isolate themselves in a hotel tend to find that the pay-off is temporary and disappointing. One wife reported:

"First I felt great. I had a lovely room. I ordered eggs Benedict and a whisky sour from room service and got them to send me up a copy of *Vogue*. After a while I did my nails and enjoyed the delicious peace around me. I wasn't angry at all. All the anger at my husband had seeped out of me when I got into my convertible and drove to the hotel.

"After a while I decided to put on a nice dress and go downstairs to see what's cooking. I sat at a little table in the hotel bar and ordered a frozen daiquiri. The place seemed to be full of lonely people and I was terrified. Finally a man spoke to me. He looked very nice and I think he was only trying to make pleasant conversation, but I got scared stiff and ran off to my room.

"The next day I was really in terror. I'd figured all along that of course I'd soon go home again, but now I started wondering whether my husband would be there when I got back. I guess that was when I began to doubt he'd even make a move to retrieve me, and I decided I'd better not take too many chances. So I called the kids and said, 'I just want you to know where I am.' They were pretty upset and I guess they must have talked to my husband right away because he was at the hotel within a couple of hours and brought me flowers and we made up on the spot. Frankly, I'm not sure I'd ever want to go through it all again."

To abort temporary exits, partners should give each other a chance to go about their separate activities in the home and to observe the fight pauses that are so necessary for them to refuel. We also recommend that spouses have a "Ready Exit Kit" handy at all times. The kit should contain toilet articles, money for transportation, some essential clothing, plus information to be left behind: the phone number of baby-sitters, for instance, and a directory of places where the exiting partner may be found in case of emergency; one place can be checked off prior to even the hastiest departure.

The idea of the kit is to facilitate a fed-up partner's trip to an explosion-free refueling area, but spouses who maintain such kits and who know that their partners have their kits ready, too, almost never use them.

Many husbands and wives, even those who love each other and know in their hearts that they don't want to change partners, can be provoked into approaching the brink of divorce very closely indeed. One husband left home after a hair-raising *Virginia Woolf* type of insult exchange and had been gone without a word for six days when his wife called us for assistance. After the husband was located through mutual friends, he and his wife agreed to give fight training a try, but at first the husband refused to move back home.

He finally did go back on a trial basis, but only after we had set up an escape hatch. He kept his motel room and arranged for a low monthly rate and two keys—one for himself and one for his wife. The room was to be their exit kit. Since this couple's frustrations were running high, they were told to observe a strict moratorium on fighting at home and, for the time being, to fight only in front of their counselor or their fight-training group. If, despite these precautions, they were to become embroiled in a bad fight, they were to take turns escaping to the motel room, with the wife starting off.

As it turned out, these safety valves helped to work out their differences in only one month of fight training. Neither partner ever used the $300 motel room, yet both later said that it had been the best investment they ever made.

When one spouse goes through with the threat to see a divorce lawyer, much depends on the lawyer. If he is sympathetic and sufficiently trained in marriage counseling, at least to encourage a splitting couple to seek professional help, nothing may be lost. But many lawyers make only *pro forma* attempts at reconciliations. They may even lack the selflessness to determine whether a divorce-seeking partner is truly serious. As a result, many couples whose marriage should have been salvaged wind up in court, spurred on by litigation-happy attorneys.

We believe the time may come when lawyers will be legislated out of the divorce business in favor of court-attached family-preservation bureaus. These could be financed by increased marriage-license fees and staffed by professional marriage counselors and family therapists. Hopefully each divorce-minded couple will also have to undergo a psychological "final incompatibility test," much as a blood test now is a prerequisite for marriage. Such safeguards are particularly desirable for couples with children aged four to 16.

When both divorce-minded partners participate in fight training with a reasonable amount of hope, this is almost always a sign that they are committed to stay together, and probably will. Many marriages, however, teeter on the brink of divorce year after year, held together only by the stalemated mutual accusations of exit fight rituals. Such fights are the ultimate in round-robin battles, and here are some reasons why they drone on and on and why these sterile partnerships don't break up faster:

1. Each partner may want the other to assume the responsibility and guilt for the actual breakup (and final rejection of the other). 2. One or both may be excessively afraid of loneliness. 3. Their separation anxiety may be pathologically extreme because of deep-rooted fears of being abandoned like orphans.

(In one case of spouse murder that we studied, the husband brought a gun instead of a pen to the lawyer's office where his divorce agreement was to be signed. He shot his wife in front of both lawyers and peacefully went to prison with a lifetime sentence. Such people can never really separate because it would require them to accept that the ex-mate will be intimate with the next mate. This possibility terrifies these people to such an excruciating extent that they may do anything to prevent it.)

Unless partners wean themselves away from each other, preferably in therapy groups that help to reduce their feelings of fear and guilt, they are likely to emerge from a divorce like battle casualties. They may congratulate themselves on their freedom, but psychologically they resemble zombies. They find it difficult to accept their changed status in the community and become extremely vulnerable to sexual and financial exploitation. Some new divorcées seek support in group psychotherapy or such excellent self-help organizations as Parents Without Partners, but the vast majority plunge into a headlong hunt for a new spouse.

As we noted near the outset of this book, such a reassertion of the mating urge is not rooted in a search for self-punishment. Most people abhor loneliness; some are even terrorized to the point where their fears can be called solophobia. Except for a few diehard loners, men and women yearn to share, to belong, to be intimate. It makes their lives meaningful. They know that when one is married, one's partner is so committed and dependent that he will put up with far more idiosyncrasies than anybody else. Besides, who else would be so willing to engage in fights and provide release for one's hostilities?

Even many sick satans have a compelling reason to remarry. Only through marriage can they indulge in their emotional orgies of pseudo-intimacy: seducing a partner, pinning him down, and then rejecting him in an almost automatic sequence of courtship-marriage-divorce. We have known spouses to drag as many as six partners through such an emotional blood bath, one after another. Alimony and child support do not deter these orgy lovers because courts always leave them enough to live on. Besides, these suitors often persuade their potential patsies to sign prenuptial agreements so that the satans won't be fined a penny for the next breakup.

Once a marriage is clearly sick and unsalvageable, divorce is the best way to assure the sanity of the partners and, especially, of children. Youngsters are infinitely better off in a clear-cut divorce situation than in a subtly crazy-making family. Furthermore, we agree heartily with the growing school of psychological and legal thought that the traditional female right to acquire the custody of children deserves to be questioned in many cases.

Just because she can give birth, a woman is not necessarily a "natural mother." Child rearing is a learned skill, not an instinctive one, and frequently it is the mother, not the father, who is the chief crazy-maker in a family. The worst thing a community can do for the children of such a couple is to award them automatically to the mother merely because she is not a prostitute and because she loves her children in her pathogenic way.

In decades to come, society will have to assume increased responsibility for millions of those children of divorce whose mothers are psychologically unfit to care for her youngsters and whose fathers are too preoccupied or possibly also incompetent as parents. The fate of these children is not enviable, whatever arrangements are made for their physical care and emotional growth. We believe, however, that society will find ways to remove these youngsters at least from influences that are clearly damaging. The only practical answer to the problem may be villages or clubs for youngsters whose mothers or fathers would abuse or neglect them.

Such a group milieu is hardly ideal. And yet it need not have anything in common with the "military academies" or socialist collectives that come to mind. Tomorrow's youth clubs and villages could be therapeutically managed learning centers, perhaps combining the functions of co-educational schools and play centers. Small groups with warmly understanding, trained counselors could impart some of the feeling for intimacy that the children's parents tragically lacked. The parents could be encouraged to visit their youngsters so the boys and girls would not feel abandoned. The best possible design for such centers may not be developed for many years, but a pressing need exists and experimentation along these lines should be encouraged. All of us owe this much to the innocent victims of marriages that no one could save.

Finally, intimates should work harder to relieve some of the pressures that overburden marriage today. Not all the hunger that exists for meaningful personal relationships can be satisfied within a twosome of husband and wife. Aggression, especially, needs additional legitimate, constructive outlets. Fair fighting with relatives, friends, office colleagues, and other outsiders should be encouraged as extensions of the Intimate System and a valuable antidote to marriage breakups that need not happen.

25. Manifesto for Intimate Living

It would be foolish, if not dishonest, to leave the impression at the end of our tour of intimate battlegrounds that constructive combat is a universal panacea. Too many husbands, wives, and lovers have tried fight training and failed to make it work for them.

Among the trainees least likely to succeed are the people who simply cannot bring themselves to drop their masks and inhibitions and come out leveling.

And the partners who would like to learn how to fight right but who cannot persuade their mates to join them in making the requisite joint effort.

And the people who take so many cocktails, sleeping pills, tranquilizers and wake-up pills that they never give their true emotions a chance to unfold.

And the emotional "empties"—people who think they have everything and need nothing and for whom the rewards of sacrificing and sharing are lost in chronic blandness, boredom, and economic "success."

And the spouses who start to fight, then turn temporarily cold toward each other, and then stop their fight training in resignation or despair, instead of using the crisis as the starting point of an intensive and informed effort to help each other grow.

And the spouses whose disparate potential for growth becomes exposed and perhaps exacerbated by realistic fighting.

And the rageolics who misuse the relative liberality of the fight rules as a license to be cruel.

As all psychotherapists know, any intervention in a natural state of affairs can at times make things worse. Invariably, an attempt to change an existing order entails some risk. In our experience with fight training, however, the system is most likely to fail because it is easily misunderstood, especially because "intimacy" and "aggression," like "love" and "hate," are conventionally believed to be mutually exclusive.

Some people choose to "misunderstand" quite deliberately.

A good example are those who—like the rageolics just cited—seize on one aspect of the training and misuse it in order to get their own way. Bona fide misunderstandings are usually the result of a failure to appreciate that fight training is part of a multi-dimensional *system* that can only be rewarding in the context of a new and intimate way of living. The system's heuristic rules and techniques are as interdependent as the parts of an engine.

To minimize risks of misunderstandings, the following summary of the dimensions and pay-offs of intimacy is offered as a model of fight training and of the way it can shape a delicately balanced new way of life.

Intimacy is, first of all, a basic outlook. It is a couple's orientation toward mutuality and their acceptance of the proposition that shared experiences are generally preferable to solo experiences. It is based on a *desire* to remain "in love" and to maintain a place in the center of the partner's heart.

Intimacy can be achieved only if the partners have adequate *information*. It cannot be achieved without a determination to be transparent, to share one's private world of thoughts and feelings with the partner. Intimates never assume where they stand. They let each other know.

Intimates accept that their relationship is never static. The state of any couple's swing *changes* constantly, and successful intimates never stop learning how to keep their love feelings alive by responding realistically to the here-and-now. Anger and aggression invariably accompany this continuing refitting process; this helps resolve crises because authentic anger brings out truth. Intimates also help each other to overcome stale routines or obsolete stances (*i.e.*, when a wife helps a husband grow to be a father).

Intimates *trust* each other. They are not afraid that their partners will exploit their weaknesses. They take turns at giving and taking but are not concerned with contractlike reciprocity. They tactfully respect each other's belt lines and temper their honesty with infinite tact so that a partner will not be cruelly hurt. They do not engage in orgies of mutual confessions (which only relieve the confessor and burden the partner). They expect to be clearly informed about how each feels about the other in any situation, but they do not feel a childlike obligation to "report everything."

Intimacy requires equal *authority*. As in all true partnerships, the leadership can change from situation to situation, depending on a partner's competence, energy, health, or other factors of the moment. Lines of command always remain reversible.

Intimacy implies *freedom* from the notion that one partner is worthless without the other as well as freedom from rigid roles. Each partner also has the freedom to pursue independent interests and to enjoy intermissions within the intimate relationship (without, however, engaging in intimacy-destroying activities).

Intimates are *loyally* devoted to each other's reciprocal commitment to be the "Number One" in each other's life and heart. They do not dwell on irrational jealous-possessive thinking, nor do they provoke or accommodate it.

Intimates are *realistic*. They keep their own and each other's feet on the ground by constant candid feedback and realize that these echoes can be positive (and rewarding) as well as negative (and punishing). They also keep each other from engaging in foolish or self-destructive pursuits.

Intimacy requires *humor*. Successful intimates can laugh at themselves and each other safely, unashamedly, without loss of face. They can be playfully laughing "children" together, ridiculing all pretenses, mimicking each other's faults, and reaping the rewards of having fun together.

Finally, intimates use *aggression* as well as affection to influence each other in the direction of better swing. They fight fairly, above the belt, out in the open, without camouflage or disloyal alliances or cowardly undermining of the opponent. From their constructive fights they learn where they stand and what they must improve, and they end up feeling better and closer for having fought.

To make these dimensions of intimacy work, husbands, wives, and lovers should bear in mind:

1. People in today's culture are so involved in playing games and wearing masks to hide their real selves that authentic intimacy, while natural to human nature, is an acquired skill that must be learned and practiced.

2. Intimate relationships are so full of paradoxes that they often seem downright mad (as when partners love and hate each other deeply at the same time). In point of fact, intimacy is a multitracked system that one must learn to understand and live with.

3. Since intimacy is a precarious, subtle quality in a relationship and since it can only emerge spontaneously, it can obviously not be subject to rigid rules. The heuristic principles outlined in this book do, however, create conditions that favor the emergence of authentic intimacy.

4. Intimacy passes through many phases. It tends to begin

with the accommodations of courtship; it evolves through power struggles, loyalty problems, the successes and failures of individual or joint "projects," and many other stages. It is helpful for intimates to realize that quarrels frequently are symptoms of the emergence of a new phase; that continual truthful confrontations about current feelings will help them through the inevitable transitions; and that the accompanying fights are anything but signs of breakup. Indeed, crises usually make it easier to restyle a relationship because intelligent partners realize that extraordinary tensions signal the end of the status quo.

Is intimacy worth all this trouble?

An overwhelming majority of our fight-training graduates believe it is, and here are some of the pay-offs they have discovered.

Intimacy is an invaluable aid to self-acceptance. It relieves excessive self-criticism, the "tyranny of the self." Most people carry feelings of guilt, failure, and shame around with them. "Loners" must forgive or punish themselves for such burdens, but intimates perform these liberating chores for each other.

Intimates realize that no one can live up to the promises and dreams of courtship, but they tend to try. This "pushing" toward courtship ideals often brings out the best in each partner because the other experiences it as evidence that he is deeply cared about.

Intimates find they can better absorb the "down" periods of their lives. Both are concerned with overcoming problems, with going on. A blow to one's self-esteem (such as losing one's job) might bring total despair to a solo-person; it can be taken in stride when shared with an intimate.

Intimacy creates a sense of sociological security. When two people are truly intimate, they can afford to be selective in their attitudes toward strangers. It follows that intimates cannot be easily manipulated by outsiders, do not need to glamorize them or depend on their promises.

Intimacy is an antidote to disorder and chaos. Its continuity—the sheer necessity that two people must coordinate their lives in order to function as a unit—insures the establishment of some direction and order.

Intimacy within a family is the most effective way of raising psychologically healthy new generations. It is society's best insurance against raising one alienated generation after another.

Perhaps most important of all, all humanity stands to benefit from intimacy. When people work off animosities among intimates and friends, they drain away aggressions that would otherwise be forced to seek outlets in the far more dangerous channels of hate groups, riots, assassinations and other criminality, and wars. The time is getting late for a thaw of the psychological ice age that threatens to engulf mankind. Inhumanity, apathy, and alienation fester behind the headlines in each day's newspapers. Realistic intimacy will bring relief if enough thoughtful husbands, wives, lovers, and parents take the trouble to understand it and make it work to enrich themselves and all the rest of us.

We are convinced, although we cannot yet scientifically prove it, that people who master the fine art of fair verbal fighting and conflict resolution will be disinclined to commit physical violence. Nor are they likely to follow leaders who exploit man's hunger for aggression release. We also believe that any disarmament system must, in order to be effective, be built on sound social-psychological thinking, not just politics. The more the values of realistic and aggressive intimacy pervade a culture, and the more people commit themselves to constructive verbal fighting, the more safely sated will be man's appalling appetite for lethal violence.

Technical Appendix

by Dr. George R. Bach

Introduction

In these pages for scientifically oriented readers, especially my colleagues and students in psychiatry, psychology, sociology, and related fields, *Fight Training* can be defined as a specific psychotherapy programmed to "cure" inept self- and other-defeating ways of coping with aggression by maximizing intimacy-generating styles of aggression and minimizing hurtful and alienating hostility.

I first presented my fight-training approach to conflict resolutions of intimates at scientific meetings: at Columbia University before the American Association of Marriage Counselors in 1960; at the annual convention of the Group Therapy Association of Southern California in 1961; at the annual meeting of the Western Psychological Association in 1962; and by invitation at the annual conference of the Orthopsychiatric Association in 1962. Here are some of the theoretical, clinical, and ethical origins of the program as described in this book:

My research in human aggression began 25 years ago with an experimental demonstration of the modifiability of hostile reactions of children in conflict situations with teachers and parents (cf. Bibliography: Bach 1944). From this evolved a therapeutic method of *conflict confrontation* through play therapy for children and group psychotherapy for adults (cf. Bach 1954).

The two anchors for my theory came first from Freud's original insight into the paradoxical and conflictful co-existence of love-eros-sex and aggression-hate (cf. Notes on Chap. 19). Secondly, my teacher, Kurt Lewin, offered a brilliant field-theory which provided concepts for *social action,* a social therapy that aimed at the resolution of this approach-avoidance conflict, not only on the intra-psychic level but also inter-personally and group-dynamically (cf. Lewin references in Bibliography). Two former professors in learning-theory, Robert Sears and Kenneth Spence, initiated a lasting interest in the application of reinforcement principles to the cognitive restructuring task inherent in direct behavior modification.

The achievement of therapeutic *behavior change* depends on a fulfillment of the desire to resolve acutely felt conflicts by acquiring *new* competence in dealing with them as they arise *here and now*. Providing historical insight into the presumably remote causes is less useful than facilitating current problem-solving through modeling (cf. Bibliography: Bandura 1962), through heuristic "programming" and through group stimulation and *practice!*

The most common and acute type of conflict that stymies the majority of my consultees cannot be resolved through traditional individually oriented personalistic approaches; they require an inter-personal, group-dynamic or "systems" orientation (cf. Bibliography: Buckley 1967). People want to combine effectively the enjoyment of close interpersonal involvements (intimacy) with the enjoyment of freedom and independence. They like to have their cake and eat it too. And they can be shown how: by learning how *interdependent systems* work and how to participate successfully in an intimate system by becoming more accessible, more transparent, more openly communicative, more assertive and less afraid of confrontations and *fair fighting*.

Theoretically, I believe that a change of state, *i.e.,* a change in levels of inter-dependence between people (in pairs and in larger groups), is brought about by instrumental aggression: fighting to get rid of (or defend) an old situation and fighting for emergence of a new order in the affairs of inter-dependent Man. Change and aggression go together, and since change is essential to growth and survival, Man has a surplus capacity for aggression and a high creativity for inventing new ways of directly and indirectly releasing it. Man is in a chronic state of aggression-overmobilization. Each individual has, therefore, an embarrassing stockpile of surplus aggression in readiness and he must do something constantly or periodically to release some of it. Consequently, man is in a constant search for enemies who can serve as safe aggression-release targets. All segments of a culture (not just politicians) share in the search for and/or invention of enemies; once found, people go after them with hostile gusto, as history amply demonstrates.

Now man has invented an aggression releaser that is a self-defeating monster: nuclear weaponry. This has rendered traditional foreign, faraway enemies obsolete. Faraway targets have to be replaced by new ones closer to home. Nuclear weaponry has brought aggression back home. Who are the most suitable enemies we can find nearby? There are many volunteer target groups—blacks vs. whites, youth vs. aged, and men against women: *the* most intimate enemies!

The tactics and strategies—even the very definition, the semantics of aggression—must change to clarify the needed change in objectives from annihilation to rational assertion in an aggression exchange, a mutual cooperation from which emerge safe, even creative ways of fully utilizing aggression for constant growth and change.

The above considerations made me more clearly conscious of the growing reservoirs of hostility within my consultees, and ten years ago I turned to the task of providing clients with a heuristic educational system which would give them a tool to deal with conflicts inherent in inter-dependence and simultaneously give them a safe, fair, *regular,* and practical aggression target and catharsis: fighting in context of intimacy.

The professional reader whose study of the technical literature is not restricted to the redundant productions of a traditional "school" will recognize that the therapeutic potential of constructive aggression is implicitly or explicitly utilized by many contemporary psychotherapists. If there should be any doubt that aggression can be turned to good advantage in human affairs, the recent book by the British psychoanalyst, Anthony Storr (cf. Bibliography), *Human Aggression,* presents ample evidence that our approach does not stand alone. Rather, it falls within the current emphasis on *authentic communication,* open *encounter* and confrontation. This trend of thought and clinical method appears in the writings of many current authors (cf. Bibliography: writings of Ackerman, Altenberg, Berlin, Berne, Bettelheim, Bugenthal, Buhler, Corsini, DeAnda, Dederich, Ellis, Erikson, Frank, Glasser, Hodge, Hogan, Kempler, Moreno, Pearson, Perls, Rosen, Sagan, Satir, Shapiro, Shostrom, Stoller, Whitaker, and Yablonsky).

A comprehensive review of the related literature also reveals a growing number of authors (cf. Bibliography: writings of Ardrey, Berkowitz, Lorenz, Rapoport, Storr, and Yablonsky) who have produced theoretical, experimental, descriptive, or comparative etiological studies of psychiatric and sociological problems posed by the existence of human aggression. But beyond general pleas for better understanding, "controls" or "substitutes" for human aggression, no practical preventive or therapeutic program is offered.

The fight training described in this book seems to be the first therapeutic educational method *specifically* designed to help people manage their aggression constructively. Its application in the context of intimate inter-personal relationships demonstrates dramatically the validity of our thesis, also advanced by Lorenz and Storr, that aggression, when properly channeled rather than repressed, suppressed, "controlled" or displaced, is a positive life force. Specifically, we submit the theory that aggressive-struggles are intrinsic to growth and *change* (see second note, Chap. 2).

Current public concern with aggression and violence has created an intellectual climate favorable for serious research and clinical work in this area. The *Zeitgeist* is possibly one of the reasons for the growing professional acceptance of our therapeutic method to utilize aggression in the service of love.

Notes & Comments on Chapter 1—"Why Intimates Must Fight."

Page 17. The standard fight-training course takes 13 sessions over three months' time. To begin, the trainee couple visits our Tuesday 8:30 P.M. open house at our Institute of Group Psychotherapy, 450 North Bedford Drive, Beverly Hills (no appointment necessary), to participate in an "information group" in which the program, fees, and duration are discussed. Interested parties are then referred to relevant literature and offered a private screening appointment where their suitability for fight training is determined by an experienced staff member from our multidisciplinary team of psychiatrist-psychologist-sociologist-physician. Accepted for fight training are those couples where *both* partners give the impression that they are genuinely concerned with improving their relationship. Excluded are severely alienated couples where one or both are ambivalent as to the value of their togetherness, or where partners are deeply convinced that the other is mentally sick and needs psychiatric treatment for his person, not his marriage. Alienated-ambivalents as well as the "psychiatry-playing" people will participate in our individual and group therapeutic sessions—each in separate programs with occasional "visitation" and conjoint sessions. Through self-growth and therapeutic development they learn to stop playing psychiatry with mates or anyone else and start to make responsible ambivalent-free decisions—such as to stay with the mate and work on enriching togetherness; or to divorce the partner in a relatively painless and rational manner.

Couples who are accepted participate in four-hour, once-a-week sessions of our fight-training therapy groups where, with the aid of tape recorders and together with four or five other couples, they are coached in the finer points of marital conflict-resolution. They are encouraged to fight with each other in front of the group (live) and/or to bring their homework to the group (their own tape-recorded fights). Their fights will be analyzed and scored as to style and effect—by the couple involved, by the "fight trainer," and by the group. Fight-style improvements and regressions are noted and discussed. Improvements are positively reinforced by approval—especially from the other couples who, although having started as a group of resistant strangers, become emotionally cohesive and deeply interested in the growth of each other's marriage.

One weekend, either during or shortly after the four months' session, the fight-training couples are invited to participate in a 24-hour, or longer nonstop marathon encounter group—invented and developed by myself in collaboration with Dr. Fred Stoller in 1963. (Ref. Bach, George R. "The Marathon Group—Intensive Practice of Intimate Interaction," *Psychological Report*, 1966. 18:995—1002.)

The marathon sessions give our trainees maximum opportunity to practice aggressive conflict-resolution—not only with each other but also with other members of the group. Aggressive leveling and feedback critique are most helpful therapeutic learning experiences in marathon groups. (Ref. Bach, George R., "Marathon Group Dynamics II—Dimensions of Helpfulness," *Psychological Report*, 1967. 20:1147–58. Bach, George R. "Marathon Group Dynamics III: Disjunctive Contacts," *Psychological Report,* 1967. 20:1163–72. Bach, George R. "Group-Leader Phobias in Marathon Groups," *Voices*, 1967. 3:41–46.)

Shortly after the marathon each couple participates in a marathon-group follow-up session and, finally, in a private conference where the future participation of the couple in one or none of our Institute's training or therapy programs is discussed. Most couples need not repeat the fight-training course. They are no longer afraid of conflict and aggression and can now fight rationally as well as emotionally with genuine style. They can stop analyzing their aggressions and start to feel and enjoy closer intimacy. Some graduate trainees have formed autonomous "fight clubs" to stay in practice.

Page 18. Chronic-redundant insult exchanges (*Virginia Woolf* style) are hostility rituals which, in cases of inability to fight out frustrations, are the only and perhaps necessary aggression catharsis available to couples who neither know how to fight fair nor foul. Yet they must somehow express their disappointment, anger, and frustration with their life together, a togetherness they do NOT want to destroy. So they either lash out ritualistically at their children (the symbol of their unhappy togetherness) or at each other. In many such cases, participation in a hostility ritual is the only experience in mutual intimacy the couple can afford. In many instances it is an essential prelude and/or sequel to the enjoyment of sexual intimacy. These irrational temper tantrums (having no issue, giving no new information) are not fights that strive for some change or solution. It is precisely the inability to attack the intolerable and to fight for change that feeds such hostility rituals. As the important psychological function of hostility-rituals are better understood, mates can differentiate them from proper fights. And when partners learn how to fight fair and without fear, *Virginia Woolf* type hostility rituals disappear from the marital scene and true intimacy takes over. However, many fight-trained couples still enjoy engaging playfully in mock-up hostility rituals—entertaining each other with a *Virginia Woolf* now and then.

Page 19. At this time we have only clinical evidence for our hypothesis that irrational group-oriented or community-directed hostility and violence decreases for individuals who have learned to make a more satisfactory and direct use of aggression in face-to-face relationships with emotionally significant others. While it is tragically clear that Man as a species has a relatively easily aroused, innate propensity for engaging in aggressive and violent action against fellow humans, it is neither instinctive nor necessarily natural for the targets of aggression to be strangers, out-groups, enemy invaders, etc. Nevertheless, this is unfortunately so, because hostility directed against an enemy group is morally and rationally sanctioned in civil and foreign wars and in aggressive competitive sports while intimate inter-personal fighting is likely to be suppressed and repressed. Group-targeted violence (however insane and life-destroying it actually is) is readily supplied with patriotic or other ethno-syntonic ideals and goals (liberty, equality, integration, democratic freedom, anti-imperialism, anti-communism, anti-Judaism, etc.). Social scientists are still collecting evidence for a bio-genetic support of group-targeted violence, the latest being the protection of territory. (Ref. Ardrey, Robert. *The Territorial Imperative.* New York: Delta Books, 1966. Lorenz, Konrad. *On Aggression.* New York: Harcourt, Brace & World Inc., 1966.)

Political leadership has traditionally thrived on the hero-making quality of providing the public with morally sanctioned, guilt-free aggression releases. We submit that the release of aggressive impulses (like the release of sexual impulses) should become a *personal responsibility*—being taken care of among friends, NOT enemies. The success of our program is proof that people, especially young children, can learn to fight out their aggression within the family, the peer group, and the playground—if they are not encouraged to displace it toward "enemies" who are far away from the real context of their personal lives. Open, constructive marital warfare can teach, by example, that homes allowing for greater immediacy and emotional satisfaction of intimate animosities are the most satisfactory. When children learn early in life to take care of their aggression where it is safest (at home) and acquire the technique for responsibly working through their hostilities as they arise—in the context of loved ones, intimate friends, and family and "tribe" (group members)—such children will not later be so easily persuaded to participate in group-oriented violence.

Page 20. Our Field-theoretical, Lewinian background helped us to see therapeutic education as a cognitive restructuring: new foreground-background relationships; new integrations of supposedly irreconcilable opposites, creating *Synergic Tolerance* for both programming and spontaneity. This is in line with the new philosophy of science. (Ref. Boguslaw, Robert. *The New Utopians—The Study of System Design & Social Change.* Englewood Cliffs, N.J.: Prentice-Hall, 1965. Kaplan, Abraham. *The Conduct of Inquiry.* San Francisco: Chandler Publishing Co., 1964.)

Page 20. Individuals can be ordered along a hostility expression dimension with "weak-control" (acting out) and "over-control" (fight-phobic) on the extreme ends. Their leanings toward face-to-face personal targets versus faraway, strange, impersonal or abstract-symbolic hostility targets can also be assessed with psychological test instruments. Moreover, these can test the reality level at which partners would not feel a personal responsibility for participating in violence. Such instruments are being developed at our Institute as part of a new research project that aims at the establishment of "Violence-prevention Centers." So far, clinical impressions suggest that the aggression-overcontrolled person (who also abhors aggressive face-to-face leveling with friendly significant others) is most ready to engage in violent, planned lethal attack toward either friend or foe when there is proper provocation by the victim and/or strong social inducement or pressure. Generally fight-phobic (quiet, peaceful nonfighting) people are, as I see it, more personally and socially dangerous than the more openly aggressive. Both "super-aggressors" and "super-fight-evaders" are initially very resistant to fight training; but with patience and good will, they too can learn to become decent fighters. (Ref. Bach, George R. "Thinging—A Sub-Theory of Intimate Aggression Illustrated by Spouse-Killing," presented at the 75th Annual Convention of the American Psychological Association in Washington, D.C., September 2, 1967.)

Page 23. Camouflaged hostility has many masks. In its offensive form it surreptitiously undermines or spoils the well-being of its victim (*i.e.*, passive-aggressive parents). In its defensive form it secretly foils the partner's destructive moves against him. There are many levels of effectiveness of camouflage, the most psychologically important being self-deception. The concept of self-deception is treated in depth by Jean-Paul Sartre. (Ref. Sartre, Jean-Paul. *Being and Nothingness*. New York: Citadel Press, 1965.)

The camouflaged aggressor refuses awareness of his own camouflaged aggressiveness. He kids himself into believing that he has no mean streak in his body. Camouflaged or indirect aggression (in both its offensive and defensive form) aims at creating the same results as victorious open aggression—but with built-in clever insurance against responsibility for either winning or losing. In cases where camouflaged aggression successfully achieves its destructive aims without the aggressor having to account for it, nor being subject to righteous counter-attacks from his victim, such aggressors can have their cake and eat it too. This is the real pay-off of their strategy. Camouflaged hostility is most prevalent in cultures such as ours that decry open, inter-personal face-to-face aggressive leveling—especially among loved ones—as "bad manners," "nasty," "ugly," etc. In America, both North and South, the practice of camouflaged aggression (the fine art of doing your friends in and getting away with it, upmanship, etc.) is a social pastime played for big psychological pay-offs. The details can be found in Dr. Eric Berne's best-seller, *Games People Play*. (Ref. Berne, Eric. *Games People Play*. New York: Grove Press, 1964.)

Interesting speculations concerning the origin of camouflaged hostility are generously supplied under "passive-aggression" in the psychoanalytic literature. (Ref. Shapiro, David. *Neurotic Styles*. New York & London: Basic Books, 1965.)

The manipulation and exploitation of others in con-man fashion for ulterior motives (a great American hostility sport) has been clearly recognized and described in current literature. (Ref. Biderman, A. D. & Zimmer, H. *The Manipulation of Human Behavior*. New York: John Wiley & Sons, Inc., 1961. Shostrom, Everett. *Man, the Manipulator*. New York & Nashville: Abingdon Press, 1967. Goffman, Erving. "On Cooling the Mark Out," *Psychiatry*, 1952. Vol. 15, No. 4, 451–63. Goffman, Erving. *The Presentation of Self in Everyday Life*. New York: Doubleday, 1959. Berne, Eric: *Games People Play*. New York: Grove Press, 1964.)

Page 25. Research into the therapeutic function of aggressive encounter has been presented (Ref. Bach, George R., ed. "Constructive Aspects of Aggression," a symposium presented to the 9th Annual Conference of the Group Psychotherapy Association of Southern California, 1962) for family groups as well as regular and marathon groups (Ref. Bach, George R. "Marathon Group Dynamics II: Dimensions of Helpfulness," *Psychological Report*, 1967. 20:1147–58. Bach, George R. "Group-Leader Phobias in Marathon Groups," *Voices*, 1967. 3:41–46. Bach, George R. "Marathon Group Dynamics III: Disjunctive Contacts," *Psychological Report*, 1967. 20:1163–72); also for individual psychotherapy (Ref. Whitaker, Carl A. "The Use of Aggression in Psychotherapy," presented to the 9th Annual Conference of the Group Psychotherapy Association of Southern California. 1962). All come to the conclusion that tension- and quarrel-free relationships are neither enduring nor deeply, emotionally involved. Autonomy-worshiping, intimacy-phobic loners can indeed get along in life without personal strife by learning techniques of extracting maximal joy from minimal (often ritualized) fleeting contacts. (Ref. Schutz, William. *Joy*. New York: Grove Press, 1967.)

Page 26. (Ref. Harlow, H. F. "Affectional Responses in Infant Monkeys," *Science*, 130, 1959. Harlow, H. F. "The Nature of Love," *American Psychologist*, 1958. 673–85.)

Page 27. (Ref. Lorenz, Konrad, *op. cit.*)

Page 27. (Ref. Erikson, Erik H. *Childhood and Society*. New York: Norton, 1950. Erikson, Erik H. *Identity and the Life Cycle*. New York: International Universities Press, 1959.)

Page 30. Dr. Albert Ellis, the founder and director of the Institute for Rational Living, invited me to a scientific conference on the use and abuse of therapeutic aggression in 1968. The concept of rationally motivated anger and "rational aggression" (a contemporary version of righteous wrath as in a fight against injustice, prejudice, and irrationality itself) emerged from this conference. (Ref. Bach, George R. "Therapeutic Uses & Abuses of Aggression," presented at the

Institute for Rational Living in New York, seminar conducted May 30, 1968.) Dr. Ellis correctly insists on helping people to clearly differentiate self-defeating, irrational hostility from constructive aggression focused on assertive concern.

Page 31. (Ref. Yablonsky, Lewis. *The Hippie Trip*. New York: Pegasus, 1968.)

Page 32. (Ref. Berne, Eric, *op. cit.*)

Notes & Comments on Chapter II—"Fighting for (and Against) Intimacy."

Page 35. Reference source of divorce and remarriage statistics: Confer Statistical Abstract of U.S. 1967, by the Department of Commerce, 1967, Washington D.C.

Page 36. Theoretically we are dealing here with social phenomenology as first developed in K. Lewin's field-theory. (Ref. Lewin, Kurt. *A Dynamic Theory of Personality*. New York: McGraw-Hill Book Co., 1935. Lewin, Kurt. *Principles of Topological Psychology*. New York: McGraw-Hill Book Co., 1935. Lewin, Kurt. *Resolving Social Conflicts*. Ed. by Gertrud Lewin. New York: Harper & Brothers, 1948. Lewin, Kurt. *Field Theory in Social Science*. Ed. by Dorwin Cartwright. New York: Harper & Brothers, 1951.)

Currently these concepts are being creatively pursued by R. D. Laing. (Ref. Laing, R. D. *The Divided Self*. London: Tavistock Publications, 1960. Laing, R. D. *The Self and Others*. London: Tavistock Publications, 1961. Laing, R. D., and Esterson, A. *Sanity, Madness and the Family*. New York: Basic Books, Inc., 1964. Laing, R. D. *The Politics of Experience*. Baltimore: Penguin Books, 1967.) Optimal distance can be conceptualized as a balanced state between autonomy and entwinement (identity-fusion), allowing the degree of freedom of movement that permits reconfirmation of individual identity boundaries that may be temporarily surrendered or, as Laing would say, "invaded." We submit that one of the natural constructive functions of aggression and fighting between members of an intimate system is to find that "balanced state" of synergy: autonomy *and* entwinement. More generally we see the function of intimate aggression (in the context of system theory and field theory) as regulating instrumentally "changes of states" within an inter-personal system, such as from autonomy to inter-dependence (or self-identity to fusion) and back again; from verbal to nonverbal communications (*e.g.*, from verbal scolding to hitting); from dyadic-contact to multiple contacts (and back to dyadics) (*e.g.*, *ménage à trois*, multiple loving, more children, death of friends, family members growing up, expansion and restriction of friendship circles and other psychoecological changes). We theorize that fighting among and between members of an inter-dependent system generates not only heat but some new light by which information is displayed which is relevant to, and necessary for, knowing the newly emerging state of affairs. They must let each other know how each experiences himself and the other during this new state of the system; how they define the new situation; and how their respective roles are changing in it. (Ref. Lewin, Kurt. *Resolving Social Conflicts* (especially chapter on marriage), *op. cit.* Laing, R. D. *op. cit.* Heider, Fritz. *The Psychology of Interpersonal Relations.* New York: John Wiley & Sons, Inc., 1958.)

Page 36. (Ref. Festinger, Leon. "Informal Social Communication," *Psychological Review,* 1950. 57:271–82. Festinger, Leon, and Kelly, Harold. *Changing Attitudes Through Social Contacts.* Ann Arbor, Mich.: Research Center for Group Dynamics, 1951. Festinger, Leon. *A Theory of Cognitive Dissonance.* New York: Harper & Row, Inc., 1957. Goldstein, A. P., Heller, K., and Sechrest, L. B. *Psychotherapy and the Psychology of Behavior Change.* New York: John Wiley & Sons, Inc., 1966. Jennings, Helen H. *Leadership and Isolation* (2nd edition). New York: Longmans, Green & Co., Inc., 1950. Newcombe, T. M. "The Prediction of Interpersonal Attraction," *American Psychologist,* 1956. 11:575–86. Pepitone, A., and Reichling, G. "Group Cohesiveness and the Expression of Hostility," *Human Relations,* 1955. 8:327–38. Schacter, Stanley. Deviation, Rejection and Communication," *Journal of Abnormal Social Psychology,* 1951. 46:190–207. Tagiuri, R., and Petrullo, L. (eds.) *Person Perception and Interpersonal Behavior.* Stanford: Stanford University Press, 1958.)

Page 44. Isolation and inability to deal constructively with interpersonal conflicts are known causes of suicide. Its prevention depends on the maintenance of intimate contact during psychological crises. For Bibliography of scientific books and papers on suicide, write: Suicide Prevention Center, 2521 West Pico Boulevard, Los Angeles, Calif. 90006.

Page 45. Marathon Research by Bach, George R. *op. cit.*

Page 45. The traditional procedure of sending each partner in a troubled marriage to a separate analyst or psychotherapist is being rapidly replaced by the newer, more effective methods of "con-joint" marriage and family therapy—where all parties involved in a conflict are seen together, frequently in the company of a group of other couples and families. The creative pioneer work of Virginia Satir exemplifies this new, theoretically sounder and clinically more effective approach. (Ref. Satir, Virginia. *Conjoint Family Therapy.* Palo Alto: Science & Behavior Books, Inc., 1964. Boszormenyi-Nagy, I., and Framo, James L. *Intensive Family Therapy.* New York: Hoeber Medical Division, Harper & Row, 1965.)

Page 45. Beyond Lewinian field-theory, our orientation is influenced by systems and communication theory and research. Especially influential has been the thinking of my friend Robert Boguslaw, professor of sociology, Washington University, St. Louis. (Ref. Boguslaw, Robert. *op. cit. See also* Walter Buckley, *Sociology and Modern Systems Theory.* Englewood Cliffs, N.J.: Prentice-Hall, 1967.)

Notes & Comments on Chapter III—"Training Lovers to be Fighters."

Page 47. The discriminating items in our confidential interviews which most clearly distinguished the 28 "card-house" couples (56%) were the *denial* of hostility to themselves and to each other—and, of course, to the outside world. The term "card-house marriages" suggested itself from follow-ups one to three years later. All of these fight-free couples eventually ended up in separation, divorce, or sought professional counseling for the real marital troubles they had brushed under the carpet, thereby creating the illusion of conflict-free marriages.

Page 47. Couples who merely played at the game of intimacy (playing at being married) made up 40% of our sociometrically selected sample of fifty "elite" couples. These 20 couples did *not* kid themselves or each other about the conflict-ridden and hostility-loaded state of affairs between them. In fact, they were "conflict-habituated," belonging to the same class of socio-economically "successful" marriage described under that category by John and Peggy Cuber's book *The Significant Americans,* a study of sexual behavior among the affluent. (Ref. Cuber, John F., and Harroff, Peggy B. *The Significant Americans.* Baltimore: Pelican Books, 1965.) Privately, these significant people engaged in *Virginia Woolf* type hostility rituals (sans guests), but they were too committed to social-economic conveniences to display their conflicts to others. Their success in camouflaging resulted in their being chosen by some of their friends as "a happy couple." Psychologically their lasting bond was strengthened by severe separation anxiety, fear of change generally—and fear of the dating game in particular. Instructive to our theory was the impression that their engagement in hostility rituals, their conflict-habituation, kept them from breaking apart; by contrast, the nonfighting, card-house dwellers broke up.

Page 48. Our 4% of true intimates (a much lower percentage than the "intrinsics" discovered by the Cubers) kept their arguments current and specific. Their fights were fresh—not redundant, not ritualized. They were not too shy to fight in front of others. And when they did, others felt the basic love, concern and the context of good will in their willingness to face, rather than deny, conflict. We have not published this research because of a serious sampling bias, which will be corrected in our future research plans. The people who selected and nominated the "marriage elite" candidates, themselves belonged to a socially self-conscious, status-oriented stratum of "successful" society. They probably did not nominate more openly fighting couples because they themselves correlated conflict-display with "marital problems." Repeating the "marriage elite" research with better sampling-controls will also clear up other contaminating factors such as: length of marriage (the "card-houses" were younger); economics (the game-players were richer); social gregariousness (true intimates may be less frantically "mixing" and thus be less exposed for "elite" nominations).

Page 49. Our preferred method of training is first to show the professional trainee (qualified psychologists, psychiatrists, and family or marriage counselors) how he or she can fight more constructively with his own mate or lover. Only after professionals go through fight training for themselves do we consider them ready to undertake the training of clients.

Page 50. The basic principles of group psychotherapy are described in Bach's *Intensive Group Psychotherapy*. New York: Ronald Press, 1954.

Page 52. As Jerome Frank (Ref. Frank, Jerome. *Persuasion and Healing*. Baltimore: Johns Hopkins Press, 1961) has demonstrated, all therapies are programmed and persuasive—only some not explicitly so. Ours are. Among the many advantages of explicitly programming a course of therapeutic re-education are: there is no "magic" or mystique; the trainee-clients know, in front, what is aimed for and can understand and judge the appropriateness and utility of every new step they are learning. Also a programmed approach can later be objectively assessed as to whether, and to what degree, it achieves its stated objectives.

Page 55. Confer *Statistical Abstract of U.S. 1967*, by the Department of Commerce, Washington, D.C.

Notes & Comments on Chapter IV—"Getting a Good Fight Started."

Page 56. (Ref. Kubie, L. S. *Practical and Theoretical Aspects of Psychoanalysis*. New York: International Universities Press, Inc., 1950.)

Page 58. Ritualized (round-robin) fights (like ritualized sex) have, in addition to the tension-relief function, the purpose of "familiarity validation." They show that each partner knows the other, has "his number"—and each knows "his lines." Fight and sex rituals demonstrate the existence of a level of familiarity and intimacy that the partners as individuals do not enjoy with anyone else. Fight and sex rituals are the "in-privilege" of established intimates. The confusion that results when strangers get mixed up in such rituals was dramatized by Edward Albee in *Virginia Woolf*. The psychotherapist and marriage counselor can, through our fight training, help couples to become more fully aware of, more tolerant with, and also amused by, these highly pair-specific fight rituals. The point of fight training is not necessarily to destroy the rituals that intimates have developed between them, but to differentiate them from real fighting over new, currently meaningful issues and positions. Fight training decontaminates conflicts from the redundant materials that make up the rituals. Once trainees learn how to keep their fights clean of "Vesuvius" outbursts, *Virginia Woolf's* and other aggression rituals, such as "psychoanalysis" (example: "Your childhood was more pathogenic than mine, you poor thing!"), then they can opt occasionally to enjoy them just like consciously chosen aggression games, such as football or bridge. The crucial importance of fight rituals in the healthy management of aggression, recognized for some time in animals (cf. K. Lorenz and H. Harlow), has recently been further clarified by Anthony Storr in *Human Aggression* (cf. Bibliography).

Page 59. Dr. Leonard Berkowitz disagrees with the concept of Catharsis. His theoretical position denies the validity of cathartic aggression. He adheres to the orthodox theory that aggression must always have a frustrated target. This appears to us as an untenable position considering our research and clinical experience with cathartic rituals. (Ref. Berkowitz, Leonard. *Aggression: A Social Psychological Analysis*. New York: McGraw-Hill Book Co., 1962.) That aggression and violence can be conforming behavior totally unrelated to frustration has been convincingly demonstrated. (Ref. Wolfgang, M. E., and Ferracuti, F. *The Subculture of Violence*. London: Tavistock, 1967. *See also* Yablonsky, L. *The Violent Gang*. New York: Macmillan, 1962.)

Page 60. The term "leveling" was first applied by my friend and colleague, Dr. Fred Stoller, to describe the kind of open, risky, transparent (and at times aggressive) process of letting others know what you think of them and where they stand with you. We promote leveling in regular and, even more particularly, in marathon group sessions. (Ref. Stoller, Frederick. "The Long Weekend," *Psychology Today*. Dec. 1967, 28–33. Stoller, Frederick. "Accelerated Interaction," *International Journal of Group Psychotherapy*, 1968. 18:220–35.)

Page 62. The nature of the "inner dialogue" gives excellent self-diagnostic information and documents the utility of the outer (interpersonal) dialogue.

The less efficient the outer dialogue has become as an instrument to process, display, and openly exchanged information about the way partners "experience" one another, the more irrational and secretive become the inner dialogues as exemplified in Hamlet's classical soliloquies. The most drastic examples are overtly nonfighting persons whose inner dialogue tends to be vicious even to a point of carefully incubating ways to get rid of the mate—including murder. (Ref. Bach, George R. "Thinging: A Sub-Theory of Intimate Aggression Illustrated by Spouse-Killing," presented at the 75th Annual Convention of the American Psychological Association in Washington, D.C., September 2, 1967.)

Page 62. A sound explanation of the reality and sanity insuring functions of healthy, rational inner dialogues can be found in the writings of Albert Ellis. (Ref. Ellis, Albert. *Reason and Emotion in Psychotherapy*. New York: Lyle Stuart, 1962.)

Notes & Comments on Chapter V—"When and Where to Fight."

Page 72. Deutero-fighting—fighting about fighting (how, when, and whether at all)—is the first step in fight training at our Institute. During this procedure the trainer-therapist helps trainees to recognize their resistance against aggressive leveling, their irrational fears of hurting and getting hurt, their feeling guilty or harboring anti-romantic resentments against loved ones, and their false expectations of further (even final) alienation resulting from any kind of fighting. This is also the appropriate occasion for the trainer-therapist to come to terms with his own aggression ideology. Unless he learns to overcome his own traditional resistances against the therapeutic use of aggression he will directly or indirectly intensify the fight-phobias of his clients. (Ref. Bach, George R., ed. "Constructive Aspects of Aggression," a symposium presented to the 9th Annual Conference of the Group Psychotherapy Association of Southern California, 1962.)

Page 73. Dr. A. W. Pearson, Medical Director of the extensive Alcohol Rehabilitation Program in the Los Angeles County Health Department, sobers alcohol-troubled couples by our marathon techniques. Dr. Pearson demonstrates to these couples and their participating and concerned friends the difference between the nonsensical, alcohol-drenched *Virginia Woolf* style hostility rituals and the genuine, involved, realistic fighting that these same couples can do when the alcohol wears off (and is not replenished) during nonstop weekend group therapy. Instant TV playback makes the participants even more clearly aware of the dramatic improvement in their conflict-confrontations when they enjoy freedom from alcohol. At our Institute we use the same approach with equally good results for couples who complicate their conflicts with alcohol. Fight-phobic couples are particularly prone to use alcohol.

Page 76. Our research into the therapeutic helpfulness among members of marathon groups has shown a similar lack of "I'll help you if you help me," "a hand for a hand," "eye for an eye" reciprocity. (Ref. Bach, George R. "Marathon Group Dynamics II: Dimensions of Helpfulness," *Psychological Report*, 1967. 20:1147–58. Bach, George R. "Marathon Group Dynamics III: Disjunctive Contacts," *Psychological Report*, 1967. 20:1163–72. Bach, George R. "Group-Leader Phobias in Marathon Groups," *Voices*, 1967. 3:41–46.) One of the sources of disappointment in love and marriage can be removed if people can be taught *not* to expect immediate reciprocity. Intrinsic to an intimate system of give-and-take are such nonreciprocal exchanges as: "Let me give to you and please take from me!" Or "I love giving to you!" Any attempt crudely and instantly to pay back or return the giving (especially with an attempt to match the value) reduces the intimate quality of the interaction and changes it to resemble contracts that govern transactions such as prostitution or even psychoanalysis. (Ref. Schofield, W. *Psychotherapy: the Purchase of Friendship*. Englewood Cliffs, N.J., Prentice-Hall, 1964.)

In true intimacy there is intrinsic joy in giving, especially when appreciatively received and taken. Intimate giving is not part of a manipulation for ulterior pay-off, as in game-playing. (Ref. Berne, Eric. *op. cit.* Shostrom, Everett. *op. cit.*)

Page 77. Trainees are counseled never to attempt a clearance-confrontation during "overload situations" when partners are burdened with immediate chores and cannot take on any added demands.

Notes & Comments on Chapter VI—"How to Fight a Fair Fight."

Page 80. Our trainer-therapists are guided by a theory of "Trust-Formation through Aggression" which differs in emphasis from conventional trust-formation theories as thoroughly researched by Jack Gibb. (Ref. Gibb, Jack R. "Climate for Trust Formation," *T Group and Laboratory Method*, by Bradford, L. P., Gibb, J. R., and Benne, K. D. New York: Wiley & Sons, Inc., 1964.)

Conventionally, trust is believed to grow with repeated demonstrations of love, positive regard, understanding, all in a climate of relatively tension-free acceptance. We believe that a more practical, reliable quality of trusting can be achieved by knowing the worst that a partner, in moments of conflict and tension, could or would do. If the treatment is too hostile-destructive, then the "mean" partner can be persuaded to recognize and respect the belt line—below which any blow is unconditionally intolerable. To the happy surprise of many fearful, mistrusting souls, partners gladly learn to respect belt lines—but they must know them and accept them as real. People are much more capable of absorbing occasional irritations of their Achilles' heels than they have irrationally told themselves. At times, it is even worth getting hit below the belt to obtain valuable information on how mean or frightened or helpless or defeated or panic-stricken a partner feels when he temporarily ignores a belt line.

Notes & Comments on Chapter VII—"Male and Female Fight Styles."

Page 89. Speculation about supposedly deep dynamic differences between the feminine and masculine psyche is a favorite intellectual pastime of an amazing number of otherwise scientifically oriented psychotherapists and marriage counselors. Worst are the psychotherapists who, in spite of the obvious difference in sex-social realities between the United States of 1969 and Vienna of 1899, still believe (and make their sex-role-curious patients believe) in the classic psycho-analytic position of women (and men) as outlined by Freud. (Ref. Freud, Sigmund. *The Psychology of Women—New Introductory Lectures on Psychoanalysis.* New York: W. W. Norton, 1933. Pp. 153–85.) According to Freud, females, being without penis, are inherently frustrated cripples, accus-tomed to masochism and passive (including frigid) receptivi-ty of the sex-aggressive penetrating male—whose penis and dominance women envy and resent. As a consequence of this feminine "castration-complex" women are supposedly afflict-ed by a "faulty super-ego development" which is interpreted to mean that they are prone to have a less developed sense of fairness and justice than men; and that women therefore feel less conflicted when they use "feminine wiles" (dirty tricks to get their way). To any competent and contemporary social scientist these Freudian speculations on femininity reflect Freud's personal and cultural timebound biases. Unfortunately for the clarification of gender-role realities, Freud's stereotypes have been grotesquely elaborated in hundreds of "learned" papers and books by less than creative followers of Freud and Jung. Fortunately for mankind and especially for woman-kind most of these Freudian sex-role myths are being contra-dicted by careful social and physiological research studies such as those conducted by Masters and Johnson. (Ref. Masters, William, and Johnson, Virginia. *Human Sexual Response.* Boston: Little & Brown, 1966.) *The Journal of Sex Research,* the publication of the Society for the Scientific Study of Sex, Inc., 12 East 41 Street, New York, N.Y. 10017, is one of the best antidotes to stereotyping Man and Woman into different "bags." Even though etiquette considers fighting to be fe-male-inappropriate behavior, young girls' minds are filled with almost as much hostility as are the minds of boys. (Ref. Bach, George R. "Young Children's Play Fantasies," *Psycho-logical Monographs,* 59, No. 2, 1945. Bandura, Albert. "So-cial Learning Through Imitation," *Nebraska Symposium on Motivation.* Lincoln, Neb.: University of Nebraska Press, 1962. Pp. 211–69.) These works show that little girls will imitate with gusto, aggressive (hitting) behavior of an adult female they earlier observed on film. It is therefore not surprising that under the strong stimulus-condition of the heat generated by the battle of the sexes, the stereotype of the nonaggressive female melts away. Psychoanalytically oriented psychotherapists and marriage counselors should acquaint themselves with Dr. Judd Marmor's Freud-corrective chapter, "Changing Patterns of Femininity: Psychoanalytic Implications," (Ref. Marmor, Judd, "Changing Patterns of Femininity: Psychoanalytic Implications,") *The Marriage Relationship: Psychoanalytic Perspectives*, edited by Salo Rosenbaum and Ian Alger. New York: Basic Books, 1968.) Despite such efforts as those by Dr. Marmor, the Freudian put-down of females continues. The most recent example of Freudian gender stereotyping is in Anthony Storr's chapter, "Aggression in the Relations Between the Sexes." This is a theoretical dinosaur in his otherwise up-to-date and enlightened *Human Aggression*. Storr's imagery of nonaggressive femininity postulates a tradition-accommodating false ideal which creates clients for the psychoanalysts' couch among women who naïvely believe that identity is achieved by conformity to sex-typing. Actually such conformity is a "crazymaker."

Page 89. In a controlled aggression-producing experiment Bach found that under certain conditions (fantasy-support) young girls can and will express extremely vicious aggression, overriding the usual negative reinforcement of the expression of aggression in girls. (Bach, 1945.)

Notes & Comments on Chapter VIII—"Ending a Good Fight."

Page 97. Our trainer-therapists must constantly counteract the notion that people who are angry cannot make love. The contrary is often true. Anger and resentment temporarily alienate—but alienation requires a bridge back to a good relationship. Sexual intimacy is the natural bridge. Conflicted partners can be taught not only to enjoy sex in the bedroom ("using," if you wish, each other to obtain some pleasure in life—even if they do not enjoy each other in the living room); the fractured intimate system *needs* joy-giving as the bonding agent to keep the system going during times of crisis.

Notes & Comments on Chapter IX—"Bad Fighters and How to Reform Them."

Page 103. Individuals with incomplete adult identity formation watch a presumably more self-defined partner for reactions through which their own identity vacuum could be filled up. They are hungry for attribution of traits and wishes unto them, which tragically is the very thing that prevents self-identity from growing and, in fact, creates or reinforces schizophrenic traits. (Ref. Erikson, Erik. *op. cit.* Bateson, G., Jackson, D. D., Haley, J., and Weakland, J. "Toward a Theory of Schizophrenia," *Behavioral Science,* 1956. 1:251–64. Cooley, C. H. *Human Nature and the Social Order.* New York: Scribner, 1902. Haley, Jay. "An Interactional Description of Schizophrenia," *Psychiatry,* 22: 321–32. Kaplan, Abraham. "Models of Self Identity," a discussion presented to the Group Psychotherapy Association of Southern California, 1967. Laing, R. D. *op. cit.* Sarbin, T. R. "Role Theory," in G. Lindzey (ed.) *Handbook of Social Psychology.* Vol. 1. Cambridge, Massachusetts: Addison-Wesley, 1954. Pp. 223–58.) The Psychological pay-off in partner-watching is not only the accumulation of negative evidence but also to collect image-reinforcement of a positive, usually romantic nature. Lovers seem to enjoy watching one another—especially in romantic moods. The real trouble with partner-watching is that it is passive parasitic and "freeloading" so far as mutual communication is concerned. Peeping Toms have no communication with their objects.

Page 104. Most damaging to intimacy are such analytic labels as: "You treat me like a father/mother" or "Naturally, after you saw your father abuse your mother, after which she left all of you, you now fear my leaving you whenever I'm angry at you." When partners go alone or to separate therapists (on whose couches they gossip about the not-present partner), they tend to do to the other partner, at home, what was done to them in the psychiatrist's office. They "analyze" the spouse or the relationship—as if they had no responsibility for creating it. Our trainees are made aware that partners choose whom they deserve and must not judgmentally pseudo-analyze each other as a defensive substitute for sharing and solving existing problems and conflicts together.

Notes & Comments on Chapter X—"When Words Fail: Fighting with Fists and Fingernails."

Page 116. Dr. Gene Sagan (Berkeley, Calif.) conducts "fight classes": partners engage in structured actual physical fighting in which individuals express, experience, and integrate the unique quality of their aggression. Serious hurting is prevented by handicapping, "contacts," and refereeing. A film and discussion of this program, "Fighting as a Therapeutic Tool," was presented by Natividad DeAnda at the 1968 annual scientific conference of the Golden Gate Group Psychotherapy Society, San Francisco. Dr. Sagan's program seems like a promising extension of our own fight-play experiments.

Page 121. A complete discussion of the conditions governing the transition from verbal aggression to physical violence would lead the reader too far afield. However, I have completed a specialized study of spouse violence, including murder. (Ref. Bach, George R. "Thinging: A Sub-Theory of Intimate Aggression Illustrated by Spouse-Killing," presented at the 75th Annual Convention of the American Psychological Association in Washington, D.C., September 2, 1967.)

Notes & Comments on Chapter XI—"The Language of Love: Communications Fights."

Page 136. In psychotherapy, silence and selective nonresponding are often deliberately used by a clinically experienced psychotherapist. His disengagement means: "I am not going to collude in your 'setup operations' in which you want to engage me so I will respond in such a way as to validate *your* definitions of our relationship." Silence and disengagement (without breaking contact) can be very effective to make psychiatric patients aware of their often unconscious manipulative intentions involving the therapist and/or a therapy group. In the context of this book, however, it must be pointed out that intimate partners are not patients and spouses are not psychotherapists; they should not try to use clinical techniques of interaction with each other. (Ref. Bach, George R. *Intensive Group Psychotherapy*. New York: Ronald Press, 1954. *See "Set-up Operations."*) The clinical use of silence and disengagement has been thoroughly researched by Dr. Ernst G. Beier. (Ref. Beier, Ernst G. *The Silent Language of Psychotherapy*. Chicago: Aldine Publish. Co., 1966.)

Notes & Comments on Chapter XII—"Fighting By Mail and Telephone."

Page 141. Our clinical experience with psychotherapy over the telephone, either with contacts between psychotherapist and patient or between therapy group members, has been generally favorable. Where extreme long distances were involved the airmail exchange by talk by tapes has on occasion helped to maintain useful contact with a therapist and/

or group. We consider it theoretically sound, mechanically feasible, and morally desirable to extend such electronic contacts to adaptations of TV and radio. An important fringe benefit would be the therapy that a large number of listeners and/or viewers would derive from bona fide two-way talk therapy; and there is no reason why fight training could not be demonstrated and taught through broadcasting.

Notes & Comments on Chapter XIII—"Dirty and Sick Fighters and How to Stop Them."

Page 147. (Ref. Goodrich, D. W., and Boomer, D. S. "Experimental Assessment of Modes of Conflict Resolution," *Family Process*, 1963. 2:15–24.)

Page 151. The most detailed and consistent focus on the nature of crazy-making tactics (such as collusion, attribution, and mystification) is shown in the highly original work of R. D. Laing. (Ref. Laing, R. D. *op. cit.*) Laing's work has helped us to recognize more clearly the patterns of pathogenic aggression in relations of self to significant others.

Page 153. *See* Berne, Eric. *Transactional Analysis in Psychotherapy.* New York: Grove Press, Inc., 1961, for a therapeutic approach specifically aimed at untangling transactions that are confusing due to incompatible or anachronistic ego-states.

Page 156. Effective, fair fighting skills in the fight for one's own identity are the best insurance against identity-corroding influences. Thus, to some extent, fight training has become part of all of our psychotherapy programs; it is very helpful for self-growth.

Page 158. Foiling or protecting oneself against sick, dirty fighters is, of course, not the same as curing them. We do not claim that fight-training alone is sufficient therapy for the severely mentally and emotionally disturbed whose psychiatric illness is often rooted in the mismanagement of their aggressive impulses.

Notes & Comments on Chapter XIV—"How to Score Intimate Fights."

Page 159. Our scoring system is an important educational aid for the professional fight trainer-therapist who, by showing his trainees how to score fight styles and fight effects, teaches them how to recognize alienating or "dirty" fighting in themselves and others. Mastering the scoring system (usually after only six fight-group sessions) and then using it to score tape-recorded fights at home and live fights in front of a trainee group (who independently score and later compare) enables trainees to reinforce the all-important belief that they *can* learn to fight fair and informatively with a minimum of injury. Trainees can retain scoring sheets and compare the beginning profiles with later ones. The accompanying chart illustrates a fairly typical case of changes in fight styles from the beginning (B) to the end or "after" (A) a successful 12-session experience. Before fight training the constructiveness score was −7. Of the 9 fight-style parameters, only one (Reality) was rated plus. Eight were rated minus. After training, the constructiveness score was +7, with only one category (humor) rated minus. This particular trainee had little capacity for healthy laughter. His humor habitually expressed itself in ridicule. Although he improved somewhat, this particular dirty tactic proved too well ingrained to be significantly changed. His struggle to change himself even in this respect brought his alienated wife (who was delighted with the improvement in the other categories) emotionally closer to him. Like other spouses she was deeply impressed to learn that her mate's lack of a healthy sense of humor was not specifically invented to torture her but was, to a significant extent, an individual personality and contact style.

Page 160. Compared with the educational use of our scoring system, the scientific research utility of these procedures is far from satisfactory. This is not the place to discuss our serious methodological problems in this and other areas of facilitating therapeutic learning experiences. The professional reader will be aware of these problems and the technical literature dealing with research in clinical behavior modification. (Ref. Eysenck, H. J. *The Effects of Psychotherapy*. New York: International Science Press, 1966. Caplan, Nathan. "Treatment Intervention and Reciprocal Interaction Effects," *Journal of Social Issues*, Vol. 14, 1968. Pp. 63–88.)

Notes & Comments on Chapter XV—"Fighting Over 'Trivia.' "

Page 183. The following conversion hypothesis may well explain the extraordinary amount of energy spent by intimates in trivial bickering. It suggested itself from comparative observations of aggressive horseplay, fighting, and teasing among sibling peers, buddies, and pals during childhood and adolescence.

Changes in Fight Styles before (B) and after (A) Fight Training

THE FIGHT STYLE PROFILE

B = BEFORE FIGHT TRAINING ▬ ▬ ▬   A = AFTER FIGHT TRAINING ▬▬▬

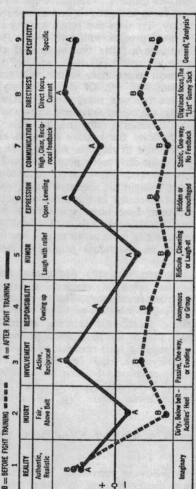

	REALITY 1	INJURY 2	INVOLVEMENT 3	RESPONSIBILITY 4	HUMOR 5	EXPRESSION 6	COMMUNICATION 7	DIRECTNESS 8	SPECIFICITY 9
+	Authentic, Realistic	Fair, Below belt – Achilles' Heel	Active, Reciprocal	Owning up	Laugh with relief	Open, Leveling	High, Clear, Reciprocal feedback	Direct focus, Current	Specific
O									
I	Imaginary	Dirty, Below belt – Achilles' Heel	Passive, One-way, or Evading	Anonymous or Group	Ridicule, Clowning or Laugh-at	Hidden or Camouflaged	Static, One-way; No Feedback	Displaced focus, The "List" Gunny Sack	General, "analysis"

The "plus" (+) positions on the profile represent good (or "bonding") styles of aggression.

The "minus" (−) positions represent poor (or "alienating") styles of aggression.

The middle (O) positions indicate styles rated as neutral, irrelevant, or unobservable.

The profile is complete when one line is drawn to connect all nine dimensions, intersecting each dimension at the appropriate level (+ or − or O). When the line stays predominantly above the "O" level, the fight was fought in a predominantly bonding style. When the line stays predominantly below the "O" level, the fight was fought in predominantly alienating style.

We suspect that trivial verbal bickering between adult intimates is the verbal equivalent of aggressive physical (but intimate) contact-plays of children. Nonverbal aggressive contact-plays of children are emotionally exciting, good exercise, sometimes erotically stimulating—and always a sign of inter-personal intimate involvement. Kids don't play as aggressively with strangers as they rough-house with a sibling or pal. Similarly, adults do not squabble and quibble with strangers—only with intimates. As my wife, Peggy Bach, has observed: "It's during adolescence that you can see childhood pushing, shoving, and wrestling changing into verbal aggression, hostile humor, teasing, and ridicule." In childhood aggressive-contact-play issues are often not involved. There is rarely anything significant to fight over. The rough-housing has its own intrinsic value. To test this hypothesis we are conducting experiments (with Hanna Thost) in which we engage adult couples in physically safe contact-aggressive, nonverbal fight-play exercises. We call this "Contact-Intensification." It enables us experimentally to reintroduce a sibling-type childlike horseplay into adult leisure-time activities as a possible method to expand the baseline for intimate contact. This experiment should permit us to test the conversion hypothesis, which would predict a re-education in verbal trivial bickering after its reconversion into physical horseplay. Initial results with the first group of subjects was confirmatory. A variation of this approach is to encourage couples to dance when they meet after a workday's separation and before they say anything to each other beyond "Hello." We have found that this contact often prevents the stupid, redundant, trivial talk rituals which couples tend to use as a way of feeling out each other's needs after the day's separation.

There is growing appreciation of the importance of nonverbal communication. Anthropologist Gregory Bateson is the prime innovator of the strong current of professional interest in all forms of nonverbal communication and nonverbal cues, signals, and emotional expressions. The technical literature in this field is vast and growing. (Ref. Bateson, G., and Ruesch, J. *Communication: The Social Matrix of Psychiatry.* New York: W. W. Norton, 1951. Ruesch, Jurgen and Kees, Wheldon. *Non-Verbal Communication.* Berkeley and Los Angeles: University of California Press, 1956. Beier, Ernst G. *op. cit.*)

Space limitations of this book limit the discussion of intimate animosities primarily to the verbal level, although the chapters on sex and physical violence deal briefly with the many, too often ignored nonverbal aspects of intimate aggression.

Page 192. The clinical discovery of a close relationship between irrationally trivial bickering and sexual enjoyment lends further support to the "conversion-theory" of trivia discussed above. In suppressing trivial bickering (because of its irrationality, absurdity, or insignificance) without reconversion to physical contact games, the "I must feel you out" function, which appears to be an important prerequisite for good sexual and passionate enjoyment is by-passed. Without contact "warm-up" there is no sex. In his erogenetic experiments with monkeys, Professor Harry Harlow at the University of Wisconsin found that animals who were deprived of contact-warmth and other bodily maternal care when they were young, later show no interest whatsoever in sex. Evidently no "animal instinct" (sex) operates without presexual contact-warmth preparation. (Harlow, H. F. *op cit.*)

Notes & Comments on Chapter XVI—"The Dream: Courtship Fights."

Page 194. Our institute operates a program to provide education and fun for people without partners. It is run on a club-membership basis and is called "Independent Intimates." While including the social and travel activities of the currently fashionable "singles" clubs, the Independent Intimates combine the social programs of most singles clubs with original activities designed to remove the anxiety from dating and bring more effective and enduring joy to the old dating game and matchmaking scene. The club is the outgrowth of an experimental marathon-type weekend which I conducted for singles in May 1968. Computer-aided matchmaking was compared with person-to-person contact selection and tryouts. The computer-type program failed miserably. For example, the most attractive and desirable bachelors (who received first choice from the most personable females) remained unmatched by the computer while some of the least compatible participants were chosen as potentially ideal mates! Selections made by simulated computerized programs overlapped with actual compatibility for only 7% of the participants.

The economic success of the mating-by-computer industry (which has failed so far to permit its procedures to be scientifically scrutinized and their selections of compatibility validated) is based on the exploitation of people who date and their rejection fears. Interpersonal contact exercises, on the other hand, maximize the display of information relevant to making selections for intimacy.

Notes & Comments on Chapter XVII—"Fighting for Realistic Romance."

Page 211. Image-making is facilitated by keeping a partner available for projections as if he were a Rorschach ink-blot card. People who "fall in love" actually are losing their identities—if not temporarily their minds. This state has an emotional intensity comparable to an acid-trip and some like to prolong this "romantic bliss" as long as possible. One sure way of bringing such a romantic romance to an end is to get married to the romancee—who, practically overnight, will turn into something else. After the "bewitching and bewildering" phase clears away and the real partner stands up, the discrepancy between dream (Chap. 16) and reality (Chap. 17) is experienced as a traumatic shock by many people. The shock can be reduced or even totally avoided if romantic mystification and image-making are, from the beginning, kept to that absolute minimum necessary to overcome the fears of realistic entwinement. It is a psychological reality (clearly demonstrated by R. D. Laing, *op. cit.*) that prolonged mystification, projections, and attribution of ego-alien traits are pathogenic and thus lethal to a healthy relationship. So are the tendencies to manipulate lovers through "setup operations" (Bach, George, *Intensive Group Psychotherapy, op. cit.*) designed to experience the love-relationship congruent with romantic imagery. Actually, these setup operations reinforce the false beliefs lovers develop in the reality of romantic expectations—and consequently, the stressful credibility gap between encouraged expectations and eventual realities. When, sooner or later, the bombardment of realistic experience brings down the house of imagery, the pangs of dissonance may cause psychiatrically severe states of depression, including suicide and homicide (crimes of passion). Dr. Leon Festinger, a student of Kurt Lewin, has focused his careful research on the conditions for the development of incongruities between cognitive structures, such as expectancy-sets, and experienced realities—an expansion of Kurt Lewin's original interest in the discrepancy between levels of aspiration and levels of achievement. (Ref. Lewin, Kurt. *A Dynamic Theory of Personality*. New York: McGraw-Hill Book Co., 1935. Pp. 250–54. Festinger, Leon. *A Theory of Cognitive*

Dissonance. New York: Harper & Row, Inc., 1957.) Our fight training for newlyweds is theoretically in line with Lewin's chapter on *Education for Reality.* (Ref. Lewin, Kurt. *A Dynamic Theory of Personality.* New York: McGraw-Hill Book Co., 1935. Pp. 171–79.) Fight training enables those caught in the *dissonance crisis* (likely to come on the heels of the honeymoon) to fight their way back from the "fallen-in-love" state to self-definition and identity without serious post-wedding depressions.

Page 227. Bernard Shaw, while clearly seeing through the romantic fallacies, was also in awe of them, thinking them insurmountable—which tragically complicated his own love life. (Ref. Shaw, George Bernard. *Pygmalion, Selected Plays.* New York: Dodd Mead, Vol. I, 1948. *Man and Superman.* George Bernard Shaw *op. cit.,* Vol. III. *Getting Married.* George Bernard Shaw. *op. cit.* Vol. IV.)

Notes & Comments on Chapter XVIII—"Sex as a Fighting Word."

Page 235. The best antidote against confusing sex myths is to stay informed by keeping in touch with current objective sex research by reading *The Journal of Sex Research.*

Notes & Comments on Chapter XIX—"Fighting Before, During, and After Sex."

Page 250. The synergic confluence of sex and aggression was first seen by Sigmund Freud, who admitted the close relationship between love-eros-sex and hostility-aggression into academia. Thus, Freud: "According to our hypothesis, human instincts are only of two kinds—those which seek to preserve and unite, which we call erotic, and those which seek to destroy and kill, which we class together as the aggressive *or* [italics mine] destructive instinct. *The phenomena of life arise from the operation of both together,* whether *acting in concert* or in opposition [italics mine]. An instinct of one sort can *scarcely ever operate in isolation*—it is always accompanied (or, as we say, allocated) with an element from the other side which modifies its aim. Thus, for instance, the instinct of self-preservation is certainly of an erotic kind; but it must have AGGRESSIVENESS at its disposal if it is to fulfill its purpose. . . . It is very rarely that a given action is the work of a *single* instinctual impulse which must in itself be compounded of Eros and Destructiveness." (Ref. Freud,

Sigmund. "Why War?" *Collected Papers*, ed. by James Strachey. London: Hogarth, 1948. Pp. 280–81.) It is not to distract from Freud's professional courage in his day and in bourgeois Vienna, as displayed in his willingness to impress the medical fraternity with the importance of the synergic confluence of eros and aggression, to point out the historical fact that artists had for centuries been honored and appreciated for rendering their interpretations of aggressive sexuality in sculptures and paintings depicting the most drastic examples of hostility with sex mergers, starting with pre-Christ works of art such as Rape of Deianira (Pollaiuola); Rape of Helen (Gozzoli); Rape of Europa (Titian) and early Greek mythology and the Old Testament of the Bible provide other references.

Page 251. Bernard Oliver had available complete records of a western regional area for all rapists on parole as of February 1, 1963. He studied 92 of them intensively and found that most of the rapists appeared to be *under*sexed rather than oversexed. (Ref. "Social Psychological Characteristics of the Rapist," paper presented at a meeting of the California State Psychological Association, December 4, 1964.) This is in accord with our own observation that people who are overtly overaggressively sexy (rape, near-rape, or rapelike) are more aggressive than sexy. They find in sex an acceptable outlet for otherwise forbidden aggressive expressions that would be severely punished in nonsexual situations. Aggressive sex (with the consent and pleasure of the cooperative "victim") may thus be a necessary preventive outlet for nonsexual socially destructive aggression. This parallels the reliable research finding by Edwin Megargee, who reported that young killers tend to be excessively overcontrolled nonfighters. (Ref. Megargee, Edwin. "Matricide and Patricide," presented at the 75th Annual Convention of the American Psychological Association, Washington, D.C., September 2, 1967.) Perhaps they are oversexed.

Page 251. Anthony Storr (cf. Bibliography) suggests reasonably that the perversion of healthy aggression into sadistic cruelty has its psychogenesis in the early suppression and repression of natural infantile hostility inherent in the young child's helpless dependency on parental care. The sadistic adult later seeks *revenge*. His old reservoir of hate makes him go far beyond realistic, healthy aggression. He behaves sadistically toward his sex partner, whose intimacy may reactivate the unresolved feelings about the early, close, overwhelming and aggression-restrictive contact with his mother.

Notes & Comments on Chapter XX—"Marital Fights
About Extramarital Sex."

Page 263. (Ref. Kinsey, Alfred, et al. *Sexual Behavior in
the Human Female*. Philadelphia: Saunders, 1953. Kinsey,
Alfred. *Sexual Behavior in the Human Male*. Philadelphia:
Saunders, 1948.)

Page 265. Not to be classified with the "con" categories
are partners who withhold information about infidelities from
their partners even when both are pledged by marathon rules
to total transparency. These otherwise open and honest people tend, for one purpose, to break the rule to answer all
questions honestly. Their choosing to become "white liars"
reflects a respect for the intolerable anxiety that total honesty
(without infinite tact) may cause in the "betrayed" spouse.
Compulsive honesty here reflects self-indulgence or a regres-
sive conformity to a "you must tell all" obligation with which
adults tend to burden young children. Honesty is, in fact,
often insisted on—not on sound principles of intimacy but for
its utility in maintaining control and manipulation of the
partner's behavior. (*See also* next note.)

Page 266. In any fight-training group of five couples or ten
partners, typically seven (70%) of the partners (usually four
men and three women) have revealed in private interviews
that they have engaged in extramarital sexual intercourse. Of
the seven infidels, typically two will have voluntarily confessed to their partners; another will be "caught," and four
remained discreet. The silent ones are strongly reinforced in
this tactful stance by what they see happening to the majority
of the unmasked infidels. The unmasked partners have only
one chance in ten to be truly forgiven, even after proper
chastisement and rehabilitative penance. In today's society,
nine of ten "betrayed" partners neither forget nor forgive,
and this holds true even for those hypocritical people who
were betrayed but who are infidels themselves.

Since this book focuses on the psychology of intimacy in
primary (usually marital or premarital or family) relationships, we have not discussed details of the interesting problems of aggressive intimacy pertaining to secondary, less
central involvement or "love affairs." The weapons system of
socially unconventional love-pairs is considerably modified by
the underground nature of "illicit love." Secrecy, generally
imposed by etiquette, outlaws emotionally and spiritually
uplifting, joy-bringing loving experiences with someone other
than the official mate. This places the burden of secrecy on
lovers who may judge that the pangs and hassles of "sneak-

iness" are not worth the game. Or else they may flaunt an affair in protest against the secrecy rule. Usually, one of the partners has a greater stake in secrecy. This makes him more vulnerable and creates a need for deeper trust in the lover than is required for marriage! Recommended reading is an article by a highly respected psychiatrist who, after 30 years of counseling couples involved in extramarital affairs, explains:

"It is well known that one of the great bulwarks against adversity ... is *memories* of having participated in some loving experiences, sexual and non-sexual. If human beings can make experiences of happy content, *including an affair*, if it must be for them, and make it work itself out as a loving experience, and shape it so that those who could be hurt by knowledge of it *aren't* hurt, it is worth being considered by society as a positive contribution to life, rather than a negative one. ... An affair to be more openly practiced, would have to have its reputation elevated before it could ever become more conventionally accepted as social behavior." (Quoted from O. Spurgeon English, M.D. "Values in Psychotherapy: The Affair," *Voices*, 1967. 3:9–13.)

Page 268. Our clinical observations of these sado-maso hostility rituals (which in nine out of ten cases accompany both disclosed and even undisclosed infidelities) suggest that sexual enjoyment with an extra partner is only one of several emotional pay-offs. In fact, the "sideshows" and aftermaths may provide more intensive emotional experiences than even the tryst.

Notes & Comments on Chapter XXI—"Fighting With (and About) Children."

Page 292. Since this book's major theme is male-female intimacy and adult partnership, this chapter on family conflict touches on only a few basic points. Our Institute maintains an active program of multiple family group therapy, and this most hopeful approach should deserve a book of its own. Our forthcoming volume for professionals, *Therapeutic Aggression*, will be explicit on our methods of training entire families how to fight right and enjoyably. Readers will appreciate the enormous complexity of the subject. One need only be reminded of Bell and Vogel's compilation of about fifty experts' writings about "The Family." (Ref. Bell, N. W., and Vogel, E. F. eds., *A Modern Introduction to the Family*, Glencoe, Illinois: Free Press, 1960.) To respect our limitations here, readers involved in family group therapy are again referred to Boszormenyi-Nagy and Framo, *op, cit.* Also: Jackson, Don D., ed. *Human Communication.* Palo Alto, Calif.: Science & Behavior Books, 1968. Ackerman, Nathan W. *Treating The Troubled Family.* New York & London: Basic Books, 1966.)

Notes & Comments on Chapter XXII—"When Kids Fight Back."

Page 293. It is obvious from the bewilderment caused by the aggressive uprising of college youth and the Gandhi-like noncooperation of hippie youth that adults have traditionally assumed that youngsters have no moral right to "fight back." Professional psychotherapists and family group therapists are trying to bridge the generation gulf and have, indeed, found in group therapeutic methods one way of channeling the mutual aggression of adults as well as youth into productive confrontations.

The youth program at our Institute has been tailored to help teen-agers fight back constructively for their own independence and identity formation. It has been coordinated by our "Junior Group Therapists," Marshall Shumsky and Roger Bach.

Our research on teen-age group therapy and marathon groups has shown that teen-agers need allies to assist them in expressing negative emotions to other teen-agers and parents. In this context, we have provided "visitation rights" for parents to participate in our teen-age groups. For a more detailed report on our youth program and research, see Shumsky, Marshall E., "Teenagers in Group Therapy and Marathon Groups," presented at the Western Psychological Association's Convention, March 30, 1968.

The hippie movement has been described by Lewis Yablonsky in the *Hippie Trip,* Pegasus, 1968. The role of black and white youth fighting back at the "establishment" has been described by Eldridge Cleaver. *Confer* Cleaver, Eldridge, *Soul on Ice,* New York: McGraw-Hill, 1968.

Page 307. We have found these guidelines clinically effective and theoretically sound, but they may differ in some respects from those suggested by other colleagues: Escalona, Sibylle, *Understanding Hostility in Children,* Chicago: Science Research Associates, 1954—a fine little book written for the layman. Ginott, H. G. (*Between Parent and Child,* New York: Macmillan, 1965) has also written for lay readers and has some relatively helpful recommendations about children's aggression as "due to curiosity and high energy"

(p. 183). Very practical is a book by Albert Ellis containing a chapter on how to deal rationally with children's often irrational hostilities. (Ref. Ellis, Albert, and others. *How to Prevent Your Child from Becoming a Neurotic Adult.* New York: Crown, 1966.)

The crucial importance of encouraging children to stand up to and be self-assertively aggressive against parents and teachers as a necessary condition for their identity-formation is explained from a neo-psychoanalytic viewpoint by Anthony Storr (cf. Bibliography). The reader is particularly referred to Chapter 5: "Aggression in Childhood Development." The British child psychologist Dr. D. W. Winnicott's paper "Aggression in Relation to Emotional Development" in *Collected Papers* (London: Tavistock, 1958) contains (p. 204) the following sentence repeatedly quoted by Dr. Storr: "If society is in danger, it is not because of man's aggressiveness, but because of the repression of personal aggressiveness in individuals." This is in line with our proposal to replace lethal, anonymous group-hostility with personal-contact aggression.

Notes & Comments on Chapter XXIII—"Family Fights."

Page 308. Properly conducted family confrontations have a stronger emotional impact than most diadic encounters, just as group therapeutic pressure is more lastingly effective than individual doctor-patient consultations (Ref. Bach, George R., *Intensive Group Psychotherapy,* New York: Ronald Press, 1954.) Several group dynamic factors contribute toward this: the presence of an audience which not only watches every move made, but also judges and, in turn, becomes the subject of group feedbacks. Furthermore, people do not display the variety of their potential gifts as freely in twosomes as they do (after proper warm-up) in the prolonged-contact group where the stimulation and instigation for response is at once more forceful (coming from several people rather than one) and more heterogeneous, stimulating a greater range of potential responsiveness. With the notable exception of Ackerman (cf. Bibliography), psychiatrists once considered family group therapy programs to be sheer heresy. One of the active innovators in this field was the psychologist Dr. J. E. Bell. (Ref. Bell John E. "Family Group Therapy," Public Health Monograph No. 64, U.S. Department of Health, Education and Welfare, 1961.)

Following Bell, the literature on family group therapy blossomed until approximately 200 authors of papers and books on the subject are now available for professionally oriented readers. The best bibliography is in Boszormenyi-Nagy, 1965, *op. cit.* Pioneers in the therapeutic use of aggression in child and family therapy are Bruno Bettelheim. (Refs. *Love Is Not Enough,* New York: Free Press, 1955; *Truants from Life,* New York: Free Press, 1955; *The Empty Fortress,* New York: Free Press, 1967; and Ackerman, Nathan W., *op. cit.*)

Historically speaking, J. L. Moreno pioneered marital and family confrontation through his psychodrama group therapy. The earliest purposely therapeutic marital fight scene on record was conducted by Dr. Moreno in Vienna in 1923, later reported in *Psychodrama,* Vol. I., 1st edition. New York: Beacon House, 1940. Pp. 4–5.

Notes & Comments on Chapter XXIV—"Exit Fights."

Page 319. The dirtiest, most satanic fighters tend to search for individuals who have pathologically high separation anxiety and dread, as an intolerable trauma, the experience of being abandoned. The satans exploit this vulnerability by omnipotently indulging in mate-hurting activities and often later trying to deliver the fatal blow of leaving their victims after all. These exciting satans play Russian roulette because, as Professor Rasch of Cologne has shown, they may get killed by the separation-over-anxious partner (Ref. Rasch, Wilfried, "Homicide and Intimacy," presented at the 75th Annual Convention of the American Psychological Association, Washington, D.C., September 2, 1967.)

Page 321. In contrast to the old trend of making a commercial legal routine out of the divorce business, our Institute receives referrals from psychologically oriented jurists, law firms, and court counselors. It is interesting to note that a large number of lawyer-referred couples had social connections with them, suggesting that one way to delay or prevent legal escalation of divorce-bound marital troubles is for a problem couple to consult an attorney who is socially involved with them. Such couples have a greater chance to be referred to marriage therapy before a usually irreversible legal commitment to get a divorce is hastily made.

Page 321. (Ref. Bach, George R. "Thinging—A Sub-Theory of Intimate Aggression Illustrated by Spouse-Killing," presented at the 75th Annual Convention of the American Psychological Association in Washington, D.C., September 2, 1967.)

Notes & Comments on Chapter XXV—"Manifesto for Intimate Living."

Page 328. Anthony Storr (cf. Bibliography) suggests that *distance and abstraction* of the enemy favor the conversion of healthy aggression into lethal hostility, whereas "it is more difficult to project images of malignant aggressors upon one's near neighbour." Anatol Rapoport in *Fights, Games and Debates* (Ann Arbor: University of Michigan Press, 1960) believes that the lethality of hostilities between combatants would be reduced if it were possible to shape their fighting into a context of ritualized gaming which requires of the opponent making the "assumption of similarity" in each other. Then irrational projections of strange and dangerous hostility would largely disappear. Independent of Storr and Rapoport, we put their theories into practice.

The Impact Theory of Aggression
A Conceptual and Semantic Clarification

by Dr. George R. Bach

My early research in human aggression (Bach, *Psychological Monographs*, 1945, No. 2) focused on inter-personal frustration, rather than influence. For the specific study of frustration-effects, I found the classic frustration-aggression (F-A) hypothesis (Berkowitz, L. *Aggression*. New York: McGraw-Hill, 1962) an adequate and convenient conceptual tool. However, as my research interests broadened to include both frustration and influence ("impact"), the old F-A theory was unable to elucidate, let alone account for, the major facts observable in our clinical practice: that when involved people fight, they fight not only to "do each other in," as the F-A theory would demand, but also to change for the better. True, they may fight to remove frustration but not necessarily to punish or injure the partner who is perceived as the frustrator. What injury, threat of injury, or punishment may be involved is instrumental in influencing the partner to change.

The expression of anger and aggression serves tension relief or cathartic purposes, as when we emit an insulting swear word upon stepping barefoot on a needle that dropped out of the partner's sewing basket. However, classical F-A theory, which unfortunately still governs most current psychological research in human aggression, explicitly excludes both influence and catharsis. This limitation renders the F-A theory useless for the scientific investigation of human aggression in the life-context of real human fight situations where influence, catharsis, and ritual factors govern intensity and form of aggression. Clinicians can train people to acquire very high tolerance levels for frustrations. But aggressive behavior often occurs without any blocking of goal-directed behavior, *i.e.*, frustration, but rather in sheer joy. People fight to provide each other with interest, entertainment, and stimulation and to reduce the enormous aggression reservoir that builds up by fight avoidance or instinctual propensities.

As an applied social scientist I believe that the aged controversy whether human aggression is innate or nurtured,

urrently revived in the writings of Ardrey, Lorenz, Mon-
ague, and Storr, is theoretically interesting but useless in
answering the urgent question of how to control aggression.
In fact, it seems socially irresponsible to tell people that they
are instinctively aggressive or that they have been taught to
become mean either because of bad modeling or man-made
usually mother-made) environmental frustrations. The instinct theories provide a rationale for a general nihilistic
acceptance of war and violence as a cogent hairshirt in
human destiny, while the environmental F-A theorists set the
irrational and therefore dangerous expectation that frustrations can be effectively removed and that freedom from
aggression can be attained.

One good and practical finding of the psychological research
guided by either the Freudian, instinctual, or the environmental F-A theories is that human aggression is modifiable,
either by regulating its instigation or by channeling its expression. Our fight training makes use of both these methods: the
instigation of fighting is by mutual consent, not just frustration; the expression is governed by mutually agreeable fair-
fight rules, and the objective of the fighting is change and
catharsis but not injury. Naturally, hurtful words and deeds
are intrinsic to all fighting, otherwise we would be dealing
with assertiveness rather than aggression and merely playing
with words.

Our Impact Theory of Aggression sees aggression as instrumental to producing change in the intimate system. Verbal as well as nonverbal aggression is primarily informative
communication about conditions that would further provoke
or maximize the injury-inflicting potentiality of aggression,
i.e., hostility, or abate it. Aggression-exchange produces useful information about desirable (tolerable) and intolerable
(alienating) positions along the dimensions of intimacy, such
as optimal distance (spacing), authority (power-hierarchy),
and loyalty (territory). In traditional F-A theory, "doing
injury is the goal response terminating the aggressive sequence" (Berkowitz, 1962, p. 199), while in our Impact
Theory, the completion of the influence process or impact is
the terminal point of the fight and the reward or "reinforcement" for it.

Semantically, the word aggression, unfortunately, is one of
many omnibus terms in the English language that has many
meanings, some of them almost contradictory. Dictionaries
define aggression as "violating by force the rights of others,"
"any offensive action or encroachment," "committing the first
act of hostility or attack," "starting a quarrel," etc. However,

"aggressive" also means to be "energetic and vigorous, full of enterprise and initiative, bold and active."

These definitions confusingly include both assertive and hostile-injurious aspects. In the more technical definition of aggression given in English and English, *Dictionary of Psychological Terms*, there is an attempt at differentiation of the various components of aggression, but the effect is confusing rather than clarifying. In view of this semantic confusion, we were forced for purposes of our own work to define clearly all terms associated with "aggression." Here are some of our major definitions:

AGGRESSION—A broad omnibus term or "dispositional" concept referring to various feelings, thoughts, actions, and interactions that naturally occur when partners frustrate or quarrel with each other as when they demand or resist change. Both instigation and expression of aggression are extremely varied, ranging from simple harmless Assertion (firm but nonnoxious) to hurtful hostility. To assert, make a demand or impact, to influence in order to put things right, is on the nonnoxious end of the aggression dimension. On the noxious side of aggression is hostility and violence, the thought or action of which involves inflicting hurts, injury, punitive damages, or elimination. (In fight training partners learn to differentiate between hostility and assertion.)

ANGER—Often an emotional reaction, but not necessarily irrational; aroused by feeling injured, interfered with, rejected, put-down, humiliated, unfairly criticized, hit below belt line, taken advantage of, manipulated or exploited. Anger has a wide range of verbal and nonverbal expressions (raised voice, facial grimaces, gesticulations, etc.). Its intensity varies from mild annoyance to uncontrollable rage.

BELT LINE—The limit of hurt-tolerance below which partners cannot absorb blows or hurts without serious injury to the relationship. Fight training teaches intimates to define clearly and expose (rather than hide) their Achilles' heel or belt lines and to adjust them if too high or too low. Hitting below a known belt line is a prototype of Dirty Fighting.

CATHARSIS—A normal healthy noninstrumental (usually ritualized) release of aggressive-hostile feelings toward displaced targets (persons, things, ideas). "Blowing off steam" without attempting, at the same time, to change or improve anything. In addition, catharsis may enhance intimacy by providing entertainment or serving as a tolerance reminder.

CONSTRUCTIVE AGGRESSION—Fair fighting between intimates which produces new authentic information. Useful in one or all of three ways: 1) to let partner know where he stands, truthfully; 2) to recognize current conflict and learn to resolve it; 3) to remind each other of existing tolerance limits on all dimensions of the intimate system. Aggressive encounters are also considered constructive to the extent that they afford one or both partners catharsis without injury, as well as fringe benefits such as entertainment (E) and contact maintenance (CM). Clinically, constructiveness of aggression is measured by the dominance of "fair" over "foul" fight styles on the fight-style chart; and by the predominance of "plus" or "minus" changes in intimacy dimensions on the fight-effects chart. Constructive aggression is expressed by the following heuristic formula:

$$CrAg = \frac{(Info) + (Cath) + (E) + (CM)}{Hurts}$$

DEUTERO-FIGHTING—To fight about fighting. In fight training partners learn to negotiate where, when, how, and what to fight about.

FAIR—Clean, responsible, clear information-producing fight tactic or style. A score above the line on fight style chart.

FIGHT—Two-way verbal aggressive confrontation of a specific, well-defined "beef" for the purpose of change (hopefully for the better) of a destructive, frustrating, or intolerable aspect of the intimate relationship.

FIGHT RITUALS—Mutually developed, understood, and tolerated (if not enjoyed) round robins of familiar and repetitive expressions of old insults, complaints, and fulminations of displaced aggression; containing no new information, producing no change but having cathartic functions.

FIGHT TRAINING—Educating intimate partners, in pairs and/or small groups of couples or families, how to engage in aggressive fights in fair rather than foul styles, showing them how to make constructive use of aggression by minimizing hurts and maximizing information and enjoying catharsis through harmless fight rituals.

FOUL—Using a dirty or alienating fight tactic or style. Scores below the line on fight-style chart.

HURTS—Pains or injuries—mental, physical, or social (humiliations, embarrassment, isolation)—incurred in the process of intimate battling. Fear of hurting the partner and of getting hurt is a major reason for fight evasion and conflict phobia with the undesirable consequences of the development of indirect passive aggression. Fight training shows these fears to be irrationally high. Partners are less vulnerable than believed and have higher hurt-tolerance and hurt-absorption than speculatively assumed and can even learn to enjoy "hurts" and find them worth-while, relative to the information obtained in the course of getting hurt. The actual experience of pain or hurting is largely regulated by irrational self-propaganda and self-defeating depressing stances such as injustice collecting. Fight training eliminates hurt-oriented self-hate and masochism.

LEVELING—Transparent, authentic, and explicit expressions about how one truly feels in an intimate relationship, especially concerning the more conflictive or hurtful aspects; sharing the "rough edges"; a two-way intimate dialogue essential for the location of conflict areas.

PASSIVE AGGRESSION—Indirect, covert, camouflaged hostility (witting or unwitting) which reduces intimacy and increases alienation more destructively than overt dirty fighting. In fight training we include, as aggression, such passive but destructive tactics as fight evasion, ambush, partner-watching, nonsharing and nonresponding, etc.

SATAN—Sadistic partners who, openly or secretly, wittingly or unwittingly, rationally or irrationally, not only enjoy the suffering, pain, or demise of intimate others but who actively pursue a line of hostile intervention (often subtle or camouflaged) injurious or even lethal to intimate others. Fight training exposes satans (who often pair with "angels" to form unholy symbiotic alliances that feed off each other's sickness) and goes to work on them therapeutically.

SYNERGY—Integrated co-existence or confluence of supposed opposites; a livable, pragmatic resolution of apparently paradoxical aspects of intimacy, such as: love vs. hate; peace vs. war; leader vs. follower; contract vs. spontaneity. Successful synergy is the ultimate goal of fight training.

VESUVIUS—A ritualized, noninjurious aggression catharsis —"blowing off steam"; may be verbally directed at anybody or anything (including the partner); a solo, not a dialogue. A Vesuvius is not a fight; its aim is hostility release or entertainment, not change. Fight training shows how to avoid the danger of converting a Vesuvius into a fight and how to use it therapeutically.

"VIRGINIA WOOLF"—A Vesuvius duet: an old, redundant insult exchange which both partners know and accept as a hostility-release ritual. Fight training shows how to make therapeutic use of these encounters and how not to turn them into real fights.

Bibliography

Ackerman, Nathan W. *Treating The Troubled Family*. New York & London: Basic Books, 1966.

Altenberg, Henry E. "Changing Priorities in Child Psychiatry," *Voices*, Vol. 4, No. 1, 1968, 36-39.

Ardrey, Robert. *The Territorial Imperative*. New York: Delta Books, 1966.

Bach, George R. "An Experimental Study of Young Children's Fantasies," Ph.D. thesis in child welfare, State University of Iowa, 1944.

———. *Young Children's Play Fantasies*, Psychological Monographs, 59, No. 2, 1945.

———. *Intensive Group Psychotherapy*. New York: Ronald Press, 1954.

———. *Constructive Aspects of Aggression*, a symposium presented to the 9th Annual Conference of the Group Psychotherapy Association of Southern California, 1962.

———. "A Theory of Intimate Aggression," *Psychological Report*, 1965. 18:449-50.

———. "The Marathon Group: Intensive Practice of Intimate Interaction," *Psychological Report*, 1966. 18:995-1002.

———. "Marathon Group Dynamics II—Dimensions of Helpfulness," *Psychological Report*, 1967. 20:1147-58.

———. "Marathon Group Dynamics III—Disjunctive Contacts," *Psychological Report*, 1967. 20:1163-72.

———. "Group-Leader Phobias in Marathon Groups," *Voices*, 1967. 3:41-46.

———. *Thinging—A Sub-Theory of Intimate Aggression Illustrated by Spouse-Killing*, presented at the 75th Annual Convention of the American Psychological Association in Washington, D.C., September 2, 1967.

———. *Therapeutic Uses and Abuses of Aggression*, presented at the Institute for Rational Living in New York, seminar conducted May 30, 1968.

———. Discussion of "Accelerated Interaction" by Frederick Stoller, *International Journal of Group Psychotherapy*, 1968. 18:244-49.

Bandura, Albert. *Social Learning Through Imitation*, Nebraska Symposium On Motivation, Lincoln, Nebraska: University of Nebraska Press, 1962. Pp. 211-69.

Bateson, G., Jackson, D.D., Haley, J., and Weakland, J. "Toward a Theory of Schizophrenia," *Behavioral Science*, 1950, 1:251-64.

Bateson, G., and Ruesch, J. *Communication: The Social Matrix of Psychiatry*. New York: W. W. Norton, 1951.

Beier, Ernst G. *The Silent Language of Psychotherapy*. Chicago: Aldine Publishing Co., 1966.

Bell, John E. *Family Group Therapy*. Public Health Monograph No. 64, U.S. Department of Health, Education and Welfare, 1961.

Bell, N. W., and Vogel, E. F. *A Modern Introduction to the Family*. Glencoe, Ill.: Free Press, 1960.

Berkowitz, Leonard. *Aggression: A Social Psychological Analysis*. New York: McGraw-Hill Book Co., 1962.

Berlin, Irving N., ed. *Training in Therapeutic Work with Children*. Palo Alto, California: Science & Behavior Books, 1967.

Berne, Eric. *Games People Play*. New York: Grove Press, 1964.

——. *Transactional Analysis in Psychotherapy*. New York: Grove Press, 1961.

Bettelheim, Bruno. *Love Is Not Enough*. New York: Free Press, 1955.

——. *Truants From Life*. New York: Free Press, 1955.

——. *The Empty Fortress*. New York: Free Press, 1967.

Biderman, A. D., and Zimmer, H. *The Manipulation of Human Behavior*. New York: John Wiley & Sons, Inc., 1961.

Boguslaw, Robert. *The New Utopians: A Study of System Design And Social Change*, Englewood Cliffs, N.J.: Prentice-Hall, 1965.

Boszormenyi-Nagy, I., and Framo, James L. *Intensive Family Therapy*. New York: Hoeber Medical Division, Harper & Row, 1965.

Buckley, Walter. *Sociology and Modern Systems Theory*. Englewood Cliffs, N.J.: Prentice-Hall, 1967.

Bugenthal, James T. *The Search for Authenticity*. New York: Holt, Rinehart and Winston, Inc., 1965.

Buhler, Charlotte. *Values in Psychotherapy*. New York: Free Press, 1962.

Cleaver, Eldridge. *Soul On Ice*. New York: McGraw-Hill Book Co., 1968.

Cooley, C. H. *Human Nature and The Social Order*. New York: Scribner, 1902.

Caplan, Nathan. "Treatment Intervention and Reciprocal Interaction Effects," *Journal of Social Issues*, Vol. XIV 1968, 83-88.

Corsini, Raymond J. *Methods of Group Psychotherapy*. New York: Blakiston Division, 1957.

Cuber, John F., and Harroff, Peggy B. *The Significant Americans*. Baltimore: Pelican Books, 1965.

DeAnda, Natividad, and DeAnda, Barbara. "Fighting as a Therapeutic Tool," presented at the 11th Annual Golden Gate Group Psychotherapy Society.

Dederich, Charles E. Originator and developer of the "Synanon Game." Described in *The Tunnel Back: Synanon,* by Lewis Yablonsky. New York: Macmillan, 1965.

Ellis, Albert. *If This Be Sexual Heresy.* New York: Lyle Stuart, 1963.

——. *The Folklore of Sex.* New York: Grove Press, 1962.

——. *The Art and Science of Love.* New York: Lyle Stuart, 1960.

——. *Reason and Emotion in Psychotherapy.* New York: Lyle Stuart, 1962.

Ellis, Albert, and Harper, Robert. *A Guide To Rational Living.* Englewood Cliffs, N.J.: Prentice-Hall, 1961.

Ellis, Albert, and Conway, Roger O. *The Art of Erotic Seduction.* New York: Lyle Stuart, 1967.

Ellis, Albert, and others. *How to Prevent Your Child from Becoming a Neurotic Adult.* New York: Crown, 1966.

English, O. S. "Values in Psychotherapy: The Affair," *Voices,* Vol. 3, No. 4, 1967, 9-14.

Erikson, Erik H. *Childhood and Society.* New York: W. W. Norton, 1950.

——. *Identity and the Life Cycle.* New York: International Universities Press, 1959.

Escalona, S. *Understanding Hostility in Children.* Chicago: Science Research Assoc., Inc., 1954.

Eysenck, H. J. *The Effects of Psychotherapy.* New York: International Science Press, 1966.

Festinger, Leon. *A Theory of Cognitive Dissonance.* New York: Harper & Row, Inc., 1957.

——. *Informal Social Communication. Psychological Review,* 57, 1950, 271-82.

Festinger, Leon, and Kelley, Harold. *Changing Attitudes Through Social Contacts.* Ann Arbor, Michigan: Research Center For Group Dynamics, 1951.

Frank, Jerome. *Persuasion And Healing.* Baltimore: Johns Hopkins Press, 1961.

Freud, Sigmund. *New Introductory Lectures on Psychoanalysis.* New York: W. W. Norton, 1933.

——. *Why War?* Collected papers, edited by James Strachey. London: Hogarth, 1948, 280-81.

Gibb, Jack. *Climate for Trust Formation T-Group Theory and Laboratory Method.* Bradford, L. I., Gibb, J. K., Benne, K. D. New York: John Wiley & Sons Inc. 1964.

Ginott, H. G. *Between Parent And Child.* New York: Macmillan, 1965.

Glasser, William. *Reality Therapy: A New Approach to Psychiatry.* New York: Harper & Row, 1965.

Goffman, Erving. *On Cooling the Mark Out. Psychiatry,* Vol. 15, No. 4, 1952, 451-63.

——. *The Presentation of Self in Everyday Life.* New York: Doubleday, 1959.

Goldstein, A. P., Heller, K., and Sechrest, L. B., *Psychotherapy and the Psychology of Behavior Change.* New York: John Wiley & Sons, Inc., 1966, 73-146.

Goodrich, D. W., and Boomer, D. S. *Experimental Assessment of Modes of Conflict Resolution. Family Process,* 2, 1963, 15-24.

Haley, Jay. "An Interactional Description of Schizophrenia," *Psychiatry,* 22:321-32.

Harlow, H. F. "Affectional Responses in Infant Monkeys," *Science,* 130, 1959.

———. *The Nature of Love, American Psychologist,* 1958, 12:673-85.

Heider, Fritz, *The Psychology of Interpersonal Relations.* New York: John Wiley & Sons, Inc., 1958.

Hodge, Marshall Bryant. *Your Fear of Love.* New York: Doubleday, 1967.

Hogan, Richard A. "Theory of Threat and Defense," *Journal of Consulting Psychology,* 1952. 16:417-24.

Jackson, Don D. *Human Communication.* Palo Alto, California: Science & Behavior Books, 1968.

Jennings, Helen H. *Leadership and Isolation* (2nd edition). New York: Longmans, Green & Co., Inc., 1950.

Kaplan, Abraham. *The Conduct of Inquiry.* San Francisco: Chandler Publishing Co., 1964.

———. *Models of Self Identity,* a discussion presented to the Group Psychotherapy Association of Southern California, 1967.

Kempler, Walter. "Experimental Family Therapy," *International Journal of Group Psychotherapy,* Vol. XV, No. 1, 1965.

Kinsey, Alfred, and others. *Sexual Behavior in the Human Female.* Philadelphia: Saunders, 1953.

———. *Sexual Behavior in the Human Male.* Philadelphia: Saunders, 1948.

Kubie, L. S. *Practical and Theoretical Aspects of Psychoanalysis.* New York: International Universities Press, Inc., 1950.

Laing, R. D. *The Divided Self.* London: Tavistock Publications, 1960.

———. *The Self and Others.* London: Tavistock Publications, 1961.

———. *The Politics of Experience.* Baltimore: Penguin Books, 1967.

Laing, R. D., and Esterson, A. *Sanity, Madness, and the Family.* New York: Basic Books, Inc., 1964.

Lewin, Kurt. *Education For Reality,* A DYNAMIC THEORY OF PERSONALITY, New York: McGraw-Hill Book Co., 1935, pp. 171-179.

———. *A Dynamic Theory Of Personality.* New York: McGraw-Hill Book Co., 1935, 250-54.

———. *Principles of Topological Psychology.* New York: McGraw-Hill Book Co., 1935.

———. *Resolving Social Conflicts,* edited by Gertrud Lewin. New York: Harper & Brothers, 1948.

———. *Field Theory in Social Science,* edited by Dorwin Cartwright. New York: Harper & Brothers, 1951.

THE INTIMATE ENEMY

Lorenz, Konrad. *On Aggression,* New York: Harcourt, Brace & World, Inc., 1966.

Marmor, Judd. "Changing Patterns of Femininity: Psychoanalytic Implications," *The Marriage Relationship—Psychoanalytic Perspectives,* edited by Salo Rosenbaum and Ian Alger. New York: Basic Books, 1968.

Masters, William, and Johnson, Virginia. *Human Sexual Response.* Boston: Little Brown, 1966.

Mead, G. H. *Mind, Self, and Society.* Chicago: University of Chicago Press, 1934.

Megargee, Edwin. "Matricide and Patricide," presented at the 75th Annual Convention of the American Psychological Association in Washington, D. C., September 2, 1967.

Menninger, Karl. *Love Against Hate.* New York: Harcourt Brace, 1959.

Moreno, J. L. *Psychodrama,* Vol. 1, (1st ed.), 4-5. New York: Beacon House, 1946.

Newcombe, T. M. *The Prediction of Interpersonal Attraction. American Psychologist,* II, 1956, 575-86.

Oliver, Bernard. "Social Psychological Characteristics of the Rapist," presented at the annual meeting of the California State Psychological Association, December 4, 1964.

Pearson, A. W., and Khoury, Nicholas J. "Alcoholism: Medical Team Approach to Treatment," *California Medicine,* Nov. 1961, 284-87.

Pepitone, A., and Reichling, G. *Group Cohesiveness and the Expression of Hostility.* Human Relations, 1955, 8:327-38.

Perls, Frederick S., and Others. *Gestalt Therapy.* New York: Julian Press, 1951.

Piaget, Jean. *Language and Thought of the Child.* London: Kegan Paul, 1926.

Rapoport, Anatol. *Fight, Games, and Debates.* Ann Arbor, Michigan: University of Michigan Press, 1960.

———. *Strategy and Conscience.* New York: Harper & Row, 1964.

Rasch, Wilfried. *Homicide and Intimacy,* presented at the 75th Annual Convention of the American Psychological Association, Washington, D.C., September 2, 1967.

Rogers, Carl R. *Client-Centered Therapy.* Boston: Houghton Mifflin, 1951.

Rosen, John N. *Psychoanalysis Direct and Indirect.* Doylestown, Pa.: Doylestown Foundation, 1964.

Ruesch, Jurgen, and Kees, Wheldon. *Non-Verbal Communication.* Berkeley and Los Angeles: University of California Press, 1956.

Sagan, Eugene. "Creative Behavior and Artistic Development in Psychotherapy," a symposium, *APA Annual Convention Program,* 1967.

Sarbin, T. R. *Role Theory,* in G. Lindzey (ed.) *Handbook of Social Psychology,* Vol. 1. Cambridge, Mass.: Addison-Wesley, 1954, 223-58.

Sartre, Jean-Paul. *Being and Nothingness.* New York: Citadel Press, 1965.

Satir, Virginia. *Conjoint Family Therapy.* Palo Alto, Calif.: Science and Behavior Books, Inc., 1964.

Schacter, Stanley. *Deviation, Rejection and Communication.* Journal of Abnormal Social Psychology, 1951, 46:190-207.

Schofield, W. *Psychotherapy: The Purchase of Friendship.* Englewood Cliffs, N. J.: Prentice-Hall, 1964.

Schutz, William. *Joy,* New York: Grove Press, 1967.

Shapiro, David. *Neurotic Styles.* New York and London: Basic Books, 1965.

Shapiro, Stewart B. "Transactional Aspects of Ego Therapy," *The Journal of Psychology,* 1963, 56:479-98.

Shaw, George Bernard. *Selected Plays.* New York: Dodd, Mead, Vols. 1, 3, 4, 1948.

Shostrom, Everett, *Man, the Manipulator.* New York and Nashville. Abingdon Press, 1967.

Shumsky, Marshall E. "Teenagers in Group Therapy and Marathon Groups," Conference, San Francisco, Calif., June 22, 1968.
    presented at the Western Psychological Association's Convention, March 30, 1968.

Stoller, Frederick. "Accelerated Interaction: A Time-Limited Approach Based on the Brief Intensive Group," *International Journal of Group Psychotherapy,* Vol. XVIII, No. 2, 1968, 220-58.

Stoller, Frederick. "The Long Weekend," *Psychology Today,* December 1967, 28-33.

Storr, Anthony. *Human Aggression.* New York: Atheneum, 1968.

Tagiuri, R., and Petrullo, L. (eds.). *Person Perception and Interpersonal Behavior.* Stanford: Stanford University Press, 1958, 316-36.

Whitaker, Carl A. *The Use of Aggression in Psychotherapy,* presented to the 9th Annual Conference of the Group Psychotherapy Association of Southern California, 1962.

Winnicott, D. W. *Aggression in Relation to Emotional Development.* Collected papers. London: Tavistock, 1958.

Wolfgang, M. E., and Ferracuti, F. *The Subculture of Violence.* London: Tavistock, 1967.

Yablonsky, Lewis. *The Hippie Trip.* New York: Pegasus, 1968.
——. *The Tunnel Back: Synanon.* New York: Macmillan, 1965.
——. *The Violent Gang.* New York: Macmillan, 1963.

Index

accommodation, 137–38, 250; pseudo-, 21

Achilles' heels, 80–82, 131; and bad fighters, 112; children's, 287–88; and sick and dirty fighters, 145

Ackerman, Nathan W., 360, 362

aggression: constructive, defined, 367; definition of, 366; and manifesto, 326; passive, defined, 368. See also specific situations

Aggression, 364, 365

Aggression: A Social Psychological Analysis, 342

Albee, Edward, 18, 342

alcohol, 73–74, 344

Alger, Ian, 347

American Association of Marriage Counsellors, 49n

American Psychologist, 337, 339

anger, defined, 366; fake, 112–13. See also specific situations

animals, 26–27, 354

Ardrey, Robert, 334

arms-control ground rules, 99

attribution, 151–53, 156–58

authority, and manifesto, 325

autonomy (self-value), and scoring, 166, 174

Bach, George R., *passim;* books and papers by, 333, 336, 337, 339, 341, 343, 344, 346, 349, 355, 361, 362

Bach, Peggy, 353

Bach, Roger, 360

bad fighters and reforming them, 103–5; notes on, 347–48

Bandura, Albert, 346

Bateson, Gregory, 348, 353

beds, sterility of, 260; twin, 247

"behavior change," 330

Behavioral Science (periodical), 348

Beier, Ernst G., 349, 353

Being and Nothingness, 336

Bell, John E., 361

Bell, N. W., 359

belt lines, 80–84, 345; defined, 366; and scoring, 160

Benne, K. D., 345

Bergman, Ingrid, 155–56

Berkowitz, Leonard, 342, 364, 365

Berne, Eric, 32, 244, 336, 337, 338, 345, 350

Bettelheim, Bruno, 305, 362

Between Parent and Child, 360

bibliography, 370–75

Biderman, A. D., 337

birds, 27

birth-control pills, 129, 252–53

blamesmanship. See scapegoating

boats, 69–70, 74

Boguslaw, Robert, 335, 340

Boomer, D. S., 350

Boszormenyi-Nagy, I., 340, 360, 362

Boyer, Charles, 155–56

Bradford, L. P., 345

brainwashing, 152

bridge table, and fun fighting, 191

Buckley, Walter, 340

bugging, 136–39, 153, 289, 298. See also bad fighters; sick and dirty fighters; specific situations

California, 31